RHETORICAL FIGURES
IN SCIENCE

Rhetorical Figures
in Science

JEANNE FAHNESTOCK

New York   Oxford
OXFORD UNIVERSITY PRESS
1999

Oxford University Press

Oxford   New York
Athens   Auckland   Bangkok   Bogotá   Buenos Aires   Calcutta
Cape Town   Chennai   Dar es Salaam   Delhi   Florence   Hong Kong   Istanbul
Karachi   Kuala Lumpur   Madrid   Melbourne   Mexico City   Mumbai
Nairobi   Paris   São Paulo   Singapore   Taipei   Tokyo   Toronto   Warsaw

and associated companies in
Berlin   Ibadan

Library of Congress Cataloging-in-Publication Data
Fahnestock, Jeanne, 1945-
Rhetorical figures in science / Jeanne Fahnestock.
p.   cm.
Includes bibliographical references and index.
ISBN 0-19-511750-6; 0-19-516542-X (pbk)
1. Figures of speech.   2. Scientific literature.   I. Title.
PN227.F34   1998
808—dc21   98-26832

A shorter version of chapter 3 appeared as "Series Reasoning in
Scientific Argument: Incrementum and Gradatio and the Case of Darwin."
Rhetoric Society Quarterly 26 (Fall 1996): 13–40.

Portions of chapter 2 appear in *Rereading Aristotle's Rhetoric.*
Edited by Alan Gross and Arthur Walzer. Forthcoming:
Southern Illinois University Press.

9   8   7   6   5   4   3   2   1

Printed in the United States of America
on acid-free paper

*In memory of my mother, Evelyn Martha Groth,
and my father, Ludwig Franz Rosenmayer*

Preface

Studies of how scientists use language and how they argue, some under the rubric "the rhetoric of science," have appeared with increasing frequency in the last ten years. Works by Charles Bazerman, Lawrence Prelli, Greg Myers, Alan Gross, Jean Dietz Moss and others anchor this new field, which has been thoroughly surveyed by Randy Allen Harris in his introduction to *Landmark Essays on Rhetoric of Science* (1997) and submitted to critique and review in *Rhetorical Hermeneutics: Invention and Interpretation in the Age of Science* (Gross and Keith 1997). Despite the variety of subjects these books examine and the diversity of approaches they employ, they all address a fundamental general question: To what extent does language do our thinking for us? How do the structures or options available in a language lead us into certain prepared lines of thought or argument?

This book also belongs in the genre of studies in the rhetoric of science, and it, too, concerns the generative power of language. But there are significant differences between the following work and others in this category that require clarification. Typically, a rhetorical analysis concentrates on a single text or a group of texts related, as the scholar chooses, by author, audience, time, genre, subject, or implication in an intellectual or social movement. There can, for example, be rhetorical analyses of *On the Origin of Species*, of Darwin's and Wallace's papers read before the Linnaen Society, of Darwin's entire oeuvre, or of arguments for evolution in the early to mid-nineteenth century, including Darwin's. (John Angus Campbell's impressive corpus of work on Darwin and evolution has taken such differing perspectives.) Rhetorical analysts draw on principles of rhetorical theory, abundantly available in the 2,500-year tradition of rhetorical commentary, to explain the means employed to present a potentially successful argument in a particular context. Thus a rhetorical analysis looks at both formal elements and historical circumstances.

This book, however, is not concerned with the rhetorical analysis of any single author, text, oeuvre, or movement, or with explanations in terms of the social or intellectual setting of any single discovery or body of thought. These approaches are fruitful and satisfying when the goal is an appreciation of a work in its intellectual or cultural moment or an assessment of its role in an argument field. But this book is more concerned with the technique of rhetoric itself, specifically with certain well-used lines of argument and their expression in certain linguistic constructions called *figures of speech*. Thus rhetoric is used in this study to illuminate scientific arguments, but, more important here, scientific arguments are used to illuminate rhetoric.

Outside of metaphor, the influence of the rhetorical structures that constitute widely applicable lines of argument has not been thoroughly explored. This work investigates the conceptual and inventive power of certain figures of speech other than metaphor and the tropes allied to metaphor, whose cognitive significance has been so thoroughly explored recently. It moves beyond analogy to consider figures less known but frequently used, including *antithesis, gradatio, incrementum, antimetabole, ploche, and polyptoton*—strange names from the Greek and Roman rhetorical lexicon that nevertheless represent common strategies of reasoning.

Two consequences follow from the interest of this work in rhetorical theory. First, rhetorical theory is very much a product of its history, and readers unfamiliar with the history of rhetoric will visit new territory (especially once they cross back over the epistemological watershed of the late eighteenth and early nineteenth centuries). Rhetoric is still a term so elided from general educated awareness that it retains only a pejorative connotation as verbal deceit. But it represents the discipline that virtually constituted higher learning in antiquity, and it remained a major portion of the university curriculum from the Middle Ages through the eighteenth century. The rhetorical tradition in classical and early modern texts is based on the conviction that there are generic skills of argument, regardless of subject matter. Rhetoric has also been valued as a teachable art, at once general and generative, which has advice to offer on everything from phrasing and premise formation to methods of behavior and action in the world. The rhetorical tradition is, furthermore, highly coherent across its 2500-year history, so that it is possible to trace similar terms across the centuries and put texts from widely different eras into conversation with each other.

Second, the following discussion assumes, in a way that might be disconcerting to some, that Aristotle, despite his associations with scholasticism and physical theories that impeded fresh observation, is still worth consulting, and that what Aristotle has to say about certain figures of speech in his *Rhetoric* and lines of argument in his *Topics* can still contribute to an understanding of how arguments in twentieth-century scientific journals are constructed and expressed. And the same is true for Quintilian, Cicero, and lesser known figures such as John Hoskins in the sixteenth century or Richard Whately in the nineteenth. Writers in this tradition provide taxonomies of naturally occurring verbal devices and of lines and methods of argument, and, more important, of the connection between or even identity of these two. The detail and particularity of the explorations in these historical works are simply missing in later treatments.

In order to revive meaningful distinctions that have been lost, and to make the rhetorical tradition accessible, some reconstruction of earlier theories concerning style and argument is required. Chapter 1 reviews the classical and early modern treatments of the figures of speech, their place in the stylistic advice offered in rhetorical treatises, and their partition into three categories. This introduction also looks at historical answers to the problem of defining the figures. Some definitions hinge on formal features, others on the presumed effects of these devices. Much was confused in the traditional view of the figures of speech, especially as it later became ossified in literary theory. Chapter 1, therefore, also examines the varying systematics of the figures and questions their underlying rationales in order to revive a minority view of the figures first introduced in antiquity: that the figures do not belong in a separate domain of language use but are rather on a continuum of constructions that are successful in varying degrees as epitomes of their functions.

Subsequent chapters feature especially effective figures of speech, ones that do significant work in many scientific arguments. To illustrate the figures and the various lines of argument they epitomize, excerpts from scientific arguments—even individual passages and lines—are chosen from various authors, texts, fields, centuries, and traditions. The examination of the same figure of speech in different kinds of works and from various authors, disciplines, and centuries, is necessary to keep the focus on the figure. As a byproduct of this variety, none of the texts sampled here is treated in the depth or with the historical detail that it would merit in a fully historicized rhetorical analysis (though the attempt has been made to present samples without distortion). The desired result is a gain in the study of rhetorical technique that scholars can then use when they construct more detailed and focused studies.

Chapter 2 begins the treatment of individual figures by concentrating on *antithesis*, using Aristotle's definition as a point of departure: an antithesis places opposed terms in symmetrical phrases (e.g., the advice to investors, "buy low, sell high"). This chapter traces the demise of the antithesis from a figure of importance equal to metaphor to an "also ran." Nevertheless, the argumentative work achieved by the antithesis is thoroughly explained in the advice on constructing arguments offered in rhetorical and dialectical treatises. Excerpts from Bacon and Darwin illustrate how arguments can draw on existing semantic oppositions, but the power of the form itself to create what Pascal called "false windows" is also discussed. The syntactic structure of the antithesis can be used to make "nonce" antonyms out of terms that were not previously opposed in the lexicon of an audience. This chapter concludes by discussing perennial controversies over whether a pair of terms represents a mediated or unmediated opposition.

Chapter 3 surveys the formal means for reuniting antithetical terms by linking them to a single predicate, flanking them with a third term, combining them into an oxymoron, or placing a mediating term or a series between them. The chapter then focuses on those figures of speech that were dedicated to constructing series, the *incrementum* and *gradatio*, and it explores additional ways in which these devices have been used in scientific arguments. The *incrementum* is a series whose members share an attribute in increasing or decreasing degree (e.g., captain, prince, king, emperor), and a *gradatio* is a series whose members overlap but need not possess the same quality (e.g., "Tribulations worketh patience; And patience experience, and experience, hope; And hope maketh not ashamed" [Romans 4:3–5]). Series reasoning is used to create places for terms—beginning, end, or middle—a case in point being the construction of fossil series to explain living forms. Incomplete series, or series with holes, can provide a rationale for identifying missing elements, a tactic used in the nineteenth century to create and fill the periodic table of elements and in the eighteenth to predict the existence of a missing planet between Mars and Jupiter. Overlapping series, on the model of the *gradatio*, are used to establish set relations and causal chains, as examples from ecological arguments demonstrate, and series are also used to dissolve established differences between categories and so to reconfigure a conceptual domain, replacing differences in kind by differences in degree. The importance of this last tactic in Darwin's *On the Origin of Species* is worked through in detail in this chapter.

Chapter 4 takes up another argumentatively useful figure of speech, the *antimetabole* (e.g., "Those who know don't tell, and those who tell don't know"). A related figure, the *chiasmus*, has been increasingly important in biblical hermeneutics, where it is usually defined as two mirror image clauses bracketing a middle term. But the antimetabole of rhetoric has no center; it is a mechanism for reversing the syntactic positions of two terms and in the process reversing their grammatical and conceptual relation to each other. Antimetaboles are frequently used to express identity claims, and illustrative cases come from geometry, especially projective geometry where "dual" or reversed theorems are taken as established a priori, and from the arguments of Louis Pasteur debunking spontaneous generation and establishing the importance of living forms in all chemical processes that produce optically active compounds. Antimetaboles also figure in causal arguments that emphasize reciprocal causality, and they can be found precisely where they might be expected in Newton's scholia for the third law of motion, in Michael Faraday's writing reporting his discovery of electromagnetic rotations, and in both Faraday's and Joseph Henry's articles on the production of electricity from magnetism, the deliberately sought-out reciprocal to the production of magnetism from electricity.

The final chapter looks at figures of repetition, singling out *ploche*, the precise repetition of a term within or across several sentences, and *polyptoton*, the recurrence of the same root in various forms. *Polyptoton* takes advantage of the natural tendency of language users to form new words off older roots and other parts of speech so that, for example, a treatise on the figures of speech will use not only the word *figure* but also the forms *figured, figural,* and *figurally,* a repetition that produces the impression that a consistent phenomenon is being talked about consistently. *Ploche* and *polyptoton* are on the point of vanishing from detection as formal devices, but they came highly recommended in rhetorical manuals. *Ploche*, perfect repetition, attempts to stabilize a term in an argument. The various expressions of Koch's postulates over the last one hundred years have all used this device. *Polyptoton* is used to create families of coordinate terms so that what is claimed about one form of a word can be transferred to another form. Chapter 5 concludes with an extended analysis of the role of these two figures in the eighteenth-century formation of a science of electricity.

The devices identified and examined in these chapters are by no means found only in scientific arguments. Arguments from other spheres are sometimes cited and many more could have been. But scientific arguments are chosen to illustrate the devices for several reasons. First is clarity. Scientific arguments, as arguments supporting claims about the way nature is or works, tend to give their main lines of reasoning a high profile; they are, in terms of the argumentative strategies looked at here, fairly open objects of analysis. Second, scientific arguers often resort to visual persuasion, so it is possible to follow certain figures of speech into their expression as "figures" in another sense. This consistency between the visual and verbal helps to underscore the fundamental conceptual processes expressed by the figures.

Third, scientific arguments are used here to weaken the old misconception that the domain of rhetoric does not extend to the sciences since rhetorical invention presumably prescribes only the reassembly of conventional truths, while scientific invention involves the discovery of new truths. The "new science" of the seventeenth century deliberately exaggerated its break with the prevailing intellectual and pedagogical tradition—that is, with rhetoric—as part of its campaign to inspire inquiry. But language does do much of our thinking for us, even in the sciences, and rather than being an unfortunate contamination, its influence has been productive historically, helping individual thinkers generate concepts and theories that can then be put to the test. The case made here for the constitutive power of figures per se supports the general point made by F. L. Holmes in a lecture addressed to the History of Science Society in 1987. A distinguished historian of medicine and chemistry, Holmes based his study of Antoine Lavoisier on the French chemist's laboratory notebooks. He later examined drafts of Lavoisier's published papers and discovered that Lavoisier wrote many versions of his papers and in the course of careful revisions gradually worked out the positions he eventually made public (Holmes, 221). Holmes, whose goal as a historian is to reconstruct the careful pathways and fine structure of scientific insights, concluded from his study of Lavoisier's drafts

> We cannot always tell whether a thought that led him to modify a passage, recast an argument, or develop an alternative interpretation occurred while he was still engaged in writing what he subsequently altered, or immediately afterward, or after some interval during which he occupied himself with something else; but the timing is, I believe, less significant than the fact that the new developments were consequences of the effort to express ideas and marshall supporting information on paper (225).

An understanding of the arguments inherent in the phrasings available in the figures would only strengthen and particularize Holmes's general point that there are subtle interactions "between writing, thought, and operations in creative scientific activity" (226).

At a more general level, this study should help to establish the centrality of the figures of speech in rhetorical theory, since these widely used devices epitomize fundamental mental operations. This point has certainly been made for metaphor, now seen as basic to linguistic and cognitive processes (thanks to George Lakoff, Mark Johnson, and Mark Turner, among others). It needs to be extended to the other figures so that they are no longer seen as decoration on the plain cloth of language but as the fabric itself. The figures epitomize lines of argument that have great applicability and durability, and though these lines can be paraphrased in roundabout ways, they gain their greatest force in the stylistic concision of a recognizable figure. In a general as well as a very particular sense, then, a style argues. Since it is impossible to argue without exploiting the structures identified in the rhetorical tradition, consciously or unconsciously, it would be better to use these devices consciously. Such a conclusion both follows from and adds to the current expansion of interest in rhetoric.

It is also hoped that this study, like others in the rhetoric of science, will help to chip away at the profound division in our culture between science and the humanities. We have so divided these two enterprises that we sort texts, disciplines, thinking styles, types of mind, and even children according to whether they belong in one domain or the other. Science students often believe they can dispense with the verbal arts, and humanities students avoid science. The polemics of the scientific revolution in the seventeenth century, debasing rhetoric to elevate science, have been too successful. Yet if the thinking styles and language habits of the two are essentially similar, as a demonstration of the figural patterning necessary to many scientific arguments suggests, there is little point in such division. We might pursue instead a "one mind" hypothesis, that the same cognitive/verbal skills serve any subject of inquiry. What matters is that these generic skills be strengthened. The consequences for our educational schemes could be profound.

I WANT TO EXPRESS MY GRATITUDE to many people for help in many forms. For their assistance and encouragement, my special thanks to my colleagues at the University of Maryland, Mark Turner in English and Stephen Brush in History and the Committee on the History and Philosophy of Science, and to my colleagues at large, Alan Gross, Carolyn Miller, Charles Bazerman, Don Freeman, Randy Allen Harris, Jack Selzer, Davida Charney, and David Kellogg; my gratitude also to Marie Secor for the sustained conversation over many years on the relations between language and argument.

My gratitude also to my editor at Oxford University Press, Peter Ohlin, for his consistent support, and to MaryBeth Branigan, Nancy Hoagland, Catharine Carlin, and Kathy Finch for their professional expertise, smoothing all phases of the manuscript-to-book process.

Finally my thanks to my husband, Stephen Fahnestock, for answering my frequent questions and for tracking down sources and texts for me, and to my sons, Peter and Derek, for being proof that it is possible to live in the two cultures at once.

Contents

CHAPTER 1 The Figures as Epitomes   3

    The Dominance of Metaphor   4

    The Classical Tradition of the Figures   6

    Theories of Figuration   15

    The Figures as Epitomes of Lines of Reasoning   23

    Boundary Problems   37

    Verbal Spread and Visual Concision   40

    The Figures in Scientific Discourse   43

CHAPTER 2 Antithesis   45

    The Aristotelian Definition of Antithesis   46

    The History of the Figure   53

    The Uses of Antithesis in Argument   58

    Arguing from Existing Semantic Contrasts   59

    The "False Window": Using the Form to Force Terms Apart   69

    Arguments that Change the Nature of Opposition   72

CHAPTER 3 Incrementum and Gradatio   86

    Undoing Antitheses   87

    Figures that Construct Series   91

    The Uses of Incrementum and Gradatio in Argument   95

    Creating Places with Series   98

    Incomplete Series   102

    Double Hierarchy Arguments   105

    The Gradatio as Sorites   108

    Merging Categories   112

    Series Reasoning in Darwin's *The Origin of Species*   114

CHAPTER 4 Antimetabole   122
        The Semantics and Syntax of the Antimetabole   123
        History of the Figure   126
        Argumentative Uses of the Antimetabole   131
        The Antimetabole and Causality   141
        Refutation by Reversal   150

CHAPTER 5 Ploche and Polyptoton   156
        Figures of Repetition   157
        Perfect Repetition: Ploche   158
        Polyptoton   168
        The Argumentative Resources of Polyptoton   170
        Ploche, Polyptoton, and the Science of Electricity
            in the Eighteenth Century   177

Notes   195

References   215

Index   227

RHETORICAL FIGURES
IN SCIENCE

1

The Figures as Epitomes

The English scientist John Dalton is credited today with bringing the elegance of whole number proportions to the understanding of chemical combination. If elements combine into compounds in simple ratios, Dalton realized, then the ancient atomic theory proposing indivisible units of matter was vindicated. But his groundbreaking insight appears only briefly and toward the end of a work preoccupied with a more pressing issue in late eighteenth-century chemical theory: the nature of heat or *caloric*. Dalton's 1808 treatise, *A New System of Chemical Philosophy*, opens with the current definition of this force become a substance. "The most probable opinion concerning the nature of caloric is, that of its being an elastic fluid of great subtilty [*sic*], the particles of which repel one another, but are attracted by all other bodies" (Dalton 1808, 1).

Theories like Dalton's have been cited as instances of the informing power of metaphorical thinking in science, for he, like others at the time, describes heat as a substance called "caloric" that has some of the properties of a liquid (Hesse 1966, 89–91; Gentner and Jeziorski 1993, 453). So when, for example, Dalton wants to illustrate for his readers the notion that every material has a different specific heat (i.e., that the same amount of different substances can contain different amounts of heat at the same temperature), he asks them to imagine "a system of cylindrical vessels of different diameters connected with each other by pipes at the bottom, and a small cylindrical tube attached to the system, all capable of holding water or any other liquid, and placed perpendicular to the horizon" (3). The small tube in this thought experiment, marked off in degrees, represents a thermometer; the cylinders of different diameters represent different substances. When water is poured in, it reaches the same level in each interconnected cylinder, and that level is recorded on the graduated cylinder. Each cylinder holds a different amount of water, illustrating the point that each substance retains a different amount of heat. But all register the same "temperature," the same level marked on the graduated cylinder.

This verbal illustration is wonderfully clear, but unfortunately it is also misleading. It obscures an essential feature of Dalton's theory: that the quantity of heat at the same temperature differs in the same volumes, not in the different volumes of differently sized cylinders. And with its foregrounding of the behavior of a liquid seeking the same level in connected containers, it gives a false impression of the importance of an analogy between liquids and caloric in Dalton's thinking. More significant in the overall conceptual economy of *A New System of Chemical Philosophy* is not the ostensible metaphor that appears in Dalton's opening sentence cited earlier, "caloric is . . . an elastic fluid," but rather the other figure of speech that occurs there, the unobvious antithesis claiming that the particles of caloric repel one another but attract all other bodies. Here, in two parallel phrases, Dalton deploys two pairs of opposite terms, repel/attract and one another/all others, matching each one with its opposite in a syntactic pattern defined over two thousand years earlier by Aristotle. The conceptual pattern epitomized by this linguistic device informs Dalton's account in a much more basic way throughout *The New System* than does an analogy between heat and liquid. Antithesis is the key to his explanation of how heat causes phase changes and promotes chemical recombination, leading in turn to his groundbreaking study of the simple ratios that describe the combinations of elements in compounds. It is, furthermore, the same linguistic device that Dalton would have encountered in the opening pages of Lavoisier's *Traité Élémentaire de Chimie* (1965), which also discusses the nature of caloric in antithetical terms.[1] Dalton's antithesis does not merely switch his thinking from one metaphorical domain to another—from a physical model of the behavior of liquids to one of attraction and repulsion, of pushing apart or pulling together. The essential feature of the antithesis that does the conceptual work in his phrasing is the matching of opposite with opposite, repelling the same and attracting the different. That analysts have concentrated only on the informing metaphors in caloric theories of heat has more to do with what they are prepared to notice than with what is conceptually dominant in a text or theory.

The Dominance of Metaphor

Currently, metaphor occupies the ground in language analysis and in studies of the mind that build on studies of language. It is a construct common across the disciplines of literary studies, linguistics, psychology, philosophy, and education, and books devoted to metaphor have come from historians, theologians, sociologists, legal theorists, and even scientists. As a fundamental mechanism in language and thinking, metaphor has been championed by the Belgian structuralists of Group μ; nominated by historian Hayden White as master of the four master tropes; and identified by the cognitive linguists and philosophers, George Lakoff, Mark Johnson, and Mark Turner, as the principle underlying all conceptual systems. A common denominator in all these studies is that, in investigating metaphor, scholars and researchers believe they have a window on a fundamental, generative cognitive process. No wonder the interest continues. There have been conferences on metaphor; metaphor has its own journal (*Metaphor and Symbolic*

Activity); special issues of other journals have been devoted to it (e.g., *Social Research* [Summer 1995]); and a recent scholarly bibliography on metaphor lists almost 3500 entries between 1985 and 1990 alone (Ortony 1993, xiii).

One field that has been particularly centered on metaphor is science studies. Stimulated by Max Black's groundbreaking 1962 study, *Models and Metaphors*, scholars in the history, philosophy, sociology, and rhetoric of science over the past 30 years have been detecting the root or core metaphors underlying or informing scientific creativity and argumentation and counting these metaphors as explanations of scientific theories and movements. The culmination of such studies appears in *The Construction of Reality*, which asserts as a grand unification principle that "scientific revolutions are, in fact, metaphoric revolutions" (Arbib and Hesse 1986, 156).

[margin note: Science and Metaphor]

It is interesting to speculate as to why this identification is so compelling to so many. One reason may be that tracing insights to metaphors seems to explain scientific creativity—the sudden genesis of ideas—in a way that preserves notions of genius and innovation. Metaphors come to people in moments of inspiration; they cannot be reached or derived systematically or procedurally. Still another reason may be that a discovery of metaphor in science releases a unifying "cluster of pieties" about how scientists and poets are basically alike because both groups use metaphor. The scientist Jacob Bronowski was fond of such encomiastic parallels in the 1950s, calling, for example, the differing views of light as particle or wave "a conflict between analogies, between poetic metaphors; and each metaphor enriches our understanding of the world without completing it" (1986, 7), and the same vaguely laudatory bracketing appears in a 1992 article by a literary scholar: "Like poets, scientists have favorite metaphors for representing their participation in an interpretation of the universe" (Papin 1992, 1261). Both groups have found this commonplace of common ground in metaphor useful.

Two final reasons may, however, come closer to explaining the dominance of metaphor in science studies. First, while metaphors are epistemological constructs, they are also identifiable, formal devices. Given an appropriate definition, they can be pointed out, providing evidence for the scholar working with texts. Second, examples of the role of metaphor in science have, in fact, been numerous and compelling: Kekulé determines the structure of benzene by day-dreaming of a chain that joins itself in a circle, like a serpent consuming its tail; Rutherford explains his atom by comparing it to the solar system. The eighteenth-century electricians vacillate between metaphors—is electricity more like water or more like fire and firearms?—a double conceptualization that has left us with terms like "current" and "flow" as well as "spark" and "discharge." Harvey's heart is a pump; Dalton's "caloric" is a fluid; Newton's 1672 particles of light act like tennis balls (that is, like seventeenth-century tennis balls); and the brain in twentieth-century cognitive science is a computer. In each of these cases, the conceptual structure of the source domain, to use cognitivist terminology, has been tapped to structure the target domain, demonstrating the heuristic power of the metaphor (Turner 1991, 52).

Despite these compelling cases, the fixation on metaphor as a stimulus in scientific creativity, as a device in scientific argument or pedagogy (Boyd 1993, 485–486), and, finally, as an explanatory resource for textual scholars overemphasizes the role of analogy in human reasoning and begs the question of whether all or even most scientific cases can be "explained" by a core metaphor. What about the gas laws, superconductivity, electromagnetic induction, the periodic table, the positron, or retroviruses? The tight focus on metaphor in science studies, like the fixation on metaphor and allied tropes in textual studies, has taken attention away from other possible conceptual and heuristic resources that are also identifiable formal features in texts and that also come from the same tradition that produced metaphor, the rhetorical tradition of the figures of speech. As Gérard Genette complained in "Rhetoric Restrained," the tendency among commentators on rhetoric (especially French commentators) from the eighteenth century on has been to reduce the whole art to the figures, the figures to the tropes, and the tropes to metaphor (1982, 104–113). Neither the Classical nor the Renaissance rhetorical traditions were so limited or limiting.

What aside from metaphor is available in the lore of the figures of speech? Some Renaissance rhetorical manuals, after all, offer well over 100 figures, most of them outside the thoroughly scrutinized category of the tropes to which metaphor belongs. What are these other categories? What is in them? Given the insights into language and cognition that have flowed from the study of metaphor, it seems plausible to ask whether other devices identified in the traditional lists of the figures have anything comparable to offer.

The Classical Tradition of the Figures

Any attempt to understand the full tradition of the figures of speech runs into immediate difficulties, difficulties that go far toward explaining why only the relatively tidy category of the tropes has been fully scrutinized. The scores of figures found in the elaborated manuals offer significant problems in definition and categorization, so that anyone browsing through a catalog of figures will wonder, first of all, how they can be united by any family resemblance. What joins a *metalepsis* like "pallid death," using the effect of a cause (death produces pallor) as a quality of that cause, with an *aposiopesis* like "And when I opened it—," breaking off a predication? Perhaps all such devices really have in common is that they can be defined ostensively as the sort of thing traditionally listed as a figure in a rhetoric.

Classical texts, Medieval summaries, and Renaissance rhetorical manuals do suggest definitions and offer schemes of organization. But not surprisingly in an art that has been revived and re-elaborated for almost 2,500 years, there are significant differences in the way the figures have been schematized and explained. Nevertheless, some attempt at an overview of these systems is a sensible place to start to see what the full doctrine of the figures has to offer. Though some of the greatest scholars of rhetoric express a curious distaste for and even embarrassment over the intricacies of the figures, deploring in particular the early modern manuals for offering needless distinctions without differences (see Vickers 1981, 105–106, and 1988, 294–295), the prodigious human effort expended on these catalogs century after century warrants a closer look.

The catalog of figures in the Rhetorica Ad Herennium

Recapturing the system that metaphor was once a part of can start with the first catalog of the figures appearing in the first century B.C.E. *Rhetorica ad Herennium*, the earliest extant manual to give them extensive treatment. Indeed, the attention to verbal devices in this early Latin text is so detailed that it is immediately apparent that the book is repeating distinctions well established in preceding Hellenistic texts now lost. The treatment of the figures in the *Ad Herennium* is important not only because it is the earliest full treatment, the only record of an even earlier system, but also because it was perhaps, thanks in part to a false attribution to Cicero, the most influential rhetorical manual from antiquity through the seventeenth century (Conley 1990, 33; Vickers 1988, 216), remaining in circulation for over a thousand years while other classical works were temporarily misplaced.

The *Ad Herennium* devotes a disproportionately long Book IV to style, introducing the figures as ornaments that confer merit and character on language [Dignitas est quae reddit ornatum orationem varietate distinguens ([Cicero] 1954, 274)]. The text divides its list of devices into two categories that will persist for centuries: figures of diction and figures of thought [Haec in verborum et in sententiarum exornationes dividitur]: "It is a figure of diction if the adornment is comprised in the fine polish of the language itself. A figure of thought derives a certain distinction from the idea, not from the words." (275). A catalog of 64 devices, 45 figures of diction, and 19 of inaptly named figures of "thought" follows this brief definition, a quantum expansion from the four Gorgianic figures associated with the Sophists or the handful of devices that Aristotle mentions in Book III of the *Rhetoric*. However, the actual grouping of these figures in the *Ad Herennium*'s list does not carry out the announced division into two kinds. There is instead a *de facto* division into three categories, since the author introduces a special set of devices at the end of the list of figures of diction.

> There remain also ten Figures of Diction, which I have intentionally not scattered at random, but have separated from those above, because they all belong in one class. They indeed all have this in common, that the language departs from the ordinary meaning of the words and is, with a certain grace, applied in another sense. (333)

Ten figures that presumably transfer or twist a word from its original meaning follow: *onomatopoeia, antonomasia, metonymy, periphrasis, hyperbaton, hyperbole, synecdoche, catachresis, metaphor,* and *allegory*. These are the tropes of later catalogs, here presented as a distinct type, though without a label, under the figures of diction. After these ten, the author merely announces that it is time to turn to the figures of thought [sententiarum exornationes].

Despite this apparent tidiness, each of the three groups of figures in the *Ad Herennium* includes devices that hardly seem to fit the principles that apparently produced the categories in the first place. An example of such misplacement among the ten "tropes" is *hyperbaton* (Latin name *transgressio*) with its two subtypes, anastrophe, and transposition. Both are concerned with altering normal word order, anastrophe by inverting sentence constituents ("From the back of the room came the sound of snoring") and transposition by altering the usual placement of sen-

tence constituents ("The food, hot and fragrant, finally appeared on the table").
Shuffling word order, far more possible in an inflected language like Latin, hardly
seems to involve transferring meaning the way the simplest metaphor does, though
the inclusion of this device does point out that the position of a word is not without effect. In addition to a confusing inclusion like that of *hyperbaton* among the
tropes, many of the devices in the *Ad Herennium* have long since left the ranks of
identifiable figures in any other than antiquarian reprises, though they have not
left the actual practice of language users. So, for example, the set of figures of diction includes *permissio*, the arousing of pity by yielding or submitting to another's
will ([Cicero] 1954, 326–327), a device that cannot be pinned down to any precise
linguistic signature or "fine polish of the language itself."

The *Ad Herennium*'s final category of 19 "figures of thought" also groups an
odd assortment of devices, ranging from *imago* (comparing one physical representation to another) to *effictio* (the physical portrayal of a person) and *notatio*
(character delineation by signs or traits of behavior), which together provide a
mini-poetics. To add to the confusion about the categories of figures in the *Ad
Herennium*, *antithesis* [contentio] appears both as a figure of diction and as a figure of thought ([Cicero] 1954, 283, 377).

Altogether then, the *Ad Herennium* announces two divisions of figures but
delivers three, roughly diction [*exornationes verborum*], tropes, and thought
[*exornationes sententiarum*], but within these three divisions it uses no consistent principles of sorting. Though most of the *exornationes verborum* can be defined linguistically and most of the *exornationes sententiarum* can be defined only
by purpose or effect, there are devices in each of these two divisions that defy
this distinction. So the *permissio* mentioned above, submitting to another's will,
which can be accomplished by different locutions, appears among the first category ([Cicero] 1954, 327), while *sermocinatio*, quoting another's exact speech in
a way that is always textually distinctive, appears among the second (395). A "good
enough" if not rigorous theory drives the *Ad Herennium*'s presentation of the
figures. Its author has inherited, from texts now lost between the fourth and first
centuries B.C.E, a wonderful elaboration of devices from commentators on the
craft of oratory. The source of these devices is the actual practice of speakers;
hence the set is open-ended and somewhat disorganized. For two thousand years,
rhetoricians will exercise their ingenuity trying to impose theoretical tidiness on
such lists of identifiable verbal practices without ever quite succeeding.

The figures in Quintilian: Distinguishing the body from the body disposed

Two hundred years after the *Ad Herennium*, Quintilian made one such attempt to
rearrange the categories of figures in Books VIII and IX of his *Institutio Oratoria*.
But his discussions only reveal the extensive disagreements that had accumulated
among rhetoricians about the nature and classification of the figures. Indicative of
these difficulties are the substantial sections interposed between Quintilian's discussion of general issues of stylistic choice and his lists of the tropes and other figures. For whereas histories and summaries of classical stylistics shift with disarm-

ing ease from concepts like the levels of style to the figures of speech, Quintilian, summarizing several centuries of rhetorical commentary, makes no such easy transition. An author's moves from one major division of a text to another, and therefore from one division of a subject to another, often reveal the ideological fault lines in a system. Before Quintilian even reaches the first group of figures, the tropes in chapter vi of Book VIII, he discusses a host of other linguistic devices for amplifying and creating reflexions or pithy sayings, many of which seem indistinguishable from the later figures.[2] His comments on these extra-figural devices are also difficult to separate from the advice on how to invent premises given earlier, as Quintilian himself acknowledges (III:269). Obviously, Quintilian does not assume that everything there is to say about verbal devices is subsumed under the figures. And there are more boundary problems to come in Books VIII and IX.

When Quintilian does reach the devices traditionally called figures, he keeps essentially the same categories established in the *Ad Herennium*, but he makes an important change in their hierarchical relationship, placing a first cut between tropes and "figures [figuræ]" (his word for the Greek term σχήματα) as he calls them in the opening of Book IX.[3] Having established a primary division between tropes and all other devices, Quintilian turns to the category of figures alone, where he has other inherited confusions to deal with. By the first century C.E., disagreements among rhetoricians about the number of genera and species of the figures, that is, non-tropes, were so extensive that they called the original term into question. Quintilian finds that "figure," or scheme, is used in two senses.

> In the first it is applied to any form in which thought is expressed, just as it is to bodies which, whatever their composition, must have some shape. In the second and special sense, in which it is called a *schema*, it means a rational change in meaning or language from ordinary and simple form, that is to say, a change analogous to that involved by sitting, lying down on something or looking back. (Quintilian 1921, III:353)[4]

A figure then is either the body itself or the body posed or disposed in a certain way. According to the first sense, the term "figure" means something like "form of expression," and since it is impossible to say anything without choosing some form of saying it, so "everything is expressed by *figures*" (III:355). But if everything is expressed figuratively, there can be no rationale for distinguishing the figures from any form of expression. Not surprisingly, Quintilian opts for the second meaning and defines figures as "a form of expression to which a new aspect is given by art" [Ergo figura sit arte aliqua novata forma dicendi] (III:355). But the minority view that Quintilian acknowledges and then sets aside makes an important breach in the definition. Why may not every form that an expression can take be a figure?

Having separated the tropes from the figures and maintained the integrity of the latter category, Quintilian next submerges the primary division found in the *Ad Herennium* between figures of thought and figures of speech into a secondary division within the overall set of figures.

> It is, however, to the best of my knowledge, generally agreed by the majority of authors that there are two classes of *figure*, namely *figures of thought* [διανοίας],

that is of the mind, feeling or conceptions, since all these terms are used, and *figures of speech* [λέξεως], that is of words, diction, expression, language or style.
(Quintilian 1921, III:357)

This distinction too had created another definition-dissolving controversy over
whether every change in words involves a change of sense and therefore over
whether figures are concerned with words or with sense. Quintilian dismisses this
problem as quibbling, "For the same things are often put in different ways and the
sense remains unaltered though the words are changed, while a *figure of thought*
[figura sententiæ] may include several *figures of speech* [habere verborum figuras
potest]" (III:357). What then is a figure of thought if it survives changes in wording and can in turn be embodied in different figures of speech? One of the oddest
passages in the *Institutes* follows as Quintilian tries to explain:

> For the former [figures of thought] lies in the conception, the latter in the expres-
> sion of our thought. The two are frequently combined, however, as in the follow-
> ing passage: "Now Dolabella, [I have no pity] either for you or for your children"
> [Iam iam, Dolabella, neque me tui neque tuorum liberum]: for the device by which
> he turns from the judges to Dolabella is a *figure of thought*, while *iam iam* ("now")
> and *liberum* ("your children") are *figures of speech*. (III:357)

A natural assumption would identify the "figure of thought" underlying Quintilian's
example as some basic proposition involving "Dolabella," "pity," and "children."
This underlying proposition could be expressed in a variety of surface forms, even
in the less-accommodating syntax of English: "Neither you nor your children deserve pity, Dolabella" or "Dolabella, you don't deserve any pity and neither do your
children" or "Pity, Dolabella, is something neither you nor your children deserve."
Thus the body of thought is posed or disposed in different ways.

But the "figure of thought" Quintilian identifies has less to do with the content
than with the context. He is quoting a passage from one of Cicero's forensic speeches
when Cicero "turns from the judges to Dolabella." The "figure of thought," then,
marks Cicero's action, his turning away from the judges and turning to speak to
Dolabella; it amounts to addressing someone directly as well as communicating
with one's adversaries and partitioning the audience by making it aware of its different members. The label for this type of interactional device in Quintilian, *figures of thought*, is particularly misleading. These figures are more like gestures, ways
of marking in speech or constructing in written texts the intentions, interactions,
and attitudes among participants. In fact, in the passage in which he sets up this
dissociation, Quintilian does not use the terms *figurae sententiarum* or *verborum*
but instead reverts to Greek terms to label these two categories, distinguishing
διανοίας from λέξεως, or the energy from the words. This "energy" of interaction resembles the twentieth-century notion of the speech act either intended
or accomplished by an utterance. Thus the "figures of thought" belong in the pragmatic or situational and functional dimension of language.[5]

The classical system then created three large categories of figures: the tropes that
involve transference of meaning, the figures of speech or schemes that include
devices of word arrangement and patterning, and the figures of thought that represent interactional gestures and either the speaker's illocutionary intent (e.g.,

descriptio, to describe vividly) or the desired perlocutionary effect of the device (e.g., *paralepsis*, to communicate presumably unmentioned content) or both (e.g., *concessio*, to concede a point). However, the two foundational treatments of the figures, the *Ad Herennium*'s and Quintilian's, differ in their primary architecture for these categories. The older text separates the *figurae verborum*, linguistically definable, from the *figurae sententiarum*, definable primarily by effect. Quintilian, however, places his major division between the tropes and the schemes, which are in turn divided between the figures of diction and thought.[6] Quintilian's practice dominates in later rhetorical manuals, causing the elevation of the tropes to a category equal to the division containing all the other figures (despite a great disproportion in the number of devices) and creating an untenable single category of "figures" combining both those that are formally definable and those that are not. In later treatises, it was easy to lose Quintilian's second-level division within the *schemata*. In the twentieth century, it is common to speak only of the tropes and schemes and to forget entirely the figures of thought as a category—though individual devices, such as the rhetorical question, have survived the demise of their category.

elevation of tropes

It would be misleading to suggest that these earliest treatments represent precise theoretical distinctions on the basis of a linguistic rationale that has since been lost. A neat division among the tropes as semantic, the schemes as syntactic, and the figures of thought as pragmatic holds only roughly when it is compared with the actual lists in the manuals. Thus, as noted previously, the *Ad Herennium* places hyperbaton, which concerns inverted word order, among that special group of "tropes" for which it has no name ([Cicero] 1954, 337) and includes among the figures of diction devices that affect only a single word by adding, deleting, and transposing letters or syllables (301–305). Later writers obviously struggled to purify the categories and make them correspond to clear and mutually exclusive divisions. But by Quintilian's time, alternate systems had accumulated, and he acknowledges the many classification problems, admitting, for example, that hyperbaton could be a scheme as well as a trope (Quintilian 1921, III:339), or that irony could be either a trope or a figure of thought (III:401). The classical doctrine of the figures could not explain why some devices were in a certain category nor whether the categories themselves were exhaustive or merely suggestive. The purpose of the system, indicated by the greater space devoted to examples than to explanation, was to foreground for practitioners some well-known and widely used devices. Implications for a theory of language were afterthoughts.

The figures in early modern treatments

In the sixteenth century, the figures of speech received more attention and elaboration than ever before, an expression of the veneration for the art rhetoric prompted in part by the newly rediscovered and disseminated treasury of classical works on rhetoric (see Vickers 1988, 254–55). This is the age of great treatises devoted solely to style and especially to the figures of speech: Erasmus' *De duplici copia verborum ac rerum commentariis* (1521), Schade's *Tabulae de schematibus et tropis* (1529), Susenbrotus' *Epitome troporum ac schematum et grammaticorum et rhetoricum* (1541), Sturmius' *De universa elocutionis rhetoricae libri tres* (1576). Texts surveying the whole art also included expanded sections on the figures. This disproportionate attention lavished on one part of the doctrine of style, itself one of the five parts of rhetoric, had profound consequences for the systematics of the figures. For not only did the early modern theorists expand the lists of figures but they also, as a byproduct of their close scrutiny, began to organize and rationalize them in different ways.

Many Renaissance manuals did depart from the two competing Classical schemes by taking essentially the same figures but imposing different categorizations. Philip Melancthon in Book II, *De Eloquentia*, of his general rhetoric, *Elementorum Rhetorices*, builds on Cicero's *De Oratore* and Quintilian's *Institutio Oratoria* and makes the expected initial division between tropes and schemes. But under schemes he rejects the usual division "into that of the textual or literal and that of the thought intended" (1969, 247) and branches instead into three subcategories.

> The first especially pertains to grammarians and concerns the position of the words or emphasis and clearness of the nouns. . . . The second type properly has to do not with words but with the thought or idea. For they are figures that give action to speech such as interrogation, wonderment, doubt, complaint, etc. The last type, for the most part, concerns the speaker and comprises the manner of enlarging, that is, the figures which embellish the speech and make it broader and more extended. (248–249)

While Melancthon put the division between tropes and schemes at a higher level than the partitions among these three types of schemes, it is nevertheless possible to read across these divisions and construct an overall four-part categorization: tropes, which involve a transference of meaning; schemes, which involve patterns of words; figures of thought, again better called figures of speech act or interaction; and a new set of figures of amplification incorporating devices Quintilian identified but did not originally place among the figures.

Melancthon's four-part division is certainly an improvement, but it does not solve the placement problems that plagued earlier systems. It is again difficult to see why some figures appear in one place rather than another, or why they could not appear under two divisions as they frequently do in Quintilian. Antithesis, for example, is listed in Melancthon's system as a figure of amplification (Melancthon 1969, 290–291), though it involves a clearly definable syntactic pattern fitting his first division; in Quintilian's system it appears as a figure of diction (Quintilian 1921, III:495) and in the *Ad Herennium*'s system as both a figure of diction ([Cicero] 1954, 283, 293) and a figure of thought (377; see chapter 2). Furthermore Melancthon's four major categories—transferring sense, patterning syntax, performing a speech act, and amplifying—do not offer a compelling partition of any broader concept, namely the concept of figure itself. Instead Melancthon is apparently grouping according to two different principles, one formal, based on the semantic or syntactic change involved, and one functional, based on what the devices should communicate or achieve for the speaker.

The greatest English work on the figures, Henry Peacham's *The Garden of Eloquence,* can serve as an accessible exemplar of how the figures were treated in manuals devoted to them exclusively. Peacham's 1593 version of this manual is especially worth looking at because he deliberately follows a formula in treating each device, including a definition of the figure, several examples, a statement about its use, and a caution about the possibilities for misuse. This lavish attention derives from the importance that Peacham places on his subject, for although he is concentrating on only a small part of the overall art of rhetoric, and although he begins his dedicatory letter with the usual gestures of humility, he is far from thinking that his subject is a despicable one. The eloquent orator is, according to Peacham, "the emperour of mens minds & affections, and next to the omnipotent God in the power of perswasion, by grace, & divine assistance." And how does the orator achieve this near divinity? "The principal instruments of mans help in this wonderfull effect, are those figures and formes of speech contained in this booke" (Peacham 1954, 4). It is no wonder that the fruit of this garden of eloquence is worth cultivating.

Peacham maintains Quintilian's major division between the tropes and schemes. The tropes, in turn, are divided according to the size of the unit affected, words or sentences; comfortably partitioned off, they pose no problems. The schemes, however, which Quintilian had divided between language and energy, require a new principle of organization. Peacham defines them overall as "those figures or formes of speaking which do take away the wearisomnesse of our common speech, and do fashion a pleasant, sharpe, and evident kind of expressing our meaning: which by the artificiall forme doth give unto matters great strength, perspicuitie and grace" (Peacham 1954, 40). He then divides the schemes, which occupy three-fourths of his treatise, into three orders, the first involving only words, and the second and third sentences or even longer passages. But Peacham also gives each of these three subcategories a different sphere of action: figures of the first order, those of words, make a speech "plaine [clear], pleasant, and beautifull" and concern harmony and pleasant proportion rather than gravity and dignity (40); in the second order are those devices "by which the sundrie affections and passions of the minde are properly and elegantly uttered" (62); and in the third are the devices of amplification, "which by large and plentifull speech moveth the mindes of the hearers" (120). Other systematizers, like Melancthon, had gone this far, basing their systems on the three traditional "offices" of rhetoric, to teach, to move, and to persuade. But Peacham goes a step further and introduces subdivisions based on new principles of partitioning. The schemes involving words are subdivided according to the kind of operation presumably performed to achieve the figure: by repetition (41), omission (50), conjunction (52), or separation (56). The figures that express the affections are ordered according to the effect the speaker wants to have: exclaiming (62), moderating (84), consulting (104), and conceding or submitting to judgment (110). And finally, the figures of amplification are ordered according to what could be called the larger scale discourse function accomplished: distribution or spreading of the content (123), description (134), comparison (156), and collection, either by leaving the sense to the hearer or by assembling the proofs and conclusions (156).

Thus in his internal sorting of these three orders of schemes, Peacham shifts from operational to functional definitions: that is, from "here is what you do to make this device" to "here is what the device does." But in any of the three subdivisions, he is as likely to include figures that can be both formally and functionally defined or only defined in one way or the other. Thus the subcategory of comparison in the third order includes antithesis and antimetabole, which are syntactically distinctive (160), and a figure called *inter se pugnantia*, "a forme of speech by which the Orator reproveth his adversarie" (163), which definitely is not. And the subcategory of exclamation in the second order includes *ecphonesis*, an outcry, which is defined by the presence of an "O" or "Alas" (62–63), and *mempsis*, the speech act of complaining and craving help (65–66), which again is not syntactically definable. Thus Peacham maintains two competing grids of explanation, one formal and the other functional, but they do not mesh or overlap consistently. Once again, an overall rationalized architecture for the figures proves impossible to construct. Peacham is not the Linnaeus of the figures. But his attention to scores of individual devices, his precise distinctions among near forms and speech acts, more than compensates for the lack of a compelling system of organization. The parts of *The Garden of Eloquence*, as indeed of all the figure manuals, are greater than the whole.

An examination of any of the Renaissance treatises elaborating the figures would require a similar description of subtle differences. Erasmus's influential schoolbook, *De Utraque Verborum ac Rerum Copia*, offering advice for expanding a text either by taking the words or the matter as the point of departure, places most tropes among the first division but maintains no distinctions among other figures dispersed in the second. Scaliger in the sixteenth century moves descriptive devices and other figures of thought into a greatly expanded category of tropes, whereas Omer Talon in the same century takes everything out of that category except metaphor, metonymy, and synecdoche. Gerhard Vossius in the seventeenth century creates new categories of schemes, including those of repetition, exaggeration, and argument.

Thus groupings shift in each author's treatment. But the actual devices listed from manual to manual remain surprisingly consistent. The mysterious inconsistencies in the categories can be explained once it is understood that the compilers are really codifying two different things: verbal forms and discourse functions or speech acts. The definitions they offer for their figures always involve either a formal marker that distinguishes the device or a functional description of its intended effect. Ideally, the placing of a figure requires both, and for some devices both form and function are specified. But in general, the more precise the formal description offered, the less precise the functional explanation, and the more precise the functional explanation, the less precise the formal. Thus all expositors of the figures detail with great accuracy the various patterns of word repetition that can occur in adjacent clauses (chapter 5), but they only say very generally that such repetitions achieve emphasis, charm, and force. Or they define with great precision the nuanced kinds of concession that a speaker can offer to an audience (confessio, deprecatio, medela, permissio, purgatio), but they cannot give a linguistic blueprint for achieving these subtly different speech acts. Ideally, a compendium of figures should do both by defining the formal means for achieving certain conceptual and persuasive functions. One or the other arm of this form/function connection might pivot with some (but not unlimited) degrees of freedom, but the central link should still hold.

Of these two modes of explanation (formal and functional), the latter, the anatomy of speech acts, was particularly liable to expansion. How long could a list be that included every possible degree of threat or apology or exhortation or promise or admonition or flattery or insult or rebuke or supplication that a speaker might want to communicate? Quintilian was aware of the open-endedness of these *figurae sententiarum* (Quintilian 1921, III:439–441), and he limited his discussion to those forms that seemed to represent indirect speech acts (e.g., making a statement in the form of asking a question). Unlike most figures of thought, those schemes that do have a precise profile, that can be both formally identified and functionally analyzed, are a much smaller core group, persisting across the centuries despite their placement in different categories. These deserve the scrutiny that so far has only been given to metaphor.

Theories of Figuration

Écart *and substitution*

In addition to explaining the individual figures either formally or functionally or both, many rhetoric texts also make claims about figuration in general. An enduring element in these overall definitions is the notion that the figures somehow represent departures from normal usage. Since this view tends to obscure a form/function rationale for the figures, it deserves some unpacking. Quintilian may be the source of this idea when he claims, in the passage cited above, that figures represent "a rational change in meaning or language from the ordinary and simple form [in sensu vel sermone aliqua a vulgari et simplici specie cum ratione mutatio]" (Quintilian 1921, III:353). The tropes depart from ordinary signifying practices, the schemes from ordinary syntax, and the figures of thought, at least in Quintilian's account, from the normal speech act implicated by a form (III:375). This equation of the figures with departures from the normal or simple has incredible longevity in the rhetorical tradition, though with significant permutations.[7] In 1593, Henry Peacham merely paraphrases Quintilian's definition in his own: "A Figure is a forme of words, oration, or sentence, made new by art, differing from the vulgar maner and custome of writing or speaking" (1). In 1953, Jean Paulhan in an essay appended to the reprint of an eighteenth-century figure manual, still speaks of expressions as either "propre ou naturelle" or "figurée" (Du Marsais 1977, 277).

Any definition of the figures as formal devices that depart from a norm in linguistic usage begs the question of how that norm should be defined. Is the normal in a language defined as the set of acceptable usages? Or is it defined in the sense of the typical, the most frequently occurring among possibilities? Clearly, none of the many figures cited and discussed so far departs from the normal in the first sense of being bizarre or unacceptable. Figures, in fact, belong to the "normal" in the sense of acceptable usage, whether they are noticed or not. Nor are they the monopoly of certain social locations, occurring more frequently in formal or ceremonial registers or situations. Instead, they occur unremarkably across situations and registers. That the figures are part of ordinary usage, normal in the first sense of the word, has been acknowledged from Aristotle, who notices in the fourth century B.C.E that "all people carry on their conversations with metaphors" (Kennedy 1991, 223), to Du Marsais, who affirms in the eighteenth century that "il n'y rien de si naturel, de si ordinaire et de si commun que les figures dans le langage des hommes" [There is nothing so natural, so ordinary, and so common as figures in human language.] (Du Marsais 1977, 8).

In a second sense, "not normal" can mean "not typical." That is, figured usage may be unremarkable or not noticed as deviant the way ungrammatical syntax would be ("table the under is lost ball the"), but figures are still not the predictable or most frequently used locutions for certain meanings or situations. In other words, figures occur under the bell curve; they are possible. But they are not under the middle of the bell curve; they are not probable.

The prospects for calculating the statistical frequency of figured as opposed to literal usage, supposing one adopts that distinction, seem remote. Even with large databases of presumably ordinary language, only the frequency of single words or certain collocations has been established, and such frequencies give no indication of figured usage. As far as the tropes are concerned (the only figures that can be involved when looking at single words), the existence of a metaphor does not depend on a word's appearance but presumably on its use in an unexpected context. It might, for example, be possible to say how often the word "boy" appears in a sample of one million words, but not how often "boy" was applied to a dog. The other figures seem beyond statistical computation. All that remains is the presumption some literate users have that figured expressions are not the most common choices that speakers and writers make. A bit of reflection on the language choices typical in certain situations—say, greetings among old friends—might weaken that presumption.

Pierre Fontanier offered a way out of the muddle that arises from the two senses of the "normal" as the typical (under the middle of the bell curve) or the possible (under the bell curve at all). In separate treatises devoted to the figures, *Manuel Classique Pour L'Étude des Tropes* and *Traité Général des Figures du Discours autres que les Tropes* written in the 1820s, Fontanier continues to base his definition of the figures on a principle of departure, of *écart.* But it is now not departure from the normal or common word or expression but from the "simple" word or expression, the unfigured or "degree zero" choice. For Fontanier, deciding whether a usage is figured requires seeing if it can be replaced with a presumably simple or straightforward expression (Fontanier 1977, 10). It doesn't matter if the figured expression is used more frequently than the "simple" expression. All that matters is whether the point expressed by the figure can be put more simply or straightforwardly. If, for example, the expression "Richard has a lion's heart" can be replaced by the presumably unremarkable "Richard has courage," then the former is figured, and if the latter cannot be replaced by anything simpler, it is not. It does not matter that the word "courage" in English is a metaphoric coinage from the Latin for heart [*cor*]. What counts in these judgments are the choices available in a synchronic slice of language. Fontanier's definition of the figures as departures from a "simple" choice works best for the tropes, but it can also be extended to the other categories. A figure of thought like the *prosopopoeia*, endowing absent persons or inanimate objects with speech—"If the halls of Congress could speak they would say, 'Where is the eloquence of Henry Clay?'"—could be replaced with a "straight-forward" sentence like "There are not many eloquent speakers in Congress these days." And a figure of speech (scheme) like the *epanalepsis* "Boys will be boys" might be translated into something like "Boys will always be polite and attentive" or "Boys will always be noisy and active," depending on the acceptable cultural paraphrase. Of course, it is certainly questionable whether such a paraphrase is really simpler or more straightforward than "Boys will be boys."

Definitions of the figures as departures from acceptable usage or from statistically normal usage or even from "simple" usage all carry with them the underlying concept that the figure is a substitution for another linguistic choice. Thus, one consistent corollary of these definitions has been an implicit division of language into two domains, the literal and the figurative. Sometimes, discussions of the literal and the figurative seem to suggest that a text, author, or reader has some master switch with two settings, on or off, figurative or literal, either/or alternatives that offer wonderful possibilities for foolery: Thus readers traveling along a text may not realize that the switch has been flipped on them and that what they are reading literally should be taken figuratively or vice versa. An either/or two-state theory is a reduction from the simultaneous fourfold senses of ancient Biblical hermeneutics, but it has been especially popular among twentieth-century French structuralists and poststructuralists who tend to model reading on cryptography, the exegesis of hidden as opposed to intended meaning (see especially Paulhan in Du Marsais [1977, 273–276]).

Even if substitution is accepted as the mechanism of figuration, identifying the mechanism still leaves a more important question unanswered: "What are these substitutions for?" And this question again changes the issue from what the figures "are" to what they "do." It cannot be answered from a formal perspective according to what syntactic or semantic substitutions have presumably been made; it has to be investigated on the functional side of the connection, by asking what speakers or writers may be accomplishing by using figures, even when unaware, and by what effect figures apparently have on listeners or readers.

Ornament and the expression of emotion and force

The figures require, and in fact they were given, a special functional place in Hellenistic and Roman theories of rhetoric. Classical stylistics, Theophrastan to Ciceronian, specifies four virtues of style: correctness, clarity, appropriateness, and ornamentation. These four represent the constraints on or criteria used by a speaker when making language choices. Expressions should be well formed by satisfying grammatical conventions, they should communicate their content, they should fit the situation of the utterance, and, to be memorable, they should have an extra distinctiveness or attractiveness. Traditionally, the figures fulfill the last of these categories. They "ornament" a text, and in the traditional characterization of the processes of rhetorical composition they are added last, the rhetor first inventing the argument, next arranging it, and then finding ways to express it aptly, good expression including embellishment with the figures. This notion of ornamenting or decorating is symbolized in the traditional medieval icon for rhetoric as a woman whose dress is ornamented with flowers that stand for the figures. Thus if language is the dress of thought, the figures are the embroidery.

Cicero's commentary on the figures seems to warrant an understanding of their function as embellishment. When introducing his brief catalogs of the figures, he advises that the "whole style of oratory is to be distinguished and frequently interspersed with brilliant lights, as it were of thoughts and words" (Cicero 1970, 252). In the *Orator*, he recommends building on a base of pure, clear, and appropriate Latin, adding that with that foundation "Only one quality will be lacking, which Theophrastus mentions fourth among the qualities of style—the charm and richness of figurative ornament [ornatum illud suave et affluens]" (1988, 364–365). These ornaments give a style its character or ideal form:

> These [lumina] will be so plentiful that no word will fall from the orator's lips that is not well chosen or impressive; there will be metaphors [tralationes] of all sorts in great abundance, because these figures by virtue of the comparison involved transport the mind and bring it back, and move it hither and thither; and this rapid stimulation of thought in itself produces pleasure. The other ornaments derived from combinations of words lend great brilliance [lumina magnum] to an oration. They are like those objects which in the embellishment of a stage or of a forum are called "ornaments" [insignia], not because they are the only ornament, but because they stand out from the others. It is the same way with the embellishments and, as it were, the ornaments of style [Eadem ratio est horum quae sunt orationis lumina et quodam modo insignia]; words are redoubled and repeated, or repeated with a slight change, or several successive phrases begin with the same words [Cicero continues with a compressed catalog of the typical schemes]. . . .
> The figures of thought [sententiarum ornamenta], however, are of greater importance; it is the frequent use of these by Demosthenes which makes some regard his eloquence as particularly admirable. As a matter of fact, scarcely any topic is treated by him without some configuration of thought. The whole essence of oratory is to embellish [illuminare] in some fashion all, or, at any rate, most of the ideas. (1988, 408–409)

Several historians of rhetoric have pointed out that the traditional conception of ornament as embellishment, or quite literally as embroidery, probably misses an essential meaning in the original term (see e.g., Vickers 1988, 314). The Latin *ornamentum* also means furniture, apparatus, and equipment, so that "ornament" may be more closely related to the notion of essential gear or "armament" than it is to adornment. There are certainly many supporting comparisons in rhetorical works for this second meaning. The *Ad Herennium*, for example, distinguishes *membrum* from *articulus*, successive short clauses from short phrases, as though both were weapons: "In the first figure it seems that the arm draws back and the hand whirls about to bring the sword to the adversary's body, while in the second his body is as it were pierced with quick and repeated thrusts" ([Cicero] 1954, 297). And in the sixteenth century Peacham readily slips into a set comparison of the figures to "martiall instruments of both defence & invasion" to be kept as "weapons alwaies readie in our handes, wherewith we may defend our selves, invade our enemies, revenge our wrongs, ayd the weake" and more ([Peacham 1954, 5] but he also points out they are better than the sword, for they do their work by persuasion rather than violence). Martianus Capella, taking no chances, endows his allegorical figure of *Rhetorica* with both weapons and jewels (Murphy 1974, 45). Comparing the *exornationes* to armament rather than to decoration certainly endows them with greater power and efficacy. But both meanings keep the figures on the surface where they can be readily removed; even Homer's heroes can be stripped of their weapons and armor when they fall.

Under either sense of the term, a view of the figures as armament or ornament fed directly into the classical theory of the three levels of style, the plain, middle, and grand, also first mentioned in the *Ad Herennium*. These levels were in part distinguished from each other on Cicero's authority (Cicero 1988, 319–321) by the frequency and kind of figures used, the plain style having the most subdued use (365), and the grand and formal style the most flamboyant (377). (Cicero never suggests that any style can be without figures.) Since the highest and most figured style was the one appropriate for themes and effects of the greatest impact, "grand, impetuous and fiery" (377), it is the style that most obviously addresses the emotions. Thus, an intimate corollary to the definition of the figures as ornament is the characterization of figures as signs of emotion in the speaker and triggers of the emotions in an audience. According to the logic of this association, if the figures abound in emotionally powerful texts, then delivering emotion is their function. The *Ad Herennium* claims, for example, of *apostrophe*, a device particularly appropriate to the grand style, that it "is the figure which expresses grief or indignation by means of an address to some man or city or place or object. . . . " ([Cicero] 1954, 283); even when used sparingly in the proper place with the proper subject, it can "instil in the hearer as much indignation as we desire" (285). Heinrich Plett believes that in the Renaissance revival of rhetoric, all theories of style, whether articulated in a full rhetoric or in a stylistic manual, seek a "functional explanation of the stylistic devices in terms of the emotions they are likely to engender" (Plett 1983, 359), and other contemporary theorists and historians of rhetoric, notably Brian Vickers (*In Defense of Rhetoric*) and Walter Nash (*Rhetoric: The Wit of Persuasion*), have emphasized the emotional functions of the figures, though they avoid tying a specific device to a specific feeling. Vickers notes the polysemous nature of this potential emotional signification. No one, he claims, can take a figure like *aposiopesis*, the sudden breaking off of a predication, and say that it will always indicate anger or doubt or embarrassment. It can convey any number of emotions, but it always indicates some strong affective content, some attitudinal overlay to the message (Vickers 1988, 317–318, 335–337). In ordinary language use, according to this rationale, listeners know that speakers break off in mid-sentence under the pressure of emotions such as rage that produce inarticulateness, so this breaking off is construed as a sign of whatever emotion seems appropriate in the context. Associating certain figures with emotional states in this way also reinforces a sense of their detachability.

A more generalized version of the functional effect of the figures sees them not as added embellishment or as the expression of emotion but as vehicles of impressiveness or vividness or force. The *Rhetorica ad Herennium*, for example, introduces four figures of repetition, the schemes *anaphora*, *epistrophe*, *symploche*, and *ploche*, and justifies the entire set by claiming that "there inheres in the repetition an elegance which the ear can distinguish more easily than words can explain" ([Cicero] 1954, 281); it praises *antithesis* for conferring "impressiveness and distinction" (283); it cites some rhetorical questions [erotema] as impressive and elegant (285). Reasoning by question and answer [hypophora] is "exceedingly well adapted to a conversational style, and both by its stylistic grace and the anticipation of the reasons, holds the hearer's attention" (289). What kinds of effects are these? The notion behind these claims seems to be that the figures are an effective delivery system for both the speaker's point and the degree of intensity or conviction behind it.

Value-added theories of the figures

All of these functional explanations of the figures as sources of emotion, charm, vividness, force, vivacity, or elegance can be grouped together as *value-added* theories of figuration. According to a "value-added" view, one begins with a plain message and then adds secondary features that make it more memorable or convincing than it would be without them. Thus the *prosopopoeia* cited earlier, "If the halls of Congress could speak they would say, 'Where is the eloquence of Henry Clay?'" adds a self-referential oratorical gesture to its imagined rhetorical question. In this way, the figures, only to be used sparingly and sprinkled here and there as the manuals advise, add some aesthetic, affective, or persuasive value and, up to a point, the more added the more the effect. But if they "add to," of course, they can also be "subtracted from." Anyone holding to a "value-added" theory of the figures is also likely to believe, at least by default, in an unfigured or degree-zero style. Value-added theories of the figures have certainly dominated in the rhetorical tradition, particularly from the Renaissance forward, when the cultural setting for politically efficacious oratory had long since disappeared, and the process of what George Kennedy has called the "letteraturizzazione" of rhetoric, its codification into a set of textual devices (and by terministic slippage, into a set of "literary" devices) took place (Kennedy 1980, 5). The figures become markers of the literary text, removed from the world of functional discourse.

Value-added theories of the figures and the notion of an unfigured style, once again reinforcing the two-domain theory of language, seem inescapably sensible. It does, at least at first glance, certainly seem possible to translate a passage out of "figurese" into some unmarked or "literal" register: "Alas! Gone are the daisies of summer" can become "Unfortunately summer is over." The first or "figured" version boasts an *ecphonesis* or affixed outcry, the syntactic inversion of *hyperbaton*, and the *metonymy* "daisies of summer" for summer itself, one device from each of the three categories tropes, schemes, and figures of thought. The second version has, apparently, nothing to which a label from even the most expanded lexicon of the figures could be attached (a point revisited below). The apparent possibility of moving from one language domain to another in this way has led to classifications of language subtypes, like C. K. Ogden and I. A. Richards' categorization of language across the span from emotive/poetic to rhetorical to scientific (Ogden and Richards 1923, 149, 234). A "scientific" version of the daisy sentence might be, "It is September 22."[8] The *reductio ad absurdum* of mapping figures onto categories of language use is the belief, sometimes held by students, that only "poetic" uses of language employ the figures or even that if figures are present the text must be poetic.

Are the figures only "value-added" rather than constitutive? That issue can be addressed first by considering the relation between figured usage and the expression of emotions. Though the emotion conveyed by a figure can only be identified in context (both the immediate context in which the figure appears and the broader social context in which the text appears), readers do attribute emotional significa-tion to some verbal devices. But does it follow, as it seems to in a value-added view, that only these devices can communicate the emotional dimension of a text? In other words, the important question is not whether certain figures express certain emotions but whether these emotions can be expressed without identifiable fig-ures. Surely they can. Even the presumably unemotional "scientific" sentence cited above, "It is September 22," can be charged with emotion depending, as all real utterances depend, on the rhetorical or contextual dimensions of its appearance: "The execution is set for September 23rd. It is September 22." This same "scien-tific" sentence would express a different emotion if it ended successive paragraphs recounting the delights of a well-spent summer. Thus, whether a sentence conveys an emotion is very much a function of its rhetorical situation, the from whom, to whom, what, and where of its occurrence. By tone of voice and gesture, a speaker can convey a wide variety of emotions in locutions that look very ordinary out of context. Certain figures of thought like the apostrophe and the aposiopesis have been linked to the emotions because they remain marked even in somewhat decon-textualized written texts. But any locution can carry such freight.

Another way to break an exclusive figure/emotion connection would be to ask whether it is really possible to say anything at all, figured or not, without emotion. The sample sentence again, "It is September 22," can certainly be put in an appar-ently unremarkable context: "It is September 22. The mail was late but the rain stopped." Yet such "flat" or "plain" or "bald" sentences can still be said to convey an emotion: the emotion of flatness or calmness, seriousness, steady-eyed contem-plation, or straight conviction. An even heartbeat is still a heartbeat. If it is impos-sible to have a text without emotion, it cannot be said that the figures add emotion to something wholly without it; they only help to express the emotion appropriate to the context. The figures of thought have been associated with the more extreme and habitually recognized kinds of emotion, but these "big ticket" emotions are on a continuum with the less remarkable kinds, rage diffusing into anger, anger into indignation, indignation into hardness of heart, and so on down the scale to mild indifference. They are not even the only ways to express or mark the extreme emotions. An understatement [litotes] can also express rage. They are merely the ways that have been traditionally and conventionally noticed in association with such emotions. They are succinct or particularly effective forms for expressing emotions, but they are not the only ways.

The analysis undertaken so far resists the assumption that an emotional dimen-sion can be factored out of an expression leaving a "content" behind. Although the profound division in the Western tradition between emotion and reason is not easily challenged, the assumption of separability is worth some probing. An *aposiopesis*, the abrupt breaking off of a predication before completion ("And then he read in the letter that . . . "), presumably conveys the speaker's sudden emotional breakdown. The context will suggest whether that is because the material is too offensive or too horrible or too revealing, or even if the speaker is just too confused to know how to finish the sentence. But the aposiopesis also tells an audience there is some material the speaker cannot or wishes not to express. The speaker conveys what may be a wonderfully useful uncertainty about the unexpressed material. A speaker could, of course, accomplish this same goal by simply saying, "I cannot say what he read in that letter." But the abrupt stop and the dangling half sentence deliver this same content iconically. The sentence does what it says.

The "what it says" is not the particular propositional content, the reference to a "he" and a "letter" in the example. The "what it says" here is the premise conveyed by the figure, which could be called its "argumentative content": there is some material the speaker does not want to reveal or cannot reveal to the audience. The unexpressed material may be scurrilous or libelous—readers and listeners will be in hot pursuit of the implications—but it can actually be more useful to the arguer to leave the precise nature of the inexpressibility murky, undefined. In *On Style*, written in the second century C.E., Hermogenes recommended this stylistic tactic as a way of adding an undefined premise (Hermogenes 1987, 89). A lump of inexpressibility stopping the speaker in mid-predication can be a useful point in the building of an argument. Nor is it really possible to factor out the emotional content from the argumentative content. Though there is a long tradition of distinguishing appeals to the reason from appeals to the emotions, the two halves that would be separated out in this analysis would not add up to the whole expressed by the aposiopesis, since inexpressibility is both an emotional and material point. Nuanced complexes of attitude plus material together constitute an argument and cannot really be untwined.

Value-added theories of the figures have, then, been seriously misleading, especially when the value presumably added is a dissociable emotional dimension, and they have mistakenly reinforced a great division in language between two domains. From the perspective of the language user, it is more useful to think of the expressions available for a particular function as a range of possibilities on a continuum. These possibilities are not divided into two separate levels, the literal and figurative. Instead, the choices available to a speaker can be thought of as less to more constitutive or iconic. The figures of speech occupy examined territory on this continuum of expressive possibilities. They have traditionally been used (and hence identified) as particularly effective ways of saying what can also be said in many other ways. They are, in other words, ideally but not exclusively constitutive of a text's many meanings, simply doing better what it is possible to do with other means, or even doing best what they are traditionally identified as doing. As Edward Surtz put it, the whole art of *elocutio* and the figures in the rhetorical tradition can be described as a search for "the perfect expression for one's ideas" (Vickers 1988, 283). Of course, the perfect expression, as far as content is concerned, may not always be the wisest in a particular situation. The fact that the aposiopesis, for example, is the best way to express inexpressibility by enacting it does not mean that it is always the best choice for that purpose; there may be situations where an announcement of intentional inexpressibility ("I cannot/will not say what he read in that letter") is a wiser rhetorical choice. But the speaker making this point with an aposiopesis is not entering a land of linguistic oddities. Once and for all the figures should come out of the cabinet of curiosities.

A view of the figures as examined territory on a continuum of possibilities explains why there has never been and never can be a fixed number of the figures. As Cicero explained in his *Topica*, while the number of types of issue is fixed in rhetoric, the number of figures of style and thought are not, for "there is no limit to this subject" (1949, 407). One can have more or fewer depending on one's patience and interest. To their great benefit, scholars in the early modern period had a great deal of such patience and interest, compiling figure catalogs of hundreds of functions and forms. The co-occurrence of such interest with the magnificence of the literary output of the time is not coincidental.

Thinking of the figures as better but not unique ways to achieve certain discourse functions also solves the considerable definitional problems they have always posed. It explains why there has never been a satisfactory definition of figurative language that rigorously separates it from an unfigured domain of usage. There never can be such a definition. The minority view that Quintilian set aside was right. Furthermore, it is not really necessary to reconcile the various definitions of the figures that have been offered because they cannot disagree. The figures may be at once acceptable usage and statistically atypical usage as well as carriers of emotion and vividness and force. They can be said to "add distinction" or other virtues in the sense that the text with appropriate figures has used the most effective linguistic means possible to do its work. Even the mechanism of substitution can be retained, so long as it means reaching into the same bag for different choices, not into an opposite sort of bag. None of these descriptions is incompatible with a more precise characterization of the figures as the formal embodiments of certain ideational or persuasive functions.

The Figures as Epitomes of Lines of Reasoning

A more useful view of the figures shifts the emphasis from what the figures are to what it is they do particularly well, what it is they express iconically. The traditional association of some of the figures with certain emotions has already been explored. In a parallel impulse, a handful of other figures can be identified with certain forms of argument or reasoning, and it is a small group of these devices that will be scrutinized in the chapters to follow. Associating certain verbal figures with general lines of reasoning, called "topics" in the rhetorical tradition, also assumes that it is possible to define these lines or arguments in the first place, a notion that for contemporary readers with no exposure to rhetoric may seem as odd as the figures themselves. While most people have a practical lexicon of the emotions that can be expressed by certain figures, they do not have a corresponding lexicon for lines of argument. When distinguishing among particular lines of argument or topics ceased to be an educational goal, it is not surprising that the cognate notion of the figures as epitomes of those lines was lost as well. A repertoire of lines of argument is also part of the material of rhetoric and of its sister art of practical reasoning, dialectic. Cicero's *Topica*, meant to be an improvement over Aristotle's *Topics,* for example, lists 17 all-purpose arguments to stimulate the construction of particular cases. Such an enterprise of cataloging or listing types of arguments and using such a prefabricated, one-size-fits-all list as an inventional resource is completely antithetical to contemporary notions of, on the one hand, the spontaneity of invention and its resources in inaccessible psychological processes, and, on the other hand, the rootedness of invention in the precise material under scrutiny. For someone to say that they are driven or inspired by general topics or lines of argument rather than by personal insight or by the evidence at hand would probably seem absurd to most people.

That is not to say that general standards or procedures of method and argument do not exist. They do. But these days they are confined to certain professions, materials, types of argument, or situations: the law, quality control management, laboratory procedure, casework in the social services, for example. The only technology of reasoning currently available that is meant to hold across many fields is the discipline of statistics, which does indeed offer a good analogy for the prestige, the aura of rigor, that topical invention and knowledge of the figures once had among the educated. Though there have been some attempts to regain a place for generic skills of argumentation, invention heuristics have nothing like the credibility they once had in the Western tradition. But understanding the figures as epitomes of certain lines of argument or reasoning does require also reinstating these durable, completely general lines. The fact that scholars have long recognized metaphor as an epitome of analogical reasoning makes the point. One need only accept that human reasoning exploits more than analogy, and that, therefore, more figures than metaphor are linked to corresponding modes of reasoning.

What does it mean to say that a verbal figure epitomizes a line of reasoning? An epitome, from the Greek verb meaning "to cut short or cut upon," is in one sense a summary, an abstract containing all the essential parts of a larger work or text, and, in a slightly different sense, it is a representative or exemplary selection from and then substitution for something longer. The figure, then, is a verbal summary that epitomizes a line of reasoning. It is a condensed or even diagram-like rendering of the relationship among a set of terms, a relationship that constitutes the argument and that could be expressed at greater length.

Antimetabole: Illustrating the figure/topic relationship

A good example of an epitomizing figure, one discussed further in chapter 4, is the *antimetabole* defined as a figure (sometimes of diction, sometimes of amplification) that reverses the relative positions of a pair of key terms in parallel phrases. A perfect example comes from a 1950s ad for the then-new wonder packaging material cellophane: "Protects what it shows/ Shows what it protects." In the ad's picture, these two phrases occupy balloons coming from the mouths of a mother holding a loaf of cellophane-wrapped bread and a daughter eating a sandwich, so

[handwritten margin note: Figure: verbal summary that epitomizes line of reasoning]

the meaning is also iconographically reinforced. This one example could be the subject of extensive analysis, but, briefly, the reversal in relative position of the two key words, "protects" and "shows," expresses succinctly the argument that the ad is making about cellophane. The new material has two interchangeable and simultaneous properties and functions; it is both transparent and nonporous, making a food product both visible and yet safe from contamination at the same time. Such a verbal figure may be, and in fact often is, used along with an expanded restatement of the argument, providing reinforcing details for the central claim. In the presence of more text, it could be said, as the old manuals would put it, that the precise phrasing of this figure adds force or vividness to the whole argument. But it also is the argument itself in the most compressed form possible. If the text were to be reduced to one sentence, that one sentence, emblematic of the whole, would be the figure.

Ad writers earn enormous sums to craft memorable phrases, and the antimetabole has had a particularly vibrant run in such copy. But the same form appeared in a very different context, in the justification given by a murderer who turned himself in many years after committing his crimes and hiding successfully under an alias. As he explained his surrender, "I would rather have my body locked up and my mind free, than living as I was, with another identity, with my mind locked up and my body free" (McFadden 1994, B4). The essence of the murderer's argument with himself is again epitomized by an <u>antimetabole</u>, a reversal of the <u>syntactic positions and semantic</u> roles of two key terms. This time, however, the terms that change places (mind and body) attach themselves in the process to different predicates (locked up and free) that maintain their relative positions. Both of these pairs, mind/body and locked up/free, express opposed or antithetical notions, adding another figure (the antithesis) and hence another argument in this instance. But it is the inversion that carries the causal argument in this case, presenting as plausible the changing of one's behavior to correct the relative state of one's body and mind.

Still another example of an argument from inversion or reciprocity perfectly epitomized in an antimetabole comes from another field and another century. In 1691, John Ray assembled the best arguments for a "natural theology," a belief, as the title of his work proclaims, that all of God's creations—the sun, moon and stars, the earth and its rivers and seas, and all the animals and plants—manifest His wisdom and beneficence. Ray's book is filled with instances of what would later be called "adaptation": sea plants grow flat and fan-like to bend with the currents (Ray 1977, 85); camels have sacks for storing water before desert crossings (344), rain falls down gradually rather than in destructive streams (88–89), and some birds have short legs for swimming but long necks for getting their food from the bottom of ponds, "For Nature makes not a long Neck to no purpose" (159). Ray is aware of the main rebuttal to his arguments.

> To elude or evade the Force of all these Instances, and innumerable others, which might be produced, to demonstrate, that the Bodies of Men and all other Animals were the Effects of the Wisdom and Power of an intelligent and almighty Agent, and the several Parts and Members of them designed to the Uses to which they now serve, the Atheist hath one Subterfuge, in which he most confides, viz. That all these Uses

of Parts are no more than what is necessary to the very Existence of the Things to whom they belong: *And that Things made Uses, and not Uses Things.* (Ray 1977, 357; italics added)

In elegant compression, Ray uses the antimetabole in a form that it frequently takes: one side as the correction of the other. The Atheists' inversion, that the animals parts determine their function and not their function those parts, will reappear 100 years later in arguments summarized by Lamarck (see chapter 4).

The arguments epitomized by antimetaboles in these three passages are not identical any more than the analogies epitomized by different metaphors are identical. The ad uses an antimetabole to express an indifference in ordering two terms and hence properties that are paradoxically simultaneous, the murderer uses an antimetabole to present a convincing motive for changing one's behavior in order to change the relationship between two sets of antithetical terms, and John Ray uses an antimetabole to express succinctly the incompatibility between two views of adaptation. Yet these arguments share a family resemblance by virtue of the fact that they can all be succinctly expressed by an antimetabole. This type of argument by reversal was identified in the rhetorical tradition almost 2500 years ago as was the durable verbal device called the antimetabole that epitomizes it, an argumentative scheme that persists across centuries and situations. There is a long tradition, especially powerful in the text-based side of rhetorical studies, of emphasis on such formal techniques and on the argumentative strategies they can express.

Recapturing an older view

There have certainly been indications of a form/function rationale for the figures in the canonical texts of the tradition, especially in what is, at least from a twentieth-century perspective, *the* canonical text, Aristotle's *Rhetoric*. Though scholarly consensus maintains that Aristotle has neither a theory of figuration nor even a general term for figures of speech (Kennedy 1991, 242, 248), Book III of the *Rhetoric*, devoted to style, does introduce a handful of verbal devices formally recognizable across instances, including metaphor, antithesis, asyndeton, and simile. At no place in Book III does Aristotle claim that these devices serve an ornamental or emotional function or that they are in any way epiphenomenal. Instead, Aristotle's somewhat dispersed discussion suggests that certain devices are compelling because they map function onto form or perfectly epitomize certain patterns of thought or argument. A case in point is his account of asyndeton, the elimination of connectives from a series, and its "opposite" in chapter 12: "Furthermore, asyndeta have a special characteristic; many things seem to be said at the same time; for the connective makes many things seem one, so that if it is taken away, clearly the opposite results: one thing will be many (256)." In other words, a series without connectives seems to Aristotle to express the separateness and therefore the multiplicity of the items mentioned; as he says of his offered example, "'I came; I spoke; I besought,' (these things seem many)" (256). Thus the special verbal device here, the elimination of the expected connective, expresses a specific meaning in itself, passing on the impression of many distinct objects, actions or notions. The form delivers this meaning regardless of the actual items in the series. Conversely, Aristotle believes that adding connectives can join items into a unity; a version like "I came and I spoke and I besought," seems to emphasize the connectedness or combination of these three separate actions. The version with asyndeton says, "I did three separate things"; the version with polysyndeton (connectives between each item) says, "I did all three of these things," a slight but potentially significant difference in the course of building an argument. By contrast, the *Ad Herennium* says only of asyndeton that it "has animation and great force, and is suited to concision" ([Cicero] 1954, 331), concision because words are removed; otherwise, the author of the *Ad Herennium*, claiming only the general *dignitas* achieved through ornamentation, pays no attention to the specific ideational work of the figure.

In chapter 10 of Book III, Aristotle singles out three devices for special attention because they are useful for creating "urbane" or smart expressions that are "well liked" (Kennedy 1991, 245). These three are metaphor, antithesis, and energeia, or "bringing before the eyes." Here it might seem that Aristotle is indeed dealing with devices that add glamor or spin to a text. But the claims he makes about these three do not sustain that interpretation. Though his pupil Theophrastus presumably added ornamentation to the three virtues of style that Aristotle does discuss—perspicuity, correctness, and appropriateness—Aristotle himself does not offer "value-added" rationales for his three special verbal devices. Instead, his comments suggest that these devices are compelling because they are perfect formal embodiments of the speaker's meanings and intentions. Even metaphor, as it is described in the *Rhetoric*, is a substitution serving some functional end. The speaker, Aristotle advises, should avoid far-fetched metaphors (226) and select only those that create "quick learning" in an audience (245). Urbanities, especially those achieved through metaphorical choices that are neither banal nor too far-fetched, make clear to a listener "that he learned something different from what he believed, and his mind seems to say, 'How true, and I was wrong'" (250). In other words, rhetorical metaphors, and indeed other lexical substitutions like epithets, are not chosen simply because they are strange and elevating but because they express perfectly, efficiently, and unobtrusively the precise idea the speaker is trying to convey. Depending on whether the speaker's purpose is blame or praise, mules are half-asses or the daughters of storm-footed mares (225).

What is true of metaphor and asyndeton in Aristotle's account is also true of the other two sources of asteia, antithesis and energeia; each accesses conviction or creates insight in a uniquely efficient way. Hence Aristotle's frequent emphasis on "learning" or imparting knowledge as the result of effective presentation of ideas and arguments, in turn the result of making the best possible verbal choices (Kennedy 1991, 242, 244, 245, 250, 252). This repeated emphasis in Book III on learning from effective presentation has to be puzzling from the later perspective that sets the figures apart as merely ornamental, which leads to a division into levels of style based in part on the extent of such ornamentation. Aristotle has no such theory of levels of prose style (like three fixed dial settings, low, middle, and high), because he has a theory of continuously tunable appropriateness based on functionally selected forms suitable to the subject, speaker, and occasion. There is, then, to reestablish the implicit connection between his theory of functional verbal devices in Book III and the opening definition of rhetoric in Book

I, a best available means or choice of lexis in every particular case (see also 225). Aristotle also seems to recognize that a theory of functionally efficient forms is dangerous, for he observes that if the "proper lexis also makes the matter credible," it becomes possible to fake the credible with the proper lexis. The speaker who can master this art can lead the listener "to draw a false inference of the truth" (235) merely because of the successful manner of presentation. His own antithesis, as demonstrated in chapter 2, is one of the most successful forms for this kind of linguistic strong-arming.

Cicero was cited above as the eloquent spokesperson for the dominant view of the figures as ornaments to a text. But a closer scrutiny of Cicero's wording in the passage quoted above (see p. 18) suggests that his theory of the figures may also be closer to a stronger functional view of what the figures can accomplish. For what the translator H. M. Hubbell renders as "embellishment," Cicero consistently describes in terms of light and illumination [lumina/illuminare]. To embellish something is to add to its surface, but to illuminate can mean to shine through as well as on something, to make it bright from within, in effect bringing out or expressing its inherent nature. Cicero actually makes this distinction himself in the *Brutus*, the rhetorical treatise he devoted to the criticism of other orators. In praising Demosthenes, and through him Antonius, he observes that the σχήματα [schemata] are the greatest ornaments of oratory, not in giving weight because they paint on words, but because they illuminate the thought ["maxime ornant oratorem eaque non tam in verbis pingendis habent pondus quam in illuminandis sententiis"] (Cicero 1988, 123–125). Again the sense Cicero seems to be after is stylistic choice that is not added as an afterthought to a text, as color is applied to a surface, but stylistic choice that shines through and therefore expresses the speaker's meaning and intention. The translator has replaced Cicero's terms with later words that represent the specifically literary understanding of the figures as epiphenomenal additions that create the aesthetic dimension of a text.

A text from the second century C.E., Hermogenes' *On Types of Style*, also provides an understanding of the functional place of figures in rhetorical stylistics within 300 years of the appearance of the first catalog in the *Rhetorica ad Herennium* and 100 years of Quintilian's careful analysis. In the tradition of Longinus' *On Sublimity*, Hermogenes analyzes not one but seven main types of style and 20 substyles in all, named generally from their overall effect: clarity, grandeur, beauty, solemnity, vehemence, and so forth. Each is described by the thoughts or content it usually expresses, the approaches that are appropriate, and the style it displays, including the characteristic word choices, figures of speech, kinds of clauses, word order, cadences, and rhythm.

Two features of Hermogenes' treatment contradict the usual understanding of the figures as after-the-fact embellishment. First is the tight continuity Hermogenes establishes between what the speaker is trying to accomplish and the best stylistic means to do it. The subject matter of the vehement speaker, for example, is the indictment of a target that the audience is pleased to have criticized, and to accomplish such an indictment, the vehement speaker should coin harsh words and use questions, direct address, pointed expressions, and pauses (Hermogenes 1987, 30–31). Second, the devices that Hermogenes identifies as figures of speech show that the category is very broad in his thinking. "The figure that is most character-istic of Purity," for example, "is the use of a straightforward construction with the noun in the nominative case" (10); in other words, Hermogenes identifies normal subject-noun predication as a figure. Another effect, sincerity, is communicated by direct address and questions, long identified as figures, but also by pointing expressions using "this" and "that" (95). Only in the case of the stylistic elements that aim at Beauty does Hermogenes speak of adornment in something like the later literary meanings of the term: "The figures that create Beauty are those that call attention to their ornamental nature and show clearly that the style has been embellished" (56). Yet, according to Hermogenes, even Demosthenes, his exem-plar of the perfect practical orator, uses these devices in persuasion, and Beauty is even valuable "where there is a need for close argument and careful reason-ing" (110). Overall then, Hermogenes' rationale for the figures extends beyond accreted adornment that draws attention to itself to a constitutive functionality, and his notion of a functional figure is broad enough to include ordinary sen-tence patterns.

Further historical support for a view of the figures as intimately linked to the argument or work of a text comes from Thomas Conley's well-documented in-terrogation of the competing meanings of the term *enthymeme*. In rhetorical theory derived from Aristotle, an enthymeme is sometimes defined as a "trun-cated" syllogism that leaves unexpressed a premise the audience supplies from its storehouse of beliefs. An argument like "We should elect X because she has moderate views" rests on the assumption that moderate views are a good or election-deserving quality; that is the missing premise or assumption that pre-sumably makes the link between the explicitly offered premise (because she has moderate views) and the conclusion (we should elect X) possible. The brief two-part form of the enthymeme could be expanded into a full syllogism, though doing so invites an application, or more often a misapplication, of the standards of formal logic that might declare invalid all kinds of perfectly convincing en-thymematic arguments. But Conley demonstrates that rhetoricians before and after Aristotle, and even some passages in the *Rhetoric* itself, express a different definition of the enthymeme.

According to one alternate view, the term *enthymeme* refers to an expression, usually brief and contained within a period, which functions as the stylistic "cap-per" of an argument. Conley's investigation of Isocrates' uses of the term, before Aristotle, demonstrates this more stylistic meaning, though such passages from Isocrates, Conley points out, have been translated in a way that conflates with the later understanding of the term.[9] Rather than drawing on an audience's system of beliefs, an enthymeme in this second sense summarizes and re-expresses material already explicit in the speeches the audience is hearing. As described in an anony-mous Byzantine commentary on Hermogenes' *On Invention*, an enthymeme de-rives its force "from its ability to draw together a large body of material and as-sertions and compress it in a particularly striking way" (Conley 1984, 173; the quotation is a paraphrase, not a translation from the source). Even the examples Aristotle cites of lines of argument or "enthymematic topoi" suggest, according to Conley, that enthymemes are "nicely turned sentences or questions raised at cli-

mactic points in the course of a speech" (171). In other sources, Conley finds the
enthymeme similarly defined as a "finishing off" (176), a "pungent" expression that
drives home a point forcefully (178).

There is then, in many rhetorical texts from the fourth century B.C.E. to the end
of the Byzantine Empire, some now rarely read, perhaps because they represent a
lost understanding, an "ambiguity—perhaps a confusion—about the line that divides argumentation from style" (Conley 1984, 176). But this is only a confusion
from the perspective that insists on a radical disjunction between style and argument. As Conley himself goes on to suggest:

> In viewing argumentation from this perspective, we can see how the notion of
> *enthymema* as a finely wrought "cap," which we encountered in our survey, could
> have a kind of legitimacy. Such a "cap," whether comprised of thoughts which link
> themselves together in the manner of a syllogism or thoughts which are linked only
> by means of the devices of style . . . can very well have legitimate argumentative force.
> Its force, however, could never be appreciated (or even perceived) outside of the
> context in which it occurs. (182)

This recovered definition of the "other" enthymeme, the "stylistic capper," surely
restores a common-sense notion about how arguments work textually. Keeping
in mind their linear dimension, the fact that arguments are experienced, whether
heard or read, in time, it makes sense to think of them as ebbing and surging,
now at a "lower" point of restatement or elaboration and now at a "higher" point
of succinct and epitomizing summation, giving the gist of the longer passage. A
stylistic enthymeme is thus that moment in a text when the argument is most
directly and emphatically expressed by the syntax and word choice. An arguer
works to achieve this high point, and there should not be, as Aristotle, Quintilian,
and others rightly observe, too many of these high points in immediate succession.
But there is no need for the dismissive "only" in Conley's text. This enthymeme-
as-stylistic-capper can take the form of a figure of speech exactly epitomizing the
line of argument employed. It was probably the recognition of this summative
potential that allowed Aristotle, picking up on the older, diffuse meaning of the
term, to emphasize the argumentative power of the enthymeme as he subtly redefined the term.[10]

The great sixteenth-century rhetorician and reformer, Philip Melancthon, also
testifies to the constitutive power of the figures that Conley traced in the older texts
and to their essential connection with the construction of arguments. After introducing a third type of scheme, the figures of amplification, Melancthon general-
izes about all the figures:

> The zealous reader will observe that all the figures, especially those that enhance
> a speech, have their origin in dialectical expressions, and if one has practical knowl-
> edge to associate them, he will be able to evaluate very many in cases subtly and
> keenly and better perceive the distinct divisions of the work. For the same expres-
> sions, when applied for the purpose of confirming or confuting, are bases for
> argument and the sinews, as they are called. When applied for the purpose of
> adorning, they are called rhetorical ornaments. And very many not only have
> been adapted to give a show of battle, but to add weight to the arguments. (263–
> 264)

Melancthon, as the author of both rhetorical and dialectical treatises, was in a unique position to appreciate the link between forms of argument and forms of expression and hence of the constitutive power of the figures in argument.

Reasons for the figure/topic separation

A different reading through key texts in the rhetorical tradition certainly warrants a more functional view of the figures and a closer link between them and the lines of argument identified as the topics. How is it then that the two systems became separated or separable? One answer requires an appreciation of the traditional partitioning of discourse skills in classical rhetoric. The canonical division known as the parts of rhetoric separates invention, the recovery or discovery of potential premises; from disposition, the optimal arrangement of these premises given the arguer's immediate situation; and from elocutio, the expression of those arguments in appropriate and effective language. This division of the subject matter of rhetoric translates too easily into a chronological sequence so that it is assumed to represent steps in the process of composition. One thinks up material, arranges it to suit the occasion, and then finds a suitable means of expressing it (let alone, in oral situations, committing it to memory and finding an appropriate mode of delivery). But there has always been an undertow working against the separation of invention and style, and it is even possible to discover arguments stylistically, as the following chapters demonstrate, by using the figures generatively, allowing the form to find the content.

Another explanation for the traditional separation of the figures and the topics comes from the accidents of history. In the centuries of its greatest development, the separate parts of rhetoric became the objects of attention in separate treatises. The youthful Cicero, for example, intended to write a separate work on each of the five parts, though only his treatise on the first part, *De Inventione*, remains. In the second century C.E., Hermogenes did produce influential separate treatises on style, the stases (a part of invention), and other elaborations that have not survived. Quintilian cites a bewildering number of treatises on separate rhetorical issues, including a work devoted exclusively to the sound *s*, and one of the most famous treatises remaining from antiquity, Longinus's *Sublimity*, is in this tradition of elaborating on a small part of a well known larger system. When, however, only some of these treatises survive and the entire system of which they were a part disintegrates, it becomes difficult to appreciate the connections among what remains. It is as though some scholar a thousand years from now came upon the "shuffle-toe-stomp" directions for a tap dance and a tape recording of the song "Blue Skies Smiling at Me" and had no idea that they were meant to be performed together. The parts of rhetoric, and particularly invention and style, were meant to be learned together and performed together, one as the expression of the other.

Curiously, methods of teaching also influenced the dismemberment of rhetoric and the isolation of the figures from argumentation. Pedagogical practice from antiquity through the Renaissance was typically divided between the work of the grammaticus teaching younger students the "language arts" and the teacher of rhetoric. The grammaticus, a teacher of Latin and Greek in the schools of Rome and a teacher primarily of Latin in the schools of medieval Europe, typically introduced students to the prestige language with the parsing of literary texts (Percival 1983, 305), a parsing that consisted not only of a word-for-word construal for meaning and grammatical case but also a rigorous identification of the figures. Medieval and early modern grammar texts typically included, along with the parts of speech and the rules of agreement, a discussion of figures, especially the syntactic figures or schemes. The precedent for this inclusion was the much used Latin grammar (*Ars Maior*) of Donatus. Thus students learned the tropes and other figures as part of the rudiments of their mastery of Latin texts and Latin composition, so that when they moved on to the study of Cicero's speeches and the drafting and delivery of *suasoriae*, persuasive speeches, they came to these tasks with a significant stylistic repertoire. Though it was only, once again, the earlier parts of a complete system of education, the study of literary texts like Homer and Virgil and the identification of figures were wedded together in school practice and to some extent they have been ever since.

Essentially the same system of education was still in place through the eighteenth century and into the beginning of the nineteenth century. The practice of partitioning the curriculum eventually produced an analogous partitioning in the figures so that, for example, when Pierre Fontanier wrote his treatise on the figures in the early nineteenth century, a treatise based on his criticism of Du Marsais' exclusive attention to the tropes, he nevertheless also wrote his text in two parts, the first a *Manuel classique pour l'etude des Tropes* (1821, with further editions in 1822, 1825, and 1830) and the second a study of *Figures autres que les tropes* [Figures other than the tropes] (1827). This division, as Gérard Genette explains in his introduction to Fontanier, was necessitated by the fact that Fontanier's first text on the tropes was used for the "second" class while the study of the non-tropes was reserved for the subsequent rhetoric class (Fontanier 1977, 5, n. 1). So, at least in France, the ancient division between the grammaticus and the teacher of rhetoric was mapped onto the figures themselves. When in 1870 the French went to a system of national education, they retained the study of *belles lettres* but dropped rhetoric from the curriculum and, as a consequence, figures that were not tropes were dropped as well.

Scholarly restorations

The teaching of the figures as functional in everyday argument and reasoning has long since disappeared from language curricula in the twentieth century. Nevertheless, if the connection is warranted, it would be amazing if it had gone unnoticed, especially in the gradual recovery of rhetoric that has been taking place since World War II. In fact, twentieth-century historians of rhetoric have been aware of the intimate connection between the figures and the topics or lines of argument. In an article published in 1990, James J. Murphy set the issue of this relationship explicitly by asking "whether the Greek *topoi* may in fact be the sources of the Roman *figuræ*" (Murphy 1990, 244). And almost twenty years ago A. Kibédi Varga called for an explication of the resulting inherently hierarchical structure of rhetoric, an elaboration of its levels of explanation that are traditionally stratified in the different parts of the art (invention, arrangement, style). In Varga's heroic recasting, "Every phenomenon should be defined at its own level but it should also be comprehended at each higher level. Every *figure* should be defined as part of elocution, but at the same time it should be mentioned in relation to the topic within which it usually appears and functions, in the chapter on invention" (Varga 1983, 86). For a rhetorical theory that is less a "pedagogical method for teaching and learning eloquence" than a "semiotic-pragmatic method for analyzing discourse," Varga envisions a hierarchy of explanatory levels ascending from grammar through elocution, the topics, the three appeals (ethos, logos, pathos), the stases, and the *genera dicendi* (the types of speeches), though the direction of explanation would always be from the higher level down. Of all these potentially interrelated levels, Varga believes that the connection between the figures and the topics has in fact received the most attention (87).

Much of the credit for that attention is, as Varga justly observes, due to a work published in 1947 by the Renaissance scholar Sister Miriam Joseph. As background to her extensive study of *Shakespeare's Use of the Arts of Language*, Sister Joseph's review of late sixteenth-century rhetorical treatises led her to several conclusions:

> first that the general theory of composition and of reading current in Shakespeare's England is to be found in one form in the contemporary works on logic and rhetoric combined; second, that it is to be found in another form in the work of the figurists which, surprisingly, treats of approximately the same matter as do the logic and rhetoric texts combined; third, that these two forms, though outwardly different, are fundamentally alike. (4)

In the almost 200 figures of speech identified in the Renaissance figure manuals there was ample scope, Sister Joseph observes, for redefining virtually every aspect of rhetorical theory in terms of verbal equivalents and memorizable exempla (17–18). To bring out the similarity in coverage between the full treatises on rhetoric and the figure manuals, she recategorized the figures into those dealing with "the aesthetic aspects of grammar" (34) and those delivering the three appeals (36). Particularly valuable is her categorization of the figures under logos according to the 17 Ciceronian topics, a categorization that will be drawn on in the following chapters. Sister Joseph's insight was reaffirmed for scholars in speech communication by J. Donald Ragsdale in an article which, based on an examination of seventeenth and eighteenth-century rhetorics, also categorizes the figures according to the three appeals. Furthermore, Ragsdale points out that, given this relationship between the figures and the appeals, it is a mistake to claim that the style manuals ignored invention (Ragsdale 1965, 164, 167). That Sister Joseph's study has received less attention than it deserves from rhetoricians is perhaps due to her dedicating her theorizing solely to the service of Shakespearean exegesis in a relentless listing (here is one of these, there is one of those) that equates less with more important forms and that consequently downplays the power of any single figure to carry an argument.[11] The net result of her prodigious scholarship is that the figures remain firmly within the tradition of belles lettres and are distanced both historically and statistically from everyday usage. They are something that literary geniuses used a long time ago.

In a work written a few years after Sister Joseph's study, *A Rhetoric of Motives* (1969b), Kenneth Burke, operating outside of the traditional academic partitioning of types of discourse and the valorizing of the literary, saw to the heart of the ability of the figures to express a particular line of argument and simultaneously to induce an audience to participate in that argument simply by virtue of their form. Burke's theory of rhetoric hinges on his principle of identification, the consubstantial unifying of speaker and audience through the devices of rhetoric. One of an arguer's ways of inducing such identification is to offer formal patterns that invite the audience's participation because they

> awaken an attitude of collaborative expectancy in us. For instance, imagine a passage built about a set of oppositions ("*we* do *this*, but *they* on the other hand do *that*; *we* stay *here*, but *they* go *there*; *we* look *up*, but *they* look *down*," etc.). Once you grasp the trend of the form, it invites participation regardless of the subject matter. Formally, you find yourself swinging along with the succession of antitheses, even though you may not agree with the proposition that is being presented in this form. Or it may even be an opponent's proposition which you resent—yet for the duration of that statement itself you might "help him out" to the extent of yielding to the formal development, surrendering to its symmetry as such. Of course, the more violent your original resistance to the proposition, the weaker will be your degree of "surrender" by "collaborating" with the form. But in cases where a decision is still to be reached, a yielding to the form prepares for assent to the matter identified with it. Thus, you are drawn to the form, not in your capacity as a partisan, but because of some "universal" appeal in it. And this attitude of assent may then be transferred to the matter which happens to be associated with the form. (58)

Burke believed that the formal appeal of some of the figures was stronger than that of others, but he had no interest in an analysis beyond that provided in a few pages on the antithesis and the gradatio, nor does he specify the lines of argument embodied in these formal devices. But he believed that he had identified the signs of a general psychological and aesthetic principle of formal persuasion whose range of applicability could easily be extended beyond his brief discussion.

It was extended in what is arguably the most important rhetorical treatise of the twentieth century, the monumental *La Nouvelle Rhetorique*, written by the Belgians Chaim Perelman (by training, a philosopher of jurisprudence) and Lucie Olbrechts-Tyteca (by training, a sociologist). Although the title of their work suggests a point of departure, it is in many ways a revival of the lost traditions of rhetoric and dialectic, a revival more necessary from a European than an American perspective. But *The New Rhetoric* does have some notable newnesses in matter and emphasis from other historically important rhetorical treatises, in particular its treatment of style in relation to argument. Rather than separating the discussion of style, and especially of the figures, from the discussion of invention, Perelman and Olbrechts-Tyteca reestablish the essential link between the two, and they recognize that when that link is broken and "the argumentative role of figures is disregarded, their study will soon seem to be a useless pastime, a search for strange names for rather farfetched and affected turns of speech" (1969, 167), precisely the disenchantment that has afflicted many commentators.

As part of their rethinking of the relation between style and argument, Perelman and Olbrechts-Tyteca necessarily explore definitions of the figures of speech. They find the same two characteristics that have been featured, either singly or together, in most definitions of the figures: an identifiable formal feature and a use "different from the normal manner of expression" (1969, 168). They recognize, however, the potential problems in these two parts of the definition of the figures: "In order that a structure be a possible object of study, it must be possible to isolate it, to recognize it as a structure; it is also necessary to know in what respect a use must be regarded as unusual" (168). Thus they realize that the *écart* definition of the figures has a trap door through which many figures will "fall" if they cease to be recognized as departures from ordinary usage: the rhetorical question, for example, is traditionally identified as a figure, but in what sense is its use abnormal? The structural or formal definition has its weak spot as well. It might be possible for anything formally identifiable to become a figure. "Theoretically," as the Belgians point out, "there is no structure incapable of becoming a figure by the way it is used" (169). The twin constraints of formal identifiability and uncommonness led some rhetoricians to reserve the label "figure" for the recognizable but deliberately artificial and by implication insincere uses of these devices. In other words, if a speaker intends the form, it is a figure, but if it is used without intention, it is not a figure. According to this view, an "Oh damn!" uttered when one stubs a toe is not a figure; an "Oh damn!" planned for the peroration of a speech is one.

To overcome these problems, Perelman and Olbrechts-Tyteca introduce a new twist in the definition of the figures, a dissociation of their own into two new classes. Putting aside the traditional division between the figures of speech and thought that they find obscuring (1969, 172), they place the dissociation, not in the speaker's intention, but in the audience's response. A traditional figure "occurs" when a hearer or reader notices it, distinguishing or dissociating its form from its substance in the process (169). But this temporary noticing can be overcome when the listener or reader perceives a justifying argumentative use of the figure: "The whole of the argumentative significance of figures arises at the moment when this distinction, which was immediately noticed, is dissolved through the effect produced by the speech" (169). "Forms which seem at first to be used in an unusual manner may come to appear normal if their use is justified by the speech taken as a whole" (169). For Perelman and Olbrechts-Tyteca, this possibility creates a new class of specifically argumentative figures.

> We consider a figure to be *argumentative,* if it brings about a change of perspective, and its use seems normal in relation to this new situation. If, on the other hand, the speech does not bring about the adherence of the hearer to this argumentative form, the figure will be considered an embellishment, a figure of style. It can excite admiration, but this will be on the aesthetic plane, or in recognition of the speaker's originality.
>
> It is apparent, then, that it is impossible to decide in advance if a given structure is or is not to be regarded as a figure, or if it will be an argumentative or a stylistic figure. The best one can do is to point out some structures that are liable to become figures. (169–170)

The New Rhetoric's redefinition of the figures has received little scholarly engagement, but it seems obvious from the start that it is highly problematic to the extent that it links the figures to an untraceable psychological experience, a perceptual moment in which a reader or listener becomes aware of a word or phrase *as* a word or phrase and then presumably accepts it because of its effectiveness in an argument, or because the text establishes its own norm and vis-à-vis this norm, the figure belongs.[12] It also seems less than useful to deprive the figures of argumentative force in proportion to their obviousness, though this point is tied to the general observation, made elsewhere in *The New Rhetoric*, that any awareness of technique on the audience's part can diminish the effectiveness of an argument. In addition to the doubtfulness of this double psycholinguistic moment of perceiving and then ignoring a device, the variability in such an awareness among consumers of the same text must be enormous. The ability to notice a figure as a figure, for example, though not necessarily the ability to notice an anomalous usage (and many figures are not anomalous), is surely tied to one's previous exposure to the figures, an exposure that was once a given for every educated person in the Western tradition, but that certainly no longer is.

Whether or not their overall definition of argumentative versus stylistic figures holds, the Belgians were innovative in tying figures to functions. They intertwine the two, dispersing figures among the techniques of argumentation identified in the book's extensive anatomy.

> Instead of embarking on an exhaustive examination of all the traditional figures, we shall inquire, in the context of a given argumentative procedure or scheme, if certain figures are of such a nature as to fulfil the function we have attributed to this procedure, if they can be regarded as one of its manifestations. This approach involves a sort of dismembering of the figures. For not only will figures range over different chapters of our study, but examples of a particular figure may occur in more than one chapter. We feel that it is this dismembering itself that best conveys the argumentative significance of the figures. (Perelman and Olbrechts-Tyteca 1969, 172)

This promise is fulfilled after an initial section (#42) devoted to what the Belgians call figures of "choice, presence, and communion," stylistic devices that accomplish a rhetor's selection of material (e.g., metonymy), or the emphasis of that material (e.g., anaphora), or the establishment of a rapport with an audience (e.g., rhetorical question). These are useful functional categories for the figures in the spirit of Henry Peacham, but more important are the figures dispersed throughout the text and tied to the specific strategies of argument. The figure *antimetabole* [as "commutation"], for example, employed in several examples cited above, is connected in *The New Rhetoric* with the general technique of dissociation as in the prizing apart of the senses of a term (428, 444). Thus the famous antimetabole "We should not live to eat but eat to live" really effects a separation, according to *The New Rhetoric*, between two different senses of "live," and perhaps of "eat" as well, by its reversal of the relationship between living and eating (428).With analyses like these, Perelman and Olbrechts-Tyteca have made the strongest technical case for an appreciation of the argumentative power of certain verbal forms.[13]

Boundary Problems

The previous two sections argue that the great treatises of the rhetorical tradition amply indicate an awareness of the fruitful figure/topic and figure/meaning linkage, and that this connection has been reestablished by many twentieth-century theorists and historians of rhetoric. Furthermore, in the last 15 years, cognitive linguists have amply demonstrated how even a metaphor, a single striking word choice from an alien semantic field, can indicate an entire conceptual system. A functional view of the figures then as "stylistic cappers," in a nonpejorative and nontrivial sense, as epitomes of the arguments in a text, is a well-warranted correction to the view of the figures as merely grace notes or verbal tinsel.

But are the figures of speech codified in the rhetorical tradition the only such form/function pairs possible? This question troubled Quintilian, who noted a competing view in his day that every locution is potentially a figure, since every thought expressed must acquire some unique "body" of expression (see p. 9). It struck Perelman and Olbrechts-Tyteca as a dangerous impasse as well: "Theoretically, there is no structure incapable of becoming a figure by the way it is used" (1969, 169), and the psychological gymnastics in their redefinition of figures owes much to their desire to avoid this free fall.

The problem of separating the figures from the category of the "literal" has long existed in the division of the tropes. An illustration of this problem is the confusion over *catachresis.* In some definitions, a catachresis is a type of metaphor, a substitute naming that occurs when a term is borrowed from another semantic field, not because the borrower wants to substitute for the "ordinary" term (e.g., "lion" for "warrior"), but because there is no ordinary term.[14] There is no word, for example, for the thing that people rest their arms on that comes out from the back of a chair (which also has no name) and is sometimes extended and attached to the seat. It takes periphrasis to describe it; some inspired user once called it an "arm," simultaneously anthropomorphizing the chair and suggesting the affected body part. That name stuck in "arm of the chair," "chair arm," and "armchair." The metaphoric origin of such coinages is well known as are theories of language growth that credit metaphoric extension as the force for such expansion. The need for catachretic naming in science in particular has been well noted and cited as, once again, a source of conceptual creativity.

The rhetor who uses catachresis, then, is not renaming, but naming. But if no substitution has gone on for an available term, how is metaphor involved? Doesn't a metaphoric usage require the presence of a competing, literal term? Yet if one looks through a dictionary with an etymologist's eye, the lexicon seems predominantly metaphoric, its abstractions traceable to catachretic borrowings from roots in its feeder languages. The problem with catachresis, then, is an instance of a general problem in a "two domain" theory of language: At what point do the figures cease and does "ordinary language" take over?

Just as it is difficult to separate catachretic coinages from metaphoric substitutions, so it should be difficult, though the problem has received scant attention, to separate figured from unfigured syntax. Again, at stake is the definition of figure. If figures are defined as departures from ordinary usage, or in Peacham's words as relief from the "wearisomnesse of our common speech," then by definition the departure must be notable. But if figures are defined as an identifiable convergence, felicity, or synergy of form and content, then separating the "figures" from ordinary usage becomes a problem. In other words, a return to a functional definition of the figures threatens to dissolve the category.

If a convergence of form and content is the essential characteristic of figures, then normal sentence patterns in English syntax figure the fixed or chosen interactions of the sentence elements. The typical pattern, subject/transitive verb/object, inevitably creates agents taking actions that affect recipients; the pattern subject/copula/complement inevitably forms the rhetoric of commentary on attributes. The unremarkable "It is September 22" cited above would be appreciated for its use of an anticipatory "it is" construction to throw the naming of the day into a position of emphasis at the end of the sentence. The language user's construction of meaning, as Richard Weaver noted in an antimetabole in 1953, is formally constrained by the conventions of grammar: "while you are doing something with it, it is doing something with you" (116). In this view, the most ordinary act of predication becomes an extraordinary act of figuration, not essentially different from the deployment of the most consciously crafted *gradatio*. Furthermore, just as rhetoricians judged whether a particular metaphoric choice served an author's purposes, it also becomes possible to judge whether the disposal of any sentence constituent seems to serve, or detract from, what the sentence should be expressing. Among rhetoricians of the past, Hugh Blair, eighteenth-century author of *Lectures on Rhetoric and Belles Lettres*, is the best practitioner of a form/function commentary on "ordinary" syntax. And the British stylisticians of this century follow this pursuit of the usual since their stylistics, as in Leech and Short's *Style in Fiction*, is predicated on normative practices, often quantitatively defined, unlike rhetorical stylistics that concentrates on the apparent departures.

The functional nature of identifiable forms in presumably nonfigured discourse can be illustrated by an analysis of the opening of Newton's celebrated 1672 paper on his "New Theory about Light and Colors [*sic*]":

> Sir, To perform my late promise to you, I shall without further ceremony acquaint you, that in the beginning of the Year 1666 (at which time I applied my self to the grinding of Optick glasses of other figures than *Spherical*,) I procured me a Triangular glass-Prisme, to try therewith the celebrated *Phenomena* of *Colours*. And in order thereto having darkened my chamber, and made a small hole in my window-shuts, to let in a convenient quantity of the Suns [*sic*] light, I placed my Prisme at his entrance, that it might be thereby refracted to the opposite wall. It was at first a very pleasing divertisement, to view the vivid and intense colours produced thereby; but after a while applying my self to consider them more circumspectly, I became surprised to see them in an *oblong* form; which, according to the received laws of Refraction, I expected should have been *circular*. (Newton 1672, 3075–3076)

The only identifiable figure in this passage is the "weak" personification of the sun as the "Sun" in the phrase "Sun's light," which has "his entrance" through a hole in Newton's shutters.[15] But this figure is left outside the room; the light that enters obeys a different rhetoric, the well-advertised transparent rhetoric of the Royal

Society, which is still a rhetoric in the sense of being a rationalizable tendency in stylistic choices.

Thus even in the absence of recognizable figures, the convergence of form and function here has not ended. Worth considering first is the "Cartesian" shape or strategy of this paragraph, the creation of exigence, of a problem requiring explanation, in the form of a personal, individual confusion at the perception of an anomaly. This strategy depends on the choice of "I" as agent, specifically in the report of mental events, "I became surprised." Noticeable next is the narrative shape, the story telling that has been heavily criticized by later historians of science as "storytelling" almost in the sense of fibbing (see Bazerman 1988, 90–95). Also worth pointing out are the grammatical choices that structure this narrative. Thus in his second sentence, Newton describes three actions, but he expresses two participially and antecedently: "having darkened my chamber" and "made a small hole in my window-shuts," thus emphasizing the action of the main predication, "I placed my Prisme." Here is the central action of the experiment to which the other actions, as preliminaries making this one possible, become subordinated while still antecedent. The sentence is a perfect formal embodiment of a certain sequence and emphasis.

In the next sentence, Newton removes himself as a perceptual agent: "It was at first a very pleasant divertisement, to view the vivid and intense colours produced thereby." He does not write "I viewed" or "I was diverted," thereby diminishing the perception of the phenomenon as uniquely personal. Even the mental act of "applying myself to consider them more circumspectly" is expressed obliquely. Personal agency in the primary predication resumes for "I became surprised." Overall the paragraph delivers a simple line of "I" agent predications after the initial announcement of the speech act of the text ("I shall without further ceremony acquaint you"). These are simply "I procured," "I placed," "I became surprised." One could call this a functional choice creating a certain emphasis on a narrative sequence and hence a figure, perhaps a dispersed anaphora in the inconspicuous repetition of "I." Newton has to make such formal choices, and these choices have consequences.

Historians of science have argued that Newton's narrative in this opening paragraph and throughout the article is more fiction than fact. His notebooks and lecture notes show a different chronology of experimental activity and thought, so that the account here is in a sense fabricated (Dear 1985, 154–155; Westfall 1980, 156–164). But any set of narrative predications and their consequent configuration of emphases would inevitably present one version as opposed to another, though some versions will certainly be "truer" in one way or another (see Holmes 1987, 229). There is no reason to assume, however, that what an experimenter physically did is the true version of an insight. Newton's opening paragraph represents one set of choices seen against other possible choices. With the exception of the personification that presumably represents a departure from the "normal"— and personification of the sun was probably more normal at the time—the choices Newton made cannot be identified in any contemporary compendium of figures. The text is nevertheless figured in the *aptness* of its choices given its author's material and purposes. As it turned out, Newton's 1672 article on light provoked more criticism than agreement when it first appeared, so "aptness" does not necessarily mean "persuasiveness" with a real audience.

Just as catachresis illustrates the problem of maintaining a definition of "metaphor" as distinct from the inevitable processes of word formation and language expansion, so does the iconic potential of *all* syntax compromise the project of separating the schemes from other, or indeed from any, syntactic orderings. Newton's second sentence subordinates two preliminary actions and heightens a third; it has a consequence. But there is no named figure, no *proparticipia*, which recommends placing anticipatory actions into participial phrases before an emphasized main action in an independent clause. The schemes, then, are very precariously, perhaps even arbitrarily, separated from the syntactic patterning available in English.

It is possible, then, for almost any identifiable structure to be called a figure in the sense that its form serves an ideational function. The only honest approach to the figures must admit that they are not unique structures from the perspective of functional efficiency. Does that mean, as Quintilian and Perelman and Olbrechts-Tyteca seemed to fear, that the category "figure" faces extinction? No, the category can be retained, though now in the sense of selection from one domain rather than from two. The formally definable devices, the ones that have been persistently noticed for centuries, can still be set aside by virtue of the kinds of functions they epitomize. Still worth the special attention that has gone along with the label "figure" are those structures tied to certain well-defined and enduring lines of argument, the subjects of analysis in the following chapters. Aside from these long-noticed forms and the basic sentence patterns in English, other identifiable forms may be tied to functions that are still to a large extent below the horizon of any function-scanning theoretical radar.

Verbal Spread and Visual Concision

A view of the figures as the epitomes of certain durable lines of argument solves the problem of the relation of the figures to the open set of unmarked, unnamed constructions. Those constructions and devices that most succinctly express a line of argument, so succinctly that the argument can be created almost automatically by creating the figure, have been singled out as the traditional figures of speech. But an argument need not be epitomized, need not be expressed succinctly. It can be phrased and paraphrased in wordier ways. The argument survives though the figure disappears. There are, in fact, many degrees of adherence to an underlying figure, as some of the passages cited in the following chapters will demonstrate. Darwin, for example, was not above interrupting a *gradatio* for a sentence of clarifying definition (see p. 114). He and so many other more recent authors "relax" the figures from their purest forms into near-figures. They do not epitomize their arguments perfectly, perhaps fearing that the epitome may be too noticeable, too bold a foregrounding of the form of an argument.

It is not unusual, for example, particularly in contemporary prose, for the relevant pieces of a figure, an epitome of a text's argument, to be worded less carefully than a textbook example and distributed more haphazardly than in the days of more conscious stylistic crafting. The antimetabole in this passage, taken from an editorial by the executive editor of *Wired* magazine, may at first escape notice.

> Some naturalists lament the fact that society is increasingly able to engineer nature— that when we poke a finger into the genes of an organism and start to rearrange its blueprints, we treat the organism as a complex machine.
>
> While this drift toward viewing nature as machinery disturbs many, the direction is at least visible. A far more shadowy shift, yet one that is equally momentous, is happening in the opposite direction: machines are coming to resemble biology. (Kelly 1995, A17)

The "opposite direction" or reversal that this passage refers to could be succinctly epitomized by joining the two separated halves of the potential *antimetabole*: "We treat the organism as a complex machine; machines are coming to resemble biology." After a little stylistic light housekeeping, this argument could be expressed in the following "stylistic capper": "We have been treating organisms as machines, but now we are beginning to treat machines as organisms."

The malleability of various lines of argument to verbal compression or expansion has been made familiar in the many studies that treat metaphor as constitutive rather than ornamental. A metaphor can be spread throughout a text in an extended analogy or allegory; it can provide a principle of organization in an extended comparison, or it can be succinctly expressed in a single word choice. It can even take all these forms in the same text. Or one can find the reasoning epitomized by the figure without necessarily finding the figure itself.

To go in the other direction, in the direction of greater compression rather than expansion, if the figures are verbal epitomes of underlying topical or argumentative moves, they can also be thought of, by a natural extension, as verbal icons approaching a visual representation of the concepts they express. A figure such as the antimetabole again, in which two key terms switch places, is very close to being, at the same time, both a verbal *and* a visual representation of the idea it expresses. One can absorb the pattern of reasoning in the figure without even understanding the words by simply noticing that two pairs of repeating units have changed places in relation to each other. Thus the nonreader of Greek can still detect the reversal in the following passage:

οἱ ἔσχατοι πρῶτοι καὶ οἱ πρῶτοι ἔσχατοι

The last (shall be) first and the first last (Matthew 20:16; see also 19:30).

Similarly, just as it is possible to arrange words in a diagrammatic way that suggests their conceptual relationship in a figure, so it is possible to arrange data and other visual units to express the same "figural logic." An example of such an arrangement, a kind of visual antimetabole, comes from a 1667/1668 issue of the Royal Society's *Philosophical Transactions*, the first science periodical in English. John Wallis, one of the founding members of the Society, had asked for volunteers in London and on the coast to measure the spring tides for several months and to gather evidence to support his mathematical hypothesis about applying the "proportion of sines." Among his patient surrogate observers was Samuel Colepresse, who measured the tides at Plymouth and who was particularly concerned to record their rate of change, which he found always greatest at mid-cycle, just as an oscillating spring has its greatest velocity at midpoint between its greatest compression and extension: "The Water," he wrote, "neither flows nor ebbs alike, in respect of equal degrees; but its Velocity increaseth with the Tide 'till just at Mid-Water, that is, half flown, or at half Flood, at which time the Velocity is strongest, and so decreaseth proportionately 'till High Water or Full-Sea" (1667, 633).

Colepresse presents his observations in the form of a diagram explaining that it was "collected from my loose Papers, containing the Observations, as they were made at several times and places; which I rather set down as a standing proportion of degrees in *general,* than to adequate every single Flux or Reflux so exactly as to half inches, or the like. . . . " (633). Colepresse, in other words, rounded off or averaged his actual observations to produce the perfectly symmetrical arrangement that he, not uncoincidentally, calls a "scheme." Rising and falling heights of the water reverse precisely like an antimetabole— in feet 1,2,4/4,2,1—and the antithetical actions of ebbing and flowing are perfectly parallel. Directions for forming Colepresse's scheme could be found in contemporary style manuals.

The *Scheme* it felf.

It is only one step, then, from the verbal iconicity of some of the figures to visual iconicity, to a representation of the ideational patterns epitomized by verbal figures in purely visual codes. Hence it is possible for the figures to be presented in diagrams and illustrations as well as in the verbal arrangements defined as figures.

The movement from verbal metaphors to literal images has been an easy one to understand. Images are consistently read metaphorically, usually from signs of a blended semiosis. It is not difficult to take the schematic relations among ideas codified in the topics and epitomized in the figures and render them in other ways. Gestalt psychology warrants the dominance of such overall patterns in the "reading" of visuals. Furthermore, an extension of the figures to visual representations helps to explain the role of the "figures" in another sense in scientific arguments where visual modes of argument are preferred. Although the visual figures are not emphasized in this study, the chapters that follow do provide examples of the visual rendering of arguments based on antithesis, incrementum, gradatio, antimetabole, ploche, and polyptoton.

The Figures in Scientific Discourse

Since figures of speech that correspond to distinct lines of reasoning can be found in arguments of any kind—political, economic, scholarly, and popular—the attention of this study to arguments from past and current scientific texts and controversies requires some explanation. Arguments from science have been chosen for two reasons. One has to do with repairing the historical divisions between rhetoric and the sciences. Part of the persuasive campaign of the fledgling scientific enterprise in the seventeenth century was its well-known polemic against rhetoric and particularly its attempt to purge its discourse of figuration.[16] But to the extent that these devices represent enduring lines of argument, it is impossible to remove them from reasoned prose. And whereas a study of their use in scientific texts corrects the notion that no figures except metaphor have ever played a role in scientific reasoning, their existence in scientific discourse, where they might not be expected, also argues, a fortiori, for their existence everywhere else.

As a second reason, corollary to the first, scientific arguments have been chosen to illustrate the figure/topic connection in order to demonstrate the continuity in patterns of reasoning across disciplines still traditionally divided between the sciences and non-sciences. It is not necessary to think in radically different ways, or to think in poetic metaphors, to think scientifically. The fact that all disciplines inevitably use the same patterns of reasoning does not, however, mean that they are all the same kind of enterprise. The last two decades have seen an enormous expansion in social and rhetorical studies of science, and for many, such studies have seemed a Jacobin dethroning of science from its epistemologically superior position. The following chapters, which find ubiquitous patterns of expression and argumentation in a variety of scientific texts, rhetorical devices that differ in no way from their counterparts in nonscientific arguments, might seem to be just another project in this leveling tradition. But, to repeat one common rejoinder, a distinction between the sciences and other fields depends less on the forms of argument used initially than on the degree of accountability demanded eventually, and in the sciences the degree of accountability is high. There is more pressure to turn an argument into a prediction or an action. A persuasive case can be made in writing for the production of an artifical analog of human insulin, but that analog must also pass the further test of producing the effects of human insulin in the bloodstream. Or if, for example, the well-visited pattern of series reasoning (see chapter three) is used to organize observational data in astronomy, and if the series produced seems to have gaps, if it calls for the existence of objects not yet discovered, those gaps will become the goal of and a motive for further observation. If that further observation is technically impossible, the enterprise will marshal its efforts to make it possible. Theories of the evolution of the stars predicted the occurrence of brown dwarfs, proto stars that had not "ignited" into sustained nuclear fusion. But it took the optical resolution of the Keck I, the largest earth-bound telescope ever built, to find the heavenly artifacts predicted by the argument. Thus the sciences differ from other disciplines less in the arguments used than in the consequences expected. The forms of argument, epitomized by the figures, are endlessly generative, but as far as outcomes are concerned, they are often spectacularly incorrect. Dalton's particles of caloric, antithetically repeling self and attracting other, do not exist.

The difference between the sciences and other disciplines is a real difference then, but it does not occur in the basic tactics of argument; these are used by everyone (Gross 1990 20, 206–207). What Richard Dawkins has written of selfish genes could be said as well of these verbal and conceptual devices, that they leap "like immortal chamois from body to body," or from text to text and mind to mind, "down the ages" (40).They are continuous across centuries, texts, and disciplines in a far richer way than the well-advertised metaphoric nature of some scientific cases. The extent of continuity demonstrated in the following study in the tactics of using opposites, series, reversals, and repetitions is intended as an illustration of the common stuff of human reasoning. This commonality should encourage students, who now believe they must choose between science or non-science on the basis of aptitude, to cross entrenched curricular boundaries, and should stimulate experts, who have the knowledge needed for important policy decisions, to have faith that basic patterns of reasoning can be used in communicating with the public.

2

Antithesis

In his speech defending Helen of Troy against blame for the Trojan War, the sophist Gorgias argues that if fate and the gods caused Helen's love of Paris, she herself was not responsible for her acts. Gorgias bases his argument on the premise that mortals like Helen are always weaker than gods, and, as everyone must acknowledge, "the stronger leads, the weaker follows" (και τὸ μὲν κρεῖσσον ἡγεῖσθαι, τὸ δὲ ἧσσον επεσθαι). In George Kennedy's translation (1991, 285) and in the original Greek (Diels 1922, 251), the grounding warrant of Gorgias' argument takes a verbal form identified over two thousand years ago: it is an antithesis. Sophists like Gorgias became famous among their contemporaries for fusing sense and sound into phrases such as the antithesis that captivate a listener's attention while delivering a trenchant argument. The device that so dazzled the Athenians in the fifth century B.C.E. was, however, in use long before the invention of writing and the early Greek attention to rhetoric. It is a frequently used form in orally transmitted wisdom literature: "A wise son makes a glad father/but a foolish son is a sorrow to his mother" (Proverbs 10:1).

Five hundred years after Gorgias, the apostle Paul, who knew both the Hebrew and Greek traditions, instructed the faithful on the essential difference between the world and the way: "To set the mind on the flesh is death, but to set the mind on the Spirit, is life and peace" (Romans 8:6 [τὸ γὰρ φρόνημα τῆς σαρκὸς θάνατος τὸ δὲ φρόνημα τοῦ πνεύματος ζωὴ καὶ εἰρήνη]). Here Saint Paul uses the profound opposition between life and death as a wedge to reinforce the antagonism between spirit and flesh, and the frame for this message too is the figure antithesis. Fifteen hundred years after St. Paul, St. Teresa of Ávila marked the tendencies in her spiritual journey in antitheses: "On one side God called me, and on the other I followed the world. All divine things gave me great pleasure; yet those of the world held me prisoner" ([Ahumada]1957, 57). And one hundred and fifty years ago, Frederick Douglass, in slavery, spoke in the same form to the ships he could see on the Chesapeake Bay: "You are loosed from your moorings, and are free; I am fast in my chains, and am a slave! You move merrily before the gentle gale, and I sadly before the bloody whip!" (1988, 96). Across centuries, languages, and cultures, the thoughts and passions of very different speakers have been poured into the same figure of speech, the antithesis.

The Aristotelian Definition of Antithesis

As a figure already marked and much imitated, antithesis received Aristotle's special attention in Book III of the *Rhetoric*. It is one of the three devices he selects, along with metaphor and energeia, for forming a polished prose style. His account is the inevitable point of departure for the discussions of antithesis that have followed through the centuries. To understand his account requires, first of all, placing it in the context of his discussion of prose style in general in Book III. Since Aristotle wants to consider the potential effects of stylistic choices, he begins by distinguishing two kinds of prose style: prose that is "strung on" or *paratactic*, loping along without closure from one predication to another, and prose that comes to points of completion or is *periodic*. Aristotle believes that the period, the unit of this second style, is an inherently satisfying syntactic unit because it has a perceivable beginning and end.

Aristotle next takes this satisfying period apart, claiming that some periods can be built from two subunits called *cola*. Not just any two cola, however, produce an artistic period that both invites the audience to anticipate its completion and leaves a memorable impression because of its "number" or prosody. First, Aristotle claims, the length of the cola making up a period is critical. Excessively short ones disappoint listeners by closing too abruptly, and long ones frustrate them by postponing the expected completion. He prefers balanced cola of equal length, not too long and not too short (the usual Aristotelian middle way), and he believes that a first colon of temperate length will create the expectation of a second colon of equal length, causing listeners (or readers) to feel a certain satisfaction when the pattern is completed and their expectation is fulfilled.

Second, the wording of the cola making up a period is critical. Since periods can be built from shorter cola, Aristotle explains that the *lexis*, the wording of these cola, can be either "divided" [διῃρημένη] or "contrasted" [ἀντικειμένη] (Kennedy 1991, 241; Freese 1926, 390). The example he offers suggests that a period with divided lexis is simply a period with parallel parts: "Often have I admired those organizing panegyric festivals and those instituting athletic games" (Kennedy, 241). But in cola containing contrasted *lexis* Aristotle stipulates, in words that echo a similar discussion in the *Topics*, "opposite lies with opposite or the same is yoked with its opposites" (241).[1] This definition is immediately followed by several examples, including the following: "It happens often in these circumstances that the wise fail/ and the foolish succeed. Either while living to hold it;/or when dead to lose it" (Kennedy 1991, 242).[2]

Based on Aristotle's commentary and examples, an antithesis can be defined as a verbal structure that places contrasted or opposed terms in parallel or balanced cola or phrases. Parallel phrasing without opposed terms does not produce an antithesis, nor do opposed terms alone without strategic positioning in symmetrical phrasing. Instead, the figure antithesis, according to Aristotle, must meet both syntactic and semantic requirements. It is shaped language [σχήματα] that delivers a contrast (Kennedy 1991, 245; Freese 1926, 396).

Aristotle's original stipulation ("opposite lies with opposite or the same with opposites") further suggests two types of antithesis. The second kind mentioned ("same with opposites") has only one pair of opposed terms, as in Pascal's aphorism, "A trifle consoles us because a trifle upsets us" (Pascal 1966, 38). This saying makes sense if "trifleness," though applied to different things, is taken to mean the same thing in the two cola. But many antitheses, like Gorgias' "the stronger leads, the weaker follows," have two pairs of opposites ("opposite lies with opposite"); these can be called double antitheses. Both single and double antitheses offer the predictability Aristotle required. After encountering the third key term in the figure, most listeners familiar with the language used can finish an antithetical predication themselves ("The night is long and the day is _____"). Double antitheses, however, are the more familiar or "default" mode of the figure, more artificial yet more expected. But either kind qualifies as the device that Aristotle promoted as at once pleasing and persuasive.

The semantics of antithesis

Antithesis as a figure of speech exploits the existence of many "natural" opposites in the vocabularies of all languages. Small children filling in workbooks and adolescents studying for the antonyms section of the SAT learn to match words to their opposites and so absorb much vocabulary as pairs of opposed terms, connecting up to down and bitter to sweet, pusillanimous to courageous and ephemeral to everlasting. Calling these antonyms "natural" simply means that pairs of words can have wide currency *as opposites* among users of a language outside any particular context of use. Word association tests give ample evidence of the consistent linking of opposites in verbal memory when subjects given one of a pair of antonyms most often respond with the other, "hot" triggering "cold" or "long" retrieving "short" (Miller 1991, 196). An antithesis as a figure of speech at the sentence level builds on these powerful natural pairs, the use of one in the first half of the figure creating the expectation of its verbal partner in the second half. Consider the defeat of such expectation and the consequent loss of force if, instead of using the natural opposites "succeed" and "fail," Kennedy had chosen to translate Aristotle's example as, "In these circumstances the wise fail/ and the foolish do much better."

In addition to pairs of opposites that have wide currency among the users of a language over centuries, there are also "local" opposites, specific to communities more narrowly definable in time and place. In the early Christian church, for example, *homoousian* and *homoiousian* were one such pair of local opposites; in the late twentieth-century United States, the pair *Reaganite* and *Clintonite* is another.[3] There are also temporary opposites constructed for a particular argument, usually by the figure antithesis itself; cases of these "nonce" oppositions will be discussed below. The point requiring emphasis here is that all of these degrees of opposition, stable to occasional, can form the semantic base of the figure.

The term that Aristotle uses in the *Rhetoric* in his definition of the figure, the word "opposite" (ἐναντίον), is for Aristotle a genus term divisible into four species. Since Aristotle opens the *Rhetoric* with the famous claim that rhetoric is the "counterpart" of dialectic, his discussion of opposition in the *Rhetoric* can be clarified from the much fuller treatment of opposition in other treatises in the *Organon*. In the *Categories*, Aristotle explains that terms can be opposed in four ways: as contraries (hot and cold); as privation/possession pairs (blindness and sight); as relatives (double and half); and as affirmation and negation pairs (being and not-being) [Barnes 1984, I, 18; In *De Interpretatione* affirmation and negation pairs are identified as contradictory opposites (27)].[4]

The contrasted lexis in the figure antithesis can use any of these four modes of opposition, but antitheses are typically constructed from contraries such as friend and enemy, near and far, good and evil, love and hate.[5] Aristotle also made a further critical division of contraries into two species: those that admit intermediates and those that do not (Barnes 1984, I, 18–19). According to his division, if one of a pair of contraries must belong to something, there will be no intermediates between that pair. A number, for example, must be either odd or even, so, according to Aristotle, there is no intermediate notion or term between these two. If, however, neither of a contrary pair need apply to an entity, then there are intermediates between them. A pair like love and hate flanks the intermediate notion of indifference. This potential for mediation turns out to be a crucial distinction in arguments that either use or form antitheses.

Antitheses can also be constructed from contradictions, pairs of words or phrases opposed, not because they can stand for the opposite ends of a scale such as the contraries hot and cold, but because they seem to represent exhaustive either/or alternatives: "rational/irrational," known/unknown," "I did see it"/ "I did not see it." Stylistically, contradictions can be formed, as in the last example given, by adding "not" or "never" or some other global negative to a sentence (I eat spinach/I never eat spinach), or they can be created by adding a negating prefix to a word so that, for example, "perfect" becomes "imperfect," "certain" "uncertain" and "tonal" "atonal." Many words seem to have both a contradiction and a contrary available: the contrary of "clean," for example, is "dirty"; its contradiction is "unclean." "Polite" has a contradictory partner, "impolite," and a contrary, "rude." Choosing a contrary instead of a contradiction for the opposite term in an antithesis can have consequences in an argument, either for premise-building or for potential refutation.

Logicians prefer contradictions over contraries when they talk of opposition, because contradictions cancel each other in a way that contraries cannot. A pair like "Jack is in the house"/ "Jack is not in the house" seems to fill the field of possibilities for Jack's relation to the house, and, as Aristotle points out, only for such affirmation/negation pairs is it "necessary always for one to be true and the other one false" (Barnes 1984, I, 21). If an arguer can set up a situation so that one or the other of two contradictory statements necessarily holds, then, as logicians in agreement with Aristotle have pointed out for centuries, to deny the one is to affirm the other. Contradictions belong to this certain world of A and not A. Contraries, on the other hand, can both be true of an object if one is looking at it from different perspectives, or at different times, or in different relations (Lloyd 1966, 87); the same person can be judged short or tall according to the height of the observer. Or, even worse from a logician's point of view, both of a pair of contrary terms can be avoided entirely; a listener can deny that a sound is either loud or soft but maintain instead that it is in some unnamed middle between those extremes.

Stylistically, contradictions form antitheses easily because they invite repetition that leads to the construction of parallel or even identical phrases: "If it does not rain, I will go; but if it does rain, I will not go." The full antithesis here approaches the redundant because the second half seems simply to rephrase the first. Oscar Wilde produced a figure from a single pair of contradictions much more elegantly: "There is only one thing in the world worse than being talked about, and that is not being talked about" (Wilde 1985, 6). Wilde could have constructed this antithesis from contraries rather than contradictories, but "The only thing worse than being talked about is being ignored" hardly has the same unexpected force.

Still another kind of contrasted lexis is important in forming antitheses. Many pairs of words are neither contraries nor contradictories but are nevertheless retrievable together in word association tests. These are correlatives. They designate reciprocal or complementary relationships between two people, things, or events, like "cause/effect," "lead/follow," "parent/child," "doctor/patient," "teacher/student."[6] Mention of one of a pair of correlative terms prepares the way for the other, so again, an arguer's ability to evoke the one by using the other makes these pairs potential candidates for antitheses. Aristotle did provide an example of an antithesis built on correlatives: "When these men were at home, they sold you; but coming to you now, they have been bought" (Kennedy 1991, 242: "buying" and "selling" are correlative actions; "at home" and "coming to you now" are better described as contraries). Aristotle's fourth type of contrasted lexis, privation/possession pairs, collapses readily into the other categories. His favorite example, blindness and sight, can be treated as a contradiction (to see or not to see) or as a pair of contraries (blind and sighted).

Aristotle did not distinguish among the four types of opposed lexis in his discussion of antithesis as a verbal device in Book III of the *Rhetoric*. It is likely he believed that any of the four types could produce an antithesis. But distinctions among the three major sources of antithesis—contraries, contradictories, and correlatives—are important in identifying how the antithesis epitomizes different lines of argument described in Book II of the *Rhetoric*, and they are crucial to the anatomy of dialectical arguments in his *Topics*.

The syntax of antithesis

Whether the opposed terms in an antithesis are contraries, contradictories, or correlatives, the figure requires two cola with if not identical then at least parallel phrasing. This parallelism, like a jeweler's setting, brings the opposed terms into relief, foregrounding them in the listener's or reader's attention. The parallelism can come from the precise repetition of all but the opposed words in each of the two parts or from similar grammatical forms. Either way, the parallel cola place the opposed terms in similar positions, heightening their difference so that the

contrast between them becomes greater than it would be if they occurred in un-
balanced cola or simply appeared randomly in one or more sentences. Furthermore, a well-structured antithesis places at least one pair of its contrasted terms
(or its only pair in the case of single antitheses) at the end of its parallel parts in
positions of emphasis. Consider the following possibilities with and without such
parallelism and end focus:

> You have a lot to gain by winning/ and if you lose, it won't cost you anything.
> You have everything to win, and you will lose nothing.
> You have everything to win/ and nothing to lose.

These sentences deliver roughly the same antithetical point, and in many situations the first might be preferred because it sounds more informal, less like pre-
packaged wisdom. The second deploys pairs of opposites and so could qualify semantically: everything and nothing, win and lose. But only the third qualifies as
the figure; here the contrast is finally shaped or epitomized into an antithesis by
using parallel forms (the complements "everything" and "nothing" and the infini-
tives "to win" and "to lose"), by placing these opposites in parallel positions, and,
as an added touch, by placing one of the pairs at the ends of the balanced cola.

Why is parallel structure the ideal form for an antithesis? One can easily invent
a perceptual rationale. An antithesis is designed to deliver a contrast, and the ability to perceive a contrast, according to a commonplace in psychology, is enhanced
by a uniform background. Red and green dots will be more obvious against a uniform white background than against a background of orange and purple dots. In
the same way, different grammatical structures in the two halves of an antithesis
would diminish the intended contrast between the paired opposites. The juxtaposition of contrasted terms in adjacent cola is also important, for as Aristotle points
out, opposites are more evident when they are placed side by side (Kennedy 1991,
223, 242). But as important as this visual rationalizing may be, auditory rationalizing is more important, for the device was first identified in Greek oral practice,
where good antitheses were not seen but heard. Audible parallelism requires aural
patterning with paired cola of similar length, cadence, and emphasis that perhaps
even rhyme. The good antithesis sounds like a jingle.

The defining importance of audible parallelism in the phrasing of antitheses is
demonstrated by the fact that rhetorical treatises in antiquity group the antithesis
with other figures that create sound patterns. Aristotle, Quintilian almost 500 years
after him, and everyone in between discuss antithesis with the other so-called
Gorgianic figures, all of which depend on "verbal resemblances," as Quintilian
calls them (1921, III, 489–495; see also Kennedy 1991, 243), created by concluding cola with the same syllable or sound (*homoeoteleuton*); balancing cola with
an equal number of syllables (*isocolon*); concluding cola with words that have
the same number of syllables (*parison*); concluding them with a different inflec-
tion of the same word (*polyptoton*); or simply concluding them with the same
word (*epistrophe*). These other devices need not be combined with opposed lexis,
but clearly any formal property that produces greater symmetry in paired phrases
is more likely to increase the listener's or reader's sense of the tightness or com-

pleteness and therefore of the presence or memorability of the phrasing and the cogency or force of the point. A perfectly formed antithesis does, in fact, combine *isocolon, parison*, and perhaps, in an inflected language, even *homoeoteleuton*; it is an overdetermined figure. The aural patterning of the antithesis, its tightness and predictability, are critical to appreciating how the syntax of the figure can be used to force semantic opposites.

The antithesis in Aristotle's rhetorical and dialectical invention

Though the term antithesis (ἀντίθεσιϛ) itself first appears in Book III of Aristotle's *Rhetoric*, other terms used in the definition of the device appear elsewhere in the *Rhetoric*. Most significantly, the definition of the figure in Book III strongly recalls the characterization of the first of the 28 lines of argument in Book II, chapter 23: "One *topos* of demonstrative [enthymemes] is that from opposites [*ek tōn enantiōn*]; for one should look to see if the opposite [predicate] is true of the opposite [subject], [thus] refuting the argument if it is not, confirming it if it is" (Kennedy 1991, 190; notably, this last piece of aphoristic advice is expressed as an antithesis). This phrasing strongly recalls Book III's definition of the antithesis as cola with contrasted lexis, when "opposite lies with opposite or the same is yoked with its opposites" (Kennedy 1991, 241). Clearly the figure and the topic are related, but unpacking that relationship requires reference to Aristotle's much fuller discussion of this line of reasoning in the *Topics*.

Aristotle's *Topics* explains in detail how arguers can build on the "reputable" opinions that are held, in his frequently repeated formula, by all, or most, or the most notable people. In Book I, chapter 10, he explains how contrasted lexis can be used to construct plausible premise/conclusion pairs which, not coincidentally, take the form of antitheses:

> Likewise, also, propositions contradicting the contraries of reputable opinions will pass as reputable; for if it is a reputable opinion that *one ought to do good to one's friends*, it will also be a reputable opinion that *one ought not to do them harm*. Here, that one ought to do harm to one's friends is the contrary, and that one ought not to do them harm is the contradictory of that contrary. . . . Also, on comparison, it will look like reputable opinion that the contrary predicate belongs to the contrary subject: e.g., *if one ought to do good to one's friends, one ought also to do evil to one's enemies*. (Barnes 1984, I, 173; italics added; for a restatement of these points in terms of properties, see Book V, Barnes I, 228–229, and in terms of definitions, see Book VII, Barnes I, 257–258)

What Aristotle explicates here are the common sense correlates of propositions that contain terms with opposites. Quite simply, if you believe something, you don't believe its opposite, and if you don't believe its opposite, you will agree with a statement that contradicts or negates that opposite. Furthermore, you will tend to believe in the consistent pairing of opposites. Given the widely recognized contraries offered in Aristotle's examples—"friend" and "enemy," "doing good" and "doing harm"—the self-evidence of these patterns seems inescapable and the reasoning based on them compelling. The possible inversions, demonstrated in the italicized passages above, fall naturally into tight antitheses as their verbal epitomes.

Essentially then, in the *Topics*, Aristotle recognizes the combinatorial potential of pairs of semantic opposites to create either single or double antitheses. As he explains in Book II, chapter 7, putting four terms, that is, two pairs of opposites, into play produces six possible combinations and hence six potential antitheses, two double and four single (Barnes 1984, I, 188–189):

1. good to friends and evil to enemies [double]
2. evil to friends and good to enemies [double]
3. good to friends and evil to friends [single]
4. good to enemies and evil to enemies [single]
5. good to friends and good to enemies [single]
6. evil to friends and evil to enemies [single].

Aristotle acknowledges that the two cola in the first two of these antitheses can be plausibly maintained simultaneously: If it is right to help or do good to one's friends, it is also right to do evil to one's enemies, and if it is wrong to do evil to one's friends, it is wrong to help one's enemies. Here "opposite [good/evil] lies with opposite [friend/enemy]," and therefore either of these statements can be used in support of the other. Of course, the support here is not compelling from a Christian per-spective,[7] and whenever such specific examples are involved, the cultural bound-aries of plausibility begin to show. But the general point remains. The cola of double antitheses are potential sources of positive premises; arguers who can construct a statement plausible to their intended audience, with the opposite of each of the terms in their claim, have support for their arguments. But the remaining four, the single antitheses with only one pair of contraries each, presumably cannot be held simultaneously. An arguer bent on refutation, even self-refutation, will try to construct one of these single antitheses to test a position. If contraries can be plau-sibly predicated of the same subject (at the same time and in the same relation and respect), the arguer has a problem. Thus double antitheses support and single an-titheses refute, or, again in the words of the *Rhetoric*, "look to see if the opposite [predicate] is true of the opposite [subject], [thus] refuting the argument if it is not, confirming it if it is" (Kennedy 1991, 190).

Once the verbal form, the figure antithesis, is recognized as the epitome of an underlying topical reasoning, it becomes possible to use the figure itself as a stylis-tic prompt or frame for invention, though nothing perhaps illustrates the differ-ence between the Classical and Renaissance versus the contemporary mind-set more than the discomfort that any such notion of purely verbal invention produces. Nevertheless, this process of stylistically or figurally prompted invention can be illustrated with the following example, starting with the hypothetical claim: "The presence of other STDs [sexually transmitted diseases] in a person increases the likelihood of HIV infection being present as well." This claim has two terms with opposed partners: presence/absence and increase/decrease. If each of these pairable terms is replaced by its opposite, the resulting statement creates a potential sup-porting premise that, added to the original claim, forms a double antithesis: "The *presence* of other STDs *increases* the likelihood of HIV infection because the *ab-sence* of other STDs *decreases* the likelihood of HIV infection." If, however, only one contrary is replaced in the original, the resulting statement flatly refutes the first: "The *absence* of other STDs increases the likelihood of HIV infection" or "The presence of other STDs *decreases* the likelihood of HIV infection." These statements could only be brought to support the original claim if they could be contradicted: for example, "It is not the case that the presence of other STDs decreases the likelihood of HIV infection; the presence of other STDs increases the likelihood." The hypothetical example here has its real-world embodiment in an ongoing study of HIV infection in sub-Saharan Africa, where a correlation has been established between the presence of genital ulcers, a sign of an STD infection, and a "greatly increased risk of HIV infection" (Nowak 1995, 1333). In scientific argument, the generation of such claim and premise pairs is usually the prelude to a search for confirming data, but the need for further support does not negate the enduring relevance of Aristotle's observations on the potential premise generation possible from the formation of single and double antitheses.

The History of the Figure

In Aristotelian stylistics, dialectic, and rhetoric, antithesis is a consistent, and consistently important, concept, at once a verbal, analytical, and persuasive device. But the Aristotelian tradition is not the only tradition in rhetoric, nor is Aristotle's *Rhetoric*, according to many historians, as important as other texts have been (Conley 1990, 17). How is antithesis featured in these other texts, and what happens to it across the centuries as it is passed from manual to manual, treatise to treatise? And how is it that a figure that was at one time as important as metaphor in stylistics and more important in dialectic has all but disappeared from attention?

A sampling of rhetorical texts over two thousand years shows that the term itself certainly survives, but its double nature as the verbal signature of a topical device uncouples, and its syntactic and semantic components diverge. By the eighteenth century, even its essential semantic feature, the deployment of opposite terms that defined it two thousand years earlier, disappears. The loss of antithesis from our current understanding of the figures and of their heuristic power becomes understandable given this history.

The *Rhetorica ad Alexandrum*, the only remaining rhetorical manual contemporary with Aristotle's *Rhetoric*, shows that Aristotle was not alone in his designation of antithesis as a figure of importance in the fourth century B.C.E. But the author of the *Ad Alexandrum* (attributed to Anaximenes of Lampaskos, 380–320 B.C.E.) dissociates antithetical thought from antithetical phrasing, marks the possibility of having one without the other, and stresses the need to combine both in the perfect figure.

> An antithesis occurs when both the wording and the sense, or one or other of them, are opposed in a contrast. The following would be an antithesis both of wording and sense: "It is not fair that my opponent should become rich by possessing what belongs to me, while I sacrifice my property and become a mere beggar" [an antithesis which has not survived translation]. In the following sentence we have a

merely verbal antithesis: "Let the rich and prosperous give to the poor and needy";
and an antithesis of sense only in the following: "I tended him when he was sick,
but he has been the cause of very great misfortunes to me." Here there is no verbal
antithesis, but the two actions are contrasted. The double antithesis (that is, both
of sense and of wording) would be the best to use: but the other two kinds are also
true antitheses." (Barnes 1984, II, 2295–2296)

The author of the *Ad Alexandrum* recognizes that the antithesis as a premise builder
need not be expressed in carefully chosen contrasted lexis positioned in balanced
phrases; at the same time, he acknowledges that it is possible to construct phrases
with semantic opposites that are not premise/conclusion pairs. Anaximanes has,
then, like many later rhetoricians, a looser definition of the antithesis. He makes
the presence of contrasted lexis a sufficient feature of the figure, without the added
stipulation of parallel phrasing in adjacent cola, so that he finds it possible to label
a single clause with essentially one pair of opposites ("Let the *rich and prosperous*
give to the *poor and needy*") an antithesis. In this departure from the Aristotelian
definition, or perhaps the expression of an earlier definition, the use of the figure
as an inventional prompt is obscured, though Anaximenes' expansion in the other
direction, marking the possibility of having an antithesis in sense if not in wording, does capture a notion of the figure as epitomizing a line of reasoning that can
be more loosely expressed.

In the Latin *Rhetorica ad Herennium*, a text written three centuries after the *Ad
Alexandrum* and Aristotle's *Rhetoric* and far more influential than either, the figure antithesis is not singled out as a uniquely effective device; it is lost in a list of 63
others as is metaphor. Furthermore, its defining features are dispersed across several figures. One form of antithesis, labeled *contentio*, "occurs when the style is built
upon contraries" [Contentio est cum contrariis rebus oratio conficitur] as in the
accompanying example, "To enemies you show yourself conciliatory, to friends
inexorable" [Inimicis te placabilem, amicis inexorabilem praebes.] ([Cicero] 1954,
282–283). Here is a typical double antithesis built on contraries (enemies and
friends, conciliatory and inexorable), but its two parts constitute a paradoxical
characterization and do not in themselves, out of context at least, interact as premise
and conclusion. A few sections later, however, the text offers *contrarium*, translated "reasoning by contraries," as a figure "which, of two opposite statements, uses
one so as neatly and directly to prove the other," a definition consistent with the
topical uses of antithesis [Contrarium est quod ex rebus diversis duabus alteram
breviter et facile contraria confirmat] (292–293). Among the list of examples of
contrarium occurs the following double antithesis, very close to the example offered under contentio: "Now, why should you think that one who is, as you have
learned, a faithless friend, can be an honourable enemy?" [Nam quem in amicitia
perfidiosum cognoveris, eum quare putes inimicitias cum fide gerere posse?] The
phrasing here is also driven by contraries, perhaps not coincidentally the "friends
and enemies" of Aristotle's *Topics*, but there is a significant difference in what is
claimed for contrarium as opposed to contentio.

This figure [contrarium] ought to be brief, and completed in an unbroken period.
Furthermore, it is not only agreeable to the ear on account of its brief and complete

rounding-off, but by means of the contrary statement it also forcibly proves what the speaker needs to prove; and from a statement which is not open to question it draws a thought which is in question, in such a way that the inference cannot be refuted, or can be refuted only with much the greatest difficulty. (293–295)

This most influential text on the figures, then, repeats the *Ad Alexandrum*'s dissociation into an antithesis of thought versus an antithesis of words, creating two figures instead of one. The contentio, as the example reveals, is presumably the purely "stylistic" half; you are conciliatory to your enemies and inexorable to your friends. The contrarium, though it too is praised for being "agreeable to the ear," presumably takes over the argumentative or topical nature of the figure: to paraphrase the example provided, "X will not be an honourable enemy because X has been a faithless friend." This dissociation of the antithesis into stylistic and probative aspects, the one a figure of diction and the other a figure of thought, first mentioned in the *Ad Alexandrum* and repeated in the *Ad Herennium*, will persist in the rhetorical tradition for centuries.[8]

Since Quintilian laboriously compiled, digested, and judged the rhetorical treatises available at the end of the first century C.E., incorporating especially the advice of his model Cicero, his *Institutio Oratoria* gives us the fullest account of antithesis as it was understood in the classical tradition. For Quintilian, the essence of an antithesis (called *contrapositum* or *contentio*) is semantic contrast, pairs of opposing terms that can be placed in a variety of settings. Quintilian lists all these possible forms of verbal antitheses that in later centuries were cataloged as different figures: single words with single words, pairs with pairs, cola with cola, and sentences with sentences (Quintilian 1921, III, 494–495).[9] Aristotle's double definition is then relaxed in Quintilian's characterization; in one direction of elaboration, antithesis becomes semantic contrast, the use of opposed terms that need not be predicated of the same or of opposite terms and need not even appear in parallel environments, although the prototypical examples of the figure still have those qualities.

At the same time, Quintilian conflates the antithesis with the argument of a text, for he also records an equivalence current in the first century C.E. between the antithesis and the enthymeme. What a reader of Aristotle or the *Ad Alexandrum* would confidently identify as an antithesis is evidently also called an enthymeme by Quintilian's contemporaries, enthymeme being an older term that may have simply meant a well-expressed argument (Conley 1984, 176–177; see also chap. 1). In Aristotle's usage, these two concepts seem distinct. Yet by the first century C.E., according to Quintilian, "the majority hold the view that an *enthymeme* is a conclusion from incompatibles: wherefore Cornificius styles it a *contrarium* or argument from contraries" (III, 203).[10] Curiously, the antithesis as both a stylistic device deploying opposites and as the epitome of an argument does satisfy both senses of the term "enthymeme" that, according to Conley, are current in the fourth century B.C.E. When this antithesis-as-enthymeme is added to Quintilian's other discussion of the forms of the figure, Quintilian's account marks two opposite trajectories for the antithesis, from any semantic opposition on the one hand to any forceful refutative enthymeme on the other. Here is the style/argument split in the making.

The antithesis/enthymeme conflation that Quintilian reports may explain why he takes the bold step of singling it out as a device that does not produce emotion. When he concludes his discussion about figures with advice about choosing figures appropriate to the time, place, and character of each occasion for speaking, he warns that

> when terror, hatred and pity are the weapons called for in the fray, who will endure the orator who expresses his anger, his sorrow or his entreaties in neat antitheses [contrapositis], balanced cadences and exact correspondences? Too much care for our words under such circumstances weakens the impression of emotional sincerity, and wherever the orator displays his art unveiled, the hearer says, "The truth is not in him." (Quintilian 1921, III, 505–507)

This caution against the coldness of too balanced a style has a long life in the rhetorical tradition. Demetrius gives the same admonition in *On Style,* pointing out the dangers of overdetermined figures before the rhetorically trained audiences of antiquity. When speakers use too many predictable periods, Demetrius warns, listeners are apt to "loudly declaim the endings of the periods which they foresee and forestall" (Demetrius 1982, 309).[11] Sixteen hundred years later, George Campbell repeats this same stricture and exaggerates it almost to the point of absurdity: "The antithesis, it is thought, is particularly unfavorable to persuasion, and therefore quite unfit for the more vehement and argumentative parts of a discourse" (Campbell 1963, 377). Frederick Douglass, who learned his figure-making power from a Ciceronian manual, *The Columbian Orator,* would have been amazed by such an observation.

In the Renaissance resuscitation of the Classical tradition, antithesis continues to lead a double life. Renaissance style manuals that focused exclusively on the figures proliferated distinctions among near-kinds, and as a result, features of the original antithesis are distributed among other figures. The semantics of opposition becomes the rationale, so that even an immediate verbal juxtaposition of one pair of contraries compressed within a comma (the shortest syntactic unit in classical stylistics) is labeled an antithesis. Thus, though Henry Peacham defines the figure as "a proper coupling together of contraries, and that either in words that be contrarie, or in contrarie sentences" (Peacham 1954, 160), most of his examples involve tight tensions of immediate opposition within phrases not between them, as in "So well sighted were the eyes of his minde, that by them he saw life in death, an exaltation in falling, glories in shame, victory in destruction. . . . " (161). Peacham does give examples of contraries in separate clauses: "Art thou rich? then robbe not the poore: if thou beest strong, tread not the weake under thy feete: if wise, beguile not the simple: if publike by authorities, oppresse not him that is private" (161). But none of these would qualify under Aristotle's topical definition. Each instance juxtaposes one pair of contraries—rich/poor, strong/weak, wise/simple, public/private—and the cola in these examples are not parallel. Furthermore, Peacham's examples make congeries of antitheses; they come in bunches and, in most of the examples Peacham provides, they come quickly (e.g., "What is more odious than labour to the idle, fasting to the glutton, want to the covetous, shame to the proude, & good lawes to the wicked.") These rapid fire pairs of antithetical terms have a cumulative effect far different from that of the antithesis in two cola. The limit of this compression of opposed terms is, of course, the oxymoron, which immediately juxtaposes contraries to shock a perceiver with a paradox: "joyful tears" and "living death." In the last of the "Renaissance" figure manuals, *Traité Général des Figures du Discours autres que les Tropes,* first published in 1827, Pierre Fontanier defines the antithesis, like the oxymoron, as the bracketing of verbal opposites. His *antithèse* either opposes two objects to each other ("Le riche et l'indigent, l'imprudent et le sage" [The rich and the indigent, the imprudent and the wise]), or one object to aspects of itself ("Vicieux, pénitent, courtisan, solitaire,/ Il prit, quitta, reprit la cuirasse et la haire"[Vicious, penitent, courtier, solitary/He takes, leaves, retakes the cuirass and the hair-shirt]) (Fontanier 1977, 379).

In a text that represents late eighteenth-century thinking on style and persuasion, Hugh Blair's influential *Lectures on Rhetoric and Belles Lettres,* a text reprinted well into the nineteenth century, antithesis appears among a miscellaneous collection of figures of secondary importance, in keeping with Blair's overall demotion of the figures into literary devices, valuable only as they serve the affect, beauty, and sublimity of a text and thus only indirectly its argumentative force.[12] Since Blair has no place for the schemes or figures of word arrangement, antithesis is not characterized as a syntactic figure. It is once again, as in the Renaissance manuals, a semantic figure. Balanced cola are not a necessity in the figure but only a possible enhancement: "In order to render an Antithesis more complete, it is always of advantage that the words and members of the sentences, expressing the contrasted objects, be . . . made to correspond to each other" (Blair 1965, I, 353).

If for Blair the antithesis is essentially semantic, for George Campbell in *The Philosophy of Rhetoric,* 1776, it is essentially syntactic.

> That kind of period [sentence] which hath most vivacity is commonly that wherein you find an antithesis in the members, *the several parts of one having a similarity to those of the other, adapted to some resemblance in the sense.* The effect produced by the corresponding members in such a sentence is like that produced in a picture where the figures of the group are not all on a side, with their faces turned the same way, but are made to contrast each other by their several positions. (Campbell 1963, 372–373; italics added)

Though Campbell does speak of "contrast," he emphasizes balance in his comparison of the antithetical period to a group portrait of persons distributed on both sides of a picture and turned toward each other or "reflected reciprocally." Campbell's antithesis, in other words, does not project to the end, driven by the expectation of an opposition; instead, it turns to the middle. It is less a movement than a composition. Thus the overall architecture of the period, its balance and parallelism, attracts Campbell, and the importance, indeed the necessity, of lexical opposition is diminished. With his looser definition, Campbell can go on in his discussion of antithesis to claim the apparently impossible, that an antithesis can affect three clauses at once or even span several sentences, not just the paired members of a single sentence.[13]

8 *Rhetorical Figures in Science*

Across the centuries, from Aristotle and the *Ad Alexandrum* to Blair and Campbell, in texts whose purpose is to explain the potential communicative effects of verbal choices, the antithesis gradually loses its identity as a frame for premises built on opposed concepts. It metamorphoses into other verbal devices that juxtapose semantic oppositions like the oxymoron and, by the eighteenth century, the term *antithesis* also becomes a generalized descriptor for a compositional style of balanced phrases, paired against each other but not necessarily driven by semantic contrast. Such "drift" in the definition of some figures of speech, as Carol Poster has pointed out (1998, 13), makes it difficult to "authorize" any one historical characterization as the correct or true figure. But if the goal is to identify those forms that best express a particular line of reasoning, it must be said that some of the definitions that "antithesis" has accumulated over the centuries only serve to obscure the possibility of inventing an argument well known in dialectic through stylistic choices. The fatal dissociation between style and content, so frequently seen in "mere rhetoric" as mere words overall, is found here as a rift within, in the loss of the Aristotelian antithesis, where opposite lies with opposite, or the same with opposites in parallel cola, functioning both to delight the ear and deliver an argument.

The Uses of Antithesis in Argument

Though the Aristotelian antithesis is rarely explicitly taught or distinctively noticed, the form survives and is still widely used. Further it is, like metaphor and the other figures discussed later, a powerful conceptual tool in the framing of arguments, particularly arguments employed in science. The argumentative uses of the double cola antithesis can be unpacked by considering whether the opposites employed are already accepted by an intended audience as opposites before the argument or whether one of the pair is in fact promoted or pushed into opposition during the argument by the other pair and by the syntactic frame of the figure. In the first case, drawing on already accepted pairs of opposed terms, the frame of the figure can be used as a prompt to invent or construct arguments; Francis Bacon was an exemplary user of antitheses in this Aristotelian manner. In the second case, the arguer constructs an argument to set terms in opposition, to make nonce contraries out of terms and notions that were not necessarily opposed before in the audience's thinking.

Finally, many arguments employing antitheses are less concerned with using existing oppositions or constructing new ones than they are with reconfiguring the nature of an existing opposition, either pushing the terms apart into mutual exclusion or placing them as extremes on a connecting continuum. The result here is not the undoing of an antithesis so familiar in poststructuralist arguments. The antithesis remains. But after the argument it is, if the argument has been persuasive, an antithesis of a different kind. In order to explore the many arguments of this type, it will be necessary to revisit the original Aristotelian distinction between contrary and contradictory terms and incorporate distinctions among opposites made by C. K. Ogden in the twentieth century.

Arguing from Existing Semantic Contrasts

The argumentative uses of the antithesis depend on the rhetorical status of the opposed lexis used to fill the syntactic frame of the figure. Given terms that are already accepted as contraries, whether local or more enduring, the form can become an inventional prompt, the first colon determining the choice of terms and the form of a second. Thus, in a sense the figure writes itself by drawing on known contrasts, and its effect with a particular audience depends on their prior recognition of these contrasts. The very first of the 28 lines of argument in Aristotle's *Rhetoric*, based on the system in the *Topics* outlined earlier, is a blueprint for creating an antithesis from such already accepted contrasts: It advises the rhetor to consider whether a subject has an opposite (that is an opposite already available in the minds of the audience), and if it does, to consider whether an opposite can be claimed of that opposite. This direction is illustrated by the first example offered to illustrate line one in 2:23 of the *Rhetoric*: "that to be temperate is a good thing for to lack self-control is harmful" (Kennedy 1991, 190–191). Temperance has a readily accepted semantic opposite in lack of self-control (or it used to) and good or good effects their recognized contrary in harm. A premise can be constructed using these existing or already accepted oppositions, and common wisdom, at least in Aristotle's day, readily accepts that temperance has good effects while lack of self-control has bad ones. Again, as the *Topics* explains, if such a believable antithetical premise cannot be constructed from a known pair of antonyms, but a single subject can take antonymical predicates, the "other side" has an argument in its favor: for example, "How can you say intervening in another country's affairs prevents disaster when, more often than not, intervening in another country's affairs has led to disaster?"

The power of the figure antithesis drawing on already existing or accepted semantic contrasts can have an even stronger influence on the construction of inferences from texts. So strong, in fact, are the implications that can come from recognized pairs of opposed terms and from familiarity with the figure, that it is possible to use what could be only half an antithesis and still secure the effect of a whole. Familiarity with the potential form and a firm grasp of accepted antonyms can fill in the gap when an audience is given only one colon and is somehow invited by the context, perhaps by a speaker's long pause, to construct a second colon that will complete the antithesis. The speaker who says simply, "I am tired of words," inevitably calls for deeds without saying so in a culture that lives with a "words/deeds" and a "giving up/turning to" dichotomy.

Antithesis in Bacon's Novum Organum

The power of antitheses using accepted oppositions as inventional prompts can be illustrated by Francis Bacon's use of the figure in the *Novum Organum*. Furthermore, it is more than likely that Bacon was specifically aware that he was following invention advice prescribed in both the dialectical and rhetorical traditions, traditions which he had deliberately winnowed for what he considered of lasting value for his new instauration. In the *Advancement of Learning*, Bacon reviewed the classical inheritance and concluded again and again that this art or that endeavor was "deficient." But when he came to the traditional parts of rhetoric, he found its art of topical invention not deficient at all, and, in perhaps the most important sentence in the *Advancement*, he transformed the method of topical invention in rhetoric into a method of empirical investigation for science: "Neither may these places serve only to apprompt our invention, but also to direct our inquiry" (Bacon 1952, 59). Though Bacon condemned figurative language in a notorious passage, he inevitably used its resources not only to achieve a magnificent prose style but at the same time, and not coincidentally, to guide his thinking and to discover material.

In the *Novum Organum*, Bacon follows his own advice given in the *Advancement*; as a result, the importance of antitheses and of antithetical reasoning to the entire project of the *Novum Organum* can hardly be exaggerated. First of all, in the manner illustrated by Peacham's examples of multiple and quick oppositions (see above, p. 56), Bacon generates great catalogs of antithetical terms when he introduces and recommends his method of empirical investigation. Far from being driven by some unstructured perceptual framework, much of his program of inquiry is driven by existing, accepted semantic antitheses. For instance, he recommends that investigators looking into changes such as "all generation and transformation of bodies" consider among other pairs of contraries—"what is expanded, what contracted, what is united, what separated, what is continued, what cut off, what propels, what impedes" (Bacon 1860, 124). The investigation of the "spirits" or "tangible essences" of bodies is also directed by opposed terms:

> whether it be copious and turgid, or meagre and scarce; whether it be fine or
> coarse, akin to air or to fire, brisk or sluggish, weak or strong, progressive or retro-
> grade, interrupted or continuous, agreeing with external and surrounding objects,
> or disagreeing, &c. (125)

Even the overall framework of this new inquiry into nature is driven by a semantics of accepted opposites as investigators turn their attention "from the complicated to the simple; from the incommensurable to the commensurable; from surds to rational quantities; from the indefinite and vague to the definite and certain" (126). The similarity is striking between these passages and those offered by Peacham a few decades earlier as examples of contentio and contrarium. There is in these passages really no separation between the means of explicating a research program and the means of rhetorical amplification.

Bacon's catalogs of amplified recommendations, taken from the opening of the second book of the *Novum Organum*, also introduce his method of induction based on tables of observations, a method that bears more than a passing resemblance to the balanced method of the rhetorical commonplace book. But instead of antithetical columns of virtues and vices in the usual manner of the commonplace book, Bacon recommends lists of positive and negative instances of the phenomenon under scrutiny, to be followed by a third table recording differences in the degree of the phenomenon when present. Although several scholars have thoroughly explored the rhetorical roots of Bacon's method (e.g., Wallace, Jardine, Vickers, and Briggs), the extent to which his investigative procedures are figure-driven, and specifically determined by the figure antithesis, has not been analyzed in detail.

To demonstrate this dependence, and in particular Bacon's use of antitheses that draw on accepted oppositions, the best available evidence is his own extensive illustration of his method, his analysis of the nature of heat in a series of tables or lists of observations. Bacon's method requires first that he provide a table of positive examples, in effect a list of sources or manifestations of heat, at least as far as human perception can detect them. Stylistically, this list of positive instances consists of fragments, only substantives and their modifiers without predicates. The predicates are omitted from most of the entries in his Table I because all of these entries have essentially the same predicate, clearly inferable from the governing purpose of the list.

1. The rays of the sun, especially in summer and at noon [give or manifest heat] (Bacon 1860, 127; all English references are to the Spedding translation). [Radii solis, praesertim aestate et meridie (Bacon 1889, 361; all Latin references are to the Fowler edition).]
2. The rays of the sun reflected and condensed, as between mountains, or on walls, and most of all in burning glasses and mirrors [give heat] (127). [Radii solis reflexi et constipati, ut inter montes, aut per parietes, et maxime omnium in speculis comburentibus (362).]
3. Fiery meteors [give heat] (127) [Meteora ignita (363).]
4. Burning thunderbolts [give heat] (127)[Fulmina comburentia (363).]

Here is the material of the scientific commonplace book without elaboration. Such concision spares Bacon from making too many distinctions and qualifications at this point, so that these positive instances appear as unifiable phenomena. But from this concise and elliptical list, the second table can be formed by an essentially stylistic process.

Bacon's method requires a second list of negative or privative examples. Where is this list to come from? How many observations could one make of phenomena that do not manifest heat? Bacon knows that such a list of negatives—in this case of phenomena manifesting an absence of heat—could continue indefinitely ("to note all these would be endless," Bacon 1860, 129). He therefore recommends that "The negatives should therefore be subjoined to the affirmatives, and the absence of the given nature inquired of in those subjects only that are most akin to the others in which it is present and forthcoming" (129). The discovery of negatives with a close connection to the items in the first list is in fact, in Bacon's practice, assisted by the figure antithesis. If the first item from his Table I is placed next to the first item in Table II, as Bacon's method recommends, the underlying process becomes obvious.

[Table I] The rays of the sun, especially in summer and at noon [give heat/produce the perception of heat] (127)

[Table II] The rays of the moon and of stars and comets are not found to be hot to the touch (129) [Lunae et stellarum et cometarum radii non inveniuntur calidi ad tactum (361).].

"The rays of the moon and of stars and comets" are opposed to "the rays of the sun." The lesser lights that rule the night, cultural opposites to the sun since Genesis and before, build on the natural contraries of day and night. If the ellipsis in the first half is filled in as directed by the wording of the second half and then the two pieces from the two tables are put together, the result is the complete figure where opposite lies with opposite: "The rays of the sun, particularly in summer and at noon, are hot to the touch; the rays of the moon, stars and comets are not found to be hot to the touch." In a similar way, item 4 in Table I, which cites "Burning thunderbolts" (127) [Fulmina comburentia (363)], can be matched to the observation in Table II that mentions "coruscations which give light but do not burn" (131), that is, nonburning lightning [Sunt quaedam coruscationes quae praebant lumen sed non urunt. (371)]. There is lightning that burns and its contradiction, lightning that does not burn. Table I also claims "All villous [hairy] substances, as wool, skins of animals, and down of birds, have heat" (127) [Omnia villosa, ut lana, pelles animalium, et plumagines, habent nonnihil teporis (363, a rare completed predication)]. Table II's matching item recommends that non-animal fibers, like linen, be tested for warmth (134) ["non ex lana aut plumis aut serico" (376)]. Table I lists piles of vegetable matter as sources of heat, an observation contradicted in Table II by the fact that single specimens of plants give off no sensible warmth. Iron and tin are listed in I as giving off heat when dissolved by acids; the contrasting softer metals mentioned in the list of negatives do not. Several items in Table I are therefore matched by antithetically generated single items in Table II. Most important, the invention here is directed by finding an obvious, accepted opposite for the term used in Table I, moon to sun, burning to non-burning, animal to vegetable, many to one, and hard to soft. Thus inquiry is firmly directed by the existing lexicon.

Table II, however, has more items than Table I (32 to 27), one entry in the first table sometimes corresponding to several in the second. Table II is longer in part for reasons that can once again be explained by the nature of the Aristotelian antithesis, for it is sometimes possible to form more than one cola antithetical to a single first colon when one of its terms has more than one opposite. A term that has two fairly obvious contraries can provide an example: The king has no power/ The queen has power or The king has no power/His subjects have power. "Queen" and "subjects" are both opposable to "king," though in different senses. In this manner, stylistically driven invention can select among possible contraries or go on to contradictions or correlatives or even to single or double antitheses, all from the same first colon. The second item in Table I generates in fact six items in Table II (numbers 2–7), each antithetical in a different way or to a different term in the single entry in Table I. Part of this fruitful item in Table I ("The rays of the sun reflected and condensed, as between mountains, or on walls, and most of all in burning-glasses and mirrors") has one potential opposite in "The rays of the sun in what is called the middle region of the air do not give heat" (Bacon 1860, 129) [Radii solis in media (quam vocant) regione aëris non calefaciunt (1889, 366)]. Here Bacon has opposed effects on Earth's surface with effects in a higher region, that is, effects on or above mountains where snow remains year-round and therefore where the rays of the sun presumably provide no heat. This middle region is the "above" and Earth with its walls and mountains the "below." Furthermore, the earthly region provides surfaces that reflect and condense; the middle region, the

entry goes on to explain, is not close enough to Earth's surface to benefit from reflection and condensation. The condensed reflections mentioned in Table I have
another potential opposite, not in absence of reflections (the contradiction) but
in diffuse and ineffective ones: "The reflexion of the rays of the sun in regions near
the polar circles is found to be very weak and ineffective in producing heat" (1860,
131) [Reflexio radiorum solis, in regionibus propre circulos polares, admodum
debilis et inefficax invenitur in calore (1889, 367)].

The next item in Table II, still corresponding to the second in Table I, picks up
on the mention of burning-glasses and, since no existing knowledge on the antithesis of a burning glass is available, Bacon recommends an experiment to fill this
slot: "Take a glass fashioned in a contrary manner to a common burning-glass"
(1860, 131) [Accipatur speculum fabricatum contra ac fit in speculis comburenitibus
(1889, 367]. This lens should be placed between the hand and the sun's rays to see
whether "it diminishes the heat of the sun, as a burning-glass increases and strengthens it" (131), an experimental design expressible once again as an antithesis. Items
5–7 recommend further experiments with the burning glass; since the original
observation in Table I credits the burning glass with the power of condensing the
sun's rays and increasing the sensation of heat, these items recommend a series of
further contraries: Instead of the sun's rays, try it on the moon's rays (#5), instead
of a celestial, try it on a terrestrial warm body that emits no rays (#6); try it on a
flame, a terrestrial body that does emit rays (#7). Once known, the results of any of
these experiments could produce either single or double antitheses of the kind
produced by matching the first items from Tables I and II. For example, the rays
of the sun condensed by the burning glass produce heat/the rays of the moon condensed by the burning glass produce heat/no heat. Bacon cannot complete these
potential antitheses because he does not know what the outcome of these experiments would be, but the syntactic vise and semantic inevitability of the figure have
determined the possible outcomes. Here inquiry is once more directed by the figure and therefore by the topic epitomized by the figure.

Table II consists of much more than a mere listing of cola antithetical to those
forming Table I. After a contrary instance is claimed, Bacon often goes on to provide supporting arguments for the claims in II, something he did not do for those
in Table I. The items in Table I are therefore like the aphorisms that comprise most
of the *Novum Organum*; they have a special status as axiomatic kernels of knowledge (Vickers 1968, 64); they are givens, having the authority of self-evidence and
hence in no need of support. However, the observations formed grammatically as
possible parallel cola in Table II do require support in some cases, precisely because they are to some extent figural in origin and therefore suppositional rather
than axiomatic. The second entry in Table II, for example (cited earlier), continues with an explanation of the absence of heat in the middle regions of the air: "for
which there is commonly assigned not a bad reason, viz. that that region is neither
near enough to the body of the sun from which the rays emanate, nor to the earth
from which they are reflected (Bacon 1860, 129; also an antithesis)," as well as an
observation supporting this explanation: "And this appears from the fact that on
the tops of mountains, unless they are very high, there is perpetual snow" (129),
followed by a collection of possibly contrary observations from travelers' tales of

mountains. Even the observations of the ancients, so contemptuously dismissed elsewhere in Bacon's writings, are here used as acceptable supporting testimony. In short, in Table II, where figurally formed potential premises appear, Bacon argues; in Table I, where he presents axioms based on widely accepted observation and knowledge, he does not.

When Bacon can find no evidence for a proposition generated by antithesis in Table II, he says so, and the claim is dismissed. Thus in many cases, an explicit negating colon is missing in Table II, though it can be reconstructed antithetically from the corresponding proposition in Table I. So, for example, entry #7 in Table I says simply "Ignited solids." Its negative partner, #12 in Table II, does not say "Non-ignited solids do not give heat." Instead, Bacon repeats the observation in Table I and claims the absence of a negative: "Every body ignited so as to turn to a fiery red, even if unaccompanied by flame, is always hot; neither is there any Negative to be subjoined to this Affirmative" (132; see also above, p. 48.). Bacon could easily have formed the contradiction of his original proposition, "Non-ignited solids give no heat," but he tends to avoid the indefinite contradictory class "not A," which is, as pointed out earlier, too open-ended.

Table II offers no negative or contrary instances lacking in heat for substances near a fire, or for sparks, friction, the heat of animals, or dung. Bacon could have ignored these items from Table I in forming Table II, but again and again, when he has no evidence to support his systematically formed antitheta, he admits "the proximate instances [are] wanting," and calls for more diligent inquiry or specific experiments. Were he driven only by existing data, he could easily have omitted any entry in Table II for which he had no information. But Bacon is influenced more by his procedure than by the available evidence, and his essentially figural method produces the holes, the unsupportable or unsubstantiated second cola formed by antithesis off the axioms in Table I. These require the program of research argued for in the *Advancement*, outlined in the *Novum Organum*, envisioned in *The New Atlantis*, and partly delivered in the fragmentary *Histories*.

Tables I and II are followed by a third that lists "Degrees or Comparative Instances of Heat." In Table III, Bacon uses a different logic, inevitably tied to a different figure epitomizing this different form of reasoning. But with all three tables prepared, Bacon is ready, in the words of his own metaphor, to press his grapes. Whenever pairing items from Tables I and II together yields contrary predicates, Bacon, essentially following the method outlined in the *Topics*, refutes a possibility.[14] Some of these intermediate conclusions appear in what, according to Bacon, is a very incomplete Table IV, "An Example of Exclusion, or Rejection of Natures from the Form of Heat." Here the fact that the sun produces heat and that common earthly fire also produces heat means that heat cannot be either solely celestial or terrestrial. With such rejections in mind, Bacon can attempt what he calls a first vintage, a pressing of the evidence so far to yield a characterization. To the astonishment of succeeding generations who have pointed out the errors and confusions in Bacon's Tables and the misapplications and fallibilities in his method, he did in this case (according to twentieth-century views, though not always in the eyes of intervening centuries) most definitely get it right: "From a survey of the instances, all and each, the nature of which Heat is a particular case appears to be Motion" (150).

Much more could be said about the importance of antithesis in the *Novum Organum*'s further listing of the kinds of "instances" that assist scientific inference, but overall it is fair to conclude that Bacon's method in the *Novum Organum,* and particularly in the tables, for all his gesturing about departing from the methods of the ancients, is still essentially topical and, given the relation between the figures and the topics, it is essentially figural as well. In particular, Bacon demonstrates how existing or acceptable pairs of contraries, fitted into a syntactic frame, can invite the invention of new arguments and direct the search for new sources of evidence. Thus it is possible to say that Bacon's empirical method of inquiry is in a sense figure-driven, and that given his epistemological commitment to the aphorism, he was predisposed to package both his arguments and his observations in epitomes such as the antithesis. Far from turning his back on the rhetorical tradition, he in fact tapped its conceptual resources epitomized in the figures.

Darwin and "The Principle of Antithesis"

Antitheses deploying widely accepted contraries, so successfully exploited by Bacon, also served to prompt the invention, and not coincidentally enhance the persuasiveness, of Charles Darwin's many arguments. Darwin inevitably uses antithesis as a figure and as a conceptual pattern in the *Origin* and elsewhere, but in one late work, *The Expression of the Emotions in Man and Animals* (1872), Darwin promotes antithesis into a major theory in his attempt to explain the connections between animal and human gestures, in itself an argument that furthered the case for an evolutionary continuum. Darwin posits three sources for expressive gestures. The first explanation is functional; gestures have an adaptive purpose, but they can remain as habits even after they cease to be serviceable (Darwin 1965, 28). So, for example, an animal suddenly facing danger will open its mouth to quiet its breathing, and this gesture remains in the gaping mouth of astonished humans. Similarly, an animal preparing to fight will expose its canine teeth, and this gesture survives in the human sneer. Second, Darwin explains some gestures as simply the result of excessive nervous force: an animal's excited "sensorium" brims over with energy that bristles the hair or causes the muscles to tremble.

It is the remaining system of explanation in *Emotions* that uses the figure of antithesis as a heuristic device. While ideally all gestures should be described by their adaptive usefulness, Darwin believed that some could only be explained as the result of "a strong and involuntary tendency to the performance of movements of a directly opposite nature, though these have never been of any service" (Darwin 1965, 50). He called this involuntary tendency "the principle of antithesis," and he used an approximation of the figure to define it: "when *actions of one kind* have become firmly associated with *any sensation or emotion,* it appears natural that *actions of a directly opposite kind,* though of no use, should be unconsciously performed through habit and association, under the influence of *a directly opposite sensation or emotion*" (65; emphasis added).

Darwin provides a key example in the behavior of dogs when greeting their master as opposed to challenging an intruder. "Instead of walking upright, the body sinks downwards or even crouches, and is thrown into flexuous movements; his tail, instead of being held stiff and upright, is lowered and wagged from side to side" (Darwin 1965, 51). Other parts of this description juxtapose the canine teeth exposed in defiance versus loosely hanging lips and ears pressed close and upwards versus ears depressed and drawn backwards. Darwin can find no explanation for these ingratiating movements except from their being "in complete opposition or antithesis to the attitude and movements which, from intelligible causes, are assumed when a dog intends to fight. . . . " (51). Darwin inserted two specially prepared drawings of dogs in these "opposite" states (see Figure 2.1).[15]

But, of course, whether these states are opposite depends primarily on whether they can be plausibly described as opposite—a matter depending in turn on whether antithetical terms and predications are already available in the language. Darwin's reliance on existing verbal oppositions to fill antithetical predications is more apparent in his description of the cat in the opposite states of affection versus rage when its gestures change from "crouching" to "upright," "hair not in the least erect" to "rather rough," tail "lashed or curled from side to side" to "[tail] held quite stiff and perpendicularly upwards," ears "closely pressed backwards" to "erect and pointed," and mouth "partially opened" to "closed" (Darwin 1965, 56–57).

Darwin manages to explain most of the human gestures he discusses as functional, at least in origin. The habit of shaking the head from side to side in negation, for example, arises, he believes, from an infant's habit of turning its head away when refusing food (Darwin 1965, 272). Two human gestures, however, elude functional explanations and instead require recourse to the principle of antithesis. The first of these is shrugging and the associated body language that expresses an emotional state that Darwin calls variously helplessness, impotence, resignation, and even the "determination not to act" (269).

> We may now inquire why men in all parts of the world when they feel . . . that they cannot or will not do something, or will not resist something if done by another, shrug their shoulders, at the same time often bending in their elbows, showing the palms of their hands with extended fingers, often throwing their heads a little on one side, raising their eyebrows, and opening their mouths. (270)

The explanation for this cluster of gestures comes simply from their being antithetical to those of someone who prepares to resist. Darwin, in other words, does not use the current contraries, fight or flight, but the contradictory pair fight/not fight,

> an indignant man, who resents, and will not submit to some injury, holds his head erect, squares his shoulders, and expands his chest. He often clenches his fists, and puts one or both arms in the proper position for attack or defence, with the muscles of his limbs rigid. He frowns—that is, he contracts and lowers his brows,—and, being determined, closes his mouth. The actions and attitude of a helpless man are, in every one of these respects, exactly the reverse. (271; compare to the previous quotation)

Another complex of gestures only to be described by antithesis are those expressing astonishment. The challenge for Darwin here is less that of coming up with opposite gestures, or a language to describe them, than it is coming up with an emotion that is the opposite of astonishment.

Figure 2.1. Visual antithesis: Darwin's "Opposite Dogs." From Charles Darwin, *The Expression of the Emotions in Man and Animals*, 3rd ed., ed. Paul Ekman (New York: Oxford University Press, 1998).

Now, a man in an ordinary frame of mind, doing nothing and thinking of nothing in particular, usually keeps his two arms suspended laxly by his sides, with his hands somewhat flexed, and the fingers near together. Therefore, to raise the arms suddenly, with the whole arms or the fore-arms, to open the palms flat, and to separate the fingers,—or, again, to straighten the arms, extending them backwards with separated fingers,—are movements in complete antithesis to those preserved under an indifferent frame of mind, and they are, in consequence, unconsciously assumed by an astonished man. (288)

In each of these cases, there has perhaps been some construction, like a deliberate back formation, of an antithetical emotion and set of gestures from the emotion and set of gestures under scrutiny, an "intent to resist" as the opposite of helplessness and an "indifferent frame of mind" as the opposite of astonishment. But despite the straining, these opposite emotions are readily recognized and then easily paired with gestures described by opposites (e.g., open/closed, together/separate, flexed/flat, lax/extended). The antithetical art in this argument is matching opposite emotions with oppositely describable gestures. Pointing out the role of well-established semantic opposites in these paired passages does not mean that Darwin is wrong or deluded in either his pairings or his principle; it simply means that his invention, matching antithetical emotions with antithetical gestures, has been guided or prompted by established semantic pairs, and that he is therefore following a prepared and hence already persuasive linguistic groove.

Darwin was also aware, long before structuralist semiotics, that opposition is a basic feature in any conventional system of signs, as in the gestural languages of Cistercian monks and the deaf (Darwin 1965, 61), but he does not follow a semiotic line of reasoning by imagining that it could also be functional for an animal to use an obviously different sign to signal an obviously different emotion. Instead, in trying to explain how these opposite gestures came about, Darwin claims that the principle of antithesis is grounded in necessary somatic or physiological oppositions; opposed sets of muscles are brought into play automatically when an animal avoids a functionally significant gesture.

Not only does Darwin rely on the availability of antithetical adjectives to describe gestures, but the ultimate grounding of his theories of expression also depends on existing semantic antitheses embodied in the conventional understanding and naming of the emotions themselves. That Darwin was aware of the oppositions built into the language of the emotions is obvious in his structuring of the chapters on the human emotions beginning with chapter 6: "My observations will be arranged according to the order which I have found most convenient, and this will generally lead to opposite emotions and sensations succeeding each other" (Darwin 1965, 146). So a chapter on low spirits is followed by one on high spirits, a discussion of disdain and disgust by helplessness and patience, and affirmation by negation. After a description of the bearing of the proud, Darwin can plausibly bypass a description of humility, once the principle of antithesis has been established, since it will obviously be the opposite (263), and when he comes to explain the sounds of laughter, he assumes that they will be

> as different as possible from the screams or cries of distress; and as in the production of the latter, the *expirations are prolonged and continuous,* with the *inspirations short and interrupted,* so it might perhaps have been expected with the sounds uttered from joy, that the *expirations would have been short and broken* with the *inspirations prolonged;* and this is the case. (205; italics added)

In his concluding chapter, Darwin reminds readers that "once a functional expression has been fixed by association with a certain frame of mind, there will be a strong and involuntary tendency to the performance of directly opposite actions, whether or not these are of any use, under the excitement of an opposite frame of mind" (348). But what is an "opposite frame of mind"? It is the other half of an a priori semantic pairing, pride to humility, joy to sorrow, love to hate, waiting to be linked in double cola with other predetermined pairs of adjectives used in descriptions of gestures like those quoted above, up and down, broken and continuous, short and long. Thus Darwin built much of his theory of emotions and their expression in animals and humans not only on the principle but also on the figure antithesis.

The "False Window": Using the Form to Force Terms Apart

The argumentative effects of an antithesis need not depend, as they do in Bacon's and Darwin's cases, on two pairs of already accepted semantic contrasts. The ability to perceive the pattern in an antithesis, to fulfill its predictions and even to feel its force, is part of the competence of an experienced user of the language. It belongs in a "stylistic vocabulary," a repertoire of prepared constructions in a language. Once a language user is familiar with the form created by placing opposed words in parallel phrases, the form can take on a life of its own, and an arguer can use it with only one set of opposed terms to in effect create another set of semantic opposites. In other words, it is possible to force or fake a double antithesis by placing one pair of words in strategic positions that are not pairs of antonyms to begin with in the existing vocabulary or prior usage of an audience. The arguer thus creates nonce antonyms out of terms not opposed before the argument. Hence the antithesis is a primary stylistic tool for a whole host of arguments whose purpose is to force a pair of terms into opposition.

In the late seventeenth century, Pascal, who distrusted this potential in the figure, compared this process to architectural *trompe l'oiel*: "Those who make antitheses by forcing words are like those who make false windows for symmetry. Their rule is not to speak accurately, but to make apt figures of speech" (Pascal 1952, 175). The false window added for the sake of symmetry in a façade corresponds to a placeholding word that completes the figure, even though it would not be recognized by an audience beforehand as the opposite of its partner. Aristotle also noticed these false antitheses (ψευδεῖς ἀντιθέσεις) briefly, giving as an example a line from the poet Epicharmus (Kennedy 1991, 243; Freese 1926, 394):

Sometimes I was in their house, sometimes I was with them

To be in someone's house and to be with them are usually synonymous notions, but the structure here, drawing on an audience's familiarity with antitheses, encourages a construal of these phrases as opposed or mutually exclusive. In the case of this example, the audience is invited to interpret the author's intention as humorous, to get the joke that it was possible to be in the house belonging to these people and yet not be with them, either because they were always in some other part of the house or gadding about elsewhere.[16]

But what is humorous here is very deadly in the use of antitheses to construct other entities such as peoples or nations into opposition. In the *History of the Peloponnesian War*, Thucydides provides an example of this process in his reconstruction of the Corinthians' speech inciting the Spartans to go to war with Athens. The Corinthians use existing semantic oppositions as wedges, hammered in by successive predications, to create opposites of terms that did not exist as opposites in the language.

> Then also we think we have as much right as anyone else to point out faults in our neighbours, especially when we consider the enormous difference between you [the Spartans] and the Athenians. To our minds, you are quite unaware of this difference; you have never yet tried to imagine what sort of people these Athenians are against whom you will have to fight—how much, indeed how completely different from you. An Athenian is always an innovator, quick to form a resolution and quick at carrying it out. You, on the other hand, are good at keeping things as they are; you never originate an idea, and your action tends to stop short of its aim. . . . Think of this, too; while you are hanging back, they never hesitate; while you stay at home, they are always abroad; for they think that the further they go the more they will get, while you think that any movement may endanger what you have already (Thucydides 1954, 75–76).

Following this passage of immediate contrasts between Athenian and Spartan qualities, Thucydides places a long passage on the Athenians and then a long contradictory passage on the Spartans, the contrast continued though without the figure. When the Corinthians were done, they succeeded in sparking ethnic hatred and 30 years of war, and the two cities, Athens and Sparta, passed into historical commonplace as opposed cultures and antithetical terms.

The antithesis has often been used in scientific arguments to construct terms into opposition that are not forceful opposites to begin with. Physiologists, for example, have long accepted a basic separation between sensory and motor nerves. The discovery of this opposition was the work of the nineteenth-century anatomists Charles Bell and François Magendie, the latter providing convincing evidence when he experimented on the spinal cords of live puppies. Magendie first cut the dorsal or posterior roots of the lumbar and sacral nerves coming from one side of an animal's spine and observed that the affected leg eventually regained motion but the animal did not respond when that limb was pricked or squeezed. Though Magendie claimed to perform this experiment without a prediction, the result suggested an exploration of potential opposites. In another animal, he cut the anterior (ventral) roots of the corresponding nerves, causing the animal to lose movement while still showing a response to painful stimuli. Magendie concluded his report on these experiments in the *Journal de Physiologie* with an epitomizing antithesis.

> Je poursuis ces recherches et j'en donnerai un récit plus détaillé dans le prochain numéro; il me suffit de pouvoir avancer aujourd'hui comme positif, que les racines antérieures et les postérieures des nerfs qui naissent à la moelle épinière, ont des fonctions différentes, *que les postérieures paraissent plus particulièrement destinées à sensibilité tandis que les antérieures semblent plus spécialement liées avec le mouvement.* (Magendie 1822, 279; italics added)

[I am pursuing this research and I shall give a more detailed description in the next issue. It is sufficient for now to be able to propose that the anterior and posterior roots of the nerves that arise from the spinal cord have different functions; that the posterior appear more especially intended for sensations, whereas the anterior seem to be more particularly linked with movement. (Holmes 1987, 232)]

"Sensation" and "movement" are not accepted antonyms in everyday French or English, but they become opposed (and eventually opposite and separate systems) by virtue of their placement in this figure, linked with the established antonyms "posterior" and "anterior." Magendie's simple antithesis only approximates the later more complex understanding when further oppositions like that between somatic and autonomic are added. But Magendie's basic opposition continues in the subsequent renaming of the sensory nerves as *afferent* (coming in) and the motor as *efferent* (going out).

The longstanding debate on the nature of the fossil "bird" archaeopteryx also concerns definitions that came to be characterized as antithetical for purposes of this specific debate: Was *archaeopteryx* a bird or a dinosaur? This debate began shortly after the discovery of the fossil in the 1850s, Richard Owen categorizing *archaeopteryx* as unequivocally a bird and T. H. Huxley characterizing it as a proto-bird, closer to the dinosaurs. The issue is still in debate, and arguments for both positions can be found in specialist and popular publications. The February 1993 issue of *Science*, for example, offers two pieces arguing that *archaeopteryx* is a true bird, one an overview piece by a science writer and the other a report written by the original researcher. The *Science* reporter summarized the debate in the following "near" antithesis:

The latest phase of the controversy pits ornithologists, who consider the 150-million-year-old creature a bird, adapted to life in the trees and capable of powered flight, against paleontologists, who claim *Archaeopteryx* was a dinosaur that spent most of its life on the ground. (Morell 1993, 764)

If a random group of twentieth-century speakers were taking a word association test and were directed to come up with an opposite, it is very unlikely that the term "bird" would trigger "dinosaur." But the argument here requires that these terms be constructed into opposition, at least temporarily. Nor does it matter that birds may be the evolutionary progeny of dinosaurs. The way to construct these terms into opposition is to tie them to more fundamental, already recognized opposites. Of the three potentially opposed pairs of terms in the science writer's sentence, ornithologist/paleontologist, bird/dinosaur and trees/ground, only the last is arguably an accepted contrast, backed by the force of the well-established pair, up and down. The antithesis between bird and dinosaur, and hence between ornithologist and paleontologist, is being constructed in this argument by strong claims that these groups and genus terms are somehow as opposite as the two locations, up in the trees versus down on the ground.

Alan Feduccia, the author of the research report appearing later in the same issue, does not engage the antitheses used by the science writer. He slices into the issues on a different plane and creates a different antithesis, not between fields or groups of people but between theories of the origin of flight that hinge on the categorization of *archaeopteryx*:

> Two major theories for the evolution of avian flight—*the cursorial theory, in which flight evolved from the ground up, and the arboreal theory, in which flight evolved from the trees down*—are based on interpretations of the paleobiology and behavior of this primal bird. (Feduccia 1993, 790; italics added)

Feduccia too builds his antithesis (see italicized phrasing) between a cursorial and arboreal theory on the "natural" semantic opposites of up and down, also reified in the simple physical distinction between trees and ground. This difference is the crucial one for Feduccia, since he builds on the "up" half of the potential bird/dinosaur antithesis, basing his argument on measurements of the curvature of *archaeopteryx*'s claws against the range of curvature in the claws of modern perching versus ground-dwelling birds. His results very definitely place *archaeopteryx* in the trees. He finds its claws similar to those of modern perching birds, and, after a rehearsal of other evidence on the aerodynamic properties of the fossil species, he concludes: "*Archaeopteryx* probably cannot tell us much about the early origins of feathers and flight in true protobirds because *Archaeopteryx* was, in modern sense, a bird." Since his argument has already established a bird/dinosaur disjunction on the opposition between up and down, to say that *archaeopteryx* is a bird amounts to saying that it is not a dinosaur. (Feduccia 1993, 792).

Arguments that Change the Nature of Opposition

C. K. Ogden's theory of opposites

Not all arguments involving antitheses are concerned with inventing second cola from accepted oppositions, as Bacon did, or with constructing new pairs of opposites, as Magendie did. They sometimes have the more modest goal of reconfiguring the kind of opposition represented by a pair of terms. The result is not the undoing of an antithesis, the familiar collapsing of some structuralist binary. The antithesis remains after these arguments, but it is now an antithesis of a different kind.

To capture these differences in constructed oppositions, the work of the natural language philosopher C. K. Ogden is particularly useful. In a brief treatise published in 1932, Ogden analyzed pairs of antonyms and reaffirmed "a very fundamental distinction in any theory of opposites—that, namely, between the Scale and the Cut. Opposites . . . may be either the two extremes of a scale or the two sides of a cut" (Ogden 1967, 58). Ogden uses the metaphors scale and cut for a distinction that Aristotle characterized with opposed terms translated as "mediated" and "unmediated." Later semanticists have adopted this distinction, using the terms "gradable" versus "ungraded" for these two kinds of opposition.

With a completely different base of evidence, the classical scholar G.E.R. Lloyd came to the same conclusion about the fundamental difference, often confused, he believed, in the earliest fragments of Greek philosophy, between pairs of opposed terms that exclude intermediates and those that admit them (95). Lloyd agrees with Aristotle that only certain pairs of contraries (like odd and even) as well as all contradictions of the form A/not A, fulfilled the criterion of excluding intermediates, so important to the development of logic (Lloyd 1966, 163). Both Ogden and Lloyd reaffirm the distinctions made by Aristotle and carefully preserved in Renaissance logic between two different kinds of opposition.[17]

When terms anchor the ends of a scale, as many contraries do, they are, in a sense, potentially connected by any number of possible intermediates, and it is even possible to imagine a hypothetical neutral midpoint between them, hate and love, for example, blending midway into indifference. When terms seem to set up either/or alternatives, as contradictions and some contraries do, they construct a different kind of antithesis. Their midpoint is not an average of properties but, to use physical analogies, a sharp boundary producing a dichotomy—a cut into two yin and yang complements or mutually destructive forces—or an empty space. Crossing over occurs at a definite point and puts a notion in a different conceptual domain. There is no middle territory to be occupied.

Ogden also realized, and here his thinking is a fertile departure from Aristotle's, that scales and cuts could be combined in antitheses in various ways. It is possible, for example, to think of a pair of opposed terms as representing two scales placed end-to-end, meeting at a cut. Furthermore, these two scales can acquire direction, moving toward or away from each other. As Ogden conceptualized them metaphorically, the pair right/left move away from each other starting at a neutral midpoint, but the pair hot/cold move toward each other. The oppositions between open/shut and visible/invisible, he believed, represent a cut with a scale on one side only. There are degrees of "openness" or "visibility," he argued, but no degrees of "shutness" or "invisibility."[18]

Ogden also believed that some terms were opposites only by definition or fiction, and that any attempt at analyzing these culturally complex pairs demanded "panoptic diagrams" schematizing several intersecting scales. Work/play, for example, incorporated scales like degrees of freedom versus restraint and pleasure versus pain, and their complexity clearly exasperated him. Finally Ogden, following Aristotle's dictum in the *Categories* (Barnes 1984, I, 7), did not believe that "real entities (movable objects) can have true opposites" unless they were referred to with modification (Ogden 1967, 93). "Objects will therefore appear as opposites only in so far as some sensational factor is involved, i.e. in so far as adjectival elements, admitting of quantification or dichotomy, enter into their descriptions or definitions" (92). This possibility troubled Ogden because pairs of opposed adjectives not based on sense perceptions—pairs like new/old, free/controlled and beautiful/ugly—can be added to nouns referring to entities and thus push them into opposition. "In proportion as they are removed from direct descriptions of perceptive elements into which they must be translated, such fictional adjectives give rise to controversy and emotive distraction" (93). These are of course, in Ogden's view, self-evidently bad outcomes.

Ogden realized that his work on opposition had "a direct bearing on the whole field of verbal controversy" (Ogden 1967, 105), but he chose not to pursue what he considered too messy a topic. His purpose in investigating the semantics of opposition was simply to shorten his Basic English Vocabulary by removing one of each pair of opposites from the list. Nevertheless, his reprise of the fundamental distinction between cuts and scales and his insight into how these kinds of opposition can be mixed are especially important for a theory of argument informed by figuration. For from a rhetorical point of view, pairs of terms cannot always be fixed as either excluding or allowing intermediates. In the stress and play of position-forming, arguers may work to turn antitheses based on cuts into those based on scales—which are inherently easier to undo—or to turn scalar oppositions into either/or cuts to keep terms separated. Furthermore, the potential for adding direction to scales, for moving the position of a cut on a scale, and for combining cuts and scales becomes especially fertile ground for the arguer manipulating types of opposition. As a semanticist, Ogden wanted to freeze the cut or scale nature of paired terms as fixed features in a language. To rhetoricians, however, changing or reinforcing the cut/scale difference, with all its potential permutations, can be the goal of an argument that works to change an audience's conception of a particular antithetical pair. Take as a simple illustration Ogden's assertion that the open/shut dichotomy has a scale on one side for degrees of openness, but then a clear cut between open and shut with no scale, no degrees on the "shut" side. Someone adopting a rhetorical view of oppositions will immediately demur and say that one can indeed argue for degrees of "shutness" that correspond to the degrees of difficulty in opening something. The possibilities of arguing a scale into place on one side of a cut or of undoing a cut entirely and replacing it with a continuous scale or of rupturing a continuous scale with an unbridgeable chasm—all of these may be the result of argument as well as, in Ogden's view, the starting point of demonstration.

Cases illustrating the cut/scale malleability

Two very simple and fundamental methods in measurement illustrate the lability of cut versus scale conceptualizations in antithetical reasoning and argumentation. The first concerns temperature which, given thermometers, seems a simple case of one-way scales. According to Ogden, however, our everyday vocabulary reveals that the opposition between hot and cold represents not extreme points on a continuous unidirectional scale but the extremes of two diverging scales, scales that meet naturally at the temperature of the skin surface. Measures of temperature increase on either side of this point of perceptual neutrality, cold, colder, coldest to one side and hot, hotter, hottest to the other. A point of neutrality in a temperature scale is of course preserved in both the Fahrenheit and Celsius scales where the midpoint (32°F and 0°C) is calibrated on the freezing point of water, not the sense of human touch. But even with this new midpoint in place, temperatures are still spoken of as either falling below or rising above freezing; they are still conceptualized on diverging scales. The Kelvin scale, however, hypothesizes a system based not on the human perception of temperature or the freezing point of a common substance but on the concept of heat as molecular motion, absolute zero being absolute lack of motion. It therefore imposes a continuous unidirectional scale; the other more humanly accommodated systems are also linear scales, but they preserve the notion of divergence from a midpoint.

Another illustration of cut versus scale thinking comes from the historical reconceptualization of acids and alkalis or bases. An older view of these two classes represented them on independent scales of increasing strength, aqua regia at the extreme on one scale and lye on the other. When acids and alkalis were redefined as complementary substances that could neutralize each other to produce salts and water, they ceased to exist on independent scales but became implicated in a single series according to what could act on what. In 1909, the opposition between acids and bases was reconceptualized along a continuous one-way scale, the pH scale, a simple numerical ranking from 1 to 14 defined as the negative of the log of the hydrogen ion concentration. The midpoint of this scale is the pH of water at 7. Thus what was once conceptualized as two diverging scales was later rationalized, according to a single underlying principle, into a continuous one-way scale. But as every high school chemistry student knows, "lab thinking" still requires an overlay of the concept of paired, abutting series diverging to extremes from a midpoint, weak to strong acids on one side (pH 7 to 1) and weak to strong bases on the other (pH 7 to 14), on top of the continuous series of the pH scale from the extremes of 1 to 14.

Human versus brute

Persistent arguments in the history of ideas have sometimes been characterized by competing metaphors. But some debates could also be described as competition between kinds of antithesis, and whether a particular pair of terms represents a mediated or unmediated opposition can be argued back and forth for centuries in the light of new theories and new kinds of evidence.

Take, for example, one of the pairs of terms on the list of 25 oppositions that Ogden considered fundamental, that between humans and animals, or, in the more loaded older phrasing of this contrast, between human and brute. Do these terms represent the end points of a continuous scale or two sides of an unbreachable cut?[19] If an arguer's purpose is to push concepts apart to either side of a gap, then one useful tactic is to link the contested terms with an already accepted pair of presumably mutually exclusive opposites and another is to establish a contradiction with a trait that one side has and the other side does not. For centuries, the favored predicate terms in the human/brute debate were "rational" versus "irrational," a pair typically taken as either/or contradictories leading to the formation of neat antitheses like "Humans are rational; brutes are irrational." But basing humanity on rationality can easily make brutes of some humans, and as long as these arguments have been made, they have been attacked, sometimes by offering evidence of animal rationality or of other animal perfections, as in Montaigne's observations in his *Apologie de Raimond Sebond*, and sometimes by ridicule as in Benjamin Franklin's observation that the rationality of humans consists in their finding a reason for whatever they want to do.

The ancient opposition between human and brute was seriously challenged in the nineteenth century when various theories of evolution, culminating in Darwin's, were publicly aired. Inevitably, theories of evolution, successors of the older "chain of being" arguments, claim a continuum instead of a rupture between humans and animals. The implications of these theories and the potential for a continuum were subject to new arguments in the mid-nineteenth century because of the recent availability of two new sources of evidence. In the 1840s and 1850s, the first reliable accounts of the four species of great ape became available to Western audiences, allowing a sorting through of three centuries worth of travelers' tales about strange man-like beasts glimpsed in the forests of Borneo or along the rivers of tropical West Africa. It was only in 1847 that the gorilla was identified and examined by an American, Dr. Thomas Savage (Huxley 1871, 32), and in the 1850s, the English paleontologist Richard Owen reported his extensive anatomical findings on the chimpanzee. And it was only in 1857 that a strangely formed but ostensibly human skull was discovered in a cave above the valley of the Neander River, a find that prompted the rediscovery of other putatively human fossils.

In the 1850s and 1860s, because of this new material, arguments were engaged again on the nature of the antithesis between humans and animals, focusing particularly on the relation between humans and the great apes. Linnaeus had placed humans, along with monkeys, lemurs, bats, and certain human-ape hybrids that he accepted from travelers' tales, in the order Primata. Buffon and Cuvier had taken humans out of this single comprehensive category by cutting it into two orders, one for the Bimana, the two-handed, containing only humans, and one for the quadrumana, the supposedly four-handed, containing all the apes and monkeys. Predictably, those who would emphasize the separation and the contradictory nature of the terms "human" and "ape" looked for evidence of human features missing or somehow presentable as radically different in the great apes. In other words, the kind of antithesis they wanted to establish dictated the kind of evidence they emphasized. Their arguments concentrated on the hand, the foot, and especially the brain, since in order to force a cut, the two terms, "human" and "ape" had to be predicated of mutually exclusive attributes, of an A and a not-A. An argument for an unmediated antithesis has no choice but to pursue an absolute.

In 1857, Richard Owen published his claim to such an either/or difference: "The posterior development [of the human brain] is so marked, that anatomists have assigned to that part the character of a third lobe; it is peculiar to the genus Homo, and equally peculiar is the posterior horn of the lateral ventricle and the 'hippocampus minor' which characterise the hind lobe of each hemisphere" (qtd. in Huxley 1871, 134). To epitomize Owen's arguments in an antithesis based on a contradiction, humans have posterior brain parts and apes do not have posterior brain parts.

The challenge of these arguments was accepted by T. H. Huxley. When Owen repeated his claims about absolute structural differences between ape and human brains at the famous meeting of the British Association in 1860, in which Huxley and Wilberforce squared off over the implications of Darwinism, Huxley vociferously denied this exclusionary claim, maintaining instead at that meeting and in the January 1861 issue of the *Natural History Review*, in the language of direct contradiction of a contradiction, "That the *hippocampus minor* is neither peculiar to, nor characteristic of, man, inasmuch as it also exists in the higher quadrumana" (Huxley 1871, 135). Huxley reviews this entire controversy in detail and assesses the evidence from comparative anatomy and fossil humans available to him in

Evidence as to Man's Place in Nature (1863). In the second essay of three comprising this volume, "The Relations of Man to the Lower Animals," Huxley predictably places the great apes close to humans by constructing a quantified scale of measurable anatomical features. After reviewing the evidence from embryology attesting to the morphologically indistinguishable origins of all vertebrates, Huxley selects the gorilla as his representative great ape species and then argues repeatedly, based on scaled measurements, that as different as the gorilla seems to be from humans, it is even more unlike the other great apes: for example, "In these respects the pelvis of the Gorilla differs very considerably from his [human's] (Fig. 16). But go no lower than the Gibbon, and see how vastly more he differs from the Gorilla than the latter does from Man, even in this structure" (92) and "So that, for the skull, no less than for the skeleton in general, the proposition holds good, that the differences between Man and the Gorilla are of smaller value than those between the Gorilla and some other Apes" (97) and "Whatever part of the animal fabric—whatever series of muscles, whatever viscera might be selected for comparison—the result would be the same—the lower Apes and the Gorilla would differ more than the Gorilla and the Man" (101).[20] This repeated formula establishes a mediated human/ape antithesis along a scale of mammals with the great apes near and the gorilla considerably nearer the human end. As Huxley concludes:

> I have endeavoured to show that no absolute structural line of demarcation, wider than that between the animals which immediately succeed us in the scale, can be drawn between the animal world and ourselves; and I may add the expression of my belief that the attempt to draw a physical [*sic*; should perhaps be psychical] distinction is equally futile, and that even the highest faculties of feeling and of intellect begin to germinate in lower forms of life. (129)

But immediately after this impassioned conclusion for a mediated opposition, Huxley reopens the divide: "At the same time no one is more strongly convinced than I am of the vastness of the gulf between civilized men and the brutes; or is more certain that whether *from* them or not, he is assuredly not *of* them" (129–130). What either/or difference could lead Huxley to claim a human/animal scale in one sentence and then a cut in the next, narrowly saving himself from self-contradiction by the hedging term "civilized" and a reinvoking of the deliberately ambiguous term "brutes"?

To reestablish a cut, Huxley returns to another ancient either/or difference frequently used to divide humans from animals, the presence of language on one side of this divide and its absence on the other. This A/not A contradiction remains firmly in place for Huxley and helps to explain his perception of a "great gulf" (Huxley 1871, 120) or "chasm" (123) between apes and humans. Huxley's salvaging argument here, carried on in a lengthy note, is subtle and hedged, but it leads him to concede that he believes

> with Cuvier, that the possession of articulate speech is the grand distinctive character of man (whether it be absolutely peculiar to him or not), I find it very easy to comprehend, that some equally inconspicuous structural difference may have been the primary cause of the immeasurable and practically infinite divergence of the Human from the Simian Stirps. (122)

In the conclusion to this essay, Huxley turns the physical continuity between animals and humans, overlaid by their linguistic discontinuity, into a celebration of human achievement on the warrant of the distance humans have progressed and their exclusive possession of the generation-spanning power of speech. "Our reverence for the nobility of manhood will not be lessened by the knowledge, that Man is, in substance and in structure, one with the brutes; for he alone possesses the marvellous endowment of intelligible and rational speech. . . . " (132).

The centuries-old language/no language dichotomy, which Huxley repeats here to reinforce the animal/human dichotomy, has received perhaps its strongest challenge in the mid-twentieth century from the many psychologists who undertook lengthy projects to teach a variety of nonhuman primates—chimpanzees, gorillas, orangutans, and bonobos—to use American Sign Language or specially constructed languages employing token systems and keyboards as interfaces for ape users. The potential of apes to communicate across species in the celebrated cases of Washoe, Koko, and others has attracted tremendous public interest, a certain sign that fundamental issues seem to be at stake in a course of research.

The targeting of apes to become a language-using species was argumentatively enhanced by the fact that, thanks to arguments like Huxley's, not only do apes occupy the position just next to humans on a phylogenetic scale, but this closeness was dramatically enhanced by the discovery in 1975 (King and Wilson) that chimpanzees and humans share 99% of their genetic profile, another source of arguments for the human/ape dichotomy as mediated. Given this extraordinary similarity and an evolutionary model of human development, it makes sense to look for language abilities in some kind of nascent form in the phylogenetic relatives closest to humans, to take up, as it were, Huxley's open question of whether speech is "absolutely peculiar" to humans. When the experimenters claimed success, the language-using apes did not, in effect, cross the boundary between human and animal to the human side; instead they colonized the gap and therefore reconfigured the either/or difference between humans and animals into a scale of continuous intelligence and linguistic ability, coinciding with the genetic and anatomical scales.

Since their inception, the ape-language experiments have been under heavy criticism aimed at restoring an either/or antithesis between animals and humans. A recent book-length critique, *Aping Language* by Joel Wallman (1992), is worth looking at in detail for the tactics it necessarily employs to restore human/ape as contradictories rather than mediated contraries. Since Wallman has to argue an A/not-A pair into place he centers, predictably, on what counts or does not count as language. According to Wallman, the apes may be doing some things that their human trainers have overinterpreted as language, but what they are doing does not amount to language in the sense of language used by humans. In the case of reference, Wallman sets up a dichotomy been goal-directed gesturing and true reference, between signing as "pragmatic rather than referential" (Wallman 1992, 65). "When the apes signed," he asks, typically offering antithetical possibilities, "were they referring to things with symbols for concepts or merely producing gestures that had reliably garnered them rewards in that context previously?" (65).

Also important to Wallman is whether apes are capable of "displaced reference," that is, whether they can refer to things not in their immediate environment and not the object of their immediate desires. Other philosophies of language might argue against this antithesis between the immediate and the displaced in Wallman's definition of reference, but his is, nevertheless, the predictable strategy given his argumentative goals, one that surfaces in his own language about his argument. He concludes his chapter critiquing the apes' reference capabilities by deciding that the best case among the ape projects, the pygmy chimpanzee Kanzi, who learned a special language called keyboard Yerkish indirectly while observing his mother's training, nevertheless "clusters with the other apes rather than with children on the instrumental/noninstrumental contrast" (Wallman 1992, 78). The underlying antitheses are as follows: "apes sign pragmatically/children refer; pragmatic reference is instrumental/true reference is noninstrumental."

What Wallman does for reference he also does for claims about the apes' abilities to use syntax. Koko the gorilla placed a modifying term before a noun in 75% of the cases in a trial. This result looks like evidence for a certain degree of one kind of syntactic ordering and hence the kind of approximation of language-using ability that one would expect when moving incrementally closer to humans. But Wallman refutes it by using still another pair of presumably unmediated opposites: "the 75 percent figure reflects a mere statistical tendency, a 'preference,' rather than a grammatical constraint. By contrast, children, according to [Roger] Brown, 'show something much stronger than a statistical preference for correct order'" (Wallman 1992, 85). The antithesis distillable from this argument could be expressed as follows: "When it comes to syntactic ordering, apes show a preference; children demonstrate a constraint." Even the evidence offered by the experimenters of apes constructing novel combinations of signs does not persuade Wallman, who again is ready with a dichotomy between words in grammatical constructions and words only tied to each other by their "separate relevance to the situation of utterance" (96). Washoe the chimpanzee's celebrated feat of signing "water bird" when first seeing a swan is questioned as possibly a signing first to the water and then to the bird in succession, not to the same thing in combination.

In his final chapters, Wallman sets aside the ape-language projects and considers the evidence from primate and human neuroanatomy and from naturalistic primate communication to see if there is any evidence for nascent language centers in the brains of apes or for communication practices in the wild that prefigure human language. Basically, Wallman's argumentative task in these chapters is once again to undo arguments, like Huxley's, that contribute to a conceptualization of animal brain architecture or animal communication as somehow only incrementally rather than profoundly different from the human. For example, despite some evidence to the contrary, ape and monkey brains, according to Wallman, seem not to show the strong lateralization that human brains presumably show in the distribution of language activity: thus, a lateralization/no lateralization pair provides the necessary contradictory predicates supporting the overall claim that there is "an exclusively human evolutionary *complex* of organic traits undergirding language" (Wallman 1992, 118). Wallman also finds lack of continuity between primates and humans in what is called "categorical perception," the ability to clump the acoustic continuum into discrete packages, an issue that in itself is a reification of the cut/scale difference.[21] He cites evidence that while humans can only per-

ceive categorically or by clumping, some primates can perceive both categorically or not, an either/both opposition, while lowly chinchillas, hardly neighbors
on the phylogenetic block, have precisely the same clumping boundaries that
English speakers have (124), making absurd the notion of an incremental approach to human abilities.

Wallman's deployment of antitheses is strongest in the chapter dealing with
evidence of how primates communicate in the wild. He divides the issues raised
by this in situ research into a number of contrasts, fully aware that "Some of these
contrasts are dichotomous [cuts], while others define a continuum of possibilities
[scales], with language at one end and primate systems, if not at the other, then at
least elsewhere" (Wallman 1992, 128). Since overall he believes that there is "more
support for the discontinuity position" (128), it is not surprising that the dichotomous pairs predominate in subsections of this chapter, titled by pairs meant to be
taken as contradictory on whether vocalizations are learned or inborn, volitional
or nonvolitional, and semantic or affective (that is, cortically versus limbically
controlled).

Finally and predictably, in the concluding chapter of *Aping Language,* where a
summarizing epitome of the arguments is expected and delivered, Wallman reprises
his case and the figure antithesis makes a strong showing:

> Apes and monkeys do not have obvious nascent versions of the language regions of
> the human brain, although there are some hints of such developments here and
> there. Nor do other primates, with a few exceptions, evince language-like principles
> in their natural systems of communication. Ours, dispensing with qualifications, is
> cortical, while theirs is limbic; our symbols are learned, their calls are inborn; our
> language is referential, their communication affective. (Wallman 1992, 152)

Thucydides would have appreciated the final sentence of this passage. By means of
antitheses like these, Wallman has unhooked a link in the phylogenetic continuum.
Humans are on one side of a cut, apes and all animals on the other, and between
them there is a "language gap wide and unexplained"(152).

Male versus female

Among the ten fundamental oppositions used by the Pythagoreans to explain the
structure of the world is the pair male/female.[22] While no opposites may seem more
permanent and absolute across all languages and cultures, the kind of antithesis
represented by this pair, whether male/female sit on opposite sides of a cut or on
opposite ends of a scale, can in fact be a matter of local argument and belief, intimately tied to other social beliefs and projects. For example, under the pressure of
polemics for equal educational access, arguments favor diminishing or even elimi-
nating the male/female antithesis, at least on the axis of mental abilities. Arguments
claiming that women could not accomplish a university education were based on
a categorical, anatomical difference between the sexes: Women menstruated and
men did not. Currently, researchers in brain anatomy and physiology are once again
constructing the male/female antithesis as an either/or cut rather than as a difference in degree on a connected scale. Their work has been reported in publications

for both expert and wider audiences, and the publications accommodated to less-expert readers tend to employ more striking antitheses pushing male/female apart.

Much of the data on male/female differences in brain anatomy have, of necessity, been based on differences in degree, since there are no absolute differences in brain anatomy as there are absolute differences in the reproductive organs. Among these reported differences in degree are the following: men have larger brains in absolute if not relative size, but women presumably have a thicker corpus callosum and more neurons in the preoptic anterior hypothalamic region (Gur et al. 1995, 528). Many of these physical differences in degree are based on samples of dissected brains, and the overall results of such studies are reported as averages for the sexes, even though individuals in the test populations may have scores or values in one another's territory. In other words, the averages can be represented as distinct, whereas the individual scores overlap. Original researchers point out these overlaps, but they are often ignored in secondary reports to wider audiences.

A newer generation of neuroanatomical studies uses the evidence from positron emission tomography (PET) scans or from functional magnetic resonance imaging. These diagnostic tools presumably pinpoint areas of brain activity on the basis of increased blood flow while subjects perform a specified cognitive task. Despite such state-of-the-art data generation, an arguer who wants to configure the results into an either/or cut versus a scaled difference must still present the data in such a way that the terms being pushed apart (male/female) are tied to other pairs of opposites deemed more absolute or at least less problematical by an audience. Thus, while differences in degree, like differences in the density of a particular kind of cell in a particular region of the brain, produce "more" versus "less" scalar antitheses, always susceptible to exaggeration or reduction by the standard rhetorical arts of amplification and minification, other kinds of differences can create a seemingly unbridgeable gulf.

An example of a recent argument for a male/female cut comes from the work of the Shaywitzes and colleagues at Yale, work that was widely reported to a variety of audiences with predictable results in the epitomizing of the arguments. The Yale group measured brain activity during tests of various language skills designed to activate visual, orthographic, phonological, and semantic recognition and processing (Shaywitz et al. 1995, 607). In the phonological component, participants were asked if pairs of nonsense words rhymed. Magnetic resonance imaging of brain activity showed that the men in the sample used only a small area on the left side of their brains when performing this task (inferior frontal gyrus), whereas the women used that area plus an area on the right side of their brains. "This was," according to reporting in the *New York Times*, "the first clear evidence that men and women can use their brains differently while they are thinking" (Kolata 1995, C7). Although there may certainly be varying degrees of activity in the same region of the brain, activity on one side versus activity on both sides amounts to an either/or distinction, a cut beyond mediation. Thus the male/female difference has been effectively tied to a pair of opposites (one/both) recognized as firm contradictions. The popularity of these arguments, the ease with which they move into the mass media, comes in part from the fact that they can be epitomized with such striking oppositions.

Two versions of the verbal figure antithesis were used in the issue of *Nature* in which the Shaywitzes' original research report appeared. According to the rhetorical practice common in both the widely read weekly science magazines *Nature* and *Science,* an introductory, assessing piece by another expert often appears as an introduction to an important research report following in the same issue (and conversely the appearance of the introductory piece creates the importance of the research report). The brain researcher who commented on the Shaywitzes' work, Michael Rugg, epitomizes the findings as follows: "Shaywitz et al. found that a task requiring rhyme judgments on pairs of visually presented nonsense words activated cortex in the inferior gyrus of the frontal lobe. This activation was *unilateral in males* but was *bilateral in their female subjects*" (Rugg 1995, 561; emphasis added). (Typically, Rugg has avoided the perfect antithesis that would have resulted had he used "females" instead of "their female subjects.") The original research report uses the pair "lateralized" and "bilaterally" (Shaywitz et al. 1995, 607–609) as well as a more diffuse antithesis: "During phonological tasks, brain activation in males is lateralized to the left inferior frontal gyrus; in females the pattern of activation is very different, engaging more diffuse neural systems that involve both the left and right inferior frontal gyrus" (607). (This sentence appears in a bolded first paragraph that functions as an abstract and hence as an epitome of the argument that follows.) A unilateral/bilateral antithesis matches well with another of the ten fundamental Pythagorean pairs: one and plurality. Here is a pair that seems to be an unbridgeable contradiction. How is it possible to mediate between one and more than one? Finding, in this case, a one/both split stabilizes a female/male dichotomy as opposed to a continuum.

In addition to the verbal antitheses in each of the pieces, *Nature* employed a striking visual antithesis on its cover, showing two shadowy cross sections of brains, the male brain on the left with illuminated pixels on one side only and the female brain on the right with illuminated pixels on both sides (see Figure 2.2). In order to make the two sides of this picture, or the two cola of this antithesis, parallel, the smaller female brain was "stretched" on a system of key anatomical points so that its outline matches that of the larger male brain. With this enhancement to absolute parallelism, the contrast between the illuminated and unilluminated portions is as amplified as the opposed terms are in the verbal figure.

Interestingly enough, the subjects in the Shaywitz test showed no differences in performance, though performance differences in such tests of mental abilities have in the past been the staple of arguments for a mediated male/female antitheses. The sum of these older investigations was epitomized as follows by science writer Gina Kolata, "Psychologists have consistently shown that *men, on average, are slightly better than women on spatial tasks,* like visualizing figures rotated in three dimensions, and *women, on average, are slightly better at verbal tasks*" (Kolata 1995, C7; italics added). In a *Science* article on similar research, this same assumption is expressed in the following figure: "*Women* perform better than men on some *verbal* tasks, whereas *men* excel in certain *spatial and motor* tasks" (Gur et al. 1995, 528). (The reference for this last figurally expressed claim is a 1974 textbook.) These antitheses pairing men and women with the terms "spatial" and "verbal" can be read as reinforcing either a mediated or unmediated antithesis, depending on how

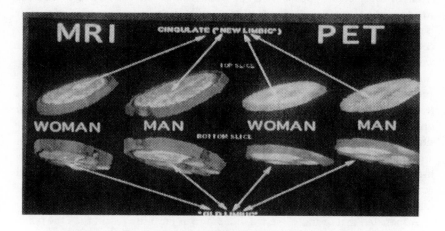

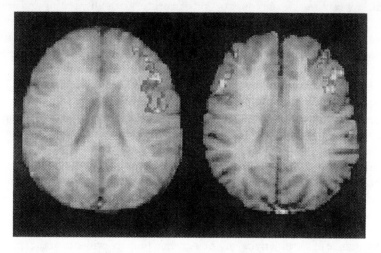

Figure 2.2. Visual antitheses. (a) Physical differences in the male and female brains at rest. From Ruben C. Gur et al., "Sex differences in regional cerebral glucose metabolism during a resting state," *Science* 267 (January 27, 1995). Reproduced with permission of Ruben C. Gur, from the Brain Behavior Laboratory, University of Pennsylvania. (b) These composite magnetic resonance images show the distribution of active areas in the brains of males (left) and females during a "rhyming task." In males activation is lateralized (confined) to the left interior frontal regions but in females the same region is active bilaterally. From Bennett A. Shaywitz et al., "Sex differences in the functional organization of the brain for language," *Nature*, 373 (February 16, 1995). Reproduced with permission of B. A. Shaywitz et al., 1995, NMR/Yale Medical School.

an audience conceptualizes the pair spatial/verbal. Do they represent merely different or completely opposed tasks and abilities? Which for most audiences is the stronger pair of contrasting words to begin with, male/female or verbal/spatial? It is possible that the pair verbal/spatial becomes more opposite than merely different by virtue of its position in claims such as those quoted above. Here, in other words, is probably a case of mutual reinforcement among pairs of opposites. According to the logic of the male versus female argument here, a mediated difference between men and women is supported by their performance tendencies on tests of different abilities; but, to take a stronger version of this same argument, an unmediated opposition between male and female is supported by a strong opposition between verbal and spatial tasks. Ideally, the opposites in the predicate of an argumentative antithesis should be more stable, that is, more readily assumed by the audience addressed, than the ones under scrutiny. But it can, of course, be asked why spatial and verbal tasks are treated as semantic opposites, why it is assumed that there is no component of the spatial in the verbal or vice versa.

A spatial/verbal or motor/verbal dichotomy is far more recent than the male/female opposition; it is the construction of a century of ability testing and grouping in the psychological literature, since become a commonplace in the twentieth century. The characterization of these two types of tasks to the point of opposition has been strengthened in turn by arguments linking them to different hemispheres in the brain described by the fundamental Pythagorean opposites of right and left. Though most neuroscientists would dissent from such a simplistic correlation, in the popular understanding, the left brain dominates in verbal and the right brain in motor skills. The results of these correspondences are mutually reinforcing sets of opposites across interconnected arguments, female/verbal/left and male/spatial/right.

An anchoring of the female/male difference to such a left/right dichotomy is by no means new; the pre-Socratics believed that female children were formed on the left side of a mother's womb or generated from a father's left testicle, and male children were correspondingly generated from the right side of the womb and the right testicle (Lloyd 1966, 17, 50). However, these similarities are probably less representative of an underlying mythology than they are evidence of the tendency to use one pair of strong opposites in antitheses that are constructed to argue for or "explain" a strong separation between another pair.

The current generation of imaging studies necessarily relies heavily on such strong spatial opposites as right and left, front and back, and top and bottom to argue for fundamental differences in cognitive processes. But it may also be that labeling skills as verbal or spatial and then positing these as in effect opposites rather than mere differences is reinforced by predicating them of what are, in fact, culturally stronger opposites to begin with, male and female, left and right. Without the antithetical pairing of such terms, the evidence for gendered brains would simply amount to the fact that men and women have a different distribution of scores on different tests, certainly evidence of difference but without the divisive power of opposites predicated of opposites.

In another study of activity differences based on PET scans, Ruben C. Gur and his colleagues found only differences of degree in the metabolic rates of the "idling" brains of men and women injected with radioactively labeled glucose. "Whereas men had higher relative metabolism [than women] in lateral and ventro-medial aspects of temporal lobe regions, they had lower relative metabolism [than women] in the middle and posterior cingulate gyrus" (Gur et al. 1995, 529). This result represents average values for females and males; 17 of the 61 subjects had scores that placed them in the opposite gender group. The Gur article concludes that "the brains of men and women are fundamentally more similar than different" (530). However, Gur's group from the Brain Behavior Laboratory at the University of Pennsylvania School of Medicine, whose goal was perhaps to find a laterality in activity that had not shown up in other scanning tests, did find some "sex x region" differences in metabolic rates. The *New York Times* article reporting on this laboratory's finding heightens these differences by importing still other pairs of recognized antonyms. Thus, the caption to a picture of hovering brain wafers with varying areas of darkness claims:

> PET scans found that *women*, on average, had more activity in a *recently evolved* part of the limbic system, the cingulate gyrus, involved in *symbolic actions*. *Men*, on average, had higher metabolic activity in the more *ancient and primitive* regions of the limbic system, involved in *direct action*." (Kolata 1995, C1; emphasis added)

"Women," "recently," and "symbolic action" are opposed here to "men," "ancient and primitive," and "direct action," and hence once again the two terms under scrutiny, female and male, are pulled further apart by association with other accepted opposites.[23] As long as the nature of the female/male opposition is debated, the tactics of constructing cuts versus scales, and the figure antithesis, will be put into play.

3

Incrementum and Gradatio

In 1857, the British Admiralty sent the H.M.S. *Cyclops* to sound the depths of the Atlantic Ocean and test the firmness of its bottom for laying a transatlantic telegraph cable. Samples from the ocean-bottom ooze hauled aboard found their way into the laboratory of Thomas Henry Huxley, once a Navy surgeon and a former shipmate of the *Cyclops'* captain (Huxley 1968, 10). When, ten years later, Huxley reexamined his bottled specimens under the microscope, his prepared eye now discerned gelatinous bodies in the muck, bodies that he took to be the preserved specimens of loosely structured living forms, amorphous masses of protoplasm newly identified as the universal stuff of life. He christened this new form *Bathybius haeckelii* after the German zoologist Ernst Haeckel, a fervent Darwinian and systematist of the "protista" or unicellular forms of life.

Huxley's discovery of the free-form *bathybius* supported both his belief in the universality of protoplasm as the material basis of all plant and animal life, announced that same year in his essay "On the Physical Basis of Life," and his need to argue around the "origin" problem raised by Darwin's *On the Origin of Species*. If species evolved from each other with no need for special creation, where did the first living form come from? How was the gulf between the inorganic and the organic first crossed? Huxley's *bathybius* offered a potential answer to this immediate question and at the same time seemed to fulfill the speculations of the early nineteenth-century *Naturphilosoph*, Lorenz Oken, who imagined that life had originated as an "Urschleim" (a term Huxley revived), a "primitive mucous substance" generating itself from inorganic constituents in pools of sea water (Rehbock 1975, 504). Haeckel seized on the possibility that *bathybius* generated itself spontaneously on the ocean floor and, as a structureless homogenous cellular material, represented the simplest of possible life forms, its "huge masses of naked, living protoplasm" covering "the greater ocean depths" (508–509, 522). In this manner, *bathybius* was rhetorically amplified by Haeckel and others into a vast layer of primitive living matter lying along the interface between rock and teeming sea, a widely distributed middle term between the inorganic and the organic worlds (Eiseley 1957, 33). Huxley had found a missing link to bridge the gap between the end terms of an unmediated antithesis, living and not living.

Within a few years, Huxley was proved wrong, and he readily admitted his error. In the 1870s, researchers aboard the ocean-exploring vessel H.M.S. *Challenger* examined material from the sea bottom again and again, but they could find no evidence of Huxley's *bathybius*. Eventually those collecting and analyzing samples on the *Challenger* realized that, by following Huxley's directions and preserving specimens in alcohol, they were creating a clear, gelatinous precipitate of calcium sulfate from sea water, a goo that was easily misinterpreted as a primitive proto-plasm (Rehbock 1975, 528).This famous case of temporary wish fulfillment has often puzzled or amused historians of science who otherwise have a justified ad-miration for Huxley's and Haeckel's scientific achievements. But they can consider the case of *bathybius* as an example of the sometimes too powerful need for a middle term to bridge an unmediated antithesis.

Undoing Antitheses

If arguers use antitheses to push concepts apart, they must have tactics available to undo antitheses and pull concepts together again, for opening or closing an oppo-sition can be a major point of contention in a wide variety of arguments in all fields. The discovery or construction of a middle term like *bathybius* is just one of several rhetorical tactics that can be used to repair the breach between antithetical terms. The following overview of these tactics will begin with the simplest and will then concentrate on the bridging devices that have been cataloged among the figures of speech. These final mediating devices, the subject of this chapter, have proved es-pecially powerful tools in scientific argument, much beyond the repair work they can perform on antithetical terms.

The most direct method of closing an opposition simply reverses the basic de-vice of opening it in the first place. Instead of predicating opposites of opposites, the arguer predicates the same of opposites. To answer the antithesis "A is x and B is y," where A and B as well as x and y are pairs of antonyms, the arguer claims "A and B are z," where z is a new term that both can be said to share. In other words, the antithetical terms under attack can be bracketed as the double subject or ob-ject of a sentence, or they can be combined in an inclusive term; either way, as partners in a grammatical unit, they preside over the same action or share the same state, and as a result their differences seem to diminish or collapse.

The Corinthians' "rhetoric of war" provided an example of successive antith-eses pushing terms, and whole peoples, into opposition (see chapter 2, p. 70). Pre-dictably, a famous instance of the "rhetoric of peace" can provide an example of the stylistic devices that undo oppositions. Lincoln's Second Inaugural Address is in some ways the benign reverse of the Corinthians' speech inciting war between the Athenians and the Spartans. According to common interpretation, Lincoln's speech, delivered shortly before his assassination, is the manifesto of a forgiving

Reconstruction that never occurred, its declared purpose to bind up the wounds of the Civil War and heal sectional disruption. Addressed to an audience of the North who had listened to war rhetoric for 4 years, who had suffered great losses to preserve the Union, and who were still at war, Lincoln's speech could hardly unite the two sides abruptly or cavalierly. Lincoln therefore concludes the first movement of his speech with a magnificent antithesis that speaks to the immediate situation: "Both parties deprecated war; but one of them would make war rather than let the nation survive; and the other would rather accept war than let it perish."

Having acknowledged the oppositions that led to the war, Lincoln can now call on another resource of the language, the pronoun system, which allows two referents to be combined into a single grammatical entity. What follows is the crucial section in the speech that works to undo the war's antithesis by combining North and South in pronouns as united agents in expectations and values.

> Neither party expected for the war the magnitude or the duration which it has already attained. Neither anticipated that the cause of the conflict might cease with, or even before, the conflict itself should cease. Each looked for an easier triumph and a result less fundamental and astounding. Both read the same Bible, and pray to the same God; and each invokes his aid against the other. . . . The prayers of both could not be answered—that of neither has been answered fully.

Here is the stylistic antithesis to the passage quoted earlier from Thucydides. Lincoln specifies eight predicates shared by the two sides, in effect uniting them in mutual suffering of a war that lasted longer and cost more lives than either side expected. The unoffending pronouns "neither" and "each" are particularly wise choices since they discriminate while still referring to the two sides, mitigating what might otherwise be an offensive yoking if "both" were used alone. After this passage, the speech surrenders agency to God: "The Almighty has his own purposes." The only time the powerfully divisive terms North and South actually appear in this speech, they are bracketed and hence united as recipients of God's wrath, for "He gives to both North and South this terrible war." On the other side of this healing passage, there are no more antitheses, only a potentially inclusive "we" ("fondly do we hope—fervently do we pray") whose immediate referent is "believers in a living God."

This last term displays a third tactic. In addition to encompassing pronouns (e.g., "both") and bracketed units ("North and South"), Lincoln also uses a potentially inclusive or bridging category, "believers in a living God." While North and South may be opposed terms in one plane, on another they are both members of a greater whole, a larger category.[1] When an arguer can find such an encompassing term, "the same" can readily be predicated of opposites. Claiming the same attributes for opposites or including them in a larger category are versions of the same tactic. In both cases, the arguer produces perfectly ordinary sentences of a kind not usually labeled figurative though these forms certainly have argumentative functions (e.g., both [North and South] pray to the same God. Both [North and South] are believers in a living God.). The tactic of uniting opposites by placing them in a larger group is often made easier by the existence of ready-made encompassing categories. Protestants and Catholics, for example, can be set against each other as opposed groups or they can be united as "Christians," and a rhetorical advantage gained from the familiarity of the ready-made term.

But what if no such prefabricated category is available? In that case, special categories or options that can include or "ingest" the opposites have to be constructed. Lincoln's "believers in a living God" is one such construction, a modest one. More daring is the coining of a composite term. In 1600, for example, William Gilbert wrote a special chapter in *De Magnete* on the distinctions between magnetic and electrical attraction, pushing these two forms apart. But 300 years later, these phenomena were united under the term "electromagnetism."

An act of composite naming, like electromagnetism, can create not only a new category but sometimes a new choice. An example of the construction of such a composite "way out" comes from the health care debates of 1993 when opponents were characterized as favoring unfettered laissez faire competition in the medical marketplace on one side, and bureaucratic government control and rationing of health care resources on the other. Some astute policy makers characterized their program as "managed competition," a miraculous third alternative that presumably combined the antithetical sides. Making the same move, clever politicians in Canada formed a "progressive conservative" party. And in quite a different field, Nobel laureate Christian de Duve used the same tactic of creative coinage in *Vital Dust*, his extended argument for a seamless synthesis of molecular biology and evolutionary theory. Faced with what he calls "finalism" on one side, a notion that the course of evolution follows a preordained plan (de Duve 1995, 10), and a radical indeterminism on the other, which sees the evolution of life as a highly improbable chance occurrence (9), de Duve opts instead for something he calls "constrained contingency," the favored outcome that existing chemical and physical conditions impose on a random event like a copying error during DNA replication (xvi, 296).

Terms like "managed competition," "progressive conservative," and "constrained contingency" qualify as *oxymorons*, compressed juxtapositions of antithetical terms, used in these cases to create new positions that bridge or mediate between deadlocked opposites. The mediation of antitheses is their purpose, as John Hoskins explained in 1599.

> Synoeciosis [Hoskins' term for the oxymoron] is a composition of contraries, and by both words intimateth the meaning of neither precisely but a moderation and mediocrity of both; as, *bravery* and *rags* are contrary [in the sixteenth century], yet somewhat better than both is *brave raggedness*. (Hoskins 1935, 36)

According to Hoskins' specifications, an oxymoron is formed when either of two opposed terms becomes a modifier of the other: "And one contrary is affirmed to be in the other directly by making one the substantive, the other the adjective . . ." (36). The result is often valued as a paradox, the achieved impossible, a combination of unreconcilables that should not exist but that, at least in the verbal pairing, amazingly does.[2]

Whether perceived as paradoxical or not, a bridging alternative can be looked at either as the ground that absorbs or unites opposites in a larger category or as a composite alternative. But a third term that mediates between antitheses can participate in still another kind of undoing. The fundamental argumentative tactic here amounts to presenting an audience with three things at a time instead of two things at a time. Two things can always be set in opposition, but three things, provided they are perceived as on the same "plane" or as part of the same grouping, cannot be. This third thing can simply be set "next to" the other two, and the net result can be a kind of flanking move on an antithesis. Thomas Henry Huxley, for example, addressed the Victorian public's perception of an antithesis between humans and apes by bringing in a third group, the old world monkeys (Huxley 1871). Suddenly the apes, and particularly the gorilla, seemed much closer to humans. With a third term on the end, Huxley's audience was presented not with an antithesis but with a series that placed the apes closer to humans than to the other primates.

Rather than flanking antithetical terms with a third, an arguer can also try to position the third term between the opposites. At least once in the history of science, as the opening example demonstrates, this procedure of "dredging up" an intermediate occurred literally. There is, however, no reason to limit antithesis-mediating to a single third term; a coherent series of terms can be used instead. Currently, the search that inspired Huxley and Haeckel for a way to bridge the antithesis between the living and nonliving is being carried on by molecular biologists and virologists, but none of these researchers is looking for a single term as a sufficient intermediate. Instead, in the last thirty years, a host of forms have been identified that qualify to create what one virologist has called a "Continuum of Molecular Life Forms" (Levine 1992, 199). Starting at one end of such a continuum, reading from the simple to the complex, just above the "nonliving" is the first self-replicating molecule, a hypothetical RNA polymer capable of both self-maintenance and information storage. Real approximations of this first "living molecule" exist in the form of viroids, relatively short strands of RNA that are capable of replication, and virusoids, "viruses of viruses," similar chains of RNA often formed into a double helix (201–202). Another potential series of intermediates involves DNA molecules, from episomes replicating independently in a cell's cytoplasm, to plasmids, vesicles containing circular DNA that can jump from cell to cell, to insertion elements (transposons and retrotransposons), stretches of DNA that move from chromosome to chromosome, to full-fledged DNA viruses. Theorists disagree about where to place the cut in such series between the living and the nonliving.[3] A few contend that even viruses, as obligatory parasites that must hijack the metabolic and replicative processes of host cells, are not really alive. But the point derived from this example is the tactic involved: Everyone now working in this field is constructing an extended series of one kind or another. And with this final device, the catalog of tactics for undoing antitheses is complete: from bracketing opposites or unifying them with pronouns, to finding inclusive categories and new composites (sometimes as oxymorons), to introducing third terms as flanking moves or intermediates, to connecting extremes with multimembered series. The final item in this series, series construction itself, is both a well-defined tactic in scientific argument and one of the most elaborately developed areas of analysis in the tradition of form/function rationalizing embodied in the rhetorical figures. The series-making figures are well worth a close look for their conceptual virtuosity.

Figures that Construct Series

A series is easily identified in a single sentence. Some sentence constituent, usually a complement or an object, exists in multiples: "I have a, b, c, and d." Two series, however, may be formally identical on the printed page and yet suggest quite different kinds of groupings. In the expansive catalogs of figures in Classical and Renaissance style manuals, different kinds of series are labeled as different figures of speech. Some of these distinctions, now usually overlooked, are worth reviewing, for these different figures can represent or epitomize correspondingly distinctive lines of argument.

A study of series-making figures can begin with the figure *articulus*, a simple listing of words or short phrases in tandem syntactically, "when many things are connected without particular emphasis" (Melancthon 1969, 249). "Many" means at least three, and such a series claims no more than some connection among the items. "Scientists attending the meeting included A, B, C, and D." The items in this series are members of the same group appearing in the same place at the same time. Such miscellaneous lists can have important argumentative effects, and whether they are construed as closed or open-ended, complete sets or random samplings (often a function of the connectives used), can be an important issue in itself (Fahnestock 1993, 170).

Other figures identify series that are more than collections of items. Some represent the common topic of division, recommended by Aristotle and other dialecticians for finding a line of argument based on partitioning a subject in a useful way, usually to serve an argument from definition. In some technical style manuals, different figures even epitomize different types of division: *merismus,* or *partitio,* is defined simply in Peacham's *The Garden of Eloquence* as "a form of speech by which the orator divideth the whole into parts" (Peacham 1954, 124; see also Melancthon 1969, 282). But *diaeresis* lists the species of a genus and *enumeratio,* a third type of division, partitions a subject into its adjuncts or features. If numbering of the parts is added to the division, labeling a first, second, and third item in a series, the figure is *eutrepismus* (Joseph 1947, 111–114). Division as an argumentative strategy (the one in use right now) can be stretched across paragraphs or pages, but to be stylistically visible or figured, any of these divisions must produce either a list of words or phrases in a single sentence constituent or contiguous predictions in a short stretch of text.

An articulus, then, is a collection of items and a partitio and its siblings a naming of parts, species, or features. But if there is any tendency, direction, or trajectory given to a series, if there is any pattern or order imposed on the list, a different kind of series is involved, a different argumentative strategy, and therefore a different figure, the *incrementum*. Melancthon defines the incrementum as "a rising mode of speech," and as "words that progress, step by step, from the least important points to the most important ones" (Melancthon 1969, 282–283). To Peacham it is "a form of speech, which by degrees ascendeth to the top of some thing or rather above the top, that is when we make our saying grow and increase by an orderly placing of wordes making the latter word alwaies exceed the former in the force of signification. . . . " (Peacham 1954, 169). He offers as examples "Neither silver, gold, nor precious stones might be compared to her vertues," and "There was never yet a noble Captaine, Prince, king or Emperour, whose honourable fame and renoune hath spred both far and wide, and also long continued, that may ever match this worthie man in vertue and honour" (169).

Peacham takes care to distinguish the incrementum from the articulus on one hand, and, on the other, from still another figure known as the *congeries*, "which respecteth not the increase of matter but multitude of wordes" (Peacham 1954, 169). A congeries is merely a "mode of massing" (Melancthon 1969, 282), a piling up of words, often synonyms, in a series. But the terms in this type of series are in no particular order nor are they parts of the same whole, species of the same genus or features of the same subject or even necessarily separate items; instead, they amplify by quantity as in the example of a series of synonyms offered by Angel Day in 1586: "There was no rakehell, no ruffian, no knave, no villain, no cogging raskell, no hatefull companion . . . but his hand was in with him" (Day 1967, 76). An incrementum, however, cannot be a congeries and need not be a partitio; instead it expresses an ordered series, a series that goes somewhere, usually, as in the examples offered in Renaissance style manuals, from the bottom to the top of an accepted hierarchy. Formally, in their appearance on the page, all the figures mentioned so far look alike, and, without additional textual directions or constraints, some cultural knowledge is required to distinguish an articulus from a partitio from a congeries from an incrementum. A list like the following, for example—The Big Bopper, Buddy Holly, Jerry Lee Lewis, and Elvis Presley—could be understood in any of these four ways.

Most Renaissance style manuals define and illustrate the figures briefly, but in Peacham's fuller treatment, the incrementum is not only characterized uniquely, it is also recommended for a particular argumentative use. Peacham follows Quintilian's advice that one way to amplify or praise a subject is to create an ordered, ascending series and then to claim that the subject tops or exceeds even the top of this series (Quintilian 1921, III, 265). Erasmus reprises this same tactic as his "Ninth Method of Enlarging," defining an incrementum "when by several steps not only is a climax reached, but sometimes, in some way, a point beyond the climax" (Erasmus 1963, 58). So, in Peacham's examples, the lady's "vertues" adorn her more than precious stones, the rarest and most valuable of adornments in his list, and the "worthie man" excels even an emperor, the highest earthly rank, in honor. There is, of course, no reason why this device cannot be run in reverse, forming a series on a decreasing scale and establishing a point in vituperation rather than praise by saying that some subject is lower than even the lowest end of a descending series. Quintilian cites such a plunging series from Cicero: "It is a sin to bind a Roman citizen, a crime to scourge him, little short of the most unnatural murder to put him to death; what then shall I call his crucifixion?" (III, 265). Whether the series ascends or descends, the object of the arguer's encomium or vituperation occurs either as a final item added on to the incrementum or as an extra element hovering just above or below it, for the figure, in Quintilian's terms, is "carried not merely to the highest degree, but sometimes even beyond it" (III, 265). Thus the arguer's subject or goal may never actually be reached or contained by the incrementum, but the series nevertheless helps the arguer approximate its value and so in a sense places it.

Redescribed in those terms, as a way to approximate "value," it is possible to see a similarity between the figures of series construction in sixteenth- and seventeenth-century rhetorical manuals and the parallel thinking about series in seventeenth-century mathematics. To enhance this parallel requires asking whether the incrementum as described in rhetorical manuals includes the notion of increasing or decreasing differences among the elements; that is, whether a verbal series can represent a geometrical as well as an arithmetical progression. Such differences in how series grow were known to the Pythagoreans, and geometrical progressions do appear in Plato's *Timaeus*. Peacham's examples certainly leave open the possibility. It could be argued that his series, "Captaine, Prince, King and Emperour" is not a linear series with equal distances between each member, but a series in which the distances between each item become progressively greater. Peacham, however, does not articulate this difference, nor do other manuals whose treatments are usually briefer than his; he cautions only that "In this figure order must be diligently observed, that the stronger may follow the weaker, & the more worthie the lesse worthie otherwise the signification shal not encrease which this figure doth especially respect" (Peacham 1954, 169).

What the rhetorical manuals define as an incrementum resembles what is sometimes called, especially in dictionaries of "poetic" terms, a *climax*. To further confuse matters, the term *climax* was originally used for still another figure of series formation, also known by its Latin name *gradatio*. As a formally distinct figure, the gradatio first appears in the *Rhetorica ad Herennium* and reappears in virtually every manual across the centuries.[4] It is an easily recognized figure, constructed from a series of phrases or clauses each of which, except the first, repeats the end of the previous item, as an example from the *Ad Herennium* demonstrates, "'The industry of Africanus brought him excellence, his excellence glory, his glory rivals.'" (315).[5] In antiquity, the favorite example—cited by the author of the *Ad Herennium*, by Quintilian, by Dionysius of Halicarnassus, and by Hermogenes—came from Demosthenes' speech *On the Crown*, "I did not speak, but fail to propose measures; I did not propose measures, but fail to serve as ambassador; I did not serve as ambassador, but fail to persuade the Thebans" (Murphy 1983, 95; 194). In Renaissance manuals, however, the favorite examples, like the following, were taken from St. Paul: "we glory in tribulations also: knowing that tribulations worketh patience; And patience, experience; and experience, hope: And hope maketh not ashamed . . . " (Romans 4: 3–5; King James version). Students of the figures probably learned them not so much by mastering their definitions as by memorizing such culturally important examples.

The gradatio is a complex figure that incorporates or builds on other figures. The Tudor rhetorician Thomas Wilson, for example, finds a kernel of the incrementum, the notion of progression, in the gradatio: "when we rehearse the word that goeth next before and bring another word thereupon that increaseth the matter," and he invented his own moral sentence as an example: "Of sloth cometh pleasure, of pleasure cometh spending, of spending cometh whoring, of whoring cometh lack, of lack cometh theft, of theft cometh hanging, and there an end for this world" (Wilson 1994, 228). Peacham, too, recommends that the succeeding "degrees" in the gradatio "ascend so that they may end with a clause of importance" (Peacham 1954, 134). The gradatio also incorporates another figure, the *anadiplosis*, which calls for repeating the close of one sentence or constituent in the opening of the next, making it an apt expression of the drawing out of one element from the previous element as in the genealogical gradatios of the Bible: "and Asa the father of Jehosh'aphat, and Jehosh'aphat that father of Joram, and Joram the father of Uzziah. . . . " (Matthew 1:8). Because of this repetition, the gradatio has sometimes been classed among figures of repeating structures in many of the attempted groupings of the figures (Joseph 1947, 83) rather than as a figure of series construction. Emphasizing this repetition and using twentieth-century terminology, the gradatio could also be described as one of the patterns of topic/comment or given/new organization identified by twentieth-century text linguists, where the new information closing one clause becomes the old information opening the next (Williams 1989, 38–40). In other words, this figure, like so many others, becomes in some of its versions indistinguishable from an unremarkable textual practice that does not count as a use of the figure. Thus, a passage that repeats only one term would not be labeled a gradatio. Illustrating this problem of what counts and what does not count are the following two passages from Richard Weaver's *Ideas Have Consequences*.

> The denial of universals carries with it the denial of everything transcending experience. The denial of everything transcending experience means inevitably—though ways are found to hedge on this—the denial of truth. With the denial of objective truth there is no escape from the relativism of "man the measure of all things." (Weaver 1948, 4)

> Hysterical optimism will prevail until the world again admits the existence of tragedy, and it cannot admit the existence of tragedy until it again distinguishes between good and evil. (11).

The first passage counts as a gradatio; the second does not. It takes, then, at least two pairs of repeated terms in three units to achieve the figure, just as it takes three items to form any of the other types of series. This requirement justifies considering the gradatio a figure of series construction, although repetition is also necessary. A passage would also not be called a gradatio if it used synonyms instead of precisely repeated terms. The passage from St. Paul quoted above, for example, might have been loosely paraphrased without repetition, "We glory in tribulation also: knowing that trials worketh patience; And endurance, experience; and knowledge, hope."

Among the figures of series formation, the gradatio has not been completely ignored by modern critics. Kenneth Burke drew attention to it, along with the antithesis, as a device of formal persuasion, because it invites the audience's participation in its construction or completion, a participation that amounts to a kind of identification with the formal device. Citing an example he found in the news, "Who controls Berlin, controls Germany; who controls Germany controls Europe; who controls Europe controls the world," Burke points out that regardless of prior beliefs about this proposition, "by the time you arrive at the second of its three stages, you feel how it is destined to develop—and on the level of purely formal assent you would collaborate to round out its symmetry by spontaneously willing its completion and perfection as an utterance" (Burke 1969, 58–59). (Burke's gradatio is surely an example of a geometrical series expressed verbally.) But even Burke's definition of the formal appeal of figures like gradatio, where assent to the manner invites assent to the matter, does not go far enough. The gradatio and the other figures of series formation can do both general conceptual work and eptiomize very specific lines of argument.

The Uses of Incrementum and Gradatio in Argument

What general conceptual work can the incrementum and the gradatio perform? Sketching their basic functions into place can help in later distinguishing the specific kinds of arguments these figures can epitomize. As its first essential feature, an incrementum has to be formed according to some principle of ordering, and by far the most common principle of ordering is by increase or decrease in some quantifier or attribute. Identifying this basic principle makes it possible to link the dialectic tradition, which identifies arguments from "the more and the less," with the figural tradition, which gives blueprints for series construction in the incrementum and gradatio. Again, as in the case of antithesis, Aristotle's *Topics* provides a manual of potential arguments derived from this general warrant.

Arguments from the more and the less or from "greater and less degrees" (Barnes 1984, I, 191) require, first of all, that subjects being ordered by degree belong to the same genus or category, at least in the perception of arguer and audience. In the language of Aristotelian dialectics, it must be possible to predicate the same thing of the subjects involved, but different members of a genus can partake of this "same thing" in different degrees. However, if the items in the incrementum are not already within the same category as far as a particular audience is concerned, then it is possible to use participation in an ordered series to establish membership or simply to beg the question by invoking the assumption that items in an ordered series must belong in the same category or genus since they are presented as sharing the same attribute in different degrees. These potential arguments work whether one takes a view of categories organized around prototypes or a more traditional view. For purposes of ordering members of the same group into a series, making use of differences in degrees of properties, Aristòtle recommends in the *Topics* that arguers

> see if what is more is a property of what is more; for then also what is less will be a property of what is less, and least of least, and most of most, and without qualification of without qualification. Thus (e.g.) inasmuch as a higher degree of perception is a property of a higher degree of life, a lower degree of perception will be a property of a lower degree of life, and the highest of the highest and the lowest of the lowest degree, and perception without qualification of life without qualification. (Barnes 1984, I, 232)

For a rough illustration of this argumentative strategy, consider the principles of triage applied by medical personnel to establish treatment priorities among a group of the variously injured; a higher chance of surviving earns a higher place in the order of attention.

Members of a genus are, then, ordered into a graded series because they have progressively more or less of something. Even a simple conventional series like Peacham's "silver, gold, and precious stones" is ordered according to increasing rarity and therefore increasing value. This ability to order objects from the same category into a series by differences in degrees of a shared property is, according to Piaget and his followers, as fundamental a cognitive process as the ability to draw analogies between members of different categories. Arguers use this fundamental process when they deliberately search for, highlight, or even construct gradable or quantifiable attributes in the items they are grouping in order to put them into a series.

Why arguers create a series depends in turn on their further purpose in arguing: They may wish to bring the end points or the intermediates or the whole series itself and its principle of gradation to an audience's attention, whether to argue for its existence or its value. Since the purpose the arguer has for constructing the series can determine the principle selected for its construction, different purposes can produce competing series based on different ordering principles. The planets, for example, can be ordered by their distance from the sun or by their size or by their density or by their number of moons, depending on what an arguer wants to do with the resulting incrementum. Promoting some entity as an origin is frequently supported by placing it at the beginning of an ordered series. Endowing it with importance can be supported by putting it at the end of an incrementum, because the end is implicitly a position of emphasis and importance in the order of things. Even arguers who wish to avoid overt evaluation in the construction of a series may have to deal with a certain inevitable "pull" from the last term as the teleological principle of the series, the purpose or goal or achievement for which it was constructed. (For example, placing the gradatio as the last in the list of series-constructing figures, a series intended as a diaeresis but readable as an incrementum, may seem to suggest that it is somehow the greatest or most important of the series-forming figures.)

If the figure incrementum gives a pattern for forming most graded series, the figure gradatio provides a somewhat different one. In a gradatio, a series can be ordered not because members have more or less of something, but because they distribute one another's properties in an overlapping way, an nth member of a series sharing one property with $n - 1$ and another property with $n + 1$, but not the same property in differing degrees with both. A familiar example of this principle of series formation can be found in paleontological time lines or "biostratigraphic schemes," where a sequence of geological ages is constructed by the characteristic fossil species that overlap. Any children's book of dinosaurs will illustrate this principle of series formation when it shows dimetrodon appearing from the Triassic to the Jurassic, overlapping with the great sauropods who persist after dimetrodon disappears and who overlap in turn with tyrannosaurus rex in the Cretaceous. Metabolic pathways are also organized according to this principle, each intermediary sharing, say, one functional group with its precursor and another with the form for which it is a precursor. Searches for "intermediates" of all kinds are sometimes conducted on this "attribute-sharing" principle. Once a series based on shared attributes has been formed, notions of sequence in time or gradable feature or even causal connection can be imposed on the overlapping series.

Series formation is not just a way of putting end points or intermediates into place. Instead, an arguer may start with potential end points as givens (perhaps, as pointed out above, in the form of a pair of antithetical terms recognized) and construct a series as a way of getting from one to the other, a way of spanning the conceptual gap between them. A series interposed between two given terms can, however, have two quite different argumentative effects: It can bring the preexisting end points together, but it can also push them further apart. It brings together when an audience sees the links that *connect* one end of the series with the other; it pushes apart by showing how many steps *intervene* between one end and the other. A goal, for example, can be made rhetorically possible by showing the series of steps needed to connect start to finish; a journey can be rhetorically lengthened by naming stages that intervene between its beginning and end. Thus rather than inevitably connecting, an intervening series can even construct two terms into opposition.

A common purpose for series in argument is the former of these two effects, making possible the conceptual passage from one end of a series to the other. An arguer may, for example, present an audience with an apparent antithesis and then undo it with a connecting series. Because the gradatio's elements are, in a sense, melded together, it is particularly effective for joining or blending, for an incrementum presents discrete steps, whereas a gradatio smoothes these over, presenting a continuum where there were once divisions. Of course, an incrementum can also be used to achieve this "passing over" effect, but to do so requires multiplying its terms so that the stages between them begin to appear insignificant.

Building on these general effects, creating or undoing the placement of terms in relation to one another, several further argumentative uses of graded or overlapping series can be distinguished. The following list of five such uses is not meant to be exhaustive; it is rather a survey of some recurring strategies.

1. An arguer can create a new series to place a term, as described above, and then use that place as a premise. If two series formed according to different principles lead to the same placing of a term, any inference from this placing is strengthened.
2. An arguer can establish a principle of gradation and only parts of the resulting series and then use this incomplete series as a rationale for finding or placing missing elements.
3. An arguer can also use an established series or hierarchy as a model for forming another; the purpose here has more to do with the construction of the whole series than with the placing of its individual elements.
4. An arguer can employ a *sorites*, an overlapping series of premises and conclusions, to establish set relations or causal connections.
5. An arguer can also use graded series to dissolve differences between categories and so reconfigure a conceptual domain, replacing differences in kind between categories by differences in degree within a new larger category.

Examples of these argumentative strategies, epitomized by the figures incrementum and gradatio, can be found in virtually any argument field; these lines of argument are truly common topics, based ultimately in the dialectical tradition of arguing from the more or the less. The following instances of the five strategies are,
however, taken from some well-known and not so well-known cases in scientific
reasoning and persuasion, where they are probably not recognized as argumentative tactics based in the rhetorical tradition, and where they are sometimes rendered in the visual rather than the verbal text. These examples are not presented in
any historical sequence in order to avoid creating the impression that these strategies somehow grew out of each other; my contention is that these devices have
been consistently available in human reasoning and argumentation.

Creating Places with Series

A famous example of forming persuasive series where they did not exist before was
the establishment of a sequence of progenitors for the modern horse, a series used
to defend Darwinian evolution in the late nineteenth century. The point of such a
series was to place modern equus at the end and therefore to argue for its features
as the result of a process of adaptive change through natural selection. An early
construction of an evolutionary series was the work of the Russian paleontologist
Vladimir Kovalevsky. He built on the work of Albert Gaudry, who in the 1860s
had identified the Miocene fossil horse *hipparion* and had shown how it was related to fossil and contemporary forms of *equus*. Using fossils available in Europe,
Kovalevsky connected *hipparion* to even earlier forms, identifying, as it turned out
incorrectly, four progenitors of the modern horse (Gould 1996, 24; 66–67).

The Yale paleontologist O. C. Marsh, using North American fossils, constructed
a more accurate series of ancestors in five steps, moving from *orohippus, mesohippus,
miohippus, protohippus, pliohippus*, to modern *equus*. For Marsh, series such as this
one provided "the stepping-stones by which the evolutionist of to-day leads the
doubting brother across the shallow remnant of the gulf once thought impassable"
(Marsh 1877, 471). In the twentieth century, the doubting brother can take shorter
steps across the gulf of uncertainty, for the sequence of North American fossil forms
on a direct line to the modern horse is now three genera longer, from *eohippus*
[*hyracotherium*],[6] through *orohippus, epihippus, mesohippus, miohippus, parahippus,
mercyhippus*, and *pliohippus*, to *equus* (Simpson 1951, 100). More convincing still
to a distinguished paleontologist like George Gaylord Simpson, who worked with
hundreds of fossil horses, is the impression that a truly dense, minutely graded series
of forms provides of continuity. "As usual," he writes, "when we have a good fossil
record from the region which was the center of evolution of such a group, the transition from one genus to the next was gradual and the line drawn between them
for purposes of classification is arbitrary" (133).

How is this argument from the establishment of a series epitomized? Kovalevsky,
as Stephen Jay Gould points out, makes his claim for an evolutionary sequence "in
a more succinct and forceful manner" by using a compressed series: "'There can
be no reasonable doubt that the four forms—Paleotherium medium, Anchi-

therium, Hipparion, and the horse—form a relationship of direct descent'" (Gould 1996, 66). Simpson expresses part of the fossil horse sequence in a way that removes any doubt about its trajectory; he puts arrows rather than commas between the terms in this evolutionary incrementum: "*Hyracotherium→ Orohippus→ Epihippus → Mesohippus → Miohippus*" (Simpson 1951, 127). But this famous series has more impact in its visual representation in textbook illustrations and museum exhibits as an incrementum of pictures or mounted specimens arranged according to increasing size, a tiny eohippus inflating in proportional steps until it becomes the modern horse (See Figure 3.1). Such a visual figure distorts somewhat the evidence known to paleontologists.[7] Nevertheless, it is the overall form of the incrementum, rendered verbally or visually, that is persuasive, especially to inexpert audiences.

The eohippus-to-equus series is an incrementum constructed from quantitative changes; the bones of the protohorses lengthen, the number of their toes decreases, their dental crowns alter, and so on. Paleontological arguments can also construct series on the overlapping gradatio principle, particularly when the argument concerns biostratigraphic schemes, for strata are in part characterized by the fact that typifying fossils become less abundant in successive layers until they are replaced by different species. An article in *Science* provides an example of such a series, a fossil plant sequence, used to support a characterization of the sedimentary sequence in a particular Australian formation. The time period at stake is the Permian-Triassic boundary, where the transition between fossil floral species is dramatic. Only four genera and one species survive into the Triassic.

> Fossil plants replacing the *Glossopteris* flora were low in diversity. Although the zonal indicator is the distinctive seed fern *D. callipteroides,* many assemblages are dominated by the conifer *Voltziopsis* (15) or the lycopod *Cylomeia* (16). [These voltzialean conifers and small Isoetes-like lycopods are most closely allied to Eurasiatic Early Triassic genera such as Annalepsis, Tomiostrobus, and Voltzia (17).] Both *Voltziopsis* and *Cylomeia* persist into diverse later floras dominated by the **Gondwanan endemic seed fern,** *Dicroidium zuberi.* Diversification of **Gondwanan endemic seed ferns** continued with the appearance in the Middle Triassic of *Dicroidium odontopteroides,* a biostratigraphic event that has been dated in New Zealand at about 244 Ma (18). The seed fern *D. odontopteroides* is a prominent element of diverse fossil floras that show regional differentiation throughout southern Pangea (19) (Retallack 1995, 77; brackets and emphasis added).

Without the bolding of critical terms, the gradatio in this passage might be difficult to detect. Furthermore, its third sentence, beginning "These voltzialean conifers" (probably inserted to connect what the author is talking about to something his readers may be more familiar with), does not link up with the next one and therefore has to be dropped to create the figure. The author was probably unaware of the figure lurking in this passage but instead may have been guided unconsciously by topic/comment patterning. Yet, paradoxically, these caveats demonstrate the connection between the gradatio and the line of reasoning it expresses. This patterning appears nowhere else in the article, and where it appears, it epitomizes perfectly the author's argument for a series constructed from overlapping members, a series used, in turn, to support his history of a particular area.

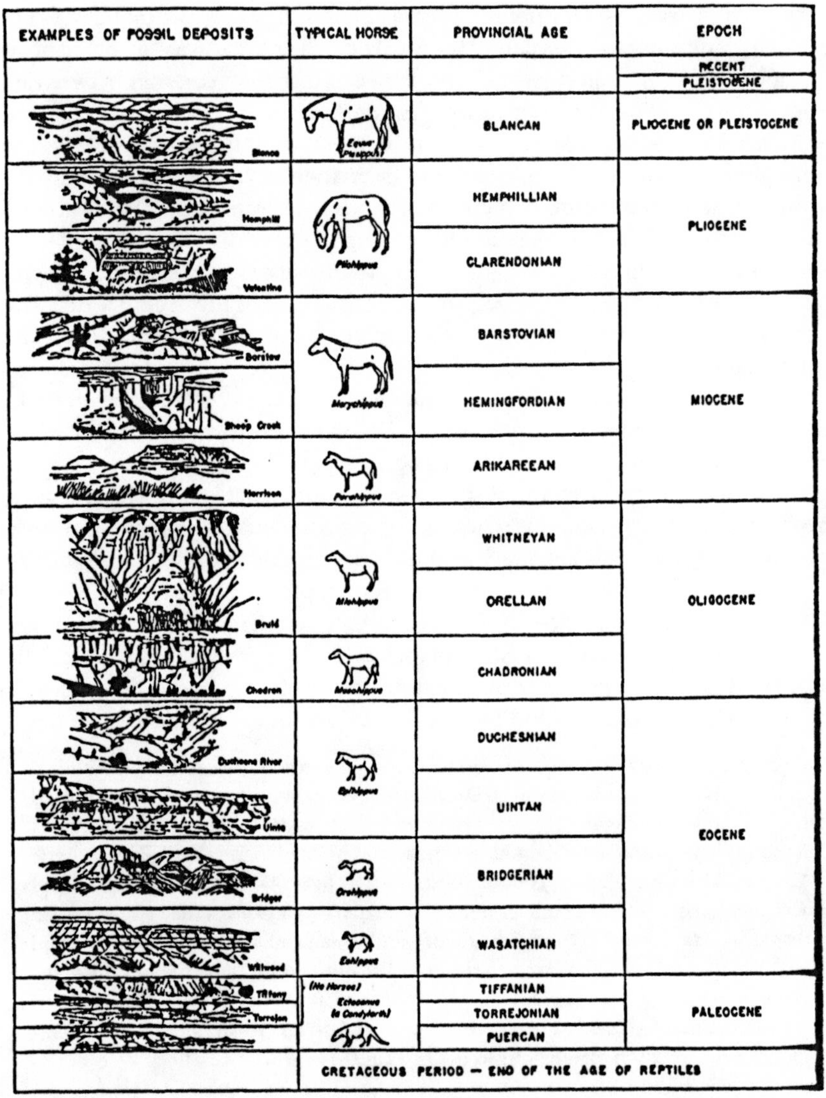

EXAMPLES OF FOSSIL DEPOSITS	TYPICAL HORSE	PROVINCIAL AGE	EPOCH
			RECENT
			PLEISTOCENE
Blanco	*Equus (Plesippus)*	BLANCAN	PLIOCENE OR PLEISTOCENE
Hemphill		HEMPHILLIAN	PLIOCENE
Valentine	*Pliohippus*	CLARENDONIAN	
Barstow		BARSTOVIAN	
Sheep Creek	*Merychippus*	HEMINGFORDIAN	MIOCENE
Harrison	*Parahippus*	ARIKAREEAN	
Brule	*Miohippus*	WHITNEYAN	
		ORELLAN	OLIGOCENE
Chadron	*Mesohippus*	CHADRONIAN	
Duchesne River	*Epihippus*	DUCHESNIAN	
Uinta		UINTAN	EOCENE
Bridger	*Orohippus*	BRIDGERIAN	
Wildwood	*Eohippus*	WASATCHIAN	
Tiffany	(No Horses) *Ketnacerus (a Condylarth)*	TIFFANIAN	
Turrejon		TORREJONIAN	PALEOCENE
		PUERCAN	
CRETACEOUS PERIOD — END OF THE AGE OF REPTILES			

Figure 3.1. Visual incrementum. From George Gaylord Simpson, *Horses* (New York: Oxford University Press, 1951). Reproduced with permission of Oxford University Press.

The examples taken from paleontological arguments, and particularly Simpson's impression of continuity, raise an interesting question: Does a longer series, that is, a series with more members, sometimes seem more persuasive than a series with fewer members, and if so why? That the longer series of fossil horses was taken as more persuasive has to do with its fulfilling the late nineteenth-century understanding that one species can be linked to another by minutely graded transitional forms. But, in general, it does seem that arguers wishing to suggest a smooth passage, an uninterrupted continuity from the beginning to the end of a series, can use not only the overlapping gradatio but also the tactic of dividing an interval into ever-smaller stages. These tend to diminish or blur the separations between the elements.

This perspective on the argumentative work of series provides, as suggested above, another possible similarity between the reasoning in rhetorical series and in mathematical series. The seventeenth century saw great advances in the mathematics of series and in their application to problems like those of calculating instantaneous rates or of finding the slope of the tangent at a particular point on a curve. Newton approached these problems by constructing an imaginary geometric series of decreasing intervals approaching a critical point. His purpose was to approximate a value that could not be directly calculated. He reasoned that the increments in this decreasing series could become so small that the term for the interval could be dropped from the calculation. The movement over the ever-smaller steps of this series, theoretically infinite in its number of terms, could then be taken as continuous (Westfall 1980, 133). Newton used the terms *fluent* for the variable quantity of an interval and *fluxion* for the rate of change or value being approximated to emphasize this continuous motion across the diminishing intervals (Kline 1972, I, 361). Though he could not defend his method rigorously and presumably resorted to "intuition" in conceiving it (Kline 1953, 232), he in a sense applied figural logic to his problem, first, by constructing a series, in this case a geometrically decreasing series, to span a gap; second, by using this series, much like the series illustrating Peacham's incrementum, to approximate a value that remains just beyond its reach: and third, by conceiving of this series as facilitating, like the gradatio or the incrementum of many elements, a continuous passage or movement over infinitely decreasing intervals. Though Newton's Cambridge reading notes show that, building on the considerable exposure to rhetoric he would have had before matriculating, he did study parts of Gerard Vossius's *Rhetorices contractae* shortly before his formulation of these methods of analysis in the 1660s (Westfall 1980, 81n, 84), and though Vossius does include the figures gradatio and incrementum in his text (Vossius 1655, 328, 359), it is highly unlikely that Newton derived his mathematical insights from his study of rhetoric. Nevertheless, these similarities do point to a continuity between rhetorical and mathematical reasoning and the possibility of moving with greater facility than is usually supposed from one system to the other.

The arguments described so far are concerned with constructing plausible series to reach an end; other series are constructed for the sake of their middles. In other words, an arguer may create a series so that some elements can be seen as intermediate, occupying "the isthmus of a middle state" in relation to the end points. Such a technique is familiar in the give-and-take of political and policy arguments, where opponents will each construct themselves into the middle of a series of possibilities to avoid appearing extreme. Brian A. Gladue and his colleagues used this technique when they conceived of and later wrote up their investigation of a biological basis for sexual orientation. They constructed three populations of volunteers, identified as "female heterosexuals, male heterosexuals, and male homosexuals" (here ordered by the authors according to overlapping attribute), injected each person with a large dose of estrogen and then measured the concentrations in blood samples, at 24-hour intervals, of luteinizing hormone and testosterone, comparing the varying levels to the baseline for each individual. They found "that men declaring a lifelong homosexual orientation had patterns of luteinizing hormone (LH) and testosterone secretion in response to estrogen that were intermediate between those of men and women declaring lifelong heterosexual orientation" (Gladue et al. 1983, 1496). This conclusion about the intermediate hormonal response of homosexuals was strengthened because the same ordering into a series resulted from two different measures. Given the actual values reported in this article, however, the term "intermediate" can literally only mean "between" and not "at midpoint." At their widest difference, for example, the levels of testosterone in female heterosexuals ($n = 12$), male heterosexuals ($n = 17$), and male homosexuals ($n = 14$) were, respectively, (in ng/ml) 0.61 compared with 4.00, and 3.31. Another arguer might have taken the same data and constructed an antithesis rather than an incrementum, but here the purpose is to bring an "in-between" state into existence, a "neuroendocrine responsiveness intermediate between that of the heterosexual men and that of the women" that could, according to the authors, serve as a biological marker for sexual orientation (1498).

Incomplete Series

In addition to forming a series to support a claim, an arguer can also present an incomplete series along with a principle of series formation, implicit or explicit, and argue a new member or members into place. A series with holes, if plausibly formed, begs for completion. Locke uses a version of this argument to support the extension of the chain of being in the following passage from Book III of *An Essay Concerning Human Understanding:*

> That there should be more species of intelligent creatures above us than there are of sensible and material below us, is probable to me from hence, that in all the visible, corporeal world, we see no chasms, or gaps. All quite down from us the descent is by easy steps, and a continued series of things, that in each remove differ very little one from the other. There are fishes that have wings, and are not strangers to the airy region: and there are some birds that are inhabitants of the water, whose blood is cold as fishes', and their flesh so like in taste that the scrupulous are allowed them on fishdays. There are animals so near of kin both to birds and beasts, that they are in the middle between both; amphibious animals link the terrestrial and aquatic together; seals live at land and at sea, and porpoises have the warm blood and entrails of a hog, not to mention what is confidently reported of mermaids or sea-men. (Locke 1995, 362)

This passage expresses gradatio reasoning without adhering to the form of the gradatio. Instead, it dwells on the points of overlap, flying fish and water-dwelling birds, animals and humans that live both on water and on land, to establish a firm principle of unbroken series construction. Locke then uses this principle and the partial series of members, "linked together" by "insensible degrees," to argue for the existence of the members missing between humans and God.

And when we consider the infinite power and wisdom of the Maker, we have reason to think that it is suitable to the magnificent harmony of the universe, and the
great design and infinite goodness of the Architect, that the species of creatures
should also, by gentle degrees, ascend upward from us towards his infinite perfection, as we see they gradually descend from us downwards. (362)

Locke confidently inferred the existence of a hierarchy completing the series, forming the "great chain of being," despite his admission in this section of the *Essay*
that it was impossible to form any distinct ideas of the spiritual creatures above
humans. Nevertheless, such confidence in the principle or source of series formation, whether the perfection of God or of nature, creates the conviction that missing members of the series exist and can be found.

A powerful example of persuasion by series formation and of the invitation to
inference and experiment offered by an incomplete series is the arrangement of
the chemical elements into an ordered overlapping series familiar to every high
school chemistry student: the periodic table. Mendeleev was only one, though arguably the most successful, of a number of chemists in the nineteenth century who
tried various schemes, various principles of series formation, to construct or elu-
cidate a natural system of the elements. The German chemist Johann Döbereiner
began in the early 1800s discovering several mini-series of three compounds or
elements grouped initially on the basis of similar properties that could then be
ordered into surprising series based on their atomic weights; bromine, for example,
turned out to have an atomic weight that is the average of the atomic weights of
chlorine and iodine (vanSpronsen 1969, 66). As more atomic weights became available, more elements were ordered into series and eventually into a single incrementum of atomic weights, which did not, however, immediately produce a clear
quantitative principle of progression despite attempts by some chemists to establish a formula for the series (Knight 1970, 10). (In fact, a perfect principle of gradation had to wait until atomic number replaced atomic weight in the twentieth
century.) In the 1860s, the British chemist John Newlands noticed, however, that
certain properties seemed to repeat after every seventh element, a principle he called
the law of octaves (vanSpronsen 1969, 107). In effect, Newlands, and others at this
time, took the linear series of the elements based on atomic weight and folded it
back on itself according to patterns of recurrence in the chemical and physical
properties of the elements, thus establishing *periodicity* or overlap within a linear
series. Newlands also assigned the elements an ordinal number (the figure eutrepismus) and left blanks where no known element could fill one of the positions created by the series. Mendeleev produced the most accurate version of this system
possible in his time with the "periodic law" as his principle of series formation. He
also presented his incomplete series visually, in tables with empty slots or question
marks (Knight 1970, 271, 273, 279), and he went further than his predecessors and
predicted the properties the missing elements would have and the compounds they
would form based on their positions in the periodic series (vanSpronsen 1969, 139).
When the elements gallium and scandium were discovered corresponding to the
unknowns he predicted, Mendeleev's version of the table became widely known
(Knight 1970, 273).

Incomplete series have been especially important in the science of astronomy. A byproduct of the Copernican solar system is a proportional ordering of the planets, an ordering possible from Copernicus' figures even without knowledge of absolute distances in the solar system (North 1995, 294). In 1772, the German astronomer J. E. Bode, claiming J. D. Titius as his source, proposed a mathematical formula to describe the underlying regularity in the disposition of the planets. Taking the distance between Earth and the sun as 1 (= 1 astronomical unit or au), the distances of the other planets can be expressed in astronomical units roughly as follows: Mercury .39; Venus .72; Mars 1.5; Jupiter 5.2; Saturn 9.5 (Smoluchowski 1983, 31). This series can also be expressed by the formula $(x + 4)/10$, where x is a number in the series 0, 3, 6, 12, 24, 48, 96, . . . , every number past the second doubling the previous number. Thus for Earth, the third planet out, one plugs the third number in this series, 6, into the equation to yield the standard, Earth's orbit at one astronomical unit: $(6 + 4)/10 = 1$; for Mars, $(12 + 4)/10 = 1.6$. Jupiter's orbit corresponds to the sixth number in the series $[(48 + 4)/10 = 5.2]$. Astronomers were quick to notice that no planet corresponded to the orbit predicted by the fifth number in this series. Was there a planet missing between Mars and Jupiter?

In March of 1781, William Herschel, master of the largest telescopes of his day, discovered the seventh planet, Uranus. When the dimensions of Uranus's orbit became known, they conformed to the Titius-Bode rule for the seventh number: $(96 + 4)/10 = 20$ (closer to 19.6), strengthening the suspicion of a missing body and leading to the formation of a club of astronomers, "the Lilienthal detectives," dedicated to finding it (North 1995, 425). The first observer to fill this void was Giuseppe Piazzi, who, in 1801, discovered an object in an orbit calculated by Gauss to fill the missing slot. But this new object proved to be extraordinarily small, and then another was found in 1802 and another in 1804 and in 1807, all with orbits between Mars and Jupiter. In 1846, the Titius-Bode law was dealt a blow with the discovery of Neptune whose orbit did not conform to the rule's prediction. (Pluto however, though not a planet like the others, does have a conforming orbit.) Yet some theories explaining the debris in the "asteroid belt" still assume that either because of a collision in the past or because of gravitational effects from the proximity of the giant Jupiter (Smoluchowski 1983, 31), there should be a planet in that slot to perfect the Titius-Bode series. Thus theorists can choose to interpret the data in the light of a principle of series formation, or allow the data eventually to undermine the principle.

A more recent case in astronomy also indicates the power of the incrementum's figural logic to direct inquiry. Based on the distribution of cataloged stars and theories of stellar evolution, astronomers had long predicted the existence of "brown dwarfs," not-quite stars whose mass is too small to generate the temperatures needed to ignite sustained nuclear fusion in their cores (Kulkarni 1997, 1350). Such brown dwarfs would occupy an extreme "end" of the standard Hertzsprung-Russell chart, inevitably presented as a visual incrementum in astronomical texts, a linear distribution of stars plotted according to magnitude and temperature, with white dwarfs, giants, and supergiants as outliers. In 1995, astronomers using the most powerful optical telescope on Earth, the 400-inch telescope at the Keck Observatory in Hawaii, confirmed the sighting of a "young" brown dwarf in the Pleiades, identified both visually and by the lithium signature of its spectrograph, an indirect measure of its temperature. That same year saw the report of a "cool" brown dwarf, Gliese 229B, companion to a normal star (Kulkarni 1997, 1353).

Placing brown dwarfs at the bottom or end of the main sequence of stars creates certain difficulties. Positions at the ends of series are more difficult to predict than internal positions. Why should a series continue beyond its known extremes? It can take more compelling arguments to tack an item onto the end of a series than to fill a missing slot in an established series. The Pleiades brown dwarf was, however, given a middle and not an end position in two differently constructed series. First, on the basis of its supposed age and luminosity, it was placed at "the boundary between low-mass objects of the brown dwarf class and the lowest-mass true stars." Second, on the basis of its size as one eighth that of the sun but eighty times that of Jupiter, it was placed in a more all-encompassing series by one of its discoverers, Dr. Geoffrey W. Marcy, who claimed that the Pleiades brown dwarf "'begins to fill the gap' between the least massive stars and the most massive planets" (Wilford 1995, B7). The same set phrase of incrementum completion appears in a 1997 *Science* article assessing the discovery of the two brown dwarfs in 1995.

> Ordering objects by mass we see that brown dwarfs lie between stars and planets. Young brown dwarfs [like the Pleiades discovery] have spectra similar to cool stars and the old brown dwarf Gliese 229B has a spectrum which is similar to that of Jupiter. Brown dwarfs fill the "gap" between stars and planets. (Kulnari 1997, 1354)

Here the two brown dwarfs discovered in 1995 are also positioned in relation to each other, one closer to the stars in the series above and one closer to the planets in the series below. But together as brown dwarfs they are two links in a now more perfect chain of celestial objects.

Double Hierarchy Arguments

Still another use of ordered series structures what *The New Rhetoric* terms double hierarchy arguments (Perelman and Olbrechts-Tyteca 1969, 337–345). Arguers use the double hierarchy strategy when they take an established series or hierarchy, one accepted by or at least familiar to an audience, and form a second series on the model of the first, in the process trying to transfer implications of order or value from the first to the second. Medieval political theorists used a double hierarchy argument when they justified the existing political system according to a hierarchy of body parts, the King serving as head of the body politic. In scientific arguments, the purpose of forming a second series from a first is presumably less that of ordering according to value than simply of ordering, like forming one strand of DNA from another. Medieval alchemists ordered the seven known metals by the hierarchy of the seven heavenly bodies, equating gold with the sun, silver with the moon, and so on. Kepler tried to order the orbits of the six known planets according to the five regular polyhedra.

The double hierarchy arguments of alchemy and astrology are regarded as epistemological curiosities, but the result of what was originally a double hierarchy argument employed by the eighteenth-century astronomer William Herschel has been more durable.[8] In the late eighteenth and early nineteenth centuries, Herschel's uniquely powerful telescopes allowed him to catalog hundreds of objects previously unobserved. He turned his attention to newly discovered star clusters, for he was able to see that the clouds of luminosity surrounding some spots of concentrated brightness were in fact resolvable into individuals stars. He realized he was looking at vastly distant collections of stars organized by gravity into globular form, and by 1789 he recommended using his catalog of more than two thousand of these nebulae or sidereal systems to reach conclusions about their development in the same way a botanist uses the collection in a herbarium: "Why should we be less inquisitive than the natural philosopher, who sometimes, even from an inconsiderable number of specimens of a plant, or an animal, is enabled to present us with a history of its rise, progress and decay?" (Herschel 1789, 214). Herschel's conceptual breakthrough was to realize that he could interpret diachronically the variety of objects he viewed in the heavens synchronically:

> This method of viewing the heavens seems to throw them into a new kind of light. They now are seen to resemble a luxuriant garden, which contains the greatest variety of productions, in different flourishing beds; and one advantage we may at least reap from it is, that we can, as it were, extend the range of our experience to immense duration. For, to continue the simile I have borrowed from the vegetable kingdom, is it not almost the same thing, whether we live successively to witness the germination, blooming, foliage, fecundity, fading, withering and corruption of a plant, or whether a vast number of specimens, selected from every stage through which the plant passes in the course of its existence, be brought at once to our view? (1789, 226)

By analogy to the stages in the life of a plant, Herschel believed he could read the stages in the formation of star systems.

Writing two years later, Herschel abandoned his assumption that all nebulae were resolvable into clusters of stars, even the ones his telescopes could not resolve. That assumption had also been based on series reasoning: "by imperceptible degrees I have been led on from the most evident congeries of stars to other groups in which the lucid points were smaller, but still very plainly to be seen; and from them to such wherein they could but barely be suspected, till I arrived at last to spots in which no trace of a star was to be discerned. But then the gradations to these latter were by such well-connected steps as left no room for doubt that all these phaenomena were equally occasioned by stars, variously dispersed in the immense expanse of the universe" (Herschel 1791, 72; see also p. 74, "A well connected series of objects, such as we have mentioned above, has led us to infer, that all nebulae consist of stars.") Herschel admits that his stepwise reasoning has been in error, and that he has been set straight by the discovery of a new object: a single star surrounded by an extensive luminous atmosphere, a "shining fluid" (1791, 71; 83).[9] Herschel realizes that he is looking not at a single series but at two different orders of objects, star clusters versus single stars surrounded by a luminous halo, like the naturalist who casts an eye "from the perfect animal to the perfect vegetable" (1791, 73).

Twenty years later, drawing on his extensive published catalogs of heavenly
objects, Herschel constructed a detailed case for the formation of stars by condensation from nebulous matter, a case that he had only suggested in the 1791 paper.
The method in Herschel's lengthy report to the Royal Society in 1811 is to arrange
the nebular objects discovered in his sweeps "in a certain successive regular order"
(Herschel 1811, 269); it is a method very self-consciously based on an incrementum
that is analogically developmental:

> It will be necessary to explain the spirit of the method of arranging the observed
> astronomical objects under consideration in such a manner, that one shall assist us
> to understand the nature and construction of the other. This end I propose to under-
> take by assorting them into as many classes as will be required to produce the most
> gradual affinity between the individuals contained in any one class with those con-
> tained in that which precedes and that which follows it: and it will certainly contri-
> bute to the perfection of this method, if this connection between various classes can
> be made to appear so clearly as not to admit of doubt. This consideration will be a
> sufficient apology for the great number of assortments into which I have thrown
> the objects under consideration; and it will be found that those contained in one
> article, are so closely allied to those in the next, that there is perhaps not so much
> difference between them, if I may use the comparison, as there would be in an an-
> nual description of the human figure, were it given from the birth of a child till he
> comes to be a man in his prime. (270–271)

Herschel's subsequent argument contains numbered sections that generally (though
with digressions) follow the path from "extensive diffused nebulosity" to "nebulae
that draw progressively towards a period of final condensation" and so on to
formed stars. In between, Herschel has not ordered single objects; he has created
classes of objects and ordered these. True to his advertisement, these classes are
constructed in a way to convince readers that they blend into each other, the intent being especially obvious in the consecutive elements in the middle of his
series: "nebulae that are gradually a little brighter in the middle" followed by
"nebulae which are gradually brighter in the middle" followed by "nebulae which
are gradually much brighter in the middle" (300–306). Here are three classes that
could just as easily have been one, though as three they strengthen Herschel's
conclusion:

> The total dissimilitude between the appearance of a diffusion of the nebulous mat-
> ter and of a star, is so striking, that an idea of the conversion of the one into the
> other can hardly occur to any one who has not before him the result of the critical
> examination of the nebulous system which has been displayed in this paper. The
> end I have had in view, by arranging my observations in the order in which they
> have been placed, has been to shew, that the above mentioned extremes may be
> connected by such nearly allied intermediate steps, as will make it highly probable
> that every succeeding state of the nebulous matter is the result of the action of gravi-
> tation upon it while in a foregoing one, and by such steps the successive condensa-
> tion of it has been brought up to the planetary condition. From this the transit to
> the stellar form, it has been shown, requires but a very small additional compres-
> sion of the nebulous matter. . . . (330–331)

Herschel's final 1811 argument is distanced from the analogical hierarchy that jump-started his thinking more than 20 years earlier. Double hierarchy arguments are not, however, as the examples from Kepler and the early Herschel might suggest, an abandoned strategy in scientific argument, though flamboyant analogies like theirs, used for heuristic rather than explanatory purposes, are uncommon. Nevertheless, subtle double hierarchies, or perhaps they would be better called "double homologies," survive. Contemporary archaeologists who come upon a new site will date its levels according to a prevailing hierarchy of developmentally and chronologically ordered tool assemblages. If that accepted hierarchy is wrong, then their dating of the new site will be wrong. Ethologists, too, who theorize about order in animal groups, often exploit double hierarchy arguments when they order members of animal communities based on arrangements among human groups.

Of all the argumentative uses of series cited so far, the double hierarchy strategy could also be described as metaphorical; the case of the alchemists' correspondences between metals and heavenly bodies has, in fact, been so described (Gentner and Jeziorski 1993, 469). But the goal of the double hierarchy strategy is not necessarily the characterization of the individual members of a series or the open-ended exploration of one domain by the conceptual richness of another; the goal, at least initially, is to make a second ordering possible and plausible. The arguer is more concerned with defending the construction of a series, subsequently enabling premises about one thing coming before or after another. Orders of the metals, for example, even if established astrologically, could still be used to argue for one metal being more or less reactive than another based on their relative places in the series.

The Gradatio as Sorites

Many of the argument strategies described so far could be epitomized by either an incrementum or a gradatio. But in the next tactic, the gradatio is required because of the necessary connection between this figure and the *sorites*, a connection noticed in both Classical and Renaissance handbooks. The distinctive feature of the gradatio, its overlapping members, is also the distinctive feature of the logical figure sorites, the argumentative tactic of interlocking enthymemes to express the results of several syllogisms in one figure, reaching a final conclusion by stages. In 1599, John Hoskins identified a type of gradatio as a sorites or "climbing argument," made for joining "the first and the last with an *ergo*" (Hoskins 1935, 12).

As a general form, the sorites, expressed in a gradatio, can be used in constructing causal chains or definitions. How it epitomizes causal reasoning is obvious even in the brief example cited above from the *Rhetorica ad Herennium*. The claim that Africanus's industry produced rivals is made plausible by connecting industry to excellence and then excellence to glory and then glory to rivals. What might at first appear an improbable causal claim when the beginning and end are immediately juxtaposed—that good character produces bad consequences—is made probable when replaced by smaller and therefore more plausible causal links, thus in Hoskins' words, connecting the first and the last with an "ergo." Similarly, the gradatio used in chapter 1 (p. 6) in the passage summarizing Genette, shows the plausible steps by which one can start out with all of rhetoric and wind up with only metaphor. This conceptual work of linkage is expressed in the essential syntactic feature of the gradatio, its repetition or overlapping of terms, fusing the steps within the series and creating a kind of verbal touching of contiguous pairs of causes and effects.[10] Such causal chains that can be expressed in a gradatio (a causes/leads to b, b to c, c to d, and so on) are common in scientific cases, from the life cycle of trypanosomes through various hosts to the explanation of how El Ninō, a warmer than usual stretch of the Pacific, causes balmy winters in the northeastern United States.

The figure itself epitomizing such a causal chain was used in a *New York Times* piece to defend the controversial attempt in the winter of 1994–1995 to reintroduce wolves into Yellowstone National Park. The wildlife biologist interviewed by the *Times* science writer about the project provided a "hypothetical example" of how the wolves would initiate changes in the ecosystem, beginning with an increase in soil fertility from the decomposition of the carcasses of its prey. The resulting causal argument is expressed twice in the piece, once buried in the text in a summary that does not have the verbal signature of the gradatio and once as part of the illustration on the front page of the science section, where it does. Here again the tendency in scientific argument to express the figures visually produces a curious hybrid of text and illustration. Each element in this gradatio is a separate sentence, the sentences are numbered, they are arranged linearly across the page, and each is accompanied by a drawing that presumably expresses its point (see Figure 3.2). The text dispersed in this visual is a splendid example of a gradatio that could have appeared in a sixteenth-century rhetoric text:

> 1. Carcasses of large prey, like elk, slaughtered by wolves will add nutrients and humus to the *soil*. 2. The more fertilized *soil* will support lush vegetation, probably attracting snowshoe *hares*. 3. The presence of *hares* will likely prove a lure for *foxes* and other predators. 4. The *foxes* will also prey on rodents like *mice* in the area. 5. A displaced *mouse predator*, like a weasel, is likely to fall prey to an owl. (Stevens 1995, C1; italics added to emphasize overlapping terms; an interesting comparison can be made with the "lax" version of the same argument expressed in the text of the article.)[11]

Concentration on the form of this argument exposes some features that are perhaps discrepancies in the reasoning. The second step, for example, condenses the series, expressing two causal links in one, that the fertilized soil leads to lush vegetation and that this lush vegetation (to stretch out this element to gradatio form) attracts hares. The overlap between steps four and five, from mice to mouse predator, is loose. Furthermore, the kind of causal connection inferable between the different steps is not consistent: The claim that vegetation attracts hares and that hares attract foxes may depend on one kind of causal warrant; that foxes displace other predators requires a different warrant, and that a displaced predator is likely (more likely?) to fall prey to another predator needs yet a third. Nevertheless, the experts at scientific accommodation who produced this hybrid of text and illustration realized that a gradatio would most persuasively express the causal reasoning for the large, mixed audience of the *New York Times*.

A Predator's Impact: Some Possibilities

1. Carcasses of large prey, like elk, slaughtered by wolves will add nutrients and humus to the soil.

2. The more fertilized soil will support lush vegetation, probably attracting snowshoe hares.

3. The presence of hares will likely prove a lure for foxes and other predators.

4. The foxes will also prey on rodents like mice in the area.

5. A displaced mouse predator, like a weasel, is likely to fall prey to an owl.

Most scavengers, like ravens, will fare well, but many coyotes will probably be killed by wolves, and other predators, like mountain lions, may be displaced.

Source: Dr. L. David Mech/National Biological Service

Figure 3.2. Visual and verbal gradatio. From William K. Stevens, "Wolf's Howl Heralds Change for Old Haunts," *New York Times* (January 31, 1995). Reproduced with permission of Dr. L. David Mech and Glen Wolf.

Using essentially the same pattern, the physicist Richard Feynman also created a sorites in the form of a gradatio. His purpose, however, was not to link causes and effects; it was rather to employ another kind of argument epitomized by the gradatio, one that uses the logic of nesting sets typical of syllogistic reasoning. This gradatio at the service of what is essentially a definition argument pins down each subsequent element in a series by progressive inclusions. Its strategy is *emboîtement*, like nesting Russian dolls. Presumably the reasonable steps across the series prevent once again the implausibility caused by jumping from the first to the last term immediately. In the Messenger Lectures for 1964, aimed at a nonspecialist audience and reprinted as *The Character of Physical Law*, Feynman sought to explain how the physical laws he was describing do "not necessarily give you an understanding of things of significance in the world in any direct way" (Feynman 1965, 124) but were necessarily connected in a hierarchy to other levels of explanation. He believed that the fundamental laws of physics, describing the interactions of subatomic particles, were at one end of a hierarchy of possible explanations. At higher levels were concepts like "heat" and "surface tension" and above these concepts like "storm" and "star" or a physically complex phenomenon like "nerve impulse." Next came constructs like "man," "history," or "political expediency" and finally ideas like "evil, and beauty, and hope. . . . " (125). Feynman finally asks, in what he calls a religious metaphor, "Which end is nearer to God . . . Beauty and hope, or the fundamental laws?" The answer, however, is epitomized not with a metaphor but with a gradatio.

> I think that the right way, of course, is to say that what we have to look at is the whole structural interconnection of the thing; and that all the sciences, and not just the sciences but all the efforts of intellectual kinds, are an endeavour to see the connections of the hierarchies, to connect beauty to history, to connect history to man's psychology, man's psychology to the working of the brain, the brain to the neural impulse, the neural impulse to the chemistry, and so forth, up and down, both ways. And today we cannot, and it is no use making believe that we can, draw carefully a line all the way from one end of this thing to the other, because we have only just begun to see that there is this relative hierarchy.
>
> And I do not think either end is nearer to God. (Feynman 1965, 125)

The purpose of Feynman's gradatio is to remove the conceptual separation between the beginning and end of the series by means of verbally overlapping intermediates, making it possible, as Hoskins put it, to connect the first and the last with an *ergo*.[12] The gradatio works as well for this conceptual nesting as it does for the causal chain.

Almost two centuries earlier, but with precisely the same device, the *Naturphilosoph* Johann Gottfried Herder went along with the "pressure" in the gradatio toward its final term in a way that is more characteristic of the amplificatory use of the figure. In his monumental *Ideen zur Philosophie der Geschichte der Menschheit* (1784–1791), Herder, like Locke, saw all of creation progressively linked and tending toward the perfection finally achieved in humanity. Herder, in other words, was sure which end of his series was nearer to God when he put the chain of being at the service of the argument from design.

Vom Stein zum Krystall, vom Krystall zu den Metallen, von diesen zur Pflanzen-
schöpfung, von den Pflanzen zum Tier von diesen zum Menschen sahen wir die *Form
der Organisation steigen,* mit ihr auch die Kräfte und Triebe des Geschöpfs vielartiger
werden und sich endlich alle, in der Gestalt des Menschen, sofern diese sie fassen
konnte, vereinen (Herder 1989, VI, 166).[13]

From stone to crystal, from crystal to the metals, from these to the plant world, from
the plants to the animals and from these to humans we saw the Form of Organization climb, and with it the powers and forces of these creations become manifold
and finally all, in the form of humanity, so far as these could be pulled together,
unite.

Herder's gradatio, which opens book five as a summary of his first four books detailing and celebrating the wonders of the rising forms, is neither precisely causal nor
definitional. Instead, it exploits the useful ambiguity of the verbal form to suggest
both. The overlapping of terms, creating parallel members in the series, suggests that
they share a common essence and hence the argument epitomized is definitional,
while the direction of the figure, its rising to a final item, suggests that this series leads
inevitably to its final term and hence is causal. This blended possibility is precisely
what Herder had in mind: "Durch diese Reihen von Wesen bemerkten wir, so weit
es die einzelne Bestimmung des Geschöpfs zuließ, eine herrschende Ähnlichkeit der
Hauptform, die auf eine unzählbare Weise abwechselnd, sich immer mehr der Men-
schengestalt nahte" [Throughout this series of beings we observe, as far as the single
destination of these creatures is readable, a prevailing similarity of the chief form,
which changing in countless ways, approaches more and more the form of human-
ity] (VI, 166).

Merging Categories

The final argumentative use of incrementum and gradatio discussed in this chapter requires an arguer to present graded series in one or two separate domains. These
separately formed series, or one series and one undivided domain, are then, in effect, lined up one above the other as though in a single vertical scale, making possible a conceptual passage from one domain to the other. In *The New Rhetoric,*
Perelman and Olbrechts-Tyteca illustrate this strategy when they point out that
the difference between "the certain" and "the uncertain" can be bridged by claiming that there are degrees of uncertainty; a less uncertain "uncertainty" will seem
closer to a certainty. "When we are confronted with two realms of a different order,"
they conclude, "the establishment of degrees within one of them is often for the
purpose of diminishing the break between them" (Perelman and Olbrechts-Tyteca
1969, 347). In other words, when the arguer's purpose is to reduce the separation
between groups, it is useful to replace a difference in kind by a difference in degree. The conceptual chasm between the two classes bird and reptile, for example,
is diminished by a continuum based on ordering members in either or both sets,
which then allows consecutive gradation across the two groups, the most reptile-
like of birds, from an evolutionary standpoint, at the bottom of one group and the
most bird-like of reptiles at the "top" of the other. There is even a verbal device

that highlights the precise suture between the previously separated categories: When Huxley described a group of extinct reptiles, the aptly named *Ornithoscelida,* as having pelvis and hind limbs more like birds, he emphasized their position spanning the gap between the two classes by referring to them as "these Bird-reptiles, or Reptile-birds" (Rudwick 1985, 353).

Researchers in learning disabilities at Yale University Medical School used this same category-dissolving strategy to contradict the prevailing wisdom about dyslexia as "a specific, discrete entity," "a biologically coherent disorder that is distinct from other, less specific reading problems" (Shaywitz et al. 1992, 145). The existence of dyslexia as a unique syndrome was based on research that presumably showed a bimodal distribution in reading ability, a persistent "hump" in the bottom of a normal distribution, suggesting the existence of a unique and separate category of readers. The Yale researchers analyzed data from a longitudinal study of several hundred grade school children, including IQ scores and achievement results, and found, contrary to the prevailing view, that "dyslexia occurs along a continuum that blends imperceptibly with normal reading ability" so that "no distinct cutoff point exists to distinguish children with dyslexia clearly from children with normal reading ability" (148). In other words, they undid sharp category differences by finding gradations that allowed them to connect one category with another. To strengthen this category elision, they pointed out that the same individuals were not always labeled "dyslexic" from grade to grade; for example, of the 25 children in the sample ($n = 414$) categorized as dyslexic in first grade and the 31 in third grade, only 7 were categorized as dyslexic in both grades. This observation supports their case because it is consistent with the intuitive notion that, while it should be difficult or even impossible to jump from one mutually exclusive category to another, it is certainly possible to move from one location to another along a continuum (147). In the *New England Journal of Medicine,* where their study was published, the Yale researchers epitomized their reasoning visually in scatterplots of combined variables rather than in a tedious verbal gradatio: a is just a little better reader than b; b is just a little better than readers c and d" (a multiplying of terms to represent the clumping in a normal distribution) and so on. Visually, the distribution of data points in the scatterplots seems graded and continuous, suggesting no unbreachable gaps.

Perhaps the most famous use of this final tactic employing "gradatio reasoning" to break down category differences is Darwin's argumentative strategy in chapter 2 of the *On the Origin of Species,* a chapter devoted in part to undoing the distinction between varieties and species and thus to undermining the stability of species. Darwin's strategy first required his pointing out the many slight differences that can exist among individuals belonging to a single variety or species, even in those parts important from a "physiological or classificatory point of view" (Darwin 1979, 102). The extent of this gradation within groups will eventually make it possible for him to follow the gradations across groups. The malleability of the species classification was also brought home to him in the inconsistent practices of systematists, a kind of indirect evidence of the absence of clear distinctions in nature. "Compare," he invites his reader, "the several floras of Great Britain, of France or of the United States, drawn up by different botanists, and see what a surprising number of forms have been ranked by one botanist as good species, and by another as mere varieties" (104). Eventually Darwin epitomized his argument in a magnificent gradatio whose syntactic overlaps represent the eliding of category differences:

> Certainly no clear line of demarcation has as yet been drawn between species and *sub-species*—that is, the forms which in the opinion of some naturalists come very near to, but do not quite arrive at the rank of species; or, again, between *sub-species* and well-marked *varieties*, or between lesser *varieties* and individual *differences*. These *differences* blend into each other in [6th ed./by] an *insensible series*; and a *series* impresses the mind with the idea of an actual passage.[14] (Darwin 1979, 107; 1958, 66 italics added; the passage continues by running this series in reverse.)

Species are graded into subspecies, subspecies into varieties, varieties into individual differences, and these in turn "blend" insensibly. The result is a smooth continuum rather than rigidly partitioned categories.

Characteristically, Darwin demonstrates a vivid awareness of the conceptual work that his language performs, as the syntax itself creates the "actual passage" he is arguing for by overlapping terms from one phrase to another. On the other side of this figure in chapter 2, Darwin declares the identity of the highest member of the variety category and the lowest member of the species category: "Hence I believe a well-marked variety may be justly called an incipient species" (Darwin 1979, 107). From this point on in the text, the terms "species" and "variety" appear frequently in constructions which stress their interchangeability (e.g., "species of all kinds are only well-marked and permanent varieties," 174; see also 197, 209, 289, 305, 390, 391, 397, 404, 406, 443, 446, 447, 452, 455).

Series Reasoning in Darwin's *The Origin of Species*

Analyses of metaphors in science have been used not only to characterize single lines of argument but also to discover "systems of metaphor" that may structure or characterize an entire text (Ortony 1993, 4). Given the importance of the gradatio in Darwin's second chapter, it is interesting to put the series-forming figures to the same test throughout Darwin's *Origin*, to in a sense pull at this one thread in the fabric of the text. Although it would be absurd to reduce so extended and complex a set of interrelated arguments as the *Origin* presents to a single dominant type, series reasoning of the kind figured by the incrementum and the gradatio is prevalent at many points and on many levels in the *Origin*. Premises based on gradation and intermediaries are pivotal in subordinate lines of reasoning that directly support Darwin's central claims, and the absence of gradation or intermediaries is a frequent challenge that Darwin tries to overcome.

Darwin's argumentative genius is often explained by his skillful use of metaphor and analogy, and these are frequently pointed out in the "origin of the *Origin*" studies, which attempt to explain the genesis or trace the developing pattern and detail of his thinking, especially the metaphorical construction of natural selection itself (Campbell 1986, 363). Domestic selection, established in the opening chapter, serves as the formative analogy for natural selection, formally introduced in chapter 4 (though mentioned in chapter 1). Just as humans have selectively chosen animals and plants with the most desirable traits for breeding, so has nature favored the hardiest individuals for survival; anyone who wants to see how nature can work to draw out species from species over time, need only observe how breeders have produced new varieties over decades. Though the analogy between a presumably more familiar circumstance and an unfamiliar one (or in the case of natural selection, a previously nonexistent one) certainly has persuasive force, analogy is not the only means Darwin uses to argue for natural selection. Darwin also tries to arrive at natural selection, at least in the version of his reasoning presented in the *Origin*, not only by analogical leap but also by a series of intermediaries. Though in an earlier stage of his thinking Darwin presumably configured natural and domestic breeding as opposites (Campbell 1990, 18), in the *Origin* he constructs a continuum between domestic and natural selection. At one extreme is the deliberate action of the professional breeder, a group Darwin much admired and often consulted. The breeder's power of selection—conscious, directed, deliberate and amplified by Darwin into an almost magical ability to discern what is invisible to the untrained eye—while serving as one-half of the analogy with natural selection, also serves as the beginning of a series. Darwin next posits a less-directed and less-deliberate form of selection:

> At the present time, eminent breeders try by methodical selection, with a distinct object in view, to make a new strain or sub-breed, superior to anything existing in the country. But, for our purpose, a kind of Selection, which may be called Unconscious, and which results from every one trying to possess and breed from the best individual animals, is more important. Thus, a man who intends keeping pointers naturally tries to get as good dogs as he can, and afterwards breeds from his own best dogs, but he has no wish or expectation of permanently altering the breed. Nevertheless I cannot doubt [6th ed./ we may infer] that this process, continued during centuries, would improve and modify any breed. (Darwin 1979, 93; 1958, 50)

Somewhat less directed than this intent to breed the best animals is the practice that becomes the next step in the series when Darwin imagines "savages" who, even if they would not think of breeding from their best animals, "yet any one animal particularly useful to them, for any special purpose, would be carefully preserved during famines and other accidents . . . and such choice animals would thus generally leave more offspring than the inferior ones; so that in this case there would be a kind of unconscious selection going on" (94). From the breeder's determination to create a certain trait, to the average person's intent to breed the best, to the so-called savage's tendency to preserve the most useful animals, Darwin has created a series of diminishing human agency and intention whose next intelligible step removes the human agent altogether and allows Nature to select.

Series reasoning also comes to Darwin's aide when he identifies the existence of complex organs, like the mammalian eye, and of complex instincts, like the hive-making abilities of the honey bee, as major stumbling blocks to belief in descent with modification under the pressure of natural selection. His answer to both of these objections is to fill in a series in order to reach these seemingly unattainable ends, or at least to try. In the case of the eye, he believes that finding "numerous gradations from a perfect and complex eye to one very imperfect and simple" (Darwin 1979, 217) could bridge the conceptual gap, the problem in imagining how so perfect and so complex an organ could be accomplished in viable stages. This bridging is difficult to achieve, however, because "lineal ancestors" of existing species are not available for observation. The next best approximation is to look at species from the same group, "to see what gradations are possible" (218).The vertebrates are no help, but in the *Articulata*, Darwin believes he can "commence a series" finding "numerous gradations of structure" and "much graduated diversity in the eyes of living crustaceans." He concludes after some brief examples that are stand-ins for a many-membered series by declaring the two ends connected: "I can see no very great difficulty [6th ed./the difficulty ceases to be very great] . . . in believing that natural selection has [6th ed./may have] converted the simple apparatus of an optic nerve merely coated with pigment and invested by transparent membrane, into an optical instrument as perfect as is possessed by any member of the great Articulate class" (1970, 218; 1958, 170).

Darwin has better success constructing a series to build a conceptual bridge to the hexagonal cells of the honeybee. "Let us," he invites, "look to the great principle of gradation, and see whether Nature does not reveal to us her method of work." "At one end of a short series," Darwin places the humble [bumble] bees who use old cocoons and sometimes roughly rounded cells of wax to store honey; "at the other end of the series" he places the hive bee, amplifying its engineering accomplishments, its ability to build each cell as a "hexagonal prism, with the basal edges of its six sides bevelled so as to join on to a pyramid, formed of three rhombs" (Darwin 1979, 248). "In the series between the extreme perfection of the cells of the hive bee and the simplicity of those of the humble-bee," Darwin places the Mexican *melipona domestica*, which builds incomplete and irregularly grouped spherical cells. When *melipona*'s cells occasionally touch, the bees build flat walls between them; when three touch, the result is "a gross imitation of the three-sided pyramidal basis of the cell of the hive bee" (249). Darwin finds in this practice by *melipona* the key to an explanation for the hive bee's building techniques, for the hive bee's comb can be seen as the result of two actions that are just a plausible next step away from the construction instincts of *melipona*. The hive bee instinctively constructs wax spheres of equal size and equal distance in symmetrical double layers. The result, almost accidentally, is the admirably complex structure of the familiar wax comb (249).

An even more telling example of Darwin's fixation on gradation through intermediaries is his explanation of the existence of neuter castes in ant colonies. These non-reproducing forms offered another significant obstacle to his belief in descent with modification, for, after all, how could natural selection operate on organic forms that did not reproduce? This famous case requires Darwin to posit selection applied to the group as well as to the individual. With that proviso, it proved easy to imagine selection for parents that produced neuters profitable to the entire colony. A further difficulty, however, came from the fact that neuter castes often differ from each other dramatically, the same species having both small, blind workers and enormous soldiers with prodigious jaws, as wide apart in their instincts as in their morphology. But these antitheses, these extremes in possibilities are, as always, rationalized away when they can be placed on the ends of a series and connected by intermediates. Darwin unearthed and sorted the ants in colonies in his garden and found that "the extreme forms can sometimes be perfectly linked [6th ed./ can be linked] together by individuals taken out of the same nest" (Darwin 1979, 260; 1958, 254). He dissected specimens of these workers and found that their eyes differed as well as their size, allowing him to use Aristotle's strategy of linking least with least and most with most, the smallest forms having rudimentary eyes and the largest functional eyes. He believed that "the workers of intermediate size have their ocelli in an exactly intermediate condition" (260). Even better evidence came from Africa in specimens taken from a single nest of the formidable driver ant, a species with soldiers of enormous proportions and huge jaws compared to the feeble workers from the same colony. In sorting individuals from a driver colony, Darwin also found that, "though the workers can be grouped into castes of different sizes, yet they graduate insensibly into each other, as does the widely-different structure of their jaws" (1979, 261). Darwin reasoned that the more useful extreme forms of neuters would be produced in greater and greater numbers until the intermediate forms all but disappeared. Thus the evidence for an incrementum of neuter ants, based on gradations in size and complexity in jaw structure, saves his theory again.

Still another line of reasoning that depends on series construction is Darwin's argument "from the practice of systematists." Darwin was aware of the inconsistency in the principles of grouping by classifiers who used rudimentary, embryological or any other handy traits as they groped for what, in Darwin's view, was really an underlying principle of genealogical descent. Common features, Darwin argued, were not always the underlying rationale for classifications as had sometimes been argued (on analogy with genus/species tactics of definition); instead systematists used "chains of affinities" (Darwin 1979, 403). As Darwin knew from his work on barnacles, a group that eluded correct classification until its free-swimming stage was discovered, "There are crustaceans at the opposite ends of the series, which have hardly a character in common; yet the species at both ends, from being plainly allied to others, and these to others, and so onwards, can be recognized as unequivocally belonging to this, and to no other class of the Articulata" (403). This observation on the Articulata becomes expressed as an axiom of classification: "Let two forms have not a single character in common, yet if these extreme forms are connected together by a chain of intermediate groups, we may at once infer their community of descent" (409).

In addition to these self-contained arguments and refutations based on series reasoning that occur throughout the text, the overall argument of the *Origin* requires Darwin to establish the presence or explain the absence of series across three great axes of variability: form, time, and space. Darwin believed the most formidable objection to his theory was the absence of the morphologically intermediate forms that were required to demonstrate in the most tangible way how one form could give rise successively to another. Darwin had no trouble explaining why such transitional forms were not present among living species: "The main cause . . . of innumerable intermediate links not now occurring everywhere throughout nature depends on the very process of natural selection, through which new varieties continually take the places of and exterminate [6th ed./supplant] their parent-forms"

(Darwin 1979, 291; 1958, 287). The very success of this defense, however, emphasized the need for fossil evidence of these innumerable intermediates that had been
displaced by their offspring. As Darwin expresses this difficulty so forcefully himself, "Why then is not every geological formation and every stratum full of such
intermediate links? Geology assuredly does not reveal any such finely graduated
organic chain; and this, perhaps, is the most obvious and gravest [6th ed./serious]
objection which can be urged against my [6th ed./the] theory" (1979, 292; 1958,
287). After explaining that the intermediates sought are not transitional between
existing species, but between an existing species and an unknown progenitor,
Darwin must nevertheless spend an entire chapter (chapter 9 in the first edition)
arguing for the imperfection of the fossil record in ingenious ways to explain why
"all the fine intermediate gradations," the "perfect gradation between two forms,"
the "close intermediate gradations," the "intermediate varieties," the "transitional
gradations," "an infinite number of those fine transitional forms," "innumerable
transitional links" (all phrases appearing 1979, pp. 303–309) are missing.

   As a counterargument to the absence of intermediate forms in the geological
record (an absence soon addressed by the fossil horse sequence), Darwin maintains in the following chapter that such evidence as was available from the fossil
record did support his views, and again, his evidence amounts to claims for graded
and overlapping series. Taking a broad view, Darwin points out that "the fauna of
each geological period undoubtedly is intermediate in character, between the preceding and succeeding faunas" (Darwin 1979, 334) and "fossils from two consecutive formations are far more closely related to each other, than are the fossils from
two remote formations" (335). Taking a more precise view when possible, Darwin
maintains that fossil forms can sometimes be used to show transitions between
existing groups, as the connection between living pachyderms and ruminants was
demonstrated by Owen who, in Darwin's words, "dissolves by fine [6th ed./"fine"
deleted] gradations the apparently wide difference [6th ed./interval] between the
pig and the camel" (1979, 331; 1958, 325).

   Darwin is, however, aware of a certain instability in series reasoning like Owen's,
especially when an arguer tries to establish one kind of series on the basis of another. Paleontologists can order specimens by morphology or by time (that is, by
the apparent age of the formation they are found in), but when mastodons and
elephants were arranged according to these two principles, two different series were
obtained: "The species extreme in character are not the oldest, or the most recent;
nor are those which are intermediate in character, intermediate in age" (Darwin
1979, 335). Darwin adds his own example from his much loved pigeons whose
arrangement according to "serial affinity" would not match the order of their appearance and disappearance in time. Darwin explains these competing gradations
by noting that species persist for different lengths of time; the parent form of pigeons, the rock pigeon, was still alive in the wild in Darwin's time, though many
forms between this parent and other living species were extinct. A series based only
on living forms might place the oldest member in the middle between two forms
that had varied in opposite directions from this parent form in the more recent
past; a series based on order of emergence might not produce a morphological
continuun. The two competing series do not, then, necessarily cancel each other

out, but one series may not be an unproblematic reflection of the other. Darwin's apologist, T. H. Huxley, is perhaps clearer on this essential problem of drawing inferences from a single series:

> Suppose A, B, C to be three forms, while B is intermediate in structure between A and C. Then the doctrine of evolution offers four possible alternatives. A may have become C by way of B; or C may have become A by way of B; or A and C may be independent modifications of B; or A, B, and C may be independent modifications of some unknown D. . . . But if it can be shown that A, B, and C exhibit successive stages in the degree of modification, or specialisation, of the same type, and if, further, it can be proved that they occur in successively newer deposits, A being in the oldest and C in the newest, then the intermediate character of B has quite another importance, and I should accept it without hesitation, as a link in the geneaology of C. (Huxley 1968, VIII, 349)

In evolutionary paleontology, then, reasoning from a morphological series should depend on the confirmation from another series, especially a fossil series, ordered according to an independent principle. In practice, Darwin believed that the absence of a morphologically ordered series in the fossil record meant the imperfection of the fossil record. In other words, he held the finely graded morphological series to be an absolute demand. More recently, some paleontologists have inverted this reasoning, arguing that the absence of evidence of gradual change in the fossil record is not evidence of an imperfect record but of punctuated equilibrium, nongradual evolutionary change (Kerr 1995, 1421). They have held the geological series as absolute and required the morphological series to conform.

Darwin's theorizing requires as ideal evidence not only graded continuities in features and continuous series in time and hence in the fossil record, it also requires continuous series in geographical distribution. There are two distinct problems in the construction of series across geographical areas that Darwin addresses. The first has to do with the problem of local distribution and the fact that Darwin conceived of this impediment at all shows a certain "conceptual saturation" with series formation. In chapter 6, where Darwin addresses the absence of transitional forms, he considers this problem from the perspective of geographical distribution at one moment in time. Darwin is aware that the geographical range of a living species is something like a normal distribution, the prevalence of a species trailing off into rarity at the extremes of its territory. Where the ranges of two species overlap, he knows that individuals of each species often intermingle and yet remain "as absolutely distinct from each other in every detail of structure as are specimens taken from the metropolis [center of distribution] inhabited by each" (Darwin 1979, 207). "But in the intermediate region, having intermediate conditions of life, why do we not now find closely-linking intermediate varieties? This difficulty for a long time quite confounded me" (207). In the process of framing a solution to this problem, the absence of a graded series in distribution, Darwin in effect created the notion of the ecological niche and of an ecological system of interdependent species adapted to a well-defined complex of conditions, "the range of any one species, depending as it does on the range of others, will tend to be sharply defined" and hence discontinuous (208). In the twentieth century, E. O. Wilson and William Brown Jr. have put Darwin's insight on firmer footing, explaining how

species living next to each other avoid competition by adapting to slightly different niches, like different species of sticklebacks evolving to feed at the bottom or
top of a lake (Weiner 1995, 31).

The second problem challenging geographical continuity was the existence of
isolated pockets of the same species. The existence of distinct populations in a single
location is easy to explain when there are physical barriers to their dispersion. But
what about the distribution across apparent barriers? Here, once again, continuity, the overlapping continuum of the same species, provides the default condition whose absence has to be explained. The separate and miraculous creation of a
species can place them anywhere, but on Darwin's theory, species originate in a
distinct locale and radiate outward from that point; therefore, a physical chain is
required to explain their existence in another location.

Darwin overcomes this problem by treating isolated populations as though
they were the end points of what was once a continuous geographical series. This
time, however, the series is not an *incrementum* of graduated forms; it is, rather,
a *gradatio*, a repeating, overlapping chain of breeding individuals of the same
variety or species. When the physically intermediate members of this series are removed, the ends of the series, now isolated populations, remain. The kind of evidence that Darwin looks for to support this notion is evidence dictated by his conception of a physical series. What made the series continuous in the first place, and
what has since broken it? Why, for instance, do mountain tops bear the same species missing from adjacent valleys? A plausible answer: Retreating glaciers have
isolated the formerly connected dispersion of Arctic forms. Why do separated fresh
water bodies contain the same species? Flooding and the transport of seeds and
larva in the mud clinging to birds' feet are two likely explanations. How do isolated oceanic islands become populated? To address this conundrum, Darwin, who
accepted the former linkage of Asia to Alaska and of England to the continent as
the means for species radiation, rejected the too-easy explanation of land bridges
connecting most islands to the nearest mainland. Instead, he argued for ingenious
possibilities of transportation, which led to his drying fruits and soaking them in
sea water, searching bird excrement for seeds, and keeping track of the 537 plants
that germinated from a breakfast cup of pond mud.

Throughout the *Origin*, then, Darwin seeks to construct or to explain the absence of unbroken series in forms, in time, and in space, series that should be
mutually reinforcing. It is because living forms are gradable and hence connected
across time that they are connected in space and in morphology or—and this
interdependence can be read in any "evidence-to-inference" order given the theory
of natural selection—it is because they are graded in morphology that they are connected in time and in space or connected in space and hence in time and morphology. Darwin firmly believed that the best evidence for descent with modification, gradation across time represented in the fossil sequence, was largely unavail-
able. The other two types of gradation, in morphology and in distribution, could
only be read inferentially and one gradation could not be translated with certainty
into another. Yet so strong was Darwin's belief in the mutual reinforcement of these
three that he can imagine in the first edition the confirming result of a thought
experiment that cancels time and fills the earth with virtually a single, continuous

organism: "if every form which has ever lived on this earth were suddenly to reappear . . . all would blend together by steps as fine as those between the finest existing varieties" (Darwin 1979, 413).

At other points in the *Origin*, arguments based on gradation, degree, and series save the day for Darwin. The problem of sterility in hybrids is countered by claiming that such sterility is not an either/or trait but that it comes in degrees. Even the problem of precedence and authorship for the theory of natural selection itself is addressed in the historical sketch, which Darwin added to later editions of the *Origin*, by a chronologically ordered series of thinkers who proposed similar ideas, a series in which Darwin and Wallace find a comfortable and supportive place toward, but not at, the end (1958, 24). Despite all these instances, Darwin did, nevertheless, occasionally feel the constraints of series reasoning. In keeping with his habit throughout his writings of commenting on his own processes of argument, he specifically acknowledged the limits of series thinking in trying to construct the lines of descent among species, genera, etc. It was to overcome this limitation that Darwin constructed the one visual that appears in the *Origin*, the geometrical diagram of branching lines crossing horizontal lines that appears in chapter 4 and that he refers to again and again throughout the work, now redefining its branching lines as individuals, now as species, and its horizontal lines now as time markers and now as geological strata.

> This natural [genealogical] arrangement is shown, as far as is possible on paper, in the diagram [from chapter four], but in much too simple a manner. If a branching diagram had not been used, *and only the names of the groups had been written in a linear series*, it would have been still less possible to have given a natural arrangement; and it is notoriously not possible to represent in a series, on a flat surface, the affinities which we discover in nature amongst the beings of the same group. (Darwin 1979, 405–406; italics added)[15]

It is not difficult to read the phrase "only the names of the groups . . . written in linear series" as a definition of the figure incrementum, an ultimately ineffective representation of the truly branching nature of descent. A verbal incrementum can be fairly easily converted into a pictorial incrementum as it was in the case of the evolution of the horse. That kind of linear representation has, however, been replaced by circular diagrams that position a progenitor species at the center and show what Darwin called the "radiating affinities" (1979, 413) of different groups branching out from this center, a visual figure for which there is no corresponding verbal figure. But even this improved visualization is an inadequate representation of the three-dimensional branching, "the circuitous lines of affinity of various lengths" (413) that Darwin tried to describe in the twelfth chapter of the *Origin* (first edition) as the true nature of the affinities among fossil and living forms. Perhaps their visualization is only just possible in the three-dimensional rotating modeling now available on computer screens.

4

Antimetabole

The prologue to the Sumerian epic, "Gilgamesh, Enkidu and the Netherworld," dating from the third millennium B.C.E., opens with a cosmic placing of its tale that makes use of a deliberate verbal device carefully preserved in translation (Smith 1981, 17):

> After heaven from earth had been moved
> After earth from heaven had been separated

The recognizable structure found in this passage also occurs in what are probably liturgical invocations preserved on tablets discovered at Ugarit in Syria and dating between 1400 and 1200 B.C.E.: "Your slave is Baal, O Yamm, / The son of Dagan [Baal again] your captive" (Welch 1981b, 40). Scholars of ancient Near Eastern texts have commented on the many uses of such inverted parallelism in the hymns, poems, epics, and inscriptions of Canaanite literature first excavated in this century. The same structure can be found throughout the Pentateuch, especially in Everett Fox's translation, which is faithful to the poetry of ancient Hebrew: "Whoever now sheds human blood/ For that human shall his blood be shed" (Genesis 9:6). Many more passages in the Old and New Testaments, notably the sayings of Jesus, take the same recognizable form: "I came from the Father and have come into the world; again, I am leaving the world and going to the Father" (ἐξῆλθον ἐκ τοῦ πατρὸς καὶ ἐλήλυθα εἰς τὸν κόσμον· πάλιν ἀφίημι τὸν κόσμον καὶ πορεύομαι πρὸς τὸν πατέρα) (John 16:28). As the translated passages just cited demonstrate, even English with its less malleable syntax readily accommodates the sentence-length verbal formula of word reversals in roughly equal phrasing. It appears in everything from nursery rhymes, "Old King Cole was a merry old soul / And a merry old soul was he," to advertising copy, "Our Flex is back, so we're back to Flex [a shampoo]," to the most frequently quoted line in Kennedy's inaugural, "Ask not what your country can do for you; ask what you can do for your country."

The Semantics and Syntax of the Antimetabole

The inverted bicolon, known in Greek rhetoric as the antimetabole (ἀντιμεταβολή),[1] is a particularly easy structure to identify. Like the antithesis, it is a period made of two cola, but instead of having one or two pairs of opposed terms in these cola, opposites are unnecessary, and any terms can be used. The only distinguishing feature of the antimetabole is that at least two terms from the first colon change their relative places in the second, appearing now in one order, now in reversed order. In the process of changing their syntactic position in relation to each other, these terms change their grammatical and conceptual relation as well. Thus in St. Augustine's declaration of a semiotic principle—"[E]very sign is also a thing . . . but not every thing is also a sign"—"sign" and "thing" switch places in propositions claiming, first, that the set of all signs is a subset of the set of all things, but, second, that the reverse conceptual relation dictated by the reverse syntax does not hold (St. Augustine 1986, 9). Seventeen hundred years later, a journalist used the same form to complain about the unfortunate relationship between members of his own profession and the politicians they report on: "Our cynicism begets their fakery and their fakery begets our cynicism" (Mayer 1996, 25). Here again the changing syntactic order changes the grammatical relation of the two terms as agent and recipient and makes, overall, reciprocal claims, this time about their causal connection to each other. In each of these examples, separated by almost two thousand years, the arguer builds on the conceptual reversal created by the syntactic and grammatical reversal.

A variant of the antimetabole, to which the name "chiasmus" is sometimes applied, abandons the constraint of repeating the same words in the second colon yet retains a pattern of inversion (Corbett 1971, 478; see also Brogan 1994, 36–37). Instead of repetition, this variant uses words related in some recognizable way— perhaps as synonyms or opposites or members of the same category—and these related words change positions.

> Napoleon was defeated by a Russian winter
> and the snows of Leningrad destroyed Hitler.

The pattern in this chiasmus might be expressed semantically as "invader: Russian winter / Russian winter: invader." Instantiations of these classes switch places. The passive voice in the first half allows the agent to appear in a prepositional phrase, and the active voice in the second half allows the agent to appear as the subject, so grammatically the pattern in this antimetabole, or chiasmus, is recipient: agent/ agent: recipient. In the flexible syntax of Latin and Greek, such grammatical chiasmus was used frequently, allowing syntactic variety for the satisfaction of metrical patterns. Homer used it in lines like "a king good and a mighty warrior" (Iliad II 3:179) and "Of words a speaker and a doer of deeds" (II 9:443; cited in Welch 1981a,

251), and some Hellenistic commentators on Homer gave this structure, especially when it could be traced over longer passages as a principle for ordering content, the special name *hysteron proteron,* "the last first" (255). The shorter device, however, compressed within two cola, abounds in Latin literature; R. B. Steele counted 1257 examples in Livy, 211 in Sallust, 365 in Caesar, 1088 in Tacitus, and 307 in Justinius (259).

Opposed lexis, a requirement in the antithesis, is sometimes used in the antimetabole, or rather in the chiasmus, which does not repeat its terms precisely. Luther translates the answer of the man blind from birth whose sight was restored by Jesus in a chiasmus: "eines aber weiss ich: dass ich blind war und bin nun sehend" [literally, "that I blind was and am now seeing" (John 9:25)]. The pairs of opposite terms are "blind/seeing" and "was/am now." The King James Version uses an antithesis for this passage that resonates in the famous hymn "Amazing Grace": "one thing I know, that, whereas I was blind, now I see." Luther's translation is more faithful to the antimetabolic pattern of the original Greek text: τυφλὸς ὢν ἄρτι βλέπω (literally, "blind being now I see"). The two versions of this passage, in antithetical or chiastic form, do not make quite the same claim.

The grammatical chiasmus and the antimetabole have neither the same "visual" signature in a text nor do they participate in looser constructions in the same way. The perfect antimetabole should, once again, consist of two balanced cola, each of which repeats the same two terms while reversing their relative positions. The result of this reversal with balance is that one colon, in effect, mirrors the other. When there is mirror-imaging in letters only, the figure is called a palindrome as in the mock attribution to Napoleon: "Able was I ere I saw Elba." But the antimetabole is a palindrome of words rather than letters as in the old soft drink slogan: "You like it/It likes you." However, in languages without case endings, it is sometimes difficult to achieve both reversals and syllabic balance or even parallelism in the two cola. Benjamin Franklin, for example, reversed terms but did not conserve parallelism when he corrected the mistaken belief about the source of an electric spark between a charged wire and a person's finger: "The fire does not proceed from the touching finger to the wire, as is supposed, but from the wire to the finger" (Cohen 1941, 182). Yet even without grammatical parallelism, the antimetabole can still be identified here in the embedded reversals of the key terms; finger-wire/wire-finger. Since the chiasmus, on the other hand, does not repeat key terms, it quickly dissolves as a recognizable structure when its grammatical signature is lost.

To the extent that a writer can preserve parallelism as well as repetition in the two cola, the antimetabole gains in predictive power, in the invitation it offers readers to anticipate how the figure should be completed. The strength of this predictive power, like that possessed by the antithesis, comes across in the ease with which an antimetabole can sustain an ellipsis, as in the following example when the president of the International Growth Foundation criticized surgical attempts to make dwarfs taller: "Instead of trying to modify the environment to fit the people, they're trying to modify the people" (Rennie 1993, 14). Most readers can complete this truncated antimetabole mentally. It might even be argued that of all the figures, the antimetabole is the most "predictive," the easiest to complete from its first colon. The antithesis requires at least three of its four terms to constrain completion, and even then, given the fact that many words have more than one opposite, the consumer of the figure may not complete it ahead of time quite as the arguer intended. But since the key terms of the antimetabole reappear in the second half, the result is sure once the first half and the strategy are known. Evidence for this predictability comes from the fact that readers can be directed to form an antimetabole by the familiar Latin directions to change by turning around: *vice versa*.

The juxtaposed reversal of the antimetabole, thanks to its visibility, can be concentrated or expanded in variations on the two-cola formula. As in the case of the antithesis with its pairs of opposites, it is possible to compress an antimetabole from its ideal configuration in two clauses and pack the reversal into immediately juxtaposed words or phrases: "blue midnight" and "midnight blue" or "the physics of music and the music of physics." This "A of B and B of A" pattern matches Aristotle's observation in the *Categories* on the nature of relatives, things that are known by virtue of being relative to something else. A true relative, in Aristotle's treatment, must survive the test of convertibility; the double is known because it is "double of a half" and the half is "half of a double."[2] At the same time, this device of reversing noun plus prepositional phrase can also be used to presuppose or argue for the symmetrical status of relatives, implying that each member of a pair can offer a point of view on the other partner, and that, therefore, the two are somehow reciprocally linked and mutually balanced.

Just as it is possible to compress an antimetabole into adjacent phrases, so it is possible to expand it and have not two terms but two whole predications exchanging their relative positions on either side of a point of equilibrium. Richard Whately provides an example from a contemporary politician in his 1846 *Elements of Rhetoric*: "Some contend that I disapprove of this plan because it is not my own; it would be more correct to say, that it is not my own, because I disapprove of it" (Whately 1963, 324). The blocks being reversed here are not single terms but clauses. It is not difficult to imagine that even larger text structures can be involved in such reversals.

The antimetabole can also be relaxed from its ideal syntactic configuration and still perform the same conceptual and argumentative work. The tight form, compressed in two cola, foregrounds the reversal, but, as the introductory chapter explains, while figures epitomize certain arguments or lines of reasoning, they are not the only means of delivering them. Thus "approximate" antimetaboles rather than pure ones are frequently used, especially in scientific prose, where the symmetry of the figures seems sometimes to be deliberately avoided. In the following passage from *The Expression of the Emotions in Man and Animals*, Darwin ponders the causal conundrum of "the association of certain kinds of sounds with certain states of mind" (Darwin 1965, 90). Given a configuration of the mouth and a consequent sound, which, he asks, comes first or which is the consequence of the other.

> There is another obscure point, namely, whether the *sounds* which are produced under various states of mind determine the *shape* of the mouth, or whether its *shape* is not determined by independent causes, and the *sound* thus modified. (91)

Despite the looseness of the syntax here, the two possibilities Darwin considers— sounds determine shape/shape determines sound—inevitably recall the antimetabole: "sound" and "shape" exchange relative positions on either side of the "or" in two clauses beginning with "whether." Here Darwin uses a loosely worded antimetabole to express his uncertainty about which relationship is the correct one, rather than an emphatic antimetabole to replace an assumed causal direction with its reverse.

History of the Figure

The antimetabole and its close relative the chiasmus are verbal devices with a very ancient lineage, long antedating their appearance in Greek rhetoric. As the examples offered above indicate, scholars of ancient texts have identified the chiasmus in Sumero-Akkadian and Ugaritic texts dating from the third millennium B.C.E. (Breck 1994, 21), and there is a very strong tradition of Biblical exegesis, beginning with the work of Nils Lund in the 1930s, which bases interpretations of passages in both the Old and New Testaments on the detection of chiastic structures. Unfortunately, in another of the terminological muddles confusing the study of the figures, the chiasmus of Biblical hermeneutics is not quite the same device as the antimetabole and chiasmus of classical rhetoric. The term *chiasmus* comes from the Greek letter χ (chi), because the visual figure of this letter captures the transposition or crossing that occurs in the verbal figure.

In this configuration, the antimetabole and the structural chiasmus, as described above, are identical, both expressed formulaically as A:B:B:A or as A:B:B':A', the addition of the prime notation indicating that the recurring terms can be replaced by cognates. However, some Biblical scholars define the chiasmus as a figure that both repeats terms and also has a center point or pivot; in other words, they "populate" the center of the X where the lines cross, thus creating a structure that can be described by the formula A:B:C:B:A or A:B:C:D:C:B:A, and so forth (Breck 1994, 18–19). This "pivotal center" is, at least for some Biblical scholars, the "essential characteristic of chiasmus," and it is often taken to indicate what the writer intended as the "conceptual center" or point of the passage (33). An example of a chiasmus with a pivotal center occurs in Jeremiah 2:27–28; it is quoted below in translation, as John Breck presents it in his study of Biblical chiasmus, with labeling and indentation to demonstrate the chiastic structure:

> A: In the time of *their trouble* they say,
>   B: *"Arise* and *save us!"*
>   C: But where are your gods that you made for yourself?
>   B': Let them *arise*, if they can *save you*,
> A': In the time of *your trouble*.

There are undoubtedly many other passages in the Old and New Testament, some much longer, that can be convincingly arranged in this pattern that Breck calls "concentric parallelism," a building up to and then a cycling away from a central point.

Breck also suggests that some passages in the Bible can only be understood properly when they are read "chiastically," from the outside members to the inside, A to A' and then B to B'. As a case in point he cites Matthew 7:6: "Give not what is holy to dogs nor throw your pearls before swine, lest they trample them under their feet and turning, tear you to pieces." As read conventionally, this passage claims that the swine will both trample the pearls and turn on the thrower. But read chiastically, the outer two phrases belong together as do the inner two: if you give what is holy to dogs, they will turn on you and tear you to pieces; if you cast pearls before swine, they will trample them (Breck 1994, 29).[3] This passage, however, lacks the telltale reversal of the rhetorical chiasmus or antimetabole; it is instead the reader's strategy, the invocation of a chiastic or antimetabolic reading frame, that relates outer and inner units containing no repeating elements.

Breck's specification of a correct "reading frame" for this passage, and of the importance of chiastic structures in general, is greatly strengthened by the available evidence on how literacy was taught in ancient Greece and Rome. School children apparently learned to recite the alphabet not only forward and backward but also from the paired extremes (alpha and omega) to the middle pair and from the middle pair to the paired extremes (Marrou 1956, 211–212). They were thus in a sense prepared to look at passages according to any of these reading strategies, and the need for such an a priori strategy is, in turn, explained by the *scriptio continua* of ancient texts, their lack of any spacing between letters, which required readers to segment the text into syllables, words, and all higher structures (Stock 1984, 25). It becomes less difficult to believe then, despite our bias for unidirectional decoding, that authors intentionally patterned portions of their texts chiastically and that readers were prepared to decode them from the extremes to the center or vice versa.

The chiasmus identified by Biblical scholars, inversion around a central element usually in the form of a tricolon or pentacolon, is a powerful figure in its own right. When the constraint of exact repetition of the inverted elements is dropped in favor of other forms of term substitution, the chiasmus can easily be generalized into a pattern detectable across passages much longer than a few cola. But it must be distinguished from the antimetabole, which can at best be classified as one of several possible chiastic patterns. The notion of a middle or pivotal colon is not part of the definition of the antimetabole in the rhetorical tradition. Centers are never mentioned. A true antimetabole is best defined as an inverted bicolon that observes the constraint of repeating its reversed terms (or at least the roots if they change case). It has no third element in the middle that it builds up to or moves away from or that summarizes it thematically. Its middle is empty; it is a mere point of folding or the axis of reflection of the two halves toward each other, revealing their reciprocal nature as mirror images. A middle term would only distort this symmetry and as a result obscure the essential argumentative work of the figure, which depends on reversing the relative positions of its terms. Of course it is possible to take an antimetabole conforming to the canonical pattern A:B:B:A and turn its two

inside terms into a single "middle": A:[B:B]:A. Concise antimetaboles with close
repetition might invite such bracketing.

> who opens and no one shall shut/who shuts and no one shall open
> ὁ ἀνοίγων καὶ οὐδεὶς κλείσει, καὶ κλείων καὶ οὐδεὶς ἀνοίγει
>   Revelation 3:7

It might be possible to claim that this passage is primarily "about" the power of
the holy one over shutting, to prevent or secure it, on the warrant that the terms
for shutting are central in the phrase. Another interpretation might emphasize the
power of the holy one over both opening and shutting. But no matter which reading seems more plausible in this particular case, the point remains that taking such
an inverted bicolon as a chiasmus with a central term or as an antimetabole that
reverses the relationship of two terms can be a matter of deliberate choice on the
part of the reader. Here is another case where the difference between two close figures cannot be decided by a formal test alone (see also chapter 3 on series figures).

The antimetabole must have earned explicit recognition in Hellenistic rhetorical theory sometime in the third or second centuries B.C.E. Aristotle does not name
or distinguish the antimetabole in Book III of the *Rhetoric*; nor does the *Rhetorica
ad Alexandrum*. But all later treatments of the figures in antiquity do, beginning
with the *Rhetorica Ad Herennium*, where it is named *commutatio*, the figure that
"occurs when two discrepant thoughts are so expressed by transposition that the
latter follows from the former although contradictory to it" ([Cicero] 1954, 325).
Several examples follow this definition, including versions of famous aphorisms
attributed to Socrates ("You must eat to live, not live to eat") and to Simonides
("A poem should be a speaking picture; a picture should be a silent poem"). By
way of explanation, the author of the *Ad Herennium* merely observes that the effect
is "commode," that is agreeable, "when in juxtaposing contrasted ideas the words
also are transposed" (327). But the unspecified ways in which the second half "follows from," or rather "originates from," the first [a priore posterior contraria priori
proficiscatur], only hinted at here, will, in fact, determine the antimetabole's argumentative force.[4]

Quintilian himself has a much weaker conception of the antimetabole than the
Ad Herennium. He repeats precisely the same example from Socrates, but he does
not regard the antimetabole as a conceptually unique figure. Instead, he groups it
under antithesis, which he has broadly redefined as the juxtaposition of semantic
contraries (see p. 55), and he further describes the antimetabole in a way that connects it with polyptoton (see chapter 5): "Antithesis may also be effected by employing that *figure*, known as ἀντιμεταβολή, by which words are repeated in different cases, tenses, moods, etc., as for instance when we say, non ut edam, vivo,
sed ut vivam edo (I do not live to eat, but eat to live)" (Quintilian 1921, III, 497).
But for this famous example, nothing in Quintilian's definition specifies reversing
the relative positions of two terms. The resemblance to polyptoton, the migration
of a word root through different grammatical cases, occurs as the inevitable result
of switching grammatical roles in an inflected language like Latin (e.g., edam/vivo
and vivam/edo). Indeed, in an inflected language it is possible to reverse grammati-

cal roles without changing the relative syntactic positions of the terms involved, and that possibility perhaps explains why Quintilian's definition does not emphasize the syntactic reversal that is so obvious in English and other uninflected languages. Yet his examples, like most examples in Classical manuals, do contain both inflectional changes *and* syntactic reversal. Perhaps the element of reversal is so obvious in both the name of the figure and the usual examples that Quintilian feels no need to mention it.

In what sense does an antimetabole amount to an antithesis, as Quintilian suggests? Clearly, according to the older or "Aristotelian" definition of the antithesis, the topically active form discussed in chapter 2, the antithesis necessarily deploys semantic opposites but the antimetabole need not. There is only one pair of critical terms in an antimetabole and they are not necessarily opposites; "eat" is not the opposite of "live," nor is the pair constructed into opposition by the figure. Instead, the kind of "antithesis" produced by the antimetabole is an antithesis between its entire two cola when one of the two contains a negative (eat to live, *not* live to eat). Quintilian probably had this kind of colon-to-colon contrast in mind when he grouped the antimetabole under the antithesis. Whether one of the cola is negated or not determines the lines of argument that the figure can epitomize; these lines differ, as the following discussion demonstrates, from those accomplished by the antithesis.

But Quintilian's apparent demotion of the antimetabole had consequences for the history of the figure in later manuals. As long as it was categorized as a type of antithesis, the antimetabole was easy to drop from the roster of figures as a superfluous distinction within a larger category. Among the ancients, Demetrius of Halicarnassus, author of *On Style*, does not distinguish it.[5] Hermogenes also never uses the term, though he does praise changing the order of the wording in parallel phrasing (chiasmus) to avoid seeming overly artificial, citing Demosthenes' practice as his model. But Hermogenes is himself the very careful user of a formulaic antimetabole in the section of *On Types of Style* devoted to identifying the best practitioners of different genres, those whose works in fact define the standard in the genre: "The best practical oratory is that of Demosthenes, and the oratory of Demosthenes, in turn, is the best practical oratory" (Hermogenes 1987, 109); "For the most beautiful of panegyric styles is that of Plato and the style of Plato is the most beautiful of panegyric styles in prose" (113). When he comes to the third genre, poetry, Hermogenes draws attention to his antimetabolic manipulation: "Here you could simply invert the propositions as we did in the case of Plato and Demosthenes: the best poetry is that of Homer, and Homer is the best of poets" (115). Clearly, though he did not name the figure, Hermogenes knew what it meant to epitomize his definition argument in a succinctly crafted antimetabole.

In the Renaissance manuals, especially those whose authors had a strong interest in dialectic as well as rhetoric, antimetabole is once again noticed separately, and, as usual in the expanded figure catalogs of the sixteenth and seventeenth centuries, it overlaps or spreads through near forms.[6] Melancthon mixes examples of antitheses with antimetaboles in his section on devices of amplification, using both the old warhorses, the antithesis, "You are to your enemies gentle and to your friends inexorable," and the antimetabole, "One must eat to live, not live to eat."

(Melancthon 1969, 291–292).[7] But he also sees how the process of inversion [inversio] can be used by speakers for pro and con positions. If, in the example he provides, the prosecution in a murder case claims "You were seen burying him, therefore you killed him," the defense can construct an answer with an antimetabole not of terms but of clauses, "'[I]f I had killed him, I should not have buried him'" (292). The logic of the response here, as old as the Sophist Antiphon's specimen forensic speeches of accusation and defense written in the late fifth century B.C.E., comes down to degrees of plausibility. The prosecutor argues that the furtive burier of a corpse is the likely murderer, and the defense responds, antimetabollically, that the true murderer is not likely to do anything so incriminating as hastily burying the corpse.

Peacham also emphasized the argumentative potential of the figure when, after defining it as Quintilian does as "A forme of speech which inverteth a sentence by the contrary," he recommends its use "to praise, dispraise, to distinguish, *but most commonly to confute* by the inversion of the sentence" (Peacham 1954, 164; italics added; see also Smith 1973, 116). Given this emphasis on refutation, two of his three examples are scriptural antimetaboles that negate the first colon and offer a correction in the second.

> Neither was the man created for the womans sake,
> but the woman for the mans sake.
> The children ought not to laie up for their parents,
> but the parents for their children
>   (Peacham 1954, 164)

The caution that Peacham offers also focuses on this potential corrective use: "it is requisite and behoveful that the sentence inversed be not false, or that it be not perversly put contrary to the truth & meaning of the speaker through the fault of memorie" (164). The danger Peacham refers to here seems to be the ease with which an antimetabole can be created so that a speaker may flip terms too readily or put the negative in the wrong half.

In the eighteenth century, Blair never mentions the antimetabole, but Campbell, like Quintilian, categorizes it as a kind of antithesis though without negation: "Sometimes the words contrasted in the second clause are mostly the same that are used in the first, only the construction and the arrangement are inverted, 'The old may inform the young; || and the young may animate the old'" (Campbell 1963, 375). Campbell believed that in Greek and Latin "this kind of antithesis generally receives an additional beauty from the change made in the inflection," an effect which can in rare instances be achieved in English as in the lines from Pope that he cites, "What'ere of mongrel no one class admits, / A wit with dunces, || and a dunce with wits" (Dunciad, Bk iv). There is no question in Campbell of joining the antimetabole or any other stylistic device to a unique line of argument. The entire category of antithesis, of which the antimetabole is one kind, is for Campbell a figure of balance (see p. 57), whose effects, he believes, are primarily aesthetic.

In the nineteenth century, Fontanier categorized the antimetabole among the non-tropes and, specifically, among his newly invented subcategory, the "figures of style," which express an entire thought in an entire phrase or at least the most essential part of it (Fontanier 1977, 226). He called the figure "Réversion" and further subsumed it, as traditional, under the antithesis.

> *La* Réversion *fait revenir sur eux-mêmes, avec un sens différent, et souvent contraire, tous les mots, au moins les plus essentiels, d'une proposition.* On peut la regarder comme une espèce particulière d'*Antithèse.* Il suffira d'en donner des exemples

> The reversion makes to return on themselves, with a different and often contrary sense, all the words, or at least the most essential, of a proposition. One can regard it as a particular type of antithesis. It suffices to give examples of it. (381; italics in original)

These sufficient examples follow thick and fast, including the inevitable chestnut about living and eating, others from Corneille, Boileau, Rousseau, among them a memorable epigram from Agésilas ("Ce ne sont pas les places qui honorent les hommes, mais les hommes qui honorent les places" [It is not places which honor men but men who honor places]) and a stunning example from Bourdaloue where not only two entire pairs change their relative positions but also the individual members within each pair ("Nous ne devons pas juger des règles et des devoirs par les moeurs et par les usages; mais nous devons juger des usages et des moeurs par les devoirs et par les règles" [We should not judge rules and duties by manners and customs, but we should judge customs and manners by duties and rules]). The student using Fontanier's texts would learn nothing explicit about the argumentative potential in such carefully crafted forms but would certainly absorb the pattern through so many memorable examples.[8]

Overall, the antimetabole has had an undistinguished and intermittent career in the tradition of the figures, perhaps because it can be explained in several ways formally. Defined by the individual lexical items in the figure as instantiated in an inflected language, the antimetabole incorporates the polyptoton: The same roots change their case endings in the two parts of the figure. Emphasizing the negation of one half, as Quintilian and many subsequent rhetoricians did, produces a description that is indistinguishable from the antithesis. Yet no one reading examples of these two figures would confuse them. Conflating them by definition obscures the unique effect of the antimetabole which, when decoded linearly, is less a static edifice than it is a movement. One enters the antimetabole at one conceptual location and comes out at another; it has the trajectory of a parabola. To capture the argumentative work accomplished by the antimetabole requires emphasizing not the case inflections or the possible overall contrast but the essential reversal of terms as its distinguishing formal feature. It is this reversal of terms that determines the distinctive lines of argument epitomized by the antimetabole.

Argumentative Uses of the Antimetabole

Understanding the lines of argument epitomized by the antimetabole begins, once again, with the relation of the figure to the topics in Aristotle's treatises on rhetoric and dialectic. Although Aristotle does not mention the antimetabole among stylistic devices in Book III of the *Rhetoric*, he does identify it by its argumentative potential as the 18th of the 28 lines of argument.

> Another is from not always choosing the same thing before and after [an event], but the reverse [ek tou anapalin haireisthai], for example, this enthymeme "[It would be terrible] if when in exile we fought to come home, but having come home we shall go into exile in order not to fight." Sometimes people have chosen to be at home at the cost of fighting, sometimes not to fight at the cost of not remaining at home. (Kennedy 1991, 199–200)

Aristotle recommends here the deliberate trial run of a transposition. What, if anything, can be made of reversing the positions of key terms, a serious stylistic playfulness that seems far from contemporary notions of how arguments are secured? In order to illustrate the resulting line of reasoning, Aristotle provides a perfect example of the figure by reversing the consequences of fighting or not fighting—exile : home/home : exile.[9]

Once again, this line of argument, just mentioned in the *Rhetoric*, is developed in the *Topics*, where such reversals are a key maneuver in Aristotle's system of dialectical logic. Understanding the role of antimetabolic reversals in dialectic requires appreciating, first of all, that according to Aristotle's theory of arguable statements, a proposition always concerns a genus, a definition, a property or an accident. Distinguishing which of these four a proposition is about depends in part on the possibility of reversing it and seeing if the result is plausible. As Aristotle explains of statements about properties,

> A property is something which does not indicate the essence of a thing, but yet belongs to that thing alone, and *is predicated convertibly of it.* Thus it is a property of man to be capable of learning grammar; for if he is a man, then he is capable of learning grammar, and if he is capable of learning grammar, he is a man. (Barnes 1984, I, 170, italics added; see also 222, 261)

Thus, forming an antimetabole is a test for a property. A genus term cannot perform this trick of convertible predication: a robin is a bird; a bird is a robin. Neither can an accident: Venus is in the house of Jupiter; what is in the house of Jupiter is Venus. A definition, however, which, unlike a property, does capture the essence of a subject, must also be convertible with it, "For every predicate of a subject must of necessity be either convertible with its subject or not: and if it is convertible, it would be its definition or property, for if it signifies the essence, it is the definition; if not, it is a property" (172; see also 215, 259). The Aristotelian sense of a property as a unique but not essential feature of an entity no longer seems part of the general understanding of the term "property." But definitions and unique properties must still survive a test of convertibility; for example, arsenic is the element with an atomic number of 33, and the element with an atomic number of 33 is arsenic.

All these distinctions among kinds of propositions and their manipulations serve the *Topics'* purpose of giving arguers advice on how to come up with premises. The antithesis, as explained in chapter 2, is one such premise-generating machine; the antimetabole, the verbal epitome of convertibility, is another. However, the antimetabole can only be used to form premises if certain restrictions on the terms

involved are observed. Aristotle carefully distinguishes among four types of opposed terms: contraries, contradictions, correlatives, and privation/possession pairs
(see p. 48). In giving advice on how to produce premises by purely formal means,
he considers how these semantic categories affect convertibility when he recommends that the arguer

> should look among the contradictories of your terms, reversing the order of their
> sequence, both when demolishing and when establishing a view; . . . E.g. if man is
> an animal, what is not an animal is not a man; and likewise also in other instances
> of contradictories. For here the sequence is reversed; for animal follows upon man,
> but not-animal does not follow upon not-man, but the reverse—not-man upon not-
> animal. In all cases, therefore, a claim of this sort should be made, (e.g.) that if the
> honourable is pleasant, what is not pleasant is not honourable, while if the latter is
> not so, neither is the former. Likewise, also, if what is not pleasant is not honourable,
> then what is honourable is pleasant. Clearly, then, reversing the sequence in the case
> of contradictories is a method convertible for both purposes. (Barnes 1984, I, 189)

The premise formation recommended here follows naturally from the convertibility
of claims about essential properties and definitions. If the claim in a definition holds
as it should and its predicate is integrally tied to its subject, then negating the predicate negates its connection to the subject. A paraphrase of the argumentative strategy involved is more complicated than Aristotle's succinct example: *if the honourable is pleasant, what is not pleasant is not honourable.* The specific relationship
between the pleasant and the honorable here is not likely to satisfy a contemporary audience, but paying attention to the form alone shows the underlying logic
of sets. Aristotle has simply codified the common sense involved in thinking about
sets and their members and epitomized this reasoning in the form of directions
for forming a precise stylistic device to test this relationship, a special antimetabole
that reverses and negates both terms in the second colon.[10]

Definition and the commutative principle

These references in the *Topics* begin to suggest the argumentative uses of the antimetabole. The antimetabole that Aristotle stipulates depends on the convertibility
of a definition and its contradiction. Other uses of the figure underscore the interchangeability of a term and its definition, thus suggesting the simultaneity,
interconvertibility, or virtual identity of two terms. The anthropologist Loren
Eiseley's gnomic characterization of the beliefs of late nineteenth-century materi-
alists can serve as an example: "Man was mud and mud was man" (Eiseley 1957,
36). Here switching the relative positions of the terms demonstrates an indifference to their syntactic order, an apparent consequence of, but also a way of establishing, their interchangeability, their simultaneous mutuality. If one of these terms
was the genus of the other, their reversal without contradiction would be impossible. So the reversal in the Eiseley example says, in effect, these terms are so close
that neither is the genus of the other. The same form can be used to declare that
two entities are emphatically not identical as in Richard Feynman's declaration,
"Physics is not mathematics, and mathematics is not physics" (Feynman 1965, 55).
What both of these "bravura" claims (Eiseley's and Feynman's) have in common is

a declaration of the underlying interchangeability of their terms, whether both are fungible either directly by identity or, paradoxically, by the fact that they mutually have nothing to do with one another.[11]

The antimetabole as a kind of identity statement also corresponds perfectly to the commutative laws of addition and multiplication made explicit in the nineteenth century, the observation that when two natural numbers are added or multiplied, their order when undergoing these operations is not important. These axioms or laws of arithmetic are usually expressed symbolically in the following way for any two numbers m and n:

$$m + n = n + m$$
$$m \times n = n \times m$$

Of course, the commutative laws hold for any number of terms in any order on either side of an equals sign, $(a + x + c + p) = (p + x + a + c)$, etc. But written in their usual abstract form with only two terms, the commutative laws provide a blueprint for a particular class of arguments epitomized by the antimetabole: The two terms amount to the same thing, no matter what the order. The commutative law also holds for other branches of mathematics: Boolean arithmetic, vector algebra, propositional logic, and set theory (Devlin 1994, 13, 43, 44, 48, 57). Yet the law itself, according to mathematician Keith Devlin, is not "provable." "Why," he then asks,

> have mathematicians adopted the commutative law, for which the numerical evidence is slim, as an axiom, and left out other assertions for which there is a huge amount of numerical evidence? The decision is essentially a judgment call. For a mathematician to adopt a certain pattern as an axiom, not only should that pattern be a useful assumption, but it has to be "believable", in keeping with her intuition, and as simple as possible. (55)

As a verbal device, the antimetabole was identified long before the commutative laws of arithmetic were formalized, though probably not before they were put to use. It arguably meets Devlin's constraints as useful and simple, but what about it is inherently believable? Both the verbal figure and the mathematical law must express a more primitive underlying conceptual pattern that somehow satisfies the mind and therefore can be used for further argumentative work.

This underlying conceptual pattern in the antimetabole certainly involves a particular kind of symmetry. Symmetry in general is the study of the transformations—like stretching, rotating, translating, and reflecting—that an object can go through and yet look the same afterward (Feynman 1965, 84; Devlin 1994, 146). Rotate a perfect heximeric snowflake 60° and it is indistinguishably the same snowflake. But the mirror imaging that produces bilateral symmetry is a somewhat special case. According to the mathematician Hermann Weyl, a body is "symmetric with respect to a given plane E if it is carried into itself by reflection in E," a reflection in turn being defined as a "mapping" according to a rule associating every point p with an image p' (Weyl 1982, 4–5). In typical bilateral symmetry, a mirror image is produced by rotating the plane in which the two-dimensional image exists around an axis of reflection by 180°. The two resulting right-hand and left-hand versions of an image or object are referred to as enantiomorphs, from the Greek word ἐναντίος meaning "opposite." Rotation of the plane in a full circle restores the original image. According to Weyl, geometrically precise bilateral symmetry involving a representation and its mirror image is allied to vaguer notions of perceptual and aesthetic balance; hence its extensive use in the decorative arts and architecture (16). An object, whether natural or constructed, that exhibits bilateral symmetry or two objects juxtaposed as enantiomorphs seem equally weighted on both sides of a hypothetical line or midpoint, and this balance can, in turn, apparently convey a sense of completeness.

Completeness is the impression produced by Eiseley's "man was mud and mud was man." There is no question, of course, of the figure antimetabole being a bilaterally symmetrical structure in the rigorous sense of having a second half formed of "mirror writing" from the first half. The bilateral symmetry is only an approximation based on key terms changing relative places; even in this less rigorous sense, the "mapping" from the first colon to the second does not necessarily produce a parallel second colon. In an inflected language, inverting the relative positions of two terms usually means that the same term appears in the two cola with different inflectional endings, and in an uninflected language, it means that different words or more words may be needed to express the changed functions. Louis Rukeyser's comment on the Whitewater investigations of 1994 typifies the required morphing: "Though there is not a shred of evidence, there is evidence of shredding." But despite such accommodations to the syntax and grammar of a particular language, the transposition of terms still produces an impression of balance and completeness that contributes to the argumentative power of the antimetabole.

The antimetabole in geometry

In the Western tradition for over 2,000 years there was, in addition to universal training in rhetoric, another universal subject, geometry, and a specific text that every educated person encountered: Euclid's *Elements*. While the *Elements* has served for centuries as the model of rigorous demonstration as opposed to probabilistic dialectical or rhetorical argumentation, its proofs are uniquely fixed to individual propositions. Where do these propositions to be proved come from in the first place? One answer is the antimetabole that can be used for generating one proposition from another, each new proposition then requiring its own proof. Propositions 47 and 48 in Book I are a case in point (Euclid 1952, 28–29). The first of these is the famous Pythagorean theorem: "In right-angled triangles the square on the side subtending the right angle is equal to the squares on the sides containing the right angle." Its converse is Proposition 48: "If in a triangle the square on one of the sides be equal to the squares on the remaining two sides of the triangle, the angle contained by the remaining two sides of the triangle is right." These two propositions together form an antimetabole, though not a stylistically well-expressed one in the translation quoted. Nevertheless, the first begins with a right triangle and claims a special relationship between the side subtending its 90° angle and the two remaining sides; the second begins with this special relationship and claims that the triangle is a right triangle. Neither of these propositions, however, proves the other according to Euclidean standards of demonstration. Both are subject to further proofs using the available rules of construction, definitions, axioms, and previously proved propositions. Nevertheless, mere convertibility suggests the second proposition as a possibility and does make it plausible as following the first: Since in a right triangle, the square of the hypotenuse equals the squares of the two remaining sides, when the squares of the two remaining sides equal the square of the side subtending the angle they form, the triangle is a right triangle.

The usefulness of conversions epitomized by the antimetabole can extend to the definitions of Euclidean geometry: If two points determine a line, then two lines determine a point. It continues in other geometries as well where it is known as "the principle of duality," a principle that has been put to great use in "projective" geometry, a branch of mathematics beginning in the seventeenth century and growing out of the practices of perspective drawing. One of the basic theorems of projective geometry was discovered by Gérard Desargues when he rationalized some of the principles behind the rules of perspective representation. According to Desargues's theorem, if two triangles are in perspective, one the projection of the other (that is, having lines from their vertices all joining in a single point), they will also have the following property: three sets of lines extended from their corresponding sides will meet in three corresponding points and, furthermore, these three points of meeting will all lie on the same line. Once Desargues's theorem is in place, a new theorem can be generated by using an antimetabole to construct the "dual" of this theorem (Kline 1955, 35; Devlin 1994, 136). The original theorem reads: "If we have two triangles such that lines joining corresponding vertices pass through one point O, then the pairs of corresponding sides of the two triangles join in three points lying on one straight line." And the dual of this theorem, like the second colon of an antimetabole, must be as follows: "If we have two triangles such that points which are the joins [*sic*] of corresponding sides lie on one line O, then the pairs of corresponding vertices of the two triangles are joined by three lines lying on one point" (Kline 1955, 34). The dual statement is the result of interchanging the hypothesis and the conclusion (34). Mathematicians have since proved that in projective geometry, every such rephrasing of a theorem, every completion of the "mapping" defined by the antimetabole, does lead to a new theorem given "the symmetry in the roles that point and line play" in projective geometry (35). That symmetry is axiomatic in projective geometry, and it allows the substitution of "point" for "line" or vice versa and of a phrase like "points lying on the same line" for "lines meeting at a single point" or the reverse (Devlin 1994, 136). In the late nineteenth century, projective geometry, with its perfectly dual theorems, was demonstrated to be more fundamental than Euclidean geometry; indeed, Euclidean and other geometries can be described as special cases of projective geometry, a discipline where antimetabole is of fundamental importance.

Why, however, is the mapping rule that exploits antimetabole in this and other areas of mathematics called a principle of "duality," a label that suggests the creation of a unique double or partner? One answer may be the determinism involved in the creation of the second colon of an antimetabole from the first. The "mapping" rule for an antimetabole—invert the relative positions of two key terms in parallel phrases—constrains the possible result. By contrast, as pointed out above, the first colon of an antithesis can produce different second cola depending on whether a single or double antithesis is formed and depending on how many opposites the terms in the first colon have. Some words like "sharp," as Aristotle pointed out, have two opposites: "flat" for sounds and "dull" for points. So the first colon of an antithesis is less restrictive than the first colon of an antimetabole, which predicts only one second colon, one "dual" or inevitable partner of the first.[12]

Mirror imaging in nature and in argument

There are many cases in the history of science where the result of a specific line of inquiry and experiment has been the characterization of physical enantiomorphs, mirror-image objects, or of complementarity, reversible or equilibrium processes. In the early nineteenth century, Jean Baptiste Biot discovered that some crystals of quartz rotated the plane of polarization of light to the left, and others to the right (Pasteur 1905, 9). In the 1970s, Alexander Rich and his colleagues announced the discovery of left-handed DNA, a rare alternative to the dominant right-handed helix (Wang 1979, 684). And in 1995, Diana Bianca and her colleagues at the New England Medical Center discovered that, in addition to the well-known phenomenon of a mother's blood occasionally crossing the placenta to a fetus, the reverse process could also occur, and fetal cells could cross over and persist in a mother's body (Travis 1996, 85).

Visual antimetaboles are also common in scientific illustration, and the ubiquity of these enantiomorphs or "physical" antimetaboles raises again the interesting issue of the participation of prepared forms in the visual representation of natural objects. Figure 4.1 contains three images taken from standard textbooks in physics and molecular biology, accompanied by their explanatory legends. The first illustration shows the pattern of "lines of force" as they are made visible by fine threads in the field between "a pair of charged parallel plates." The second displays the pattern revealed by streamers of dye in the flow of water from a source to a drain. The final image is the familiar bilaterally symmetrical snapshot of a cell in the telophase of mitosis. These, of course, are not the only "antimetabolic" illustrations that could be found in science texts. They have been chosen for their visual similarity to one another and the particular kind of bilateral symmetry they demonstrate, despite the fact that they come from very different areas of investigation. Clearly they all represent the architecture of the field created by opposing but balanced "forces" or pulls. This pattern is certainly discoverable in nature. These images are found, and yet they are constructed as well, by manipulation and selection, to approximate a familiar conceptual pattern.

Does the verbal antimetabole have a role in the discovery of these physical antimetaboles? Not necessarily. Among the most famous findings of physical enantiomorphism was Louis Pasteur's revelation that many organic compounds come in left- and right-handed versions or isomers. In experiments performed in 1848, he was able to separate the left and right-handed crystals of sodium ammonium paratartrate according to the orientation of their hemihedral or asymmetric edges. But Pasteur's laboratory writings and published arguments about this discovery

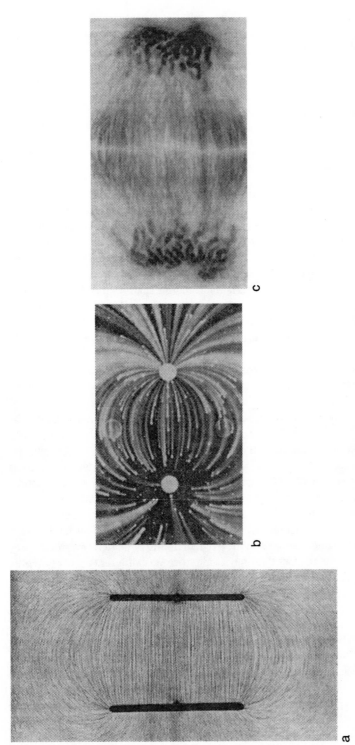

Figure 4.1. "Physical" antimetaboles. (a) Field lines between a pair of charged parallel plates. From Hans C. Ohanian, *Physics*, 2nd ed. (New York: W. W. Norton and Sons, 1989). Reproduced with permission of Robert P. Matthews. (b) Streamers of dye indicating the streamlines in water flowing from a source to a sink. From W. E. Rogers, *Introduction to Electric Fields* (New York: McGraw-Hill, 1954). Illustration by A. D. Moore. Reproduced with permission of McGraw-Hill. (c) Light micrograph of cytokinesis in a plant cell in telophase. From Bruce Alberts et al., *Molecular Biology of the Cell*, 3rd ed. (New York: Garland, 1994). Reproduced with permission of Andrew S. Bajer.

of mirror-imaging in nature do not employ verbal antimetabole, for the actual arguments he used to estabish the plausibility of his findings are not reversals. To argue for the existence of his crystalline enantiomorphs, Pasteur relied instead on antithesis, for the genesis of his research was the confusing observation that solutions of sodium ammonium tartrate rotated light to the right, whereas solutions of the paratartrate produced no such rotation (Geison 1995, 77; Pasteur 1905, 26). This difference could have been described in terms of three possibilities: light passed through a solution rotates to the right, or not at all, or to the left. But in a rhetorically more effective choice, Pasteur characterized this difference antithetically as an opposition between the "optically active" (rotating either to the right or left) and "inactive" (no rotation). He eventually discovered that the tartrate was composed of only right-handed crystals, whereas the paratartrate was composed of equal numbers of left- and right-handed crystals producing rotations that canceled each other out. In the crucial experiment, he separated out the two types of paratartrate crystal; the right-handed crystals rotated the plane of polarized light to the right and the left-handed crystals rotated it to the left, opposite lying with opposite. The results were mirror-image entities; the argument depended on antithesis.

Pasteur is justly famous for his experimental skills, but his considerable rhetorical skills have also been commented on recently by historians and sociologists of science (Latour 1988; Geison 1995). During his years of traditional French schooling at the College d'Arbois and the College Royal de Basançon from 1830 to 1842, Pasteur received the standard rhetorically intense training, and it is even likely that he used Fontanier's texts on the tropes and "other figures" that had been adopted in the colleges at the time (Fontanier 1977, 5). He did, at any rate, certainly use figures as apt epitomes in his arguments, the antimetabole among them. In one memorable case, it does not, however, appear in a reversal argument but in a famous identity or dependence formulation.

In the 1850s and 1860s, Pasteur was engaged in controversies with the German chemist Justus von Liebig over whether fermentation was an organic or inorganic process and with the French chemist and biologist George Pouchet over whether microbes could arise in sterile media by spontaneous generation. In refuting Pouchet, Pasteur both pointed out the flaws in his supposedly sterile techniques and then performed striking experiments of his own, most notably placing sterile medium in flasks with long, curiously curved necks that allowed the entrance of air but not of the air-born dust that carried microbes and spores. In a speech given at the Sorbonne in April 1864, Pasteur pointedly summed up the conclusion of his experiments against Pouchet by describing what he had effectively removed from the sterile flasks in his experiment:

> c'est que j'ai éloigné d'elle, et que j'éloigne encore en ce moment, la seule chose qu'il n'ait pas été donné à l'homme de produire, j'ai éloigneé d'elle les germes qui flottent dans l'air, j'ai éloigné d'elle la vie, car la vie c'est le germe et le germe c'est la vie. Jamais la doctrine de la génération spontanée ne se relèvera du coup mortel que cette simple expérience lui porte.

> what I have removed from it, and what I remove still at this moment, the single thing which it has not been given to humans to produce, I have removed from it the germs

which float in the air, I have removed from it life, for life is the germ and the germ
is life. Never will the doctrine of spontaneous generation recover from such as mortal
blow as this experiment delivers. (Pasteur 1922, II, 342) (also notable in this passage is the repetition of forms of the verb "to remove")

Pasteur's striking antimetabole here is more than a convenient phrase for the moment. It not only epitomizes his line of reasoning in his case against spontaneous
generation, it epitomizes the central dogma of his entire scientific career. From his
earliest studies on molecular asymmetry (or rather the symmetry of right- and left-
hand forms), Pasteur came to believe that only "naturally occurring" organic forms
could give rise to optically active compounds. Given that the soup of all fermentations was filled with compounds capable of rotating polarized light, he argued against
Liebig that the process of fermentation must therefore be carried on by living organisms. So not only was spontaneous generation impossible but fermentation could
never occur without the introduction of a living form. And given the similarity between the processes of fermentation and disease, it also seemed reasonable to agree
with the developing nineteenth-century consensus that microbial life was the origin
of disease (see Geison 1995, 96, 138). There was then, in Pasteur's thinking, a deep
association between living forms and their unique processes and products. When he
stressed this point in a summative lecture delivered in 1883, the antimetabole fundamental to his thinking was worth emphatic repetition.

> La ligne de démarcation dont nous parlons [entre le règne minéral et le règne
> organique] n'est pas une question de chimie pure et d'obtention de produits tels
> ou tels, c'est une question de forces; la vie est dominée par des actions dissymétriques
> dont nous pressentons l'existence enveloppante et cosmique. Je pressens même que
> toutes les espèces vivantes sont primordialement, dans leur structure, dans leurs
> formes extérieures, des fonctions de la dissymétrie cosmique. La vie, c'est le germe
> et le germe, c'est la vie

> The line of demarcation of which we have spoken (between the mineral [inorganic]
> kingdom and the organic kingdom) is not a question of pure chemistry and the
> obtaining of such and such products, it is a question of forces; life is dominated by
> unsymmetrical/asymmetrical processes which give us a presentiment of an envel-
> oping, cosmic existence. I even have a presentiment that all living species are pri-
> mordially, in their structures, in their exterior forms, the functions of a cosmic
> assymtery. Life is the germ and the germ is life. (Pasteur 1922, I, 377–378)

Certainly Pasteur uses the antimetabole as a "stylistic capper" here to epitomize his
line of reasoning. Since the figure displays an indifference to the order of subject and
complement, and by implication to which of two terms is the member and which
the genus, it expresses identity more accurately than the single predication, "Le germe,
c'est la vie," could. Furthermore, the antimetabole allows Pasteur a certain useful
ambiguity in the implications of his argument. For the "germe," the microorganism, is not only the irreducible principle of life, always present if life is present, but it
is also the cause of life and of all its processes and products. Such causal arguments
can also be epitomized by the antimetabole, and thus the figure allows a certain slippage from definition to causal argument or from causal argument to definition.

The Antimetabole and Causality

The line of reasoning that Aristotle illustrates with an antimetabole, the 18th of the 28 general topics listed in the *Rhetoric*, concerns reversing a "before" and "after." Try, he advises, "not always choosing the same thing before and after" (Kennedy 1991, 199–200). To say that an "after" is potentially or also a "before" is to change the implied chronological, procedural, or causal relationship between them, leading to another set of arguments that can be epitomized by the antimetabole. When the figure is used to express a causal claim, the second half of the antimetabole reverses the direction of the relationship expressed in the first half. In John F. Kennedy's famous line for example, "country" and "you" change the roles of agent and recipient: "Ask not what your country [agent] can do for you [recipient]; ask what you [agent] can do for your country [recipient]." Consistency of terms in the two cola and their traceable displacement or reordering from one colon to the other creates either an inflectional or syntactic icon, or both, for the intended reversal of conceptual roles.

Antimetaboles can express not only causal reversals but, providing that one of the cola does not have a negative (a special case discussed below), an even stronger causal interdependence, a sense that two entities always require each other and therefore cannot be separated. Kenneth Burke uses an antimetabole to express such strong interdependence without, however, a suggestion of cyclic patterning in: "you cannot have ideas without persons or persons without ideas" (Burke 1969a, 512). This is not a statement of identity, nor is it a statement of a causal relationship. It is somewhere in between. And the same sense of mutual dependence is intended in the two uses of the figure that open and close a back page editorial in the *The Chronicle of Higher Education*: "Television and college athletics. College athletics and television. They have become inseparable" and "Television needs college athletics every bit as much as college athletics needs television." In these examples, the antimetabole expresses an interchangeability that suggests not identity but mutual constitution. Since one term so depends on the other, it does not matter which comes first, an indifference displayed iconically in the syntax of the figure.

Reciprocal causality: "If you press a stone with your finger"

Typically, the antimetabole epitomizes arguments concerning reciprocal causality, a causal influence that goes in opposite directions, or a reversible process. It is not surprising that Heraclitus' philosophy of eternal flux in nature can be expressed in this form: "Cool things become warm, and the warm grows cool" or "The moist dries and the parched becomes moist." The simplest model of such a relationship has a single cause and a single effect: A causes B, B causes A. Given the necessary connection between the verbal form of this argument and its substance, it might be possible to hazard a prediction on the basis of figural logic. Given an argument whose outcome is some model of reciprocal causality, is it likely (even highly likely) that an antimetabole will be featured in that argument?

Reciprocal causality is enshrined in the heart of mechanics as Newton's Third Law of Motion.

> To every action there is always opposed an equal reaction:
> or, the mutual actions of two bodies upon each other are always
> equal, and directed to contrary parts.

Newton did not express his law in an antimetabole. If anything, the figure polyptoton has more to do with the wording of the first formulation, given the wonderfully matched cognates "action" and "reaction."[13] The second part of the statement, however, does vaguely recall the figure with its description of two equal bodies, or parts, directed contrary to each other. Newton does more, however, than merely state his laws of motion in the first book of the *Principia*, which otherwise imitates Euclid's *Elements*. He also argues for them briefly through clarifying restatements and examples, and it is here, finally, that the predicted antimetabole appears:

> Whatever draws or presses another is as much drawn or pressed by that other. *If you press a stone with your finger, the finger is also pressed by the stone.* [Si quis lapidem digito premit, premitur et hujus digitus a lapide.] If a horse draws a stone tied to a rope, the horse (if I may say so) will be equally drawn back to the stone; for the distended rope, by the same endeavor to relax or unbend itself, will *draw the horse as much towards the stone as it does the stone towards the horse* [urgebit equum versus lapidem, ac lapidem versus equum], and will obstruct the progress of the one as much as it advances that of the other. (Newton 1822, 16; 1952, 14; italics added)

Newton's first antimetabole of finger and stone pairs the active and passive voices of the verb "press" (premit/premitur) in the two cola of the antimetabole. Ideally, he should have used the active voice on both sides for a better epitome of the reciprocal, or simultaneous, causality expressed in the Third Law: the finger presses the stone and the stone presses the finger. After all, the active and passive can be paired without the inversion of the antimetabole as in Newton's second illustration where the "horse draws" and is "equally drawn" in parallel cola. However, the second time Newton gives this same illustration, he does frame it in the form that once again perfectly epitomizes the Third Law: "will draw the horse as much towards the stone as it does the stone towards the horse." Much more could be said about Newton's rhetorical choices in this brief argument, especially about the choice of "stone" in both examples, a presumptively immovable object that is nevertheless animated to press back at a human finger, or the addition of a third agent in each illustration, "you" and the "rope." But the verbal formula does appear where expected and it reappears frequently whenever the Third Law is explained.[14]

Historians of science have nominated Newton's Third Law as the source of his insight into universal gravitation (Newton 1952, 111). In his original mathematical demonstration of Kepler's laws of planetary motion, he had imagined that a planet travels around a sun fixed at one focus of the planet's elliptical orbit. This ideal model fit the available astronomical data only approximately. Newton eventually realized, in keeping with the Third Law, that the antimetabole must hold in the heavens as well, and that if the sun attracts Earth, then Earth must also attract the sun. Indeed, the actual problem in the solar system is more complicated, because all of the bodies attract each other proportional to their mass and inversely proportional to their distance, but mathematically Newton could only solve the two-body problem figured in the antimetabole.

Newton had a conventional, and therefore very thorough, seventeenth-century education in rhetoric, both at Cambridge and before (see chapter 3). He would have been familiar with all the verbal formulas represented in the figures. But the antimetabole may not only iconically express key insights in his physics; it may also come closest to epitomizing his overall philosophy of science as well. In the preface to the first edition of the *Principia Mathematica*, written in 1686, Newton introduces readers to the method and achievement of the work. After explaining the importance of rational mechanics defined antimetabolically as "the science of motions resulting from any forces whatsoever, and of the forces required to produce any motions [scientia motuum, qui ex viribus quibuscunque resultant, et virium quae ad motus quoscunque requiruntur]," Newton then writes of his own somewhat different agenda, proposing a philosophy not of manual but of natural powers such as gravity, levity, elasticity, and resistance in fluids:

> and therefore I offer this work as the mathematical principles of philosophy, for the whole burden of philosophy seems to consist in this—from the phenomena of motions to investigate the forces of nature, and then from these forces to demonstrate other phenomena [a phaenomenis motuum investigemus vires naturae, deinde ab his viribus demonstremus phaenomena reliqua]. (Newton 1952, 1; 1822, xi)

The method epitomized in this antimetabole establishes the structure of the individual books of the *Principia*, including the third on the "System of the World" (which for a long time he did not want to include):

> for by the propositions mathematically demonstrated in the former books in the third I derive from the celestial phenomena the forces of gravity with which bodies tend to the sun and the several planets. Then from these forces, by other propositions which are also mathematical, I deduce the motions of the planets, the comets, the moon, and the sea.

> Ibi enim, ex phaenomenis coelestibus, per propositiones in libris prioribus mathematicè demonstratas, derivantur vires gravitatis, quibis corpora ad sole et planetas singulos tendunt. Deinde exhis viribus per propositiones etiam mathematicas, deducuntur motus planetarum, cometarum, lunae et maris." (Newton 1952, 1–2; 1822, xi)

Thus, within a short passage of the first preface, Newton uses three antimetaboles to express the same point about his method of examining phenomena to deduce forces and using the forces for examining further phenomena. Admittedly, the phenomena that enter this process are only generally but not precisely the same as the phenomena that are explained by it in the end. In this respect, Newton's antimetaboles anticipate that variant on this line of reasoning known as the cascade, where successive iterations of a reciprocal process produce amplified or slightly different outcomes.[15] Nevertheless, it is interesting to note how one verbal formula dominates Newton's conceptualizing in this critical passage of his most important work.

Faraday's and Henry's reversals

The figural logic of reciprocal causality has had perhaps its greatest success in electrodynamics. The early nineteenth century, like the early eighteenth, was a time of intense experimentation on electrical phenomena, especially on the relationship between magnetism and electricity, and perhaps no name is more closely associated with these investigations than Michael Faraday. Fortunately for those interested in the process of scientific research, from its inception to its persuasive demonstration, Faraday kept an extensive diary of his experimental trials and musings. These diary entries led very directly, sometimes within a few weeks, to his publications in the *Quarterly Journal of Science* or the *Philosophical Transactions*. His articles in these journals were, in turn, edited for multivolumed collections of his writings that appeared during his lifetime. Thus it is possible to trace the same ideas through several textual incarnations intended for different audiences.

As a laboratory assistant at the Royal Institution in London in the 1820s, Faraday was asked by an editor to write a review of recent discoveries in the relationship between electricity and magnetism (Holton and Brush 1985, 417). He began to investigate these relationships, first established by Oersted, Ampère, and his mentor, Sir Humphrey Davy, on his own. In particular, Faraday examined the movements of a freely suspended magnetized needle brought near a vertically fixed wire conducting a current. The magnetized needle seemed to be attracted or repulsed in the vicinity of the wire according to where it was held. Faraday could have interpreted these movements as linear displacements, and indeed he first represented the phenomena to himself that way. Faraday knew, however, that the pattern of magnetic attraction around a conducting wire could also be illustrated as a circular force "field." Davy had established that pattern by fixing a disc like a collar around a current-carrying wire and sprinkling iron filings on it; the filings arranged themselves in a circular pattern (Gooding 1985, 114). Faraday's entries in his *Diary* for September 3, his usual mixture of diagram and commentary, show how he eventually used antimetabole to reconcile possible interpretations of the effects he observed (see Figure 4.2).

Signs of a conceptual breakthrough appear in the illustration accompanying entry 5 where Faraday, after changing the point of view in entry 4 by imagining himself looking down the wire at the positions of the needles, now visualizes his experiment as though it is the wire moving around a stationary needle and not the needle moving around a stationary wire. He therefore depicts the wire in multiple cross sections rather than the needle. The resulting mirror image reversal in the diagram under 5 is enhanced in the illustration accompanying entry 6. The alternating positions of A and R, positions where the wire would be attracted to or repulsed by the needle, are connected with reversed circles at the poles, constituting a visual antimetabole. This visual antimetabole is then followed by a perfectly expressed verbal one: "Hence the wire moves in opposite circles round each pole and/or the poles move in opposite circles round the wire."

According to Faraday scholar David Gooding, when Faraday wrote this figured claim, it was half established observation and half a prediction he had yet to observe (Gooding 1985, 118). Why he would have conceptualized the movement of the displaced needle as circular seems easily understood on the basis of previous discover-

2. Positions at first ascertained were as follows

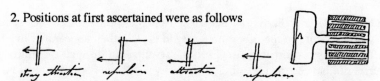

3. On examining these more minutely found that each pole had 4 positions,

2 of attraction and 2 of repulsion, thus

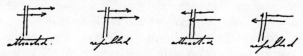

4. Or looking from above down on to sections of the wire

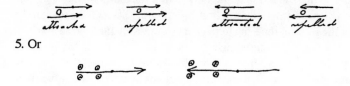

5. Or

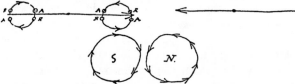

6. These indicate motions in circles round each pole, this

Hence the wire moves in opposite circles round each pole and/or

the poles move in opposite circles round the wire.

Figure 4.2. Visual and verbal antimetaboles. From Michael Faraday, *Faraday's Diary: Being the Various Philosophical Notes of Experimental Investigation Made by Michael Faraday during the Years 1820–1862*, vol. 1, ed. Thomas Martin (London: G. Bell & Sons, 1932). Reproduced with permission of HarperCollins.

ies he knew about, but why he would have reconceived the circular movement of the needle around the wire as the movement of the wire around the needle seems an inexplicable leap of genius, the kind of insight usually explained by the inspiration of a metaphor. Gooding also suggests pragmatically that, "This transformation— imagining that it is the *wire* which describes the circle instead of the needle" probably solved the problem of reducing a sequence of positions into a single spatial arrangement and three dimensions into two (118). However, Faraday's recourse to the figural logic of the antimetabole, forming the prediction from the observation by allowing the first colon to write the second, is another possible explanation.

Is it plausible to suggest that Faraday would have been familiar enough with a presumably arcane rhetorical device to have had it ready as a stimulus to invention? Figures of speech like the antimetabole are actually common enough in usage so that no exposure to rhetoric is necessary to explain their appearance in a passage. Nevertheless, most scientists from the seventeenth through the nineteenth centuries did have formal training in rhetoric, but Faraday is an exception. He taught himself the arts and skills he needed to know through assiduous self-discipline. But a source of Faraday's familiarity with structures like the antithesis and the antimetabole can readily be found through his life-long affiliation with the Sandemanians, an austere sect of Protestants who followed the teachings of the eighteenth-century Scottish reformers John Glas and Robert Sandeman. The Sandemanians were "people of the Book," intense students of the Bible who sought to live in pure conformity with scriptural truths (Cantor 1985, 70). Without a clergy, the Sandemanians expected their members to engage in constant scrutiny of the Scriptures on their own. Faraday publicly joined the Sandemanians in 1821, the year in which he performed the rotation experiments described above. In his life-long study of the Bible in the King James version (Cantor 1985, 80), Faraday would have encountered and pondered many antithetical and chiastic or antimetabolic passages, especially in the sayings of Jesus. It is likely, therefore, that Faraday had a deeper appreciation of the figures from his intense study of the Bible than even those who had had the standard exposure provided in a formal education.

Once Faraday had conceptualized the potential reversal of effects, the possibility that the wire could rotate around the magnet in addition to the already observed rotation of the magnetized needle around the wire, his challenge was to achieve this reversed effect physically. He first succeeded by shaping part of a conducting wire into a "C", which allowed it to rotate from one side to the other over a magnetic pole. He found that if he quickly removed the magnet before the wire hit it and inserted it the other way, the C-shaped wire would continue its revolution.

When Faraday wrote up this insight for an article published just a few weeks after his diary entries, he retained the antimetabole at several points, but also departed from the perfect pattern: "the true pole, as it may be called, is not at the extremity of the needle, but may be represented by a point generally in the axis of the needle, at some little distance from the end. It was evident, also, that this point had a tendency to revolve round the wire, and necessarily, therefore, the wire round the point" (Faraday 1952, 797). When, two paragraphs later, Faraday offers experimental evidence for this observation, he summarizes without the figure in language that unifies the paired phenomena but also draws attention to the mutuality epitomized by the figure: "The revolution of the wire and the pole round each other being the first important thing required to prove the nature of the force mutually exerted by them" (797). The further description of his procedures for giving physical reality to his notions does use the antimetabole, but the first half of the figure, "the wire immediately began to revolve round the pole of the magnet," is separated by several paragraphs from the perfectly parallel second half "the upper pole immediately began to revolve around the wire" (798). Each half serves as a "stylistic capper" or conclusion sitting on top of supporting detail, but the pattern is less noticeable when the two halves are separated in the developed argument. Without the evidence from Faraday's notebook, where the antimetabole exists in forceful isolation, it is easy to miss its conceptual importance as the epitome of his reasoning.

Faraday's appointment at the Royal Institution required that he not only pursue his research but that he also periodically lecture and demonstrate his findings. He was extremely successful on these occasions for public scientific persuasion, especially when it came to inventing physical evidence for his arguments. To demonstrate his discovery of "electromagnetic rotations," Faraday designed an apparatus that is an amazing physical instantiation of the verbal figure. Constructed by a skilled instrument maker to Faraday's instructions, it allows the two opposed rotary motions, like the two cola of the antimetabole, to be presented simultaneously. On one side a pivoted magnet moves freely around a fixed wire, and on the other side a pivoted wire moves freely about a fixed magnet. On both sides, fluid mercury conducts the charge. The engraving of this apparatus that then appeared in the *Quarterly Journal of Science* and later reprints (see Figure 4.3) amounts to a visual representation of the figure, the relative positions of magnet and stiff wire, stiff wire and magnet, read from left to right, expressing the figural logic of the antimetabole. Even the angular displacements of first the bar magnet and then the wire reflect in a way the grammatical alterations that are often required in a verbal antimetabole to allow the two key terms to switch places.

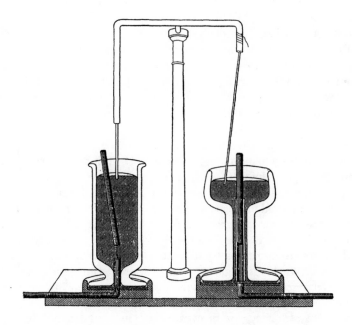

Figure 4.3. Faraday's visual antimetabole. From Michael Faraday, "Electro-magnetic Rotation Apparatus," *The Quarterly Journal of Science*, 12 (January 1822).

Ten years later, Faraday used the same figural logic in a discovery of much greater importance, the discovery that makes possible the generation of all commercial electricity in use today. Once researchers knew that an electric current generated a magnetic field, the search was on to discover if this process were reversible, if a magnetic field could generate an electric current. In the early nineteenth-century experimenters knew that they could create magnets by wrapping a current carrying wire around an iron bar. It was Michael Faraday who in 1831 first demonstrated that it was also possible to use a magnet to induce a current in an electric coil.

Faraday began his quest for this effect with every expectation of finding it since "every electric current was accompanied by a corresponding intensity of magnetic action at right angles to the current" (265). Nevertheless, in addition to this a priori hunch in the symmetry of reciprocal effects, there was also a sequential and material logic leading up to Faraday's discovery, at least as he recounts it in a paper read before the Royal Society in November 1831. Faraday had been experimenting with induction by wrapping helices of wire around wooden cylinders in layers insulated from each other. One helix was connected to a galvanometer, the other to a voltaic battery. Faraday discovered that when the battery connection was either first made or broken, the galvanometer linked to the interwoven nonconducting helix of wire nevertheless registered a charge in opposite directions. While the contact continued, the needle of the galvanometer registered no current. Predictably, Faraday epitomized these findings in an antithesis: "that the slight deflection of the needle occurring at the moment of completing the connexion, was always in one direction, and that the equally slight deflection produced when the contact was broken, was in the other direction" (Faraday 1952, 266).

Next Faraday wrapped two independent helices of wire around an iron ring, one helix again connected to a galvanometer and the other to a source of current. Once more he found that starting or stopping the current on one side induced a current in the other side, though this time "to a degree far beyond what has been described when . . . helices without iron were used" (Faraday 1952, 269). To test the effect of an iron core, Faraday first constructed helices of wire around a hollow cylinder of pasteboard. The effects on the galvanometer were barely noticeable until he inserted an iron bar into the pasteboard tube: "then the induced current affected the galvanometer powerfully" (270). The next step was to remove the external source of current. Faraday brought the opposite poles of bar magnets into contact with the iron bar inserted in a helix of wire attached to a galvanometer. In other words, he momentarily magnetized the iron bar. When he either established or broke contact with these two external magnets, opposite currents registered. Finally, in the *experimentum crucis*, Faraday replaced the iron cylinder with a cylindrical bar magnet. When this magnet was abruptly inserted into or withdrawn from a coil of wire, momentary opposite currents were generated (270). Faraday next received permission to use a much more powerful "horseshoe" magnet that belonged to the Royal Society, and he eventually found that merely inserting and removing a helix or even a single wire between the poles of this powerful magnet was enough to induce a current (271–272). He concluded that his experiments "prove, I think, most completely the production of electricity from ordinary magnetism" (272).

Faraday did not use an antimetabole to epitomize his results as the reversal of the already known ability of an electric current to produce a magnetic field. Instead, he put the logic of his reversal into an act of naming. When he had written ten years earlier on his discovery of the reciprocal rotations of a bar magnet and a current-carrying wire, he had used the then-established term for producing magnetism from electricity in his title; "Electro-Magnetical Motions" (Faraday 1952, 795). Now in 1831, Faraday, who was always scrupulous with nomenclature, coined a new term for the new phenomenon: "I propose to call the agency thus exerted by ordinary magnets, magneto-electric or magnelectric induction" (273). Thus the antimetabolic terms in Faraday's usage, electro-magnetic and magneto-electric, aptly express the reciprocal power of magnetism or electricity to induce one another.

Several months before Faraday's discovery of magneto-electric induction, an American, Joseph Henry, had produced the same results. In his summers, free from heavy teaching responsibilities at the Albany Academy, Henry had experimented with electro-magnets, creating monstrous iron horseshoes wound with coils of insulated wire that could lift hundreds of pounds (Wilson 1954, 64). Anticipating the experimental design that Faraday used with the Royal Society's strong magnet, Henry placed an iron bar wrapped with wire and connected to a galvanometer across the face of his horseshoe electro-magnet. When his assistant sent a charge through the electro magnet, Henry observed a charge recorded on a galvanometer at the moment of closing and then breaking the circuit (Henry 1886, I, 75). Henry postponed writing up his results, only to learn early in the following year from a short notice in the Library of Useful Knowledge (Henry 1886, I, 73; Wilson 1982, 65), that Faraday had already reached the goal.[16] Henry was, nevertheless, encouraged by Benjamin Silliman of Yale to write up his results for the *American Journal of Science*, which published his version of the experiment in July 1832.

There is a significant difference in Henry's experimental design, leading in turn to a significant difference in his manner of characterizing his discoveries. Faraday used permanent magnets and achieved his best results when he used the largest of these then available to him, a large compound magnet built up of bar magnets and kept in a basement in Greenwich. But Henry, following the previous path of his work, used large electro-magnets of his own devising. As a result, his entire apparatus in itself depicted the reciprocal causal relationship between magnetism and electricity, as Henry thoroughly understood. He also understood how to express that relationship figurally.[17]

> This experiment illustrates most strikingly the reciprocal action of the two principles of electricity and magnetism, if indeed it does not establish their absolute identity. In the first place, magnetism is developed in the soft iron of the galvanic magnet by the action of the currents of electricity from the battery, and secondly the armature, rendered magnetic by contact with the poles of the magnet, induces in its turn currents of electricity in the helix which surrounds it; we have thus as it were electricity converted into magnetism and this magnetism again into electricity. (Henry 1886, I, 76)

The antimetabole that closes this passage also expresses the interesting possibility that opens it, the possibility that the reciprocal relationship between magnetism and electricity indicates an underlying identity. Here again, the two possible readings of the antimetabole invite this slippage, from cause to constitution, and the next 30 years of research brought this possibility to fruition. In the 1860s, James Clerk Maxwell established the dynamic connection between electricity and magnetism as components of a propagating wave of "electromagnetic" radiation, inseparable physically and semantically. Their connection can, in fact, be understood and described as a perpetuating series of antimetaboles, one overlapping or initiating another: A changing electric field induces a magnetic field and this magnetic field in turn induces an electric field, which then goes on, participating in another antimetabolic relationship to induce a magnetic field initiating an electric field, and so on, in an inevitable reciprocal constitution that unifies electric and magnetic phenomena.

The last word on the reciprocal induction of magnetism from electricity or electricity from magnetism has yet to be written. In February 1996, scientists on the Space Shuttle released a satellite on a 12-mile tether hoping to generate electricity by dragging it through Earth's magnetic field. Before the tether snapped, the copper wire, wrapped in nylon and teflon and moving in Earth's magnetic field like a giant amplification of Faraday's original experiment with wire and the poles of a horseshoe magnet, generated 3500 Volts of electrical power for the Shuttle.

Refutation by Reversal

As they are actually found in use, many antimetaboles contain a negative in one of the two cola so that the overall pattern is "Not A . . . B but B . . . A" or sometimes "A . . . B, Not B . . . A." These are a special class of "corrective" or "refutative" antimetaboles. An arguer typically uses the first half of the figure for an assumed but mistaken relationship, one perhaps held by the audience addressed or by some misguided group. The second colon reveals that, surprisingly, this widely held belief is incorrect and the reverse is the case. The antimetaboles discussed so far, which express identity or mutual constitution or causal reciprocity, are obviously not corrective. To do its work of refutation by reversal, one half of a corrective antimetabole must be negative and the other half positive; these are the antimetaboles that Quintilian categorized as a type of antithesis (see above p. 129). St. Paul uses this form for its corrective effect when he promises to visit the church at Corinth, but not to be a burden to them, "for children ought not to lay up for their parents, but parents for their children (2 Cor. 12: 14–15; other antimetaboles follow).

Only refutative or corrective antimetaboles are enthymemes, paired statements that function as claim and support for each other. Following the 18th of Aristotle's 28 common topics in the *Rhetoric*, an arguer searching for premises in causal arguments can try switching a "before and after" to see what happens. The first colon, with the denial, can be taken as the conclusion—A does not cause B—because of the second colon, the premise—B causes A. Or the first of the pair, as a denial, can be taken as the premise and the second as the conclusion. "Since A does not cause B, B causes A." Such pairs can function as enthymemes only if the warrant or missing premise that links the two cola is a belief that of these two entities and the two alone,

one must be the cause or the effect of the other. In expanded form, the overall reasoning follows one of these two formulas: Either A causes B or B causes A; A does not cause B, therefore B causes A; Either A causes B or B causes A; A does not cause B because B causes A. Both these forms rely on the same warrant or major premise, but rhetorically, it is usually more effective for an arguer to use the first colon for the prevailing belief that is presumably wrong and therefore has to be replaced with the correct belief.

It is doubtful, however, that the corrective causal antimetabole functions with audiences primarily as a logical device inviting the reconstruction of a missing premise about the exclusive interdependence of A and B. Here, instead, is another instance of the difference between a formal logic of entailments and a figural logic of pattern completion or satisfaction. Instead of relying on preexisting assumptions, the form of the antimetabole itself, its tightness and tidiness, encourages the simultaneous construction of a belief in the dependence of the two terms. It need not invoke an existing belief; it can bring the so-called missing warrant into existence and thus effectively "beg the question." It appeals to perceptions of symmetry, to an appreciation of the possibility of inversion.

Correcting set relationships

The corrective or refutative antimetaboles cited so far involve causality. When refutative antimetaboles concern claims about definition, they are used to show that expectations or assumptions about set inclusion, about what belongs in what category, are misleading or mistaken. These constructions typically take the form "A . . . B, Not B . . . A." Unlike corrections involving causal relations, here the negation is typically reserved for the second colon. Aristotle is fond of these clarifying antimetaboles in statements like "Now a thesis also is a problem, though a problem is not always a thesis" (*Topics*, 174). St. Augustine provides another example in his aphoristic sorting out of the relations among things and signs cited above: "Thus every sign is also a thing . . . but not every thing is also a sign" (St. Augustine 1986 9). In other words, the set of things contains the set of signs but is not identical with it. A familiar-sounding phrase like the following—"All pro-lifers are conservative, but not all conservatives are pro-lifers"—intends the same adjustment in the audience's understanding of which of two terms is the containing set or genus and which the subset or species. Thus, the corrective antimetabole that concerns definition restores the appropriate hyponymic relationship between two terms when they might otherwise be understood in the opposite way or might even be confused as synonyms: "All stories are narratives, but not all narratives are stories."

Unlike the causal correctives, antimetaboles that invert set relations do not seem to function as enthymemes. To work as premise/conclusion pairs, definitional antimetaboles require, as Aristotle specifies (see above) in the *Topics*, a careful placing of two contradictory terms in the second colon: "A . . . B because Not B . . . Not A." The difference is illustrated in the following pair: "All humans are animals but not all animals are humans" and "All humans are animals because all not-animals are not-humans." The first is not an enthymeme, the second is. There is no point reconstructing a missing warrant for the first like "Either all humans are animals or all animals are humans" for the corrective antimetabole. Both sides work more like independent claims that do not necessarily support each other directly. They are only bracketed momentarily by virtue of their appearance together in the figure. Thus, the balance of the antimetabole seems almost misleading in the case of these corrected set relations, for rather than reversing a relationship symmetrically, one member of the pair is diminished and the other enhanced, a lopsided result. Thus, why the antimetabole, a form suggesting completeness and balance, serves so well as an epitome of correcting set relations, remains something of a mystery.

Lamarck's corrective inversion

The cases of scientific arguments epitomized by antimetaboles that have been cited so far in this chapter are all famous and successful ones. But there is no necessary connection between the outcome of a line of scientific investigation and the figural strategy that stimulates or epitomizes it. Following a line of figural logic may just as readily lead to fruitless concepts and experimental failure. So an illustration of this final corrective use of the antimetabole will be a spectacular if useful misconception: Lamarck's theory of evolution by the inheritance of acquired characteristics. As a systematist of invertebrates at the Museum of Natural History in Paris, Lamarck adopted the view typical of his time that living forms could be ordered in a hierarchy of increasing complexity; the informing figural logic here is based on the incrementum. Curiously however, unlike many of his contemporaries, Lamarck tended to "read" these series of increasingly complex forms in reverse, from perfection to degradation. He was also struck by the irregularities and discontinuities in what, he firmly believed, should be a smooth continuum of forms. He believed that life would proceed toward an unvarying and gradual perfection but for the intervention of causes working against this vital force.[18] Eventually, he traced these alterations and offshoots to an organism's changing environment, reasoning that alterations in an organism's environment produced certain demands on it, and these demands in turn affected the organism's habits. Changed habits, in turn, led to the use or disuse of certain organs or parts of the body, and these somatic changes could be passed on to the next generation if both parents shared them. The figural logic in this part of his argument is based on the gradatio. But Lamarck's main argument about the direction of these diversionary changes that interfere with the trajectory of increasing complexity, is, as detailed in chapter 7 of the first volume of his *Philosophie Zoologique*, based on the antimetabole.

Lamarck uses the antimetabole no less than five times in this critical chapter. In its first use, occurring in the second paragraph, the form corrects a maxim, the traditional form for a widely held belief, with an inversion:

> A la vérité, depuis assez long-temps on a remarqué l'influence des différens états de *notre organisation* sur notre caractére, nos penchans, *nos actions*, et même nos idées; mais il me semble que personne encore n'a fait connoître celle de *nos actions* et de nos habitudes sur *notre organisation* même.
>
> Truthfully, for a long time now one has noticed the influence of different states of our organization on our character, our thoughts, our actions and even our ideas;

but it seems to me no one has recognized that of our actions and habits on our organization itself. (Lamarck 1960, I, 218; emphasis added)[19]

This is a "relaxed" antimetabole; Lamarck has not gone to great pains to use parallel structure or to preserve the same words on either side of the midpoint of the figure, though his argumentative strategy is still clear in the reversed positions of "actions" and "organization." The same corrective reversal is made again in terms of an example from the constitution and behavior of a sloth, an animal believed at the time to be so weak and slow as to be incapable of moving more than 50 steps a day. Again, the first half gives the mistaken belief and the second half the correct view.

> De là, supposant que cet animal avoit reçu de la nature l'organisation qu'on lui connoît, on a dit que cette organisation le forçoit à ses habitudes et à l'état misérable où il se trouve. . . .
> Je suis bien éloigné de penser ainsi; car je suis convaincu ques les habitudes que les individus de la race de l'aï ont été forcés de contracter originairement, ont dû nécessairement amener leur organisation à son état actuel.

> Suppose that this animal had received from nature the organization by which one knows it, one would say that this organization forced on it the habits and the miserable state in which it is found. . . .
> I am far from thinking so, for I am convinced that the habits that the individuals of a race have, they have been forced to contract orginally, have of necessity led to the organization of their present state. (Lamarck 1960, I, 263)

Finally, having opened chapter 7 with a corrective antimetabole, Lamarck concludes the chapter with his central claim, expressed this final time in the best approximation of the perfect figure.

> Tout concourt donc à prouver mon assertion; savoir: que ce n'est point la forme, soit du corps, soit de ses parties, qui donne lieu aux habitudes et à la manière de vivre des animaux; mais que se sont, au contraire, les habitudes, la manière de vivre, et toutes les autres circonstances influentes qui ont, avec les temps, constitué la forme du corps et des parties des animaux.

> Simply to prove my assertion; know: that it is not the form, or the body, or its parts which give rise to the animals' habits and manner of living; but it is, on the contrary, the habits, the manner of living, and the other influential circumstances which have, with time, constituted the form of the body and the parts of the animals. (Lamarck 1960, I, 268)

The correction or replacement of one view by another, need not, of course, take the form of an antimetabole, even when the new and better view being promoted is the inversion of the previous incorrect one. But such an argument is obviously helped by an assumption that the two views in evidence in the argument, the wrong one and the better one, are really the only two views possible. The reduction to only one of two mirror-image possibilities, and hence the argumentative force of the case overall, is a byproduct of compression into the figure. In other words, a reversal argument is more believable, irrespective of its other support, because when it is expressed in an antimetabole, it satisfies some underlying symmetry condition. The figure locks in two possibilities and seems to say that the relationship must be between these two, so if it is not in one direction it must be in the other. The figure, as Burke would say, invites participation in this formal constraint, loading the case in favor of the arguer's choice of direction.

Lewontin's correction of Lamarck and Darwin

In the continuing cycle of position-forming and reforming in arguments about organisms and the environment, Lamarck himself and the major schools of biological thinking in the nineteenth century have been the subject of a twentieth-century antimetabolic reversal by the population geneticist Richard Lewontin. In "Genes, Environment, and Organisms," Lewontin seeks to correct what he believes is a persistent misunderstanding of the relationship between the environment and organisms. German embryologists of the nineteenth century favored a view of the organism as the product of invariable stages of development, unrolling themselves according to a programmed sequence, isolated from outside forces other than perhaps a triggering event. Lewontin refutes this position as an extreme by pointing out evidence of genetically identical organisms developing in very different ways according to environmental factors. He favors a view in which the history of an organism counts, "in which influences outside the structures themselves play an important role in determining their function" (Lewontin 1995, 119–120). This may sound superficially like Lamarckism, but it is not.

Erring to some extent in the opposite way, Darwin-inspired evolutionists also divorced the inside and outside, regarding the environment as a set of pre-existing conditions to which the organism, by the chance appearance of favorable somatic or behavioral changes, adapts. But where does this environment come from? Lewontin points out that the oxygen in the atmosphere is the product of organisms, the soil surrounding roots is the product of their biochemical action, and white pines create a forest too dark for their own seedlings. Lewontin makes the case then that the "environment" does not exist independently of an organism but is in fact a construction of it.

> Lamarck was wrong to believe that organisms could incorporate the outer world into their heredity, Darwin was wrong in asserting the autonomy of the external world. The environment of an organism is not an independent, preexistent set of problems to which organisms must find solutions, for organisms not only solve problems, they create them in the first place. Just as there is no organism without an environment, there is no environment without an organism." (Lewontin 1995, 131)

The antimetabole that expresses reciprocal constitution by negating both sides is the best possible epitome of Lewontin's synthesizing revision of the nature/nurture debate: "Therefore," as he reiterates a few paragraphs later in the same form, "just as the information needed to specify an organism is not contained entirely in its genes, but also in its environment, so the environmental problems of the organism are a consequence of its genes" (132). Lewontin does express his central claim without the figure antimetabole: "The proper view of evolution is then of co-evolution of organisms and their environments, each change in an organism being both the cause and effect of changes in the environment" (137). Here he is assisted by another kind of figural logic, that of repetition, the subject of the next chapter. But the parallelism and reversal established by the antimetaboles add balance and a sense of completeness to his insight, making it seem harder than ever to break the organism/environment pair apart again and assert the dominance of one over the other.[20]

5

Ploche and Polyptoton

In a 1992 issue of *Science*, two aeronautical engineers explained a new approach in the manufacturing of advanced materials for aircraft engines, an approach known as intelligent processing of materials (IPM), which they defined as "an integrated, comprehensive effort to apply mathematical modeling, sensor technologies, and control system methods to improve materials processes." IPM, they claimed, applied the scientific method "to deduce process behavior and establish extensible theories governing process performance" (Backman and Williams 1992, 1086). As part of their explanation of how IPM works, they wrote the following paragraph:

> Materials process understanding is established early in the process development cycle by conducting statistically designed experiments and formulating physics-based models of the process. The derived knowledge is encoded in a process simulator. Process sensors are established to validate process models and to characterize the material product and process conditions for the designed experiments. The models and sensors serve as the foundation for subsequent process control development and act as the vehicle for technology transfer between the development and production environments. Process control can be applied at a variety of levels. Closed-loop control is used to counteract process disturbances that have short time constants, whereas supervisory and expert system control modules mimic the process corrections made by process operators and engineers. (1086–1087)

After taking this paragraph in, a reader should be convinced that there are some well formulated procedures in place for monitoring materials processing. The language of management and engineering combined in this sample is a well known if sometimes lamented linguistic register whose typical features include a high level of abstraction and a penchant for using noun clusters as prenoun modifiers (e.g., "materials process understanding"). There certainly appear to be no figures of speech in this passage, particularly none of those discussed so far, antithesis, incrementum, or antimetabole. Yet this passage is as highly figured as any example from Henry Peacham's sixteenth-century *Garden of Eloquence*. Anyone reading it with some attention to the writers' choices is likely to notice the frequent repetition of the word "process." It appears twelve times, and its closest competitors are fairly distant, "control" occurring four times and "development" three. It is, in fact, the insistent repetition of the word "process," primarily as an adjective and once as a noun, that epitomizes the arguers' point in this passage: That there is a specific kind of awareness and control being exercised throughout a manufacturing process by systems, equipment, and people especially dedicated to their task.

Figures of Repetition

Rhetoricians have always recognized the need for emphasizing key points and terms in an argument, and one device consistently praised in rhetorical manuals for achieving such emphasis is repetition. Quintilian recommended repetition as a hedge against wandering attention and idiosyncratic interpretation when he discussed the essentials of good style for the forensic orator before a judge who will

> have many other thoughts to distract him unless what we say is so clear that our words will thrust themselves into his mind even when he is not giving his attention, just as the sunlight forces itself upon the eyes. Therefore our aim must be not to put him in a position to understand our argument, but to force him to understand it. Consequently we shall frequently repeat anything which we think the judge has failed to take in as he should. (Quintilian 1921, III, 211)

The kind of repetition of key points that Quintilian talks of here can, of course, be accomplished by paraphrase, by saying the same thing again in different words. But another kind of repetition has an important place in the stylistic repertoire of classical rhetoric: not just the repetition of ideas but the repetition of the same words and phrases.[1] Speakers who repeat the same words seem to stay on the same subject and make a place for that subject in the imperfect memories of their listeners; writers who repeat do the same and in addition provide visual chains across a text. Listeners and readers who absorb repetition, consciously or unconsciously, are also likely to infer that repeated terms have significance. Why else would they be repeated?

In the Classical and Renaissance lore of the figures, repetitions were categorized according to where they appeared in consecutive phrases or clauses. From the *Ad Herennium* on, the following schemes distinguished the strategic places for repetition:

Anaphora:[2] Repetition of the openings of successive structures.
(e.g., No one was there in the beginning; no one saw how it was put together.)

Epistrophe: Repetition of the endings of successive structures.
(e.g., When my hand works, my brain works.)

Epanalepsis: Repetition of the opening of a structure at its ending.
(e.g., Time heals the sorrows inflicted by time.)

Anadiplosis: Repetition of the ending of one structure in the opening of the next. (e.g., Cinderella loved the Prince. The Prince ignored her.)

Symploche: Repetition of both the beginning and the ending in successive structures. (e.g., Time stays for no one. Time leaps for no one.)

Subjunctio: Immediate repetition of a word with nothing intervening. (e.g., The camel came up short, short by Bedouin standards.)

Obviously more ingenious patterns of repetition can be identified, but these are the dominant ones marked in rhetorical texts over the centuries. There is nothing to prevent these patterns extending over three of four adjacent syntactic units or skipping sentence constituents and occurring in a first and third or second and fifth, etc., though the manuals stress repetition in immediately adjacent units.

Repetition in the openings and closings of phrases and clauses, already positions of emphasis, creates patterns that can presumably be picked out or even registered only subliminally in the experience of a text. The importance of such patterns in aural texts is obvious; as a modern example, one thinks of the incantatory anaphora of Martin Luther King, Jr.'s "I have a dream" speech. Such structurally strategic repetition is a kind of aural glue. Listeners, and readers as crypto-listeners, are invited to detect the patterns superimposed by these repetitions, creating potential mini-schemes of organization across a text.

Perfect Repetition: Ploche

In addition to the basic schemes of strategic repetition cited above, Classical and Renaissance treatments of the figures also marked repetitions that do not occur in structurally significant slots. Perhaps in keeping with its protean character, versions of this formal feature of random repetition went by many names. The name preferred in this study is *ploche* (from the Greek πλοκή), referring to anything plaited or woven, a single word reappearing like a single strand in a braid or fabric. According to the first definition of this figure in the *Ad Herennium* (where its Latin name is *traductio*), the same word is "frequently reintroduced, not only without offense to good taste, but even so as to render the style more elegant, as follows: 'One who has nothing in life more desirable than life cannot cultivate a virtuous life'" ([Cicero] 1954, 279).[3]

Repetitions may occur in similar grammatical slots, the same word reappearing as an adjective within a sentence or across several. But these repetitions need not coincide with a syntactic pattern, like the opening and closing of a sentence. This lack of convergence with any other pattern makes ploche virtually disappear as a recognizable figure, and without a detectable pattern in the repetition, the signs of special authorial intention diminish. After all, it is normal practice for speakers and writers to repeat words occasionally. But the very invisibility of this figure makes it potentially more effective, and thus this least marked of the forms of repetition becomes, of all the figures discussed so far, an *experimentum crucis* in understanding the argumentative power of chosen forms of expression.

The figure of random repetition thrives in Renaissance manuals under a variety of aliases: *heratio, duplicatio, palilogia, diaphora* and *traductio,* as well as *ploche.* Some of these corollary figures concern repetition that is formal but not semantic; the same word is repeated orthographically, but the same exact meaning is not intended. In Susenbrotus, for example, ploche is a scheme "When the same word is repeated emphasizing by the repetition a particular aspect of its meaning" and Scaliger points out that "The meaning is inevitably altered on the second appearance of the word" (Sonnino 1968, 103). In Peacham, the device called *ploche* is very narrowly defined as one involving only proper names, but again with the stipulation that when repeated the name "signifieth another thing" (Peacham 1954, 44). As an example Peacham offers, "In that great victorie Caesar was Caesar, that is, a mercifull conquerer" (44), a use that also employs the trope *antonomasia,* in which a proper name becomes a term for a category or type of person (as in "Pol Pot was a Hitler"). These distinctions surely capture a valid insight about what sometimes happens when a term recurs. Readers may or may not understand the second appearance in the same way. From the perspective of logic and an insistence on univocal reference, a statement that repeats terms like "Caesar was Caesar," for example, is tautological nonsense. But no one would take this statement as meaningless when encountering it outside a logic text. To avoid the tautology, interpreters take the first instance of the term to mean one thing (the individual Caesar) and the second to mean another (in Peacham's version, the type, a "mercifull conquerer"). As *The New Rhetoric* puts it, "The formulation of an identity puts us on the track of an opposition" (Perelman and Olbrechts-Tyteca 1969, 217). Of course, the same strategy can be used even when the two terms are not proper names, as in "Boys will be boys," or in the alchemists naming of purified from impure sulphur as "the sulphur of sulphur" (Crosland 1962, 129). This repetition of ordinary terms in a way that exploits possible differences is identified by Quintilian as *antanaclasis,* "where the same word is used in two different meanings" (Quintilian 1921, III, 485) and by Peacham as *diaphora,* a figure that comes with the advice that "the word which is to be repeated, be a word of importance . . . and not every common word, for that were absurd: considering that many words may be repeated without change of signification" (Peacham 1954, 45).[4] In their careful distinctions among these figures, the rhetorical manuals are clearly marking intentional uses of the same word in different senses, but it is always possible for any repetition to be taken this way. Deconstructive readers obviously favor the unintended uses of antonomasia and antanaclasis in their pursuit of potential and presumably unconscious fissures in a text, and of course an interpreter need not wait for a word to be repeated but can find these potential double readings in a single occurrence.

But the argumentative intent of repetition may just as well be to keep the same signification from instance to instance as a common thread, maintaining consistency of concepts in consistency of terms, a notion inherent in the original Greek name for the figure, πλοκή, emphasizing braided interconnections, the tying together achieved by the repetition of something. When André Lwoff gave his exasperated definition, "A virus is a virus!" he did not mean the second instance of the term in a different sense; he intended a circular prediction to indicate an entity so unique it could not be defined (Eigen 1993, 43). Repetition of terms in the same sense is distinguished by Peacham, ever the most careful of catalogers, as *traductio*: "a forme of speech which repeateth one word often times in one sentence, making the oration more pleasant to the eare" (Peacham 1954, 49). Nowhere does Peacham mention changing meanings in his definition of this figure whose effect he compares to "pleasant repetitions and divisions in Musicke," and whose chief use is "either to garnish the sentence with oft repetition, or to note well the importance of the word repeated" (49). Furthermore, in all three of the examples Peacham offers of traductio [ploche], a word is repeated three times, a number of repetitions that certainly works against changing its meaning, while at the same time it suggests an author's deliberate choice. The fact that traductio marks repetition without change of meaning is also reinforced by Peacham's caution where the "disgrace" in this figure is lapsing into "Tautologia, which is a tedious and wearisome repetition of one word" (49). As an example of traductio [ploche] well used, Peacham offers no less than John 1:1, "In the beginning was the word, and the word was with God, and God was the word," a passage that is transformed significantly depending on whether it is read as traductio or diaphora, that is, on whether the repeated "word" is to be taken in different senses or in one.[5]

The argumentative effects of ploche

The New Rhetoric emphasizes the rhetorical importance of presence, of foregrounding notions in an audience's consciousness, and it asserts that the "simplest way of creating this presence is repetition" (Perelman and Olbrechts-Tyteca 1969, 144). Here again is the general claim that the figures are like the fans in a stadium who are waving their hands, making them more visible than those sitting quietly. It is, however, possible to distinguish more specific argumentative effects from repetition than simply foregrounding.

Repetition can bring concepts together by giving them the same name or attributing the same property or action to them. It is, then, like gradatio, another device that can undo the work of antithesis, but only if the repeated term is taken to mean the same thing from use to use. If one predicates the same thing of two terms, then these two things are joined, at least provisionally, in the act of listening or reading. If these two terms started out as antithetical in the minds of the audience, then this co-predication can have the effect of diminishing their opposition (see p. 87).

The predication of the same qualities need not be drawn out or foregrounded in separate categorical propositions: X is A and Y is A. This work can occur more subtly anywhere in a sentence or across several sentences in repeated objects or verbs or adjectives positioned before nouns, and so on, although in each case the precise effect will depend on what function is repeated. Furthermore, in breaking with Peacham's examples, though not with his definition, repeating only twice in the same sense can still be argumentatively significant.

An illustration comes from the opening sentence of Roger Fowler and Gunther Kress's "Critical Linguistics," the concluding essay in *Language and Control*. "The language materials analyzed in this book suggest that there are strong and pervasive connections between linguistic structure and social structure" (Fowler and Kress 1979, 185). Here ploche carries the burden of the claim. The authors want to maintain that language and social organization map onto each other in significant ways; they could have said, "there are strong and pervasive connections between language and social organization," or "between language and society." Instead, they find pervasive connections between "linguistic structure and social structure," two entities that can be named by the same superordinate noun or genus term "structure." Since they are already the same thing by virtue of being named by the same noun—both are "structures"—it is less surprising that there should be "strong and pervasive" connections between them. Making a claim less surprising and therefore more convincing is precisely the work of a figure of argument, illustrating once again that there are pervasive connections between linguistic structure and argumentative structure.

Stability in the phenomena under discussion can be an arguer's goal achieved by stability, that is, precise repetition of the nouns, the substance terms. The identity of the terms figures the identity of the reference, though of course these identities can be as vulnerable to refutation as any other attempted stability in an argument. Repetition of modifiers secures another kind of stability; it is a linguistic device used to produce connections among phenomena that are named differently.

Darwin's use of argumentative repetition is notable. Though in a corpus as large as Darwin's one can find examples of virtually any figure, Darwin generally avoids the more obvious devices of strategically positioned repetition such as anaphora, epanalepsis, and so forth. Instead he favors ploche, the subtler repetitions that declare identity in reference or the interconnections among phenomena. Darwin adeptly repeats strategic adjectives in the following critical passage that contains his defense of the concept of a struggle for existence.

> The dependency of one organic being on another, as of a parasite on his prey, lies generally between beings remote in the scale of nature. This is likewise sometimes the case with those which may be strictly said to struggle with each other for existence, as in the case of locusts and grass-feeding quadrupeds. But the struggle will almost invariably be most severe between individuals of the same species, for they frequent the same districts, require the same food, and are exposed to the same dangers. (Darwin 1965, 60)

It would be no exaggeration to say that the repetition of "same" carries the argument in this passage. Darwin is, in his usual manner, establishing a quantitatively graded series, ordered degrees in the severity of the struggle for existence (see chapter 3). To reach the final item in this series, intraspecific competition, and to make this item a "most," requires amplification of the causes of competition among members of the same species, since the more they have in common, the more they struggle. The repetition of "same" accomplishes this intensification, linking districts, food sources, and dangers as common properties of the "same" species. The point could have been made without the repetition of "same," but the repetition epitomizes the argument.

The repetition of "different" proves critical in an article that appeared in *Science*, which in many ways typifies a generation of arguments in neurophysiology once functional magnetic resonance imaging technology became available. Brain researchers attempt to localize specific areas associated with cognitive tasks by MRIs indicating blood flow patterns. The goal of much of this research is to make robust distinctions in the tasks performed and then to associate those tasks with certain areas of the brain in ways more precise than have been possible before. The following passage summarizes the results of one such set of experiments on visual processing: "The main result was that different regions of extrastriate visual cortex were activated when [a subject was] attending to different attributes of a visual display" (Corbetta et al. 1990, 1556). This sentence delivers the primary claim of its authors: That there is a correlation between parts of the brain and parts of a specially constructed visual task. (There is no surprise in the localization of function, but some in the precision of division of the visual task.) The argument for this claim is carried by the repetition of the key word "different," the verbal trace of the standard correlation argument. Activation of *different* parts of the brain corresponds with *different* parts of the visual display. Two entities or concepts that can be modified by the same adjective are more likely to be taken as connected in some way. The logical appeal of adjective repetition, so simple and even simplistic when unpacked, nevertheless moves by quickly, without drawing the attention and potential refutation of explicit claims. Across a longer passage, the repetition of an unstressed adjective can work to associate a set of concepts that might otherwise remain dispersed. In a single sentence, the closer juxtaposition of repeated words is even more likely to take effect.[6] Ploche confounds the stylistic rule that repeating the same word in the same or in an adjacent sentence is inartistic, the result of an impoverished vocabulary. Yet what is sometimes seen as an aesthetic defect can be an argumentative virtue in a case like the following.

Koch's postulates

One of the most celebrated events in the history of medicine, made famous by Paul De Kruif's hyperbolic account in *The Microbe Hunters*, was Robert Koch's discovery of the tuberculosis bacillus in 1882. A corollary of this discovery, as famous among microbiologists, were Koch's procedural innovations. In a popular book on viruses written in 1992, Arnold Levine of Princeton University, a distinguished researcher on tumor viruses and a former editor of the *Journal of Virology*, explains that a series of criteria first established by Koch is still in use as the standard for identifying a microbial disease agent. Levine phrases what are now widely known as "Koch's postulates" in the following way:

> (1) the organism must be regularly found in the lesions of the disease, (2) the organism must be isolated in pure culture (hence the need for sterile techniques) (3) inoculation of such a culture of pure organisms into the host should initiate the disease, and (4) the organism must be recovered once again from the lesions of this host (Levine 5; see the note for similar textbook versions of the postulates).[7]

What is stylistically noticeable about this version of Koch's postulates is the repetition of the word "organism" in each of the four elements. This use of ploche epitomizes perfectly the standard demanded by the postulates: that a consistent disease-causing agent persist through a precise experimental route, from an infected disease-ridden host to a pure culture to a new host that manifests the disease to another isolation and identification procedure. If an organism maintains its identity through each step of this process, the way the word itself is maintained in each sentence of the postulates, then there is "proof" that it is a disease-causing agent. Ploche, then, is the figurative epitome of Koch's postulates, stability of the term representing stability of the referent and, in this case, of the organism under scrutiny.

Koch's postulates figure in the recent controversy over whether the HIV virus is the true causal agent of AIDS and, indirectly, of its many end-stage pathologies. Peter Duesberg, outspoken critic of the prevailing view, bases his main charge against the HIV paradigm on the fact that the virus has never been consistently identified through each of the required stages of Koch's postulates (Duesberg 1996, 35).[8] It is not always recoverable from the tissues of patients with full-blown AIDS nor has it proved possible to reproduce it for transmission to hosts of other species (174–186). In practice, however, the stage of isolation and in vitro culturing of the potential disease-causing organism is not a requirement. In experiments to identify the agent in the transmission of Bovine Spongiform Encephalopathy (BSE or "mad cow disease"), an agent not assumed to be self-replicating anyway, the brains of infected mice are ground up and injected directly into new mice (Lasmézas et al. 1997, 403–404; a method closer to that used by Pasteur to study rabies than that used by Koch to study tuberculosis). Nevertheless, if the presumed disease-causing agent is not detectable in animals down the chain when aspects of the disease are present, it is ruled out as a sufficient cause. Researchers in France have in fact been unable to complete Koch's ploche in the case of the malformed prion supposedly capable of causing spongiform encephalopathies across species and so have been forced to conclude that "a further unidentified agent may actually transmit BSE." (402)

Given the continuing importance of Koch's postulates and the consequent insistence on ploche in epitomes of research on microbial disease-causing agents, it is interesting to question how Koch himself phrased the frequently paraphrased postulates attributed to him. K. Codell Carter examined Koch's extensive writings and identified at least two variants of general criteria for identifying disease-causing agents (Carter 1985, 357, 361). Nowhere, according to Carter, does Koch produce a clear version of the multistep formula currently disseminated under his name. Perhaps the closest approximation to a general set of standards occurs in his most famous paper, his 1884 account of his tuberculosis research, "Die Aetiologie der Tuberkulose":

> First, it was necessary to determine whether the diseased organs contained elements that were not constituents of the body or composed of such constituents. If such alien *structures* [*Gebilde*] could be demonstrated, it was necessary to determine whether they were organized and showed any sign of independent life. Such signs include motility—which is often confused with molecular motion—growth, propagation, and fructification. Moreover, it was necessary to consider the relation of such *structures* [not in the original] to their surroundings, their relation to nearby tissues, their distribution in the body, their occurrence in various states of the disease,

and other similar considerations. Such considerations enable one to conclude, with more or less probability, that there is a causal connection between these *structures and the disease* [*Gebilden und der Krankheit*] itself. Facts gained in these ways can provide so much evidence that only the most extreme skeptic would still object that the microorganism may not be the cause, but only a concomitant of the disease. Often this objection has a certain justice, and, therefore, establishing the coincidence of *the disease and the parasite* [*der Krankheit und der Parasiten*] is not a complete proof. One requires, in addition, a direct proof that the *parasite* [*Parasiten*] is the actual cause. This can only be achieved by completely separating the *parasites* [*Parasiten*] from the diseased organism and from all products of the disease to which one could ascribe a causal significance. The isolated *parasites* [*Parasiten*], if introduced into healthy organisms, must then cause the disease with all its characteristics (see note for original passage in German).[9] (Koch 1987, 131)

This version of Koch's generalized procedures uses two repeating terms. The first stage of inquiry involves identification of "structures" that are not, to begin with, necessarily microorganisms. Though a master of the then best available techniques for mounting and staining tissue specimens and the inventor of many new techniques, Koch no doubt appreciated the potentially confusing artifacts observable under the microscopes of the late nineteenth century. Alien structures were not always easy to distinguish from the normal constituents of a cell. If they could be— and Koch includes illustrations with his 1884 article of tissues filled with a nightmarish ploche of identical black rods—correlation at least could be established. The part of the passage dealing with "structures" concerns such correlation.[10] The passage then hands off causal agency to "parasites" (by overlapping with the term "disease") if they can be separated, isolated, and introduced into healthy animals, which then manifest the original disease. Koch's ploche with "parasites" in this passage is an adequate if not rigorous epitome of his method, but once formulated, the postulates themselves have undergone a ploche-like repetition from text to text for over one hundred years.

The pathway established by the postulates for a potential disease-causing entity in an experimental trial can be followed even in the absence of actually establishing that the entity exists. In other words, it is possible to move an agent verbally through the postulates without a physical referent. The discovery of viruses, in fact, followed that route. In the late 1880s, Adolf Mayr identified a disease of the tobacco plant that discolored its leaves. By grinding up the infected areas and soaking them in water, he produced a supernatant that easily caused the same effect when it was spread on healthy leaves. But Mayr could never identify a microorganism in his leaf cultures. Instead, "something" could be extracted from the infected tissue, "something" could sustain itself in a separate solution, and "something" could infect a new host. A consistent term was inferable from the protocol but its referent could not be isolated. Mayr was, of course, working with a virus (once a term for an infectious agent in general), a then submicroscopic form whose existence was eventually hypothesized because of the persistence of "something" when filtrations of preparations that would remove any known bacteria still yielded an infectious agent. Viruses were not identified visually until the 1930s, when Wendell Stanley succeeded in crystallizing the tobacco mosaic virus, and it was later observed in the newly available electron microscope (Levine 1992, 6–8). Until then, research with viruses could not visually identify them as demanded in Koch's postulates, yet viruses could be written about, and they were widely believed to be stable, disease-causing agents in animals, plants, and even bacteria long before their physical identification.

The current understanding of the interaction of a virus with its host cell stretches even further any application of Koch's postulates. Many viruses are now understood to follow two different pathways of infection. They can enter a cell, release their DNA or RNA, multiply exponentially, create their own structural proteins, reassemble, break out of the cell, usually killing it in the process, and go on to infect new cells, as though following Koch's postulates on their own. Or they can enter a cell and insert their DNA into the DNA of the host, where it can wait for years. In that latent form, the viral genome is difficult to distinguish from the host's genes, and the virus ceases to be recognizable as an independent entity until the viral genes are somehow turned on again, the viral constituents manufactured, and the reproduced virus released. Tracing out this pathway represented a significant conceptual achievement, but it is questionable whether the "organism" really maintains its identity through the middle step (prophage) of the second process (see the citation from Davis et al., note 7, which deletes an identifiable entity from step 3). Either pathway, however, can be epitomized not only verbally, by a custom version of Koch's postulates using the special strain name, but also visually, in diagrams that employ an icon for the infectious agent. The precise replication of the icon claims that the agent remains consistently identifiable when it enters and exits a cell (see Figure 5.1). In actual fact, given the high rate of mutation and recombination during replication, especially of RNA viruses, many of the progeny that exit a cell are likely to differ genetically from the virus that entered it. In some ways, the figure polyptoton, discussed below, would be a better verbal icon for the process than the exact replication implied by exact repetition, the ploche of words or images.

Partial repetition: agnominatio

In addition to perfect repetition, the figural tradition also marked the partial or near repetition that occurs when words look or sound alike.[11] Students of poetry are familiar with figures in this category (alliteration, the repetition of initial sounds or consonants, and assonance, the repetition of vowel sounds) as factors in the aural architecture of a text. But a more general device, identified in the figure manuals, encompasses these and extends their significance beyond aesthetic effects to argumentative ends.

Under the name *agnomination* or *agnominatio*, John Hoskins defines this figure as the repetition of "some syllables" in consecutive words and offers a simple example from Sidney's *Arcadia*: "Alas, what can saying make them believe whom seeing cannot persuade" (Hoskins 1935, 16). "Saying" and "seeing" here share initial consonants, the same final syllables, and an equal number of syllables, and their resemblance enhances their role as parallel modes of persuasion, verbal and visual, although overall the phrase suggests an a fortiori argument: If "they" do not respond

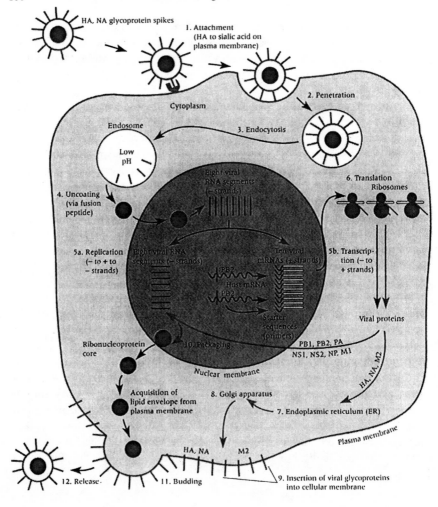

Figure 5.1. Visual ploche: Consistency of the virion (dark circle) entering and leaving a cell. From *Viruses* by Arnold J. Levine. Copyright 1992 by Scientific American Library. Reproduced with permission of W. H. Freeman and Company.

to the much stronger appeal of showing, why should "they" respond to telling? When the resemblance of words is pushed, it can approach *paronomasia*, the pun, as in Hoskins' example from a sermon indulging in half-comic denunciations: "Our paradise is a pair of dice, our almes-deed are turned into all misdeeds, our praying into playing, our fasting into feasting" (Hoskins 1935, 16). The first two of the four transformations in this passage turn on puns, but the last two are "agnominations," the strong resemblance between "praying" and "playing" and between "fasting" and "feasting" enhancing the ease with which frail humanity slides into sin.

Agnominatio has constructed many temporary and more enduring maxims: "Use it or lose it" (more aural than visual); "America. Love it or leave it"; "Praise the Lord and pass the ammunition." Citing Plato's use of sôma and sêma in "the body is a tomb," Olivier Reboul points out that the force of the repetition of phonemes in this pair disappears as soon as the phrase is translated. As Reboul explains, such verbal resemblance functions "as if—an 'as if' which quite exactly constitutes the figure—the arbitrariness of the sign were abolished, as if the sequence of phonemes responded to a sequence of thoughts to which it brought an added measure of proof" (Reboul 1989, 170). Such a figure seems "to show that the resemblance between words attests to a relationship between things" (a claim that in translation uses agnominatio) (178).

An agnominatio that has had enduring force in psychology and genetics is Francis Galton's powerful construction of two forces shaping bodies and behavior as "nature" and "nurture."[12] First introduced in 1874, this pair, sometimes in the agonistic formulation "nature versus nurture," has divided between them the complex factors that produce the observable organism and all its actions. In the 1860s and 1870s, Galton studied the consequences of his cousin Charles Darwin's theories of evolution as they might apply to human populations, eventually advocating policies that would encourage the "fit" to breed, for which he coined the name "eugenics." In 1869 he published his first treatise on the importance of lineage in creativity and talent. In response to Alphonse de Candolle's 1872 rebuttal of his work (with Candolle maintaining the influence of broad social factors in the promotion of scientific talent), Galton did his own survey-based research of over a hundred members of the Royal Society, concluding that their scientific inclinations were innate and hence due primarily to heredity. Galton's published version of his results appeared in 1874 as *English Men of Science: Their Nature and Nurture*. Galton was aware of the cleverness of the coinage in his subtitle and its powerful role in setting the conditions of his argument.

> The phrase "nature and nurture" is a convenient jingle of words, for it separates under two distinct heads the innumerable elements of which personality is composed. Nature is all that a man brings with himself into the world; nurture is every influence from without that affects him after his birth. (Galton 1970, 12)

Undoubtedly the agnominatio "nature and nurture" has had a great deal to do with constructing the following decades of debate, for the close resemblance of Galton's terms suggests the parity of these forces. Nurture, of course, has a more restricted connotation than Galton's stipulated definition allows. It meant then, and still does, an overseeing benevolence surrounding the developing organism, so Galton's pair also suggests an antithesis between what is beyond human control and what is not, an antithesis reinforced in the figure that concludes the passage quoted above. Since the two terms are so close in sound and appearance, differing only in one phoneme, it becomes more plausible to believe that they represent well-matched rivals. Parity is their theoretical condition in Galton's mind, though he believed as a result of his research that the more familiar and resonant of the two, "nature," was dominant: "When nature and nurture compete for supremacy on equal terms in the sense to be explained, the former proves the stronger" (12). Contemporary students of psychology and behavioral genetics have replaced Galton's agnominatio with the unfigured pair "heredity and environment," but the terms of the debate between these two are still set by Galton's agnominatio in the sense that there is still a presumption of two forces in conflict in the creation of a fully realized organism and sometimes even a presumption that one should normally expect a fifty-fifty contribution from these two (see Gottesman 1997, 1522–1523). Though the pair "nature and nurture" may only appear now as self-consciously used synonyms, the relative contributions of genetic makeup and individual surroundings are still being prized apart according to the size of their respective shares of a "whole" in studies of intelligence, disease, violence, and addiction.

Polyptoton

The example of ploche offered by the *Ad Herennium*, "One who has nothing in life more desirable than life cannot cultivate a virtuous life," reads in Latin as follows, "Qui nihil habet in vita iucundius vita, cum virtute vitam non potest colere" ([Cicero] 1954, 278, 280). The repeated word "vita" here appears also in the ablative "vita" and the accusative "vitam." If ploche is defined as the precise repetition of a word, it is obvious that an inflected language provides far fewer opportunities for ploche than an uninflected language like English. Yet the rhetorical manuals written for the highly inflected languages of Greek and Latin do distinguish between repeating a word precisely and repeating it in different grammatical cases. The latter device, called *polyptoton*, depends on "a change of case in one or more proper nouns." Translated into English, the example that follows this definition is incomprehensible.

> Alexander of Macedon with consummate toil from boyhood trained his mind to virtue. Alexander's virtues have been broadcast with fame and glory throughout the world. All men greatly feared Alexander, yet deeply loved him. Had longer life been granted Alexander, the Macedonian lances would have flown across the ocean. (307)

Here Alexander merely appears four times, once with the inflectional ending of a possessive, in several different positions. But in the Latin original, the proper noun Alexander remains at the opening of each successive sentence though changing its grammatical function and hence its ending each time: Alexander (nominative), Alexandri (genitive), Alexandrum (accusative), Alexandro (dative). Of course, Alexander's semantic roles change in each sentence in the English version as well, as a case grammar analysis would point out, but the name itself is not stylistically marked. Hence English will inevitably seem to employ more ploche than polyptoton.

As an analytic rather than synthetic language, English is poor in case endings. The entire inflectional system in Modern English marks only plurality and possession in nouns (-s, -es, -'s and -s'), degree in adjectives (-er, -est), and tense, person, and aspect in verbs (-s, -ed, -en, -ing). Inflectional endings are therefore less important as sources of polyptoton in English than derivational endings that shift a word from one syntactic category, or part of speech, to another (rubber/rubberize), or of affixes that change gender (poet/poetess) or otherwise alter meaning without changing the part of speech (like/dislike; neighbor/neighborhood). In the prefixes and suffixes that perform these changes, English is particularly rich, and furthermore, it allows multiple affixes to pile up on either end of a word, producing extensive word families around the same root, as in a set like colony, colonial, colonize, colonization, decolonize, precolonial, and so on. To be sure, this system is also derived from Latin and Greek, which are rich in word-building affixes, and from German, a language in which compounds are easily constructed, also leading to the formation of extensive word families.

The great sixteenth-century rhetorics like Melancthon's and Susenbrotus's are still Latin rhetorics, written to guide appreciation of Latin texts and composition in Latin. In the English vernacular rhetorics of the Renaissance, like Puttenham's, Peacham's, and Sherry's, the figures are adapted to English usage, relinquishing any restriction of polyptoton to changes of case, thanks to the impossibility of tracing such changes morphologically. Polyptoton of necessity becomes a figure of derivational change. Puttenham's *The Arte of English Poesie* (1589), a text which aggressively domesticates the figures to English, shows by its examples that endings altering parts of speech rather than grammatical cases are now at issue.

> Then have ye a figure which the Latines call traductio, and I the tranlacer: which is when ye turne and tranlace a word into many sundry shapes as the Tailor doth his garment, and after that sort do play with him in your dittie; as thus
>
>> Who lives in love his life is full of feares,
>> To lose his love, livelode or libertie
>> But lively sprites that young and recklesse be,
>> Thinke that there is no living like to theirs
>
> Here ye see how in the former rime this word life is tranlaced into live, living, lively, livelode. (Puttenham 1970, 214)[13]

Ploche defined as the exact repetition of a lexical item and polyptoton in the sense of changing the part of speech do overlap in one case, when a word migrates from one part of speech to another without changing form. English has many such homonyms that can function as both noun and verb (sign/sign, lease/lease), or noun and adjective (blue/blue, weak/weak), or even noun, verb, and adjective (love/love/love, paper/paper/paper: *To paper your walls, choose a paper that has a paper and not a cloth surface*). As mentioned above, these permutations are also examples of antanaclasis, a device that clearly belongs in the family of punning figures.[14]

With several figures of repetition in place, it is possible to schematize the basic permutations that the manual writers were consistently characterizing, albeit under a bewildering shifting of terms.

Ploche	Antanaclasis	Polyptoton
Precise repetition of form and function	Precise repetition of form but change of function	Permutation of form and change of function

The change of function (including the function of referring) mentioned under polyptoton means only that an inevitable change occurs when forms derived from the same root represent different syntactic categories. "Love" as a verb and "lover" as a noun can never have the same function in a sentence. But the spirit or intent of the figure polyptoton, as of ploche, is still the conservation of a core of meaning when a word or word root is repeated. In this sense, they both differ from the middle member of this series of permutations, the *antanaclasis*, which highlights the potential change in meaning lurking in identity of form. No external sign differentiates between ploche and antanaclasis; instead they mark opposite interpretive strategies. Potential change of meaning despite exact repetition has occupied the attention of interpreters, especially those intent on destabilizing readings. But, as in the cases of ploche examined above, the attempt at consistency, at carrying on and extending a term's range of application, is a much more important argumentative effect.

The Argumentative Resources of Polyptoton

Depending on a consistent core of meaning, polyptoton is the figural signature of one of the major reasoning strategies listed in Aristotle's *Rhetoric* and detailed in his *Topics*. It is the second of the 28 cryptic lines of argument:[15]

> Another [topic] is from [different] grammatical forms of the same word [*ek tōn homoiōn ptōseōn*]; for the same [predicate] should be true or not true, for example, [to say] that the just is not entirely good; for then what is done justly would be a good, but as it is, to be put to death justly is not desirable. (Kennedy 1991, 191)

As usual, the tactic hinted at here in the *Rhetoric* is explained more fully in the *Topics*, where the strategies described encompass the argumentative work of both ploche and polyptoton. In Book II, Aristotle introduces arguments involving "co-ordinate" terms and inflections of the same word. Co-ordinates are sets of words that belong together in part because they can be modified by the same word, a practice whose verbal signature is ploche: "By co-ordinates are meant things such as the following: just deeds and the just man are co-ordinates of justice." By inflections, Aristotle means not only case changes but also derivatives such as "justly" from "justice" and "courageously" from "courage" (Barnes 1984, I, 190). Co-ordinates and derivatives together form families of related terms, as in the example Aristotle provides: "justice, just man, just deed, justly" (190). In dialectical reasoning, Aristotle believes a claim supported for one co-ordinate term or one form of a word can be plausibly extended to the entire family of forms created from the same root as well as to terms plausibly modified by the same word.

> Clearly, then, when any one member, whatever its kind, of the same series is proved to be good or praiseworthy, then all the rest as well come to be proved to be so: e.g. if justice is something praiseworthy, then so will a just man, and a just deed, and 'justly' connote something praiseworthy. Then 'justly' will be rendered also 'praiseworthily', derived by the same inflexion from the praiseworthy as 'justly' is derived from justice. (Barnes 1984, I, 190–191; see also Bk V, sec. 7, where the same line of reasoning is run in reverse for refutation; and Bk VI, sec. 10)

The creation of premises from grammatical migration seems particularly distant from modern notions of good arguing. It may even seem somewhat occult, like an operation in sympathetic magic where the shaman manipulates an object by manipulating a token or sign for that object (in this case a word) or gains control of a force by changing its name. But what Aristotle explicates in this line of reasoning is the linguistic machinery of common sense, as his frequent references to this strategy throughout the *Topics* make clear.

It is sometimes the goal of an argument to take a concept accepted by an audience in one role or category of sentence action and transfer it to others, an agent becoming an action or an action becoming an attribute and so on. This work is epitomized by polyptoton, the grammatical morphing of the word, as Aristotle explains repeatedly in the *Topics*. For once he has introduced coordinates and inflexions, that is, derivatives, they reappear throughout his treatment of arguments involving value judgments and the four kinds of arguable propositions about definitions, genera, properties, and accidents. He points out, for example, how people's judgments follow a term as it changes from one part of speech to another. So, for example, an audience who believes that acting justly is better than acting courageously will also believe that justice is better than courage and vice versa. (Barnes 1984, I, 198). Similarly, what they believe about actions will transfer to what they believe about objects and abstractions: "if what happens unjustly is in some cases good, then some unjust things are good" (200). Attributes will accompany terms through the same grammatical changes: "if justice is a particular form of knowledge, then also justly is knowingly and the just man is a man of knowledge" (208). So will relations of similarity (255) and genus/definition connections: "Thus if forgetfulness is loss of knowledge, to forget is to lose knowledge, and to have forgotten is to have lost knowledge. If, then, anyone whatever of these is agreed to, the others must of necessity be agreed to as well" (258). As these examples illustrate once again, the *Topics* is not concerned with immutable rules of validity but with the patterns of reasoning that most people follow most of the time, and most people will indeed follow the logic of polyptotonic morphing as Aristotle describes it.

As in the case of antimetabole (see chapter 4), a polyptoton can epitomize both causal arguments as well as those involving set inclusion or definition. To argue that something is the agent of an action by naming both with forms of the same word is a valuable strategy in causal arguments, and one of Aristotle's examples in the *Topics* illustrates how ploche and polyptoton can serve such arguments: "Likewise also things that tend to produce and to preserve anything are co-ordinates of that which they tend to produce and to preserve, as e.g. healthy habits are co-ordinates of health and vigorous habits of vigour" (Barnes 1984, I, 190). Thus an arguer aiming to convince an audience that certain habits produce health might modify the recommended habits with the adjective "healthy." What kind of habits produce health? Why, healthy habits, habits that somehow already have as their property the outcome they produce. It is easier to believe that certain habits cause health if those habits are somehow inherently healthy to begin with. There is, of course, supposed to be a linear or chronological separation in this usage: The healthy habits come before the health, avoiding the equally plausible implication that the healthy habits are the health.

In a similar way, one can argue not from an effecter to an effect (healthy habits to health) but from an effect to an effecter, that is, from a result to a causal agent by the polyptotonic move of coining a noun from a verb. If there is an action, say *to glue,* then an agent can be created with the appropriate derivational ending, a *gluer.* Even an action that has already been rendered as an abstract noun can yield a causal agent by polyptoton: Acceleration is caused by an accelerator and thrust by a thruster. This agent can specify either a human or an intermediate instrument or even an unlocalized abstraction subject to later reification. This particular polyptotonic move, from abstract property to abstract cause, has been critical at many points in the history of science.

One of the most famous arguments in nineteenth-century science, first published in 1802 and perpetuated many times after in its polyptotonic epitome, is William Paley's case in *Natural Theology* that the existence of God can be inferred from the order and pattern of creation. Contemporary scholars might class Paley's as a philosophical or theological rather than a scientific argument, but most of it is devoted to evidence from "natural history," especially from comparative anatomy and physiology. After 23 chapters compiling details that substantiate the exquisite evidence of "contrivance" in the natural world, of the suitableness of every organ to its function and of the failure of any other explanation for the source of this economy, Paley concludes his 23rd chapter with these memorable lines: "Upon the whole, after all the schemes and struggles of a reluctant philosophy, the necessary resort is to a Deity. The marks of *design* are too strong to be gotten over. Design must have had a designer. That designer must have been a person. That person is God" (Paley 1963, 44).[16] Here Paley gives succinct expression to an ancient argument that the Creation shows the signs of its Creator: "The earth declareth the glory of God and the firmament showeth his handiwork." Paley's epitome in the passage just cited, whose frequent quotation indicates its success at being memorable, depends on naming the agent from the effect, the designer from the design, and, in the passage quoted, by the strategic repetition of designer and person, in the pattern known as gradatio (see chapter 3), to create an overlapping sorites that effectively connects the beginning and ending terms of the series: design and God.

Polyptoton in nomenclature and taxonomy

In some sciences, polyptotonic practices have been codified to form systems of nomenclature that embody the fundamental principles of that science. The history of chemistry has as one of its foundational episodes the late eighteenth-century reform, or rather creation, of the system for naming inorganic compounds that is still in use. The 1787 *Méthode de Nomenclature Chimique,* the joint work of De Morveau, Lavoisier, Fourcroy, and Bertholet, established the principle that compounds should be named from their constituents, and they codified, among other items, the derivational suffixes that distinguish acids and salts by their oxygen "saturation" (sulphurous from sulphuric and sulphite from sulphate). In his section of the *Méthode,* Lavoisier argued for the necessity of an accurate language to foster the development of the discipline by pointing out that a confused system was an impediment. Facts, ideas, and words were related in a chain of representation, in his thinking, and no matter how true the facts or just the ideas formed from them, false impressions will result "si on n'avoit pas les expressions exacte pour les rendre," [if one does not have exact expressions for them] (Lavoisier 1787, 14).

The perfection of chemistry's nomenclature would render ideas and facts in their exact truth, without suppressing or adding anything. It would be a faithful mirror: miroir fidèle (14). But it would be much more as well, for Lavoisier knew that the discipline was incomplete and that this initial nomenclature would be far from perfection too:

> mais pourvu qu'elle ait été entreprise sur de bon principes; pourvu que ce soit une méthode de nommer, plutôt qu'une nomenclature, elle s'adaptera naturellement aux travaux qui seront faits dans la suite; elle marquera d'avance la place & la nom des nouvelles substances qui pourront être découvertes, & elle n'exigera que quelques réformes locales & particulières

> but provided that it has been undertaken on good principles, provided that it is a method of naming, rather a nomenclature, it will adapt itself to the work which will be done subsequently; it will mark in advance the place and the name of new substances which can be discovered and it will only require local and particular reforms. (Lavoisier 1787, 16–17)

A widely accepted nomenclature that marks in advance the name and the place of substances yet to be discovered is a polyptotonic system that prepares the way for acceptable lines of research and the accompanying acceptable premises in arguments from knowns to unknowns.

In no discipline is the importance of patterned nomenclature more obvious than in organic chemistry, where entry-level competence involves gaining control of the derivational system, the licensed polyptotonic moves. Students learn, for example, that hydrocarbons are divided into three subgroups, alkanes, alkenes, and alkynes, according to whether the bonds between the carbon atoms are single, double, or triple. These endings are then conserved in the naming of particular compounds, such as ethane, ethene, and ethyne. Such naming conventions in chemistry are imposed by the International Union of Pure and Applied Chemistry (IUPAC), which began in 1892 to specify how the vast variety of organic compounds discovered or constructed in the nineteenth century could be comprehended and controlled by an organized nomenclature. The resulting systematization has served the science well by establishing derivational patterns that encode agreements about the nature of compounds. Thus the class of organic compounds known as esters, which decompose on hydrolysis to an alcohol and an acid, are systematically named from their components, IUPAC specifying that the portion derived from the alcohol comes first, in its combined form ending in *yl*, followed by the combined acid ending in *ate* or *oate*. The initiate can encounter the name of a new compound and immediately classify it by recognizing how the term was formed.

Such conventions of naming may be viewed as preliminary to argument, but they also serve as inventional prompts in the same way that series with missing elements invite completion (see chapter 3). For once a derivational paradigm has been established, it can become a research goal to fill it with homologous sets, the terms not only marking "in advance the place and name of new substances," in Lavoisier's words, but prompting the discovery as well. Filling a slot in a recognized paradigm can, in turn, serve as an argument in favor of a particular result. This process is particularly obvious in molecular biology, which has its own derivational rules and resulting sets of nomenclature. An enzyme that degrades a protein, for example, is named from that protein, as collagenase from collagen, as is a precursor molecule in a synthetic pathway, like procollagen from collagen. Only proteins whose concentrations and degradation are critical may have specific degradative enzymes, but the existence of the category determined by the naming convention can stimulate the search for the molecule. The inventional prompt suggested here may seem no different from the invitation that any category, once established, offers for the discovery of new members. But in the case of sciences that have coined the available polyptotonic moves, the specific name of the new member is also waiting.

Arguing new members into existing sets is also very much the work of biologists who believe they have come upon a new species or genus or even higher grouping. The first of these discoveries, a new species, is the easiest to make, since moving a piece into the bottom of an articulated hierarchy does the least potential damage to the systematic alignments above; a new species requires only a new "second" name, its prepared genus name being conferred by the argument. Examples of such taxonomic arguments for newly identified species were studied by Alan Gross in *The Rhetoric of Science*, and one argument in his sample merits reinterpretation from the perspective of the epitomizing figure polyptoton. In *The Wilson Bulletin* for 1979, three ornithologists present "A New Species of Hummingbird from Peru," *Heliangelus regalis*. The rhetorical tactics identified in this argument by Gross include the conferring of rhetorical presence on the bird through "over-description," the massing of physical and statistical detail about the specimens collected, as well as the act of naming itself and the use of illustrations (Gross 1990, 42–45). Among the illustrations included for their "clear display of likenesses and differences," Gross singles out and reproduces one that emphasizes "the family resemblances crucial for genus identity and the contrastive features essential for within-genus differentiation" (36; see Figure 5.2). Elsewhere he refers to the visual rhetoric in this illustration as "tendentious simplification" (45).

The argumentative tactic deployed in this drawing could, however, also be described as visual polyptoton. It presents part of the authors' case for the inclusion of their discovery in the genus *Heliangelus* despite some arguments to the contrary. Those counterarguments include the fact that all other males of species within *Heliangelus* display patches of brilliant color on their throats, whereas the male of this putative new species is uniformly deep blue, closer to the coloration of a different genus, *Eriocnemis* (Fitzpatrick et al., 1979, 181). The authors present as their strongest argument for including the new bird within *Heliangelus* the fact that the female bears a breast band that resembles that of other females in the genus. The illustration reinforces this argument. The emphasis is on inclusion in a larger set, since that is the point in jeopardy in the argument, by overall visual homogeneity, just as sharing of the common defining root is the conceptual core of the polyptoton. The conventional iconography for presenting specimens in such illustrations (see also Figure 5.3), the rigorous similarity in the alignment of the birds' bodies, and the sketchy presentation of distinctive features to diminish differences, both assist the underlying argumentative gesture. Notably, the authors have avoided imposing any ordering (incrementum or gradatio) on their illustration, an otherwise

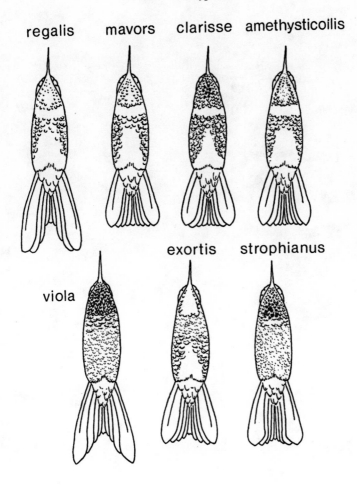

Figure 5.2. Visual polyptoton. From John W. Fitzpatrick, David E. Willard, John. W. Terbrogh, "A New Species of Hummingbird from Peru," *The Wilson Bulletin*, 91 (June 1979). Reproduced with permission of Robert C. Beason.

common tactic in illustrations of speciation.[17] *Regalis* is close to *mavors* in breast banding, close to *viola* in the length and shape of its tail, but they admit that they cannot give it an "exact position," or create a place for it in a series in *Heliangelus* (181). The best they can do is polyptoton. It has enough in common with the others, sharing the same "root," to belong in the group.

A similar example of visual polyptoton is reproduced in Martin Rudwick's well-known study *The Meaning of Fossils: Episodes in the History of Paleontology.* Rudwick details the gradual perception of a connection between objects "dug up" and the living forms they resemble, rather than the mineral material they were composed from. One of the earliest to argue for the organic origin of fossils was the naturalist

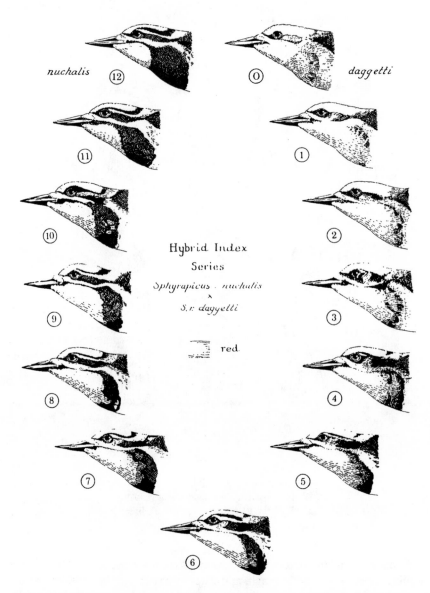

Figure 5.3. Visual polyptoton with incrementum: An argument for linking species through an ordered series of hybrids. From Ned K. Johnson and Carla Bowman Johnson, "Speciation in Sapsuckers (Sphyrapicus): II," *The Auk* 102 (January 1985). Reproduced with permission of Jeff Marks.

Fabio Colonna. In his 1616 treatise *Observations on Some Aquatic and Territorial Animals*, he included in an engraving of several whelk shells from living species one fossil shell, "within the same scheme and the same plate" (Rudwick 1985, 43). Set in the corner of the crowded illustration, the fossil shell is only distinguishable from the others by the broken outline around it representing the stone matrix in which it is fixed. But visually the entire plate argues polyptotonically that this fossil belongs with the others by virtue of sharing the same core identity.

Ploche, Polyptoton, and the Science of Electricity
in the Eighteenth Century

An extended example of the power of both ploche and polyptoton as rhetorical and conceptual strategies can be found in the texts of the early "electricians" who created the science of electricity in the first half of the eighteenth century. The figural study of this developing science has been dominated, as the introduction mentions, by an analysis of the metaphors used by the early electricians. Texts from the 1740s and 1750s refer variously to electricity as a fire or a fluid, and these competing terms (if they are indeed metaphors) suggest different ways of thinking about experimental phenomena. But perhaps more has been made of these differences than is warranted. "Fire" and "fluid" were occasionally used interchangeably in early texts. Benjamin Franklin, for example, uses both terms intermittently (see Cohen 1941, 234) and writes of "electrical fire or fluid" in the same sentence (228). In 1757 he even identifies electrical fire *as* a fluid (340, 342, 412). Second, the terms "electric fire" and "electric fluid" competed with a host of other less obviously metaphoric terms such as "electric effluvia," "electrick vertue," "electric aether," and "electric matter." Third, uses of "fire" or "fluid" were perhaps less the product of deliberate theorizing than the byproduct of experimental purpose and materials. Thus the electricians who talked of fire (Bose, Watson, and Winkler) were largely concerned with generating sparks to ignite flammable substances, and they frequently used a gun barrel as a conveniently sized, hollow metallic object to collect an electrical charge. The electricians who used the term "fluid," on the other hand, usually did so when explaining how electricity flowed through their apparatus and how it could be pumped from the ground. Some found that they could generate more electricity when they ran a wire out the door and down the pump at the garden well.

Certainly the use of metaphors informed early theorizing about electrical phenomena. It would also be possible, as well as instructive, to study the role of antithesis in the early discussions of electricity, for the "electrical" lexicon of the eighteenth century offers many pairs of opposite terms (e.g., electrics and nonelectrics as two classes of bodies), and there were any number of attempts to theorize the phenomenon into opposite types. Thus the Frenchman Charles Dufay (or Du Fay) characterized two kinds of electricity in the 1730s, vitreous and resinous, typically forcing these new terms apart by connecting them to a pair of recognized opposites: "If it [a body] attracts [an electrified silk thread], 'tis certainly of that kind of Electricity which I call vitreous; if on the contrary it repels, 'tis of the same kind of

Electricity with the Silk, that is, of the resinous" (Dufay 1734, 265). The German Georg Bose attempted to distinguish two kinds of electrical fire (or sparks) by tying them to the strong opposites male and female (Heilbron 1979, 326). The Frenchman Nollet wrote of effluent and affluent forces or currents to explain attraction and repulsion, and finally, Benjamin Franklin hit on the more successful pairs positive and negative or plus and minus to characterize a surplus or deficiency of electricity and argued for replacing the pair electrics and nonelectrics with conductors and nonconductors (Cohen 1941, 175–176; 247).

But the creation of the "science" of electricity perhaps owes as much to the figures ploche and polyptoton as to metaphor or antithesis. The first foregrounds the presence of a term simply by multiplying it, and the second foregrounds the variety of its functions by creating new forms off the root. A simple example of the importance of ploche comes from the competition among preparadigmatic schools of electrical thought in the early eighteenth-century when, according to Kuhn, "there were almost as many views about the nature of electricity as there were important electrical experimenters" (Kuhn, 1970, 13). It could be argued that the differences between these early terms for the origin of electrical phenomena, whether electric effluvia, electric fire, electric matter, electric aether, electric fluid, or electric vertue (all terms used in the 1740s), are less significant than the fact that they were all modified and hence unified by the same adjective.

Also, in purely descriptive terms, the difference between experimental reports having to do with electrical phenomena in the first decades of the eighteenth century and those that appeared in the 1740s–1760s can be characterized in terms of the frequency with which words formed from the root *electri* appear in the articles. In early texts by Hauksbee and even Gray, some form of the term may appear one, two, or a few times in a whole article. In writings from the 1740s on, repeated forms of the root occur several times on a single page. Thus the radical *electri* has a grammatical triumph by mid-century, colonizing every part of speech and reappearing through repetition in a constant refrain. Furthermore, its uses are a significant indicator of the conceptual territory conquered by the term; the spread of the root *electri*, part of the development of a dedicated nomenclature, can serve then as an index of the development of the science. What parts of speech are colonized first? When do significant extensions to other forms occur? What environment do these terms appear in (that is, what collocations occur) suggesting restrictions on their usage, and how and when do these words begin to change meaning without changing form?

Noun and modifiers

William Gilbert has the credit for inaugurating the science of electricity, not because he had anything like a later understanding of the phenomenon, but primarily because he was the first to coin certain key terms in Latin in 1600 (Heilbron 1979, 169). In his groundbreaking treatise on magnetism, Gilbert digresses for a chapter to distinguish a very different kind of attraction often confused with the pull of the lodestone. To talk about this other attraction, Gilbert borrows the Greek word for amber, ἤλεκτρον (Latin *electrum*), known from antiquity as a substance capable of attracting bits of chaff when rubbed. Any other body that exhibits this property becomes amber-like or, to use the English form of the adjective, "electric" or "electrical." Gilbert found many more substances that exhibit this property of attraction, discovering that not only amber and jet possess it but also 24 others, including glass, resin, sealing wax, and sulphur, all important in later experiments. With so many substances exhibiting the same amber-like property of attraction, Gilbert in effect created a new genus for which he needed a term. In his Latin text, he calls these collectively *electrica corpora*, electric bodies, or simply *electrica*, electrics, plural of the neuter *electricum*. Then, by default, this genus of "electrics" creates a genus of "non-electrics." Gilbert also coined the adverb *electrice* to describe the manner of attracting like amber.

The questions that Gilbert asks about the amber-like power of attraction naturally lead to further expansions of the term, not necessarily to new derivatives but to what Aristotle would call a growing family of co-ordinate terms implicated as a connected set in further arguments. How, Gilbert asks, do electrics manifest this attraction? They must have a special power, "vim illam electricam nobis placet appellare quae ab humore provenit" (Heathcote 1967, 269); this observed power of attracting like amber in turn requires an agent, and Gilbert offers a material agent as an explanation consistent with the facts as he knows them, an *electrica effluvia* (274), a stream of matter more subtle than air, gently released when an electric is rubbed, capable of easy interruption by water or light cloth but, when allowed to travel without interference, capable of "lay[ing] hold of the bodies with which they unite, enfold[ing] them, as it were, in their arms, and bring[ing] them into union with the electrics" (Gilbert 1952, 33).

Latin derives some nouns from adjectives by adding the suffix *-itas*, so the property of attracting light matter can easily become the quality inherent in the genus of *electrica corpora*, namely *electricitas*. Gilbert does not coin this term. It apparently first appears in its English form, "electricity," in Sir Thomas Browne's *Pseudo-doxia Epidemica* of 1646 (Heathcote 1967, 261): "Crystal will calefie unto electricity; that is, a power to attract strawes and light bodies, and convert the needle freely placed" (261). Here is the first critical polyptotonic move in the formation of the science, the creation of an abstract notion from a set of objects and observable physical properties. Amber-like electrics exhibit an electrical quality or electricity. This term *electricity*, however, will drastically change its meaning in the following century and a half without changing its form.

Over a century after Gilbert's digressive chapter on *electrica corpora*, the Royal Society's demonstrator of experiments, Francis Hauksbee, investigated the appearance of light in mercury-filled barometers and the effects of rubbing bodies against each other inside evacuated glass globes. Eventually focusing on the glass itself, he reported over several years on a set of experiments using globes mounted in a frame where they could be vigorously rotated and "excited," to use the words of the later electrical lexicon, with the pressure of a hand or other material. Hauksbee described his ingenious experiments in letters published in the *Philosophical Transactions* and later collected these notices in a volume of *Physico-Mechanical Experiments on Various Subjects*, published first in 1709 and expanded in a second edition in 1719.

These papers were later classified as reports of electrical experiments, but few of them use any term formed from the root "electri," and when Hauksbee does finally employ the label, he uses only the same nouns and adjectival forms that Gilbert and Browne used. His entire electrical lexicon in the *Philosophical Transactions* consists of the following three terms: *electricity, electrical quality,* and, once only, *electrical effluvia.* That the coinage "electricity" is still somewhat unfamiliar in Hauksbee's day is perhaps indicated by the fact that in Hauksbee's fifth report, the first to use any form of the term, it appears in the title over the letter as "Elistricity" (Hauksbee 1706, 2327).[18]

When Hauksbee succeeded in attracting threads dangling from a hoop to a rubbed glass globe, he referred to these experiments as seeming "to Illustrate Attraction or Electricity, by the Ends of the surrounding Threads pointing to the Axis of the Affricated Glass" (Hauksbee 1707a, 2372). And when he coated the inside of a glass globe with sealing wax, whirled it around applying his hand to the outside, and found that it attracted threads in the same way his empty glass globes did, threads that also were repelled by the approach of his finger, he writes, "in all Respects relating to Electricity, the *Effluvia* of Wax seems very agreeable to those producible on the Attrition of Glass" (Hauksbee 1708, 87). Further along in this letter he refers to the thread-attracting property of rosin as a much stronger "Electrical Quality." He discovers that a warmed rosin-coated cylinder will attract leaf brass without being rubbed, "But next day when I came to repeat the Experiment, its Electricity was so inconsiderable, as well as that of the Sulphur, that I did not think them worthy to trouble the Society" (90). All these whirlings and thread motions are labeled, ultimately, "Experiments on the Electricity of different Bodies" (89). It is, however, easy to misread these passages and think that Hauksbee is talking about an agency or force within the glass or wax or rosin cylinder. He is not. Instead the word "Electricity" in his usage could be replaced by the phrase "its ability to attract leaf brass or threads." Electricity is not for Hauksbee an agent in a body; effluvia are the agents in the bodies. Instead the label "electricity" stands, as Niels Heathcote has made clear from his study of the early usage of the term, only for the property that some substances have of giving motion to light bodies (Heathcote 1967, 261). Hauksbee's usage in this limited sense is consistent in the 11 times he uses the word "electricity" and the five times he uses "electrical quality" in 13 letters published between 1705 and 1711 in the *Philosophical Transactions,* and that sense dominates in the writing of other experimenters for the following two decades. Electricity as the quality or property of attracting or giving motion to light bodies can occasionally spin off an adjective or a manner adverb, as it did for Gilbert and Hauksbee in "electrice" or "electrical quality," but it is more difficult to derive a verb from a term used in this sense.

Despite the fact that Hauksbee made no changes in the electrical lexicon, his place as a founder of the science of electricity was in part secured by the attention he received in Joseph Priestley's mid-eighteenth century compendium, *The History and Present State of Electricity,* which first appeared in 1767. Indeed, the eighteenth-century's success in creating the science of electricity owes much to the declaration of that success in Priestley's compendium, his textbook in the form of a chronological accounting of successful experiments, deliberately omitting "mistakes, misapprehensions, and altercations" (Priestley 1775, I, xi). Priestley's *History* begins with Gilbert's observations in *De Magnete,* 1600, but concentrates on work in the early eighteenth century, ending at 1766, the period singled out by Thomas Kuhn to exemplify a preparadigmatic science, until the work of Franklin and others at mid-century provided subsequent researchers with "a common paradigm for its research" (Kuhn 1970, 15). Kuhn, however, does not discuss the rhetorical work required to achieve such a paradigm or body of agreement among researchers. Priestley's *History* is recognized as a key work in achieving this agreement, but its rhetorical mechanisms have not been elucidated. It is taken as a transparent work, elegant and notable for its clarity and simplicity, but these are terms that describe readers' impressions rather than rhetorical means. Certainly one of Priestley's rhetorical devices was his redescription of the older experiments with a greater frequency of terms formed on "electri."

When Priestley redescribes Hauksbee's experiments in his *History,* he does to some extent remain faithful to Hauksbee's descriptive language, but in order to earn Hauksbee his place as a significant forerunner, he must re-present Hauksbee's work in a way that makes it relevant. He accomplishes this feat simply by a more liberal use of the adjectives "electric" and "electrical." Thus Hauksbee's reports of experiments on the light produced by the attrition of glass globes either never mention electricity at all, or mention it only as described above, applying to the separate issue of attracting bits of thread. But Priestley praises Hauksbee for "The varieties he observed on the appearances and properties of the *electric light*(Priestley 1775, I, 21), and how he made this transition to "electric light" (I, 21) after having worked with phosphorus. He writes that "The greatest electric light Mr. Hauksbee produced, was when he enclosed one exhausted cylinder within another not exhausted" (I, 25). When Hauksbee originally described this experiment, he wrote only about producing Light ["I think, the greatest as yet that has been produc'd" (Hauksbee 1707b, 2414)], never mentioning electricity in this article. Again, Priestley writes of "the great copiousness, and extreme subtility of electric light" (Priestley 1775, I, 26) that Hauksbee produced when he partially coated the inside of glass globes with wax, pitch, and common sulphur, whirled them on his apparatus and then: "I no sooner held my Hand on that part of it, under which it was lin'd with the premention'd Wax, but the Figure of the Parts that touch'd it, was as visible on the inward Surface of the Sealing-Wax, as when the Glass alone is us'd for that purpose (Hauksbee 1708b, 219)." Hauksbee speaks of the electricity of these globes again only in his usual sense of their ability to attract light bodies such as threads.

> As to the Electricity of the Globe lin'd with this sort of Matter [flowers of sulphur which proved ineffective]; after the Attrition of it had been continued for some time, and the Glass was become pretty warm (at the same time full of common Air) the Hoop of Threads was held over it; but the Attraction was very inconsiderable on the lin'd part. (Hauksbee 1709b, 439; see also Hauksbee 1708b, 219; 1709a, 392)

Hauksbee never used the term "electric light" as Priestley did. And although he was aware of the mixed movements of matter toward and away from an "affricated" body, he never wrote confidently as Priestley did in his account: "The varieties he observed on the appearances and properties of the *electric light,* are even more curious and surprising than his discoveries concerning *electric attraction and repulsion* (Priestley 1775, I, 21, see also 19, 20). Nor did Hauksbee ever write of the "electric power of glass" (I, 28) or of the "power of electricity" (I, 29). There is nothing dishonest in Priestley's more liberal application of forms of the term *electri*, nor is Priestley unaware of his renaming: for example, "He [Hauksbee] also found, that this appearance of electric light (which he still calls the mercurial phosphorus)" (I, 22). Priestley's use of polyptoton and ploche is the essential marker of interpretation and assimilation, presenting a message originally promulgated in one lexicon or register in another and inserting a dominant term in the process. Such changes are always open to refutation and reinterpretation (a matter of using yet another register and set of dominant terms), but they are also inevitable.

Expansion to verbal forms

Between Gilbert who brings the root *electri* into modern Latin in 1600 and Hauksbee who in the first decade of the 18th century dutifully generates effluvia exhibiting electricity as attraction by the "motion and attrition" of glass globes and cylinders of wax, rosin, and sulphur, the polyptotonic expansion of "electri" did not advance at all. It is still a genus term and a modifier for a handful of words like "quality" and "effluvia." By contrast, when Benjamin Franklin begins in the late 1740s to write his letters on electricity to Peter Collinson, who has them read to the Royal Society, the root has expanded to verbal and adverbial forms, and the frequency of its appearance in the accounts of experiments that are now confidently described as "electrical" has increased enormously. What happened in between?

It was Stephen Gray who, in a series of experiments from 1729 to 1731, began to put electricity into motion, eventually creating the need for coining a verb from the root. Gray discovered that the corks he had used to close the ends of a glass tube would attract a feather just as well as the rubbed glass tube itself. He then placed a stick with an ivory ball at the end into the cork and found that this ball attracted the feather as well as the cork did. From this point on, Gray, with his collaborators Granvil Wheler and John Godfrey, established that the ability to attract substances (the Gilbert-Hauksbee meaning of the term) could be transferred to objects farther and farther from contact with an excited tube, "shewing that the Electrick Vertue of a Glass Tube may be conveyed to any other Bodies, so as to give them the same Property of attracting and repelling light Bodies, as the Tube does, when excited by rubbing" (Gray 1731, 18–19).

Yet curiously enough, in the ten letters he wrote to the Royal Society on his electrical experiments, from a 1708 letter to Hans Sloane that was never published in the *Philosophical Transactions* to a communication made on his deathbed to the Secretary of the Royal Society, Gray himself does not coin any form of active verb to describe this propagation; he does not make the easy grammatical move from saying something like "the glass tube conveys electricity to other bodies," to a construction a step away like "the glass tube electrifies other bodies." Instead, to focus on his lengthy letter published in 1731, which was widely influential, he relies on all-purpose verbs to describe this process of transference. "Conveyed" is his choice in the passage quoted above; "communicated" is also used, particularly as a past participle. He writes of his initial observation of the feather-drawing cork ball that there was "an attractive Vertue communicated to the Cork by the excited Tube"

(Gray 1731, 20), and that a fire shovel, tongs, iron poker, copper tea kettle (with and without hot or cold water), flint stone, bricks, and even vegetables "had all of them an Electrick Vertue communicated to them" (22). But his most frequent choice is the verb "carry" in passive constructions like the following: "I next proceeded to try at what greater Distances the Electrick Vertue might be carried" (22). Gray discovers that this electrick vertue "might be carried" across 3, 26, 52, 147, 293, 765, and eventually 886 feet of ingeniously suspended packthread or "Line of Communication" (e.g., 30). "Carry," like "communicate" and "convey," even in active constructions, is a particularly neutral choice. In sharp contrast to later views, an electricity that is "carried" seems to lack any movement or activity of its own. Against this background of bland verbs, there is one surprising sentence in which Gray describes what happened when he put nails into wood to suspend his lines and found no attraction at the end. "Upon this I concluded, that when the Electrick Vertue came to the Loop that was suspended on the Beam, it went up the same to the Beam" (25). Here one suddenly sees the "vertue" endowed with its own motion and activity.

But despite this exception and three other occasions in the 1731 letter using active constructions with the verb "pass" (e.g., "the Electrick Effluvia pass through all the interior Parts of the solid Cube" [35]), Gray distinctly prefers passive to active constructions, 13 times to three, using his more noncommittal verbs: The electrick vertue "is carried," "may be carried," "would have been carried," "might not be conveyed," "is not so strongly communicated." The passive is presumably the default choice for anyone who wishes to avoid attributions of agency or at least to divorce a mapping of agent over grammatical subject, but that standard explanation is not especially helpful in this context. Typically, Gray's passive constructions allow him to focus on what is being communicated, not on its source, the tube, or the agent in its generation (Gray himself rubbing the tube), or even on the means of its conveyance. The subject of all these passive constructions in the 1731 letter is either "Electrick Vertue" or "Electricity." Since the actual source and agent, a glass tube and Gray rubbing it, remain constant in all his experiments, he need not repeat the identical preliminaries in each trial.

Gray may also have preferred passive constructions and for the most part avoided attributing agency to the tube or to himself, the experimenter, because, as he reports in the later part of his lengthy 1731 letter, he can produce the same effects, that is, making an object attract leaf brass, when the rubbed tube only comes near without touching his lines of packthread or wooden hoops or live charity boys suspended in silk (that is, by induction rather than conduction). He therefore cannot make the tube unambiguously an active agent in the sense that physical contact is required for the transmission of effects, though of course the tube remains a source of whatever is the actual agent, still called either an electrick vertue or electrick effluvia in his lexicon. Thus the passive in Gray is not a default preference coming from some presumed favoring of this voice in a scientific or reportorial style. It seems instead to be a deliberate choice that reflects his sense of what should be grammatically salient in his sentences as well as a scrupulous avoidance of direct attribution of cause and effect, since direct physical contact is not necessary for passing on the ability to attract leaf brass.

It is also likely that the physical circumstances of electrical experiments in the Gray manner throughout the 1730s through the 1750s—the ingenious interposition of people, swords, pokers, packthread, or spoons in chains between the excited tube and the body attracting leaf brass, or later between the Leyden jar and the recipients of its considerable shocks—visually reinforced the separation of the source at one end and the manifestation of the effect at the other, a separation that has its analog in his grammatical constructions. The point of these experiments was not from what electricity could be excited (a point on which Gray had no news to offer) but how far and to what it could be communicated.

In 1733, the French academician Charles Dufay repeated Stephen Gray's experiments, effusively acknowledging Gray's inspiration, but he also extended and clarified them, and began theorizing to explain the sometimes confusing results. He described his experiments and theories in a letter to the Royal Society that was translated into English and published in the first number of the *Philosophical Transactions* for January/February 1734. This letter employs two kinds of locutions to describe the transference of electricity. When Dufay describes most directly his repetitions of Gray's experiments, for example, "Having communicated the Electricity of the Tube by means of a Packthread, after Mr. Gray's manner" (Dufay 1734, 260), he also uses Gray's language, which carefully preserves the distance in effects between an excited tube and the ultimate body displaying the attracting property. But Dufay found that through a combination of heating and rubbing he could make just about any substance, except metallic and fluid ones, display the property of attracting light bodies. The favored locution for this result reappears frequently in this letter: "all Bodies . . . may be made Electrick," (258) they "became Electrick" (258); "Water may be made Electrical" (259); bodies "became Electrical" (259).[19] In the last section of his letter, the phrases describing this endowing phenomenon repeatedly use the same terms, with typical eighteenth-century disregard for consistency in spelling: "is thereby render'd electrical," "when render'd electrick," "though render'd electrical likewise," "one need only render Electrical a Silk Thread," "that Body, render'd electrical, attracts," "be render'd electrick by the Tube," "be rendered as electrical as possible" (263–265). Though all but one of these is a passive or participial construction, a function of focus on the recipient of the electricity in these experiments, here finally is a usage that seems only a step away from a verb formed from the root: To render electrical is to electrify.

The final move to a verb formed from the root *electri* apparently occurs for the first time not in the English *Philosophical Transactions* but in its French counterpart, the journal produced by the Academie Royale des Sciences in Paris. The yearly publications of this journal have an unusual format. Each consists of two sections, a *Histoire de L'Academie Royale des Sciences* and the *Mémoires de Mathematique et de Physique*. The latter, the *Mémoires*, contain the actual signed communications from the Academy's scientific correspondents. The *Histoire* provides background and fundamentals for uninitiated readers on highlighted subjects and both summarizes the year's work and previews the contents of the *Mémoires*. The *Mémoires* for 1833 contain four lengthy articles by Dufay detailing his experiments; but it is the *Histoire*'s prefatory piece, authorship unknown, which introduces the verb *s'électriser* in the context of a basic explanation of how other bodies can receive electricity from a rubbed glass tube.

> Tout corps devenu électrique communique sa vertu à un autre corps qu'il touche, ou seulement qu'on en approche suffisamment, même aux Métaux qui ne peuvant pas devenir électriques *par eux mêmes*, c'est-à-dire, étant chauffés & frotté. Il n'y a que le Fer qui s'aimante, mais tout *s'électrise*, & même les liqueurs. De l'eau, dont on a suffisamment approché un Tube de verre rendu électrique, attire des brins de fil, des cheveux. La main de celui qui fait ces expériences s'électrise. Il faut que le Tourbillon du corps électrique par lui-même aille s'attacher à celui qui le devient *par communication*, ou plutôt se partage entre les deux.

> Any body become electric communicates its virtue to another which it touches, or which it only approaches sufficiently, even to metals which cannot become electric by themselves, that is to say, being heated and rubbed. It is not only iron which is magnetized, but all are electrised, even liquids. Water, to which one has sufficiently approached a tube of glass rendered electric, attracts bits of thread, of hair. The hand of those who make these experiments is electrised. It is necessary that the vortex of the electric body by itself sticks to that which becomes [electric] by communication, or rather is divided between the two. ("Sur L'Électricitie" 1733, 8; italics in original. See also pp. 9, 10, 11, 12).

The use of italics and the introduction of the new verb immediately after a cognate (*s'aimanter*, to be magnetized or to magnetize itself) suggests a self-conscious coinage on the unknown author's part. Furthermore, the French author has been assisted by the extensive category of reflexive verbs available in French. In English, reflexives are verbs that can take the same subject and object: she dressed herself. Reflexives from the French are often translated as passives in English, but they can be thought of as in a sense intermediate between active and passive constructions as in the series *occuper*, to occupy, *s'occuper*, to occupy oneself or be occupied, and *est occupée*, is occupied. As such, a reflexive hedges against agent or recipient status for its grammatical subject: "mais tout s'électrise"—everything is electrised or electrises itself. Perhaps the greater availability of the reflexive in French made it easier for the verb to appear first in that language.

Inevitably, when Priestley retells Gray's and Dufay's work 35 years later, and fully 20 years after the verb "to electrify" has spread and the noun "electricity" has changed its meaning, he occasionally slips into the more convenient lexicon, especially when he is summarizing rather than paraphrasing. Where Gray writes that his friend Wheler "proposed a Silk Line to support the Line, by which the Electrick Vertue was to pass" (Gray 1731, 26), Priestley writes "Mr Wheeler [*sic*] proposed to suspend the line to be electrified by another of *silk*" (Priestley 1775, I, 37). Gray says that when he and Wheler hung a large map of the world and a table cloth from a rubbed glass tube, they "became electrical" (Gray 1731, 32); Priestley writes of their "electrifying a large map, table cloth, &c" (I, 40). Where Gray must "circumlocute" about a "red hot poker" that "the Attraction was the same as when cold" (33), Priestley can simply write that the experimenter "electrified the red hot poker" (I, 40).

Furthermore, although Priestley occasionally retains Gray's quaint locution, "electrick vertue," the experimenters that Priestley speaks to have long accepted "electricity" as a term not for the effect of attraction but for something that moves and causes that attraction. So where Gray explains that using brass wire to support his lines of communication ruined the result, for "though the Tube was well rubbed, yet there was not the least Motion or Attraction given by the Ball" (Gray 1731, 29), Priestley can write simply of the failure of the brass wire experiment, "upon rubbing the tube, no electricity was perceived at the end of the line" (Priestley 1775, I, 39). Thus Priestley's changes to the early electricians' lexicon, while not elaborate, are telling. He knows better than the early experimenters what they actually did and what their results showed.

Curiously, despite the groundbreaking coinage in 1733 of the convenient past participle and the verb, this expansion did not quickly migrate into English. Gray read the translation of Dufay's letter in the *Philosophical Transactions* and in 1735 acknowledged his gratification for Dufay's confirmation of his work and reported on his own attempts to imitate Dufay's experiments for producing light and sparks rather than merely attraction; this letter contains Gray's first and only mention of "Electrick Fire" and speaks of electricity communicated and "Communicative Electricity" (Gray 1735, 24), but otherwise, Gray's lexicon of *electri* words is unchanged. When Gray's collaborator Granvile Wheler finally wrote on his own in 1739 after Gray's death, clarifying alternating attraction and repulsion in a series of Newtonian appearing propositions, corollaries, and scholia, he too does not make the jump to the newer term, but instead uses again and again the phrase "made Electrical" (Wheler 1739, 99,103, 108, 109). Yet Wheler reports having read not only the 1734 English letter by Dufay but also accounts of his work in the Memoirs of the Academy of Sciences for 1735 (98).

By 1745, however, the verb in all its forms had come into the English electrical lexicon. But what forms were used and how they were used deserve attention, for words do not immediately appear in every possible environment in a language. One of the first to use forms of "electrify" in English was William Watson, an apothecary turned electrical experimenter who, as a member of the Royal Society was for many years its "chief link between English and Continental electricians" (Heilbron 296). His first four letters to the Society, published together as *Experiments and Observations tending to illustrate the Nature and Properties of Electricity* (1745), can be taken as typical of mid-century usage in the *Philosophical Transactions*. Furthermore, though Watson's were not the first works read by Franklin, they were nevertheless influential on experimenters in Europe and America (Watson won the Copley Medal in 1745 for his electrical experiments), so the peculiarities in Watson's usage deserve examination.

Watson's first experiments were attempts, following the recent successes of the Germans (Heilbron 1979, 272–273), to set flammable spirits on fire with an electrical spark. He followed the usual stepwise, mediated procedure, hanging a poker by insulating silk threads and attaching ordinary, foot-long threads to one end. Here is a passage describing such a procedure without using any form of the verb, but which has circumlocutions where the verb could have been used in describing the typical experimental procedure.

Among these Threads, which were all attracted by the rubbed Tube, I excited the greatest electrical Fire I was capable, whilst an Assistant, near the End of the Poker, held in his Hand a Spoon, in which were the warm Spirits. Thus the Thread communicated the Electricity to the Poker, and the Spirit was fired at the other End. (Watson 1745, 483)

Letters to the Royal Society on electrical experiments in the first half of the eighteenth century tend to be accounts, like to above, of multiple experiments performed as ingenious variations on a theme, polyptotonic in another sense, so as further trials are recounted by an experimenter, some ellipsis or shorthand naturally occurs. Watson's most frequently used form of the verb "to electrify" is, in fact, as a modifier. The past participle "electrified" occurs 22 times in either prenoun or postnoun positions: "a Person electrified" (Watson 1745, 484), "In electrified Bodies" (485), "the Man electrified" (489), "Person not electrified," "the electrified Person" (491), "electrified Sword" (497), "ice not electrified" (Watson, 1746, 42), etc. Four of these uses occur in the elliptical construction "when electrified": "From this cold Mixture, when electrified [Watson wanted to see if the electrical fire was inhibited by the cold], the Flashes were as powerful, and the Stroke as smart, as from the red-hot Iron" (1746; 49). All these forms are abbreviations indicating to an initiated audience that an experimental procedure like that described above has gone on. Someone in touch with the ground, the reader assumes that it is Watson, has rubbed a glass tube among threads connected to a poker that is either hanging from silk or held in the hands of a person standing on a cake of wax, as a result electrifying either him and whatever he is holding or whatever is suspended by itself in silk lines. To electrify in the context of Watson's reports, quite different from Gray's, means to endow with the property of sparking or snapping on the approach of a nonexcited body. These precise procedures become less important than the expected and frequently replicated and reliable result. Hence more shorthand formulations can occur after the things and processes they refer to have been described at least once in detail. This accumulation of familiarity that can occur in one article is as likely to occur across articles.

The past participle is an essential part of passive constructions, and predictably, these occur eight times in Watson's four early letters: "Suppose that either a Man standing upon a Cake of Wax, or a Sword suspended in silk Lines, are electrified" (Watson 1745, 489); "If an electrical Cake is dipp'd in Water . . . a Person standing thereon can by no means be electrified" (492); "the Water, which had ceased dropping when the Sponge was not electrified, drops again upon its being electrified" (498). The passive construction here, as in Gray, comes not from a desire to hide the agent or agency, but from the emphasis on what is being electrified, on the recipient of the electrical virtue, since what is doing the electrifying remains the same in each experiment while the recipient frequently changes. All the other 22 uses of "electrified" as a modifier can be described as elliptical passive constructions: an "electrified Person" is a person who has been electrified. The net effect of the total of 30 uses is to maintain the focus overwhelmingly on the recipient, in keeping with the early eighteenth century's interest in electricity as a demonstrator's art, a source of entertaining spectacles.

But in four instances Watson does employ the present participle "electrifying"; once in the elliptical and agentless (or agent understood) construction "upon electrifying *A*" (Watson 1745, 493), "*A*" standing for one of two people on cakes of wax. Twice Watson uses the present participle in unusual ways. "it once happen'd, that whilst the Bar was at one End electrifying, a Spoon lay upon the other; and, upon an Assistant's pouring some warm Spirit into the Spoon, the electrical Flash from the Spoon snapped, and fired the first Drop of the Spirit (1745, 490–491).

On a later occasion, when Watson was trying to electrify a piece of ice, in part to see if he could achieve the oxymoronic feat of having ice set fire to a spoonful of spirits, he discovered that he lost too much electricity as the ice melted. "In order to obviate this, I caused my Assistant, while he was electrifying, to be continually wiping the Ice dry upon a Napkin hung to the Buttons of his Coat; and this being electrified as well as the Ice, prevented any Loss of the Force of the Electricity (1746, 41)."

What is happening at the end "electrifying" or to the Assistant "electrifying" is of course that they are receiving a static charge as Watson rubs the tube among the threads. A more expected construction here than the past progressive would be the passive "was being electrified"; instead the phrases "the Bar was at one end electrifying" and "while he was electrifying" suggest a process that is continuing almost independently, as in the expression, "the stew was cooking." Perhaps this use of the past progressive is also Watson's way of distinguishing, to some extent, effects that are occurring "downstream" of where he is applying the tube but not at the very end of whatever combination of threads, rods, and human assistants he has rigged together for any particular trial. Another way to describe this restricted sphere of usage would be to say that the progressive is used whenever Watson speaks of a part of his apparatus as an intermediary, and the passive is used whenever he speaks of a part as a recipient, no matter where it appears. The verb forms, in other words, seem accommodated to the physical parameters.

To reinforce this impression that the verb forms are adjusted to the position in the line of transfer being emphasized or described are the few instances when Watson does use the active voice. In his practice, the active voice is only used with a human agent as grammatical subject, corresponding to the initiating event in an electrical experiment (see the first passage without a verb cited above). "I placed a Man upon a Cake of Wax, who held in one of his Hands a Spoon with the warm Spirits, and in the other a Poker with the Thread. I rubbed the Tube amongst the Thread, and electrified him as before (Watson 1745, 485)."

> I was desirous of being satisfy'd, whether or no the Fire emitted would not be greater or less in proportion to the Volume of the electrified Body. In order to this [*sic*], I procured an iron Bar about 5 Feet long, and near 170 Pounds in Weight; this I electrified lying on Cakes of Wax and Resin. (Watson 1745, 490) [The bar and not Watson is lying on the cakes of wax.]

The action that Watson performs, once again, is rubbing his long glass tube among the threads or applying it to or near an iron bar, but "I rubbed and electrified" can easily be shortened to "I electrified" since these two verbs in sequence mean not "I did this and then that" but "I did this and as a result that." The grammatical subject is a human agent, since in these experiments the human operator is very much the initiator and source of the electricity, especially in the 1730s and 1740s when experimenters rubbed their tubes with their hands or applied their hands to whirling glass globes. No wonder then that early experimenters in electricity believed that it represented a mysterious vital force.

Watson also uses a human agent as grammatical subject and "electrify" as a transitive verb in three constructions where he speaks conditionally of what can happen under certain experimental conditions.[20] Thus, though a glowing poker will not fire spirits or oil, "if you electrify this heated Poker, the electrical Flashes presently kindle Flame in either" (1745; 499); in experiments with gunpowder, "if you electrify the Powder, it will fly off at the Approach of any non-electrified Substance" (1745; 500); and "if, instead of the Ice, you electrify the Spirit" (1746; 41). Since the clauses in which these verbs appear are hypothetical constructions, the verb forms in these sentences could be described as subjunctive, marked in English only in auxiliary verbs (e.g., "If you were to electrify"). But Watson is here describing experiments he actually performed while suggesting that any performer would find the same result.

When the use of auxiliaries dictates that the main verb will be an infinitive, the grammatical subjects are still human agents in Watson's early usage: "as long as you continue to electrify the Man" (Watson, 1745, 494– 495); "I was desirous to know if I was able to electrify a Drop of cold Water" (498). There is, however, one exception to the collocation of the active or infinitive forms of "electrify" with human subjects toward the end of Watson's second letter, but before examining this important instance, another question has to be asked. What other agents could Watson have used in his descriptions? One obvious candidate is the Tube itself, which, in contemporary theories, was seen as the immediate source of the "electric Effluvia" that caused the attractive or sparking effects. Yet Watson never makes the Tube an agent in a construction like "the Tube electrified the threads." Instead, the Tube is always a recipient of human action and furthermore, in what is perhaps a more telling omission, it is never described as "electrified" itself. Instead, Watson's verb of choice is "excited," as in "I excited the greatest electrical Fire I was capable" (483), and when the immediate recipient of this action is described at all it is an "excited glass Tube" (1746, 44). The separated spheres of these verbs and modifiers may represent a separation in the understanding of the forces involved. When Watson acts on the tube he is applying mechanical energy; when the tube communicates its effluvia or virtue to the threads or poker, a different kind of force is involved, one that Watson avoids describing.

In the one instance when a human is not the grammatical subject of a form of the verb "electrify," Watson has chosen the closest and hence safest polyptotonic abstraction. "Ist, I conceive, that the Air itself (as has been observed by Dr. *Desaguliers*) is an Electric *per se*, and of the vitreous Kind; therefore it repels the Electricity arising from the glass Tube, and disposes it to electrify whatever non-electrical Bodies receive the *Effluvia* from the Tube" (Watson 1745, 486). The "it" that is doing the electrifying could refer to the tube or to electricity itself; given Watson's practice elsewhere, the latter is actually the likely alternative. Watson imagines a Newtonian scheme here where the air resists the effluvia rising from the tube, forcing a transfer of the effluvia to the poker instead of its dissipation in the surrounding atmosphere. There has, of course, been a significant change in the meaning of the noun "electricity" in this passage, but polyptotonic logic makes it easily possible to say that what is doing the electrifying, aside from the obvious human agent, is electricity itself. In this move from phenomenological to abstract redescription of experimental results, a polyptotonically tied subject and verb (electricity electrifies) represents perhaps the safest construction that a cautious theorizer can make.

An examination of Watson's circumscribed use of the verb and its past participle and a comparison with what other writers before and after could do, offer an example of figural and grammatical analysis at the service of the history of ideas. In general, the coining of the verb "electriser" or "to electrify" allowed experimenters to condense their descriptions as they came more reliably to assume an initiated audience of readers. The verb also unified the description of the operations in an experiment: The experimenter electrifies the prime conductor; the prime conductor is then electrified. These are now reciprocal actions, thanks to the active and passive forms of the same verb, far from the disconnected locutions like "I rubbed the tube" and "the cork attracted the leaf brass." Electricity is now a unitary phenomenon from its source to the manifestation of its effect. Furthermore, the verb and its ubiquitous past participle used to describe a newly created or transferred state, suggest that electricity is a more active principle.[21] Conceptual changes are marked by these small polyptotonic conquests.

The root electri *in Franklin*

Benjamin Franklin remains the most well-known electrical experimenter of the eighteenth century, a reputation that is not borrowed from his greater fame in other areas but one that he earned while alive. Because of the importance of his letters on electricity at the time and their later dissemination in English editions and French translations (Cohen 1941, 139–148), Franklin's usage can be taken as the sign not only of his own thinking but also of the elaborated electrical lexicon achieved by the mid-eighteenth century. For Franklin thought of himself as a contributor to a preexisting and advancing European community of experimenters.

The origin of Franklin's interest in electrical experiments, according to his own account, was a 1743 encounter with an itinerant demonstrator, one Dr. Spence or Spencer (Heilbron 1979, 324), and a subsequent gift from the London agent of the Philadelphia Library Company, Peter Collinson, who sent the colonists an electrical tube with instructions on how to use it. But more was arriving in those boxes from London than apparatus. Collinson also sent the five-volume abridged edition of the *Philosophical Transactions* in his first shipment as well as later numbers and separate works on electricity. Thus, he sent not only the physical means for producing a static charge, but he also sent samples of the verbal means for writing about the phenomena. By the time Franklin writes his letters on electricity to Peter Collinson in London in the late 1740s and early 1750s, the inflexions and co-ordinates formed around *electri* are extensive. There are some 137 uses in Franklin's first three letters, published together as a pamphlet and containing some of his most innovative work (Heilbron 1979, 330). Of these 137 uses, the majority are adjectival and verbal.

Most notable in Franklin is ploche of "electric," "electrical," "electrified," and "electrised" as modifiers braided throughout his detailed descriptions of experiments and theoretical musings on the results. In each case, half the instances of *electri* forms in one of these three early letters are adjectival (18 of 36 in the first, 24 of 50 in the second, 27 of 51 in the third). The default effect of this repetition is to place the work described in a defined lexical community of endeavor. In, for instance, his first substantive communication written in 1747 (printed as Letter II in later collections), Franklin informs Collinson that he and his colleagues are pursuing "electrical enquiries" in the tradition of the "electrical experiments" being performed in England. He understands that there is a distinct sphere of electrical investigation manipulating the "electrical fire" (visible sparks or brush discharges) using distinctive apparatus like the "electrical sphere" and achieving famous effects like the "electrical kiss" (Cohen 1941, 171–178). The adjectival use of the past participle of "electrify" or, closer to the original French term, of "electrise" is also notable: Franklin writes of the "electrised bottle" or "electrified phial" when referring to the Leyden jar. Prenoun modifiers, like all of the examples cited here, are always more closely associated with the noun they modify than postnoun modifiers, which can seem more detached; an "electrical experiment" is a dedicated effort inevitably producing electrical phenomena, whereas an "experiment that produces electrical effects" might produce other results. Among experimenters in the late seventeenth and early eighteenth centuries, it was far from clear what effects of experiments were "electrical" (Kuhn 1970, 16). But Franklin's electrical experiments using electrical equipment result reliably in manifestations of electricity, so that he can confidently send an account of "American Electricity" to the European community of researchers.

Of more importance than usage that places Franklin's text in a particular discourse community is the repetition of modifiers that suggests the spread and ubiquity of the phenomenon. Substances in the 1740s and 1750s were still classified as either "electrics" or "electrics per se," which by friction could, like amber, generate a charge, and as "non-electrics," which could not generate but could receive a charge and thus become "electrised." The polyptotonic tongue twister, "a non-electric electrised," often appears in texts in the 1740s. Like most researchers of the time, Franklin was also concerned in the dynamics of transferring electricity from one object to another, and his observations on these transfers led to his innovative theories of positive and negative electrical states. Whatever could receive a charge and could then either transfer a charge or be discharged could be described as "electrified" or "electrised." Verbally, one transfers a charge by transferring the word, as Franklin did in his first letter describing his thoughts on lightning and electricity. The problem that Franklin had first to think through was how an electrical charge accumulates in clouds. The answer is that it is transferred from water.

> Water being electrified, the vapours arising from it will be equally electrified; and floating in the air, in the form of clouds, or otherwise, will retain that quantity of electrical fire, till they meet with other clouds or bodies not so much electrified, and then will communicate as before-mentioned." (Cohen 1941, 201–202)

Franklin at first believed but later abandoned the idea that the water became electrified in the first place due to friction between the particles of water and particles of salt in the ocean as evidenced, he wrongly thought, by the luminescence of the sea at night. "The detach'd particles of water then repelled from the electrified surface, continually carry off the fire as it is collected; they rise and form clouds, and those clouds are highly electrified" (Cohen 1941, 203).

The discovery of the first condenser, the Leyden jar, or the "phial" or "bottle" in Franklin's writings, allowed for stronger charges and more visible effects, and Franklin and his cohorts tried to improve on the source by creating an "electrical battery," a series of lead-coated glass plates that could be collectively discharged. Most of the ingenuity in the apparatus and the experiments was spurred by the use of electricity as a form of entertainment as well as enquiry, culminating in the Abbe Nollet's spectacles for French royalty, making hundreds of suddenly electrified Carthusians jump at once. In a tour de force of both experimental ingenuity and of ploche and polyptoton in the description afterward, the electricians of Philadelphia organized a fête on the banks of the Skuylkill River to demonstrate the power of electricity as well as their power over it. Using the river as a conductor, they sent a spark across it to ignite alcoholic "spirits" on the other side, an experiment they had done before "to the amazement of many" (Cohen 1941, 200).

> A turkey is to be killed for our dinner by the *electrical shock*, and roasted by the *electrical jack*, before a fire kindled by the *electrified bottle*: when the healths of all the famous *electricians* in England, Holland, France, and Germany are to be drank in *electrified bumpers* [charged glasses], under the discharge of guns from the *electrical battery*. (Cohen 1941, 200) (italics in the original)

Franklin is also thoroughly comfortable with the two forms of the verb, "to electrify" and "to electrise," and he uses them liberally and interchangeably, even as late as 1762 (Cohen 1941, 360), for he works in the tradition of both the English and French experimenters who propagated electricity across great distances and odd intermediaries and the German experimenters who created stunning effects with their discovery of stronger sources of static charge. Thus, for Franklin electricity is, from the beginning, something in motion and the cause of a state known by its powerful effects. Hence verbal forms account for 12 of 36, 14 of 50, and 13 of 51 repetitions of the root in the first three letters.

Historians of science disagree over the extent of William Watson's influence on Franklin's electrical experiments and theories. Whatever merits of the case either way, Franklin does tend to use forms of the verb in the same way Watson does. Passive constructions predominate, 28 instances to eight, always in the same manner of allowing the recipient of a charge to be the grammatical subject as in the sentence introducing his groundbreaking antithetical terminology: "Hence have arisen some new terms among us: we say *B* [a person on a cake of wax], (and bodies like circumstanced) is electrised *positively; A, negatively.* Or rather *B* is electrised *plus; A, minus* (Cohen 1941, 175). In most of Franklin's active constructions, the verb collocates with a human subject: "you cannot electrise the shot" (172); "We electrise a person twenty or more times running" (176); "we electrified the bottle again" (191); and so forth. However, in three instances, Franklin does nominate other agents. He describes a wheel set in motion by the alternate attraction of bullets fixed to it surrounded by 12 pillars of glass topped by thimbles: "the bullet nearest to a pillar moves towards the thimble on that pillar, and passing by electrifies it" (196). In the same letter he writes that the wire from a Leyden jar will "electrify" an iron shot (199). In a more daring locution, he speaks of Watson being in error when he imagined that "the electrical fire came down the wire from the ceiling to the gun barrel, thence to the sphere, and so electrised the machine and the man turning the wheel" (176). With forms of the root available in all parts of speech, Franklin could have written a completely self-contained polyptotonic expression like "the electrical fire electrised the electrical machine."

With the verb in place, the process of polyptoton could continue in the formation of a noun from the verb, from electrify to electrification or from electrise to electrisation. Franklin makes this move in 1752 when he writes of the "electrification" of the clouds (Cohen 1941, 316) as does his defender, David Colden in 1753, when he refers to the "electrisation" of a conductor (290). Theorists could now speak abstractly of the process of a body becoming electrified, a considerable conceptual distance from "electricity" as an abstraction standing for the ability to attract tiny bits of matter.

The polyptotonic path of electri

The polyptotonic path of the root *electri* from Gilbert in 1600 to Priestley in 1766 can now be roughly traced out. First comes the adjective coined from the noun for amber and meaning amber-like in the sense of having the property of attracting light matter when rubbed. According to Heathcote, the Latin form of this adjective was actually in use as early as the mid-thirteenth century in the writings of Roger Bacon (Heathcote 1967, 266). Gilbert uses the adjective and an adverbial form, and, since he finds this amber-like property in many substances, he groups them as *electrica corpora* then shortened to *electrica*, a new noun standing for all substances that exhibit this power of attraction. By default, a genus of electrics brings a genus of non-electrics or *anelectrica* into existence. These two, electrics and nonelectrics, came to divide the world of substances between them.

Since any noun is available to be modified, an *electric* could in turn gain other properties. The choice of the frequently used adjective *excited*, for example, to describe an electric that had been rubbed—from the Latin *excitare*, meaning to call out, bring out, or waken—commits the user to the notion of a power which is in the material itself, but which can be stimulated and drawn out from it. A different choice of adjectives would have committed a user to a different conception of the relation of the quality to the substance exhibiting it as, for example, a "saturated electric" or an "imbued electric," where the ability to attract is put into and not drawn out from.

A key polyptotonic move comes next. The lexicon expands, from an adjective describing a quality (*electrical*) and a noun naming a group of objects displaying that quality (*electircs*), to a new noun, an abstraction that stands for the quality those objects demonstrate: *electricity*. The creation of a noun standing for the quality itself, which can be separated from the objects that exhibit it, is perhaps the most important lexical moment in a developing science. From the mid-seventeenth century until well into the eighteenth, electricity stands for the property that certain bodies possess of attracting light substances. But as the experimental effects attributable to this "electricity" change dramatically in the 1730s and 1740s, since this property of attracting can be collected, intensified, and give rise to sparks, a new need arises for a term that can stand for whatever it is that can cause these more dramatic effects. Two choices are available. One can use a more or less general noun for this unknown cause or origin and modify it with an adjective describing it by its effects: early electricians used many such combinations, mentioned above, including electric effluvia, electric matter, electric fire, electric aether, etc. Or one can continue to use the abstract noun, "electricity," but allow its sense to slide metonymically from effect to cause. For much of the eighteenth century, authors exploited both possibilities, though eventually the terms using "electric" as a modifier disappeared (see, for example, Priestley's indifferent use of both [1775, I, 44]). Again, the noun *electricity*, conveniently an *antanaclasis* whose sense as cause or effect depends on context, can behave as nouns always behave. It can become a plural and indeed from Dufay in the 1730s on, theorists begin to speak of *electricities*, modified as resinous or vitreous, positive or negative, effluent or affluent.

An abstract noun standing for a source or cause is available to become a verb when there is a need for one. (The opposite path from verb to abstract noun for "the act of," like *run* to *running*, is more familiar.) In the case of electricity, Gray's discovery of electrical conduction and induction created the need for a verb to describe this transfer or movement. Non-electrics could indeed become electrified, that is they could exhibit the properties of attraction by receiving its cause. At first the passive form of the verb and the past participle as modifier predominate in an experimental culture that focuses on ever-new recipients of an electrified state. Agency for the active form of the verb resides at first only with humans, but, with the discovery of the Leyden jar and ways to generate larger charges, agency could be expanded to key pieces of the apparatus. The identification of lightning as electricity in the 1750s also loosened the limitation to a human agent. Once created, the verb in turn gave rise to a new abstract noun, in this case for the process of acquiring a new state, *electrification*, a term that could grow in turn as a site of theorizing.

Every developing science will present a path of polyptotonic expansion in its key terms, the unique signature of its conceptual growth. Many more case studies would be needed to see if the sequence exhibited by the science of electricity, from adjective to category noun to abstract noun to verb, is typical. More such studies could also indicate which forms were the most useful in which sciences. In the case of electricity in the eighteenth century, the adjective was undoubtedly the conceptual workhorse. Its expansion through ploche, creating a cohort of co-ordinate terms, helped persuade early experimenters that there were indeed uniquely electrical effects generated by special electrical apparatus caused by an elemental electrical matter or aether or fluid or fire, allowing those who worked in these arts to create an informal social organization that would further the science and to make yet another polyptotonic move by calling themselves *electricians*.

Notes

Chapter 1

1. The first chapter of Lavoisier's *Traité Élémentaire de Chimie*, published 19 years before Dalton's *New Philosophy*, amply illustrates the prevailing conception of caloric as a repulsive force, the antithesis of the attraction of affinity that holds the particles of bodies together.

> Si après avoir *échauffé* jusqu'à un certain point un corps solide, & en avoir ainsi *écarté* de plus en plus toutes les molécules, on le laisse *refroidir*, ces mêmes molécules *se rapprochent* les unes des autres dans la même proportion, suivant laquelle elles avoient été écartées; (Lavoisier 1789 [1965], 2; italics added to indicate antithetical pairs of terms)

> When we have heated a solid body to a certain degree and have thereby caused its particles to separate from each other, if we allow the body to cool, its particles again approach each other in the same proportion in which they were separated. (Lavoisier 1952, 9)

Lavoisier infers from the existence of solids that there must be some power of attraction in nature that counteracts the repulsive power of heat. "Ainsi les molécules des corps peuvent être considérées comme obéissant à deux forces, l'une répulsive, l'autre attractive, entre lesquelles elles sont en équilibre" [Thus the particles of all bodies may be considered as subjected to the action of two opposite powers, the one repulsive, the other attractive, between which they remain *in equilibrio*] (1965, 3; 1952, 9). Lavoisier acknowledged the tendency to think of heat as a substance: "It is difficult to comprehend these phenomena, without admitting them as the effects of a real and material substance, or very subtle fluid, which, insinuating itself between the particles of bodies, separates them from each other" (1952, 9–10). Not wanting to have the same word express both cause and effect, Lavoisier coins for the cause, the hypothetical fluid, the term "caloric" (10).

This opening section of Lavoisier's celebrated chemical treatise amply illustrates the formative power of antithesis in his thinking. Dalton's refinement over Lavoisier's account amounts to matching a different pair of antithetical terms (same/other instead of heat/cool) on Lavoisier's opposed forces of separation and attraction. Thus Dalton imagines that the particles of heat are repeled from each other but attracted to whatever is not also a particle of caloric.

2. Among the four devices of augmentation is a form of climax (Quintilian 1921, III: 265–267) and among the devices that create reflexions, anatomized in chapter 5 of Book VIII, is the "noema" (III:289), which resembles emphasis (III:413) and another pattern of reflexion that resembles either an antimetabole or an antithesis (III:291).

3. Quintilian acknowledges that other rhetoricians have found it difficult to make the same move, to separate the "figures" from the tropes, for devices in both sets have a specifiable form and effect alterations in language, and both categories are used in the same way to "add force and charm to our matter" (Quintilian 1921, III:349). But though other rhetoricians, following the *Ad Herennium*, grouped the tropes and schemes, Quintilian wants to keep these categories apart:

> The name of *trope* is applied to the transference of expressions from their natural and principal signification to another . . . or, as the majority of grammarians define it, the transference of words and phrases from the place which is strictly theirs to another to which they do not properly belong. A *figure*, on the other hand, as is clear from the name itself, is the term employed when we give our language a conformation other than the obvious and ordinary. . . . [A figure does not, however] necessarily involve any alteration either of the order or the strict sense of words. (III:349–351)

In this passage, Quintilian sets up the often-repeated distinction between the tropes and schemes, the first affecting the semantics and the second the syntax or "conformation" of language. But for both categories, Quintilian maintains an overall definition of the figures as departures from "obvious and ordinary" usage, the tropes from common signification and the schemes from common forms of expression.

4. This same comparison to the posing of bodies and to sculpture is echoed in an earlier passage from Book II discussing when it is expedient and becoming to change a "time-honoured order."

> We see the same thing in pictures and statues. Dress, expression and attitude are frequently varied. The body when held bolt upright has but little grace, for the face looks straight forward, the arms hang by the side, the feet are joined and the whole figure [not Quintilian's word] is stiff from top to toe. But that curve, I might almost call it motion, with which we are so familiar, gives an impression of action and animation. So, too, the hands will not always be represented in the same position, and the variety given to the expression will be infinite. Some figures [again not his word] are represented as running or rushing forward, others sit or recline, some are nude, others clothed, while some again are half-dressed, half-naked. . . . A similar impression of grace and charm is produced by rhetorical figures, whether they be *figures of thought* or *figures of speech* [figurae quaeque in sensibus quaeque in verbis sunt]. For they involve a certain departure from the straight line and have the merit of variation from the ordinary usage. (Quintilian 1921, I:293–295)

Yet another link between a form in words and a disposition of the body comes from the fact that the word σχῆμα in Greek, which the Latin *figura* approximates, means not only form or bearing but also the steps in a dance.

5. The figures in this category that Quintilian goes on to catalog in Book IX include many of those that first appeared almost two centuries earlier in the *Ad Herennium*. These figures of interaction include such enduring devices as the rhetorical question (*erotema*) and its forgotten siblings, such as asking *and* answering a question (*hypophora*) or answering a question different from the question asked: "Did you strike the victim?" "He hit me first." They include *prosopopoeia*, incorporating the imagined speech of an absent person or in-

animate being, and a host of variants on the device of invoking other speakers in one's own voice. Many of the figures of thought, in other words, specify interactions between speaker and audience and reciprocal intentions and effects. Quintilian, however, aware of the impossibility of naming all of these, limits his discussion to those devices that "depart from the direct method of statement" (Quintilian 1921, III:375), such as questions that are asked with the intent of making an assertion or denials of taking up a topic that are made with the express purpose of introducing it.

More interesting are the ones since lost, ones less easily named but quite easily recognized from their definitions. Take, for example, *communicatio* (Quintilian 1921, III:386), the device of consulting one's opponent or the judges. Quintilian provides an example from Domitius Afer's defense of Cloatilla: "'It may be that chance has brought you into contact with the unhappy woman in her helpless plight. What counsel do you give her, you her brother, and you, her father's friends?'" (III:387). Or the advocate turns to the judge and asks, "What do you advise?" Though all of Quintilian's examples concern the forensic setting and the easily identified roles or sites of address in the courtroom, it is easy to imagine this gestural device constructing a reader's role in all kinds of texts. In fact, much of the rhetoric of fiction and reader response criticism has involved the surprised rediscovery of these ancient interactional devices.

Yet another "figure of thought" embodying the energy of interaction is "freedom of speech," called *licentia* in the *Ad Herennium* and defined there as the act of speaking freely before those who have power over us. Speaking freely includes insulting, taunting, pointing out the faults of the audience, or even admitting to a fault or crime. The author of the *Ad Herennium* recommends that such raw frankness be palliated by claiming trust in an audience's higher virtues. The gesture implies, "If I tell you how wrong you are here, it is only because I know how much you want to do the right thing." Yet another twist on this figure involves explicitly introducing such an approach to frankness, "I know that I can trust you to hear the flaws in your character pointed out without taking offense," and then following this preparation with a compliment such as: "But I have to tell you that your generosity is excessive in this case" (Quintilian 1921, III: 389–391). In the twentieth century, these devices have been rediscovered by experts in interpersonal communication, Erving Goffman and others, under the rubrics of footing and face.

6. In this division, Quintilian is actually following the lead of Cicero, his model in all things rhetorical, who in both the *Orator* (1988, 407–414) and the *De Oratore* (1970, 252–255) suggests these three divisions and quickly lists figures without, however, saying anything about what they are or what they should accomplish. Cicero imagines that these categories and their members are thoroughly known.

7. In the setting of a grammar text used to teach correctness such as Guarino Veronese's *Regulae Grammatica* from the early fifteenth century, figures are defined not just as departures but even as errors made for a reason ["Figura est vitium cum ratione factum" (Percival 1983, 317)]. To take a simple example, a construction such as *milites et tribunus currunt,* "the soldiers and the tribune are running," was listed as a figure because *tribunus,* a singular noun, is immediately conjoined with *currunt,* a plural verb. According to Percival, medieval grammarians worked out lists of such permissible deviations from strict syntactic rules (317).

8. A more recent classification of the same type as Ogden and Richards' is M. A. K. Halliday's division of language functions among the ideational, expressing content, the interpersonal, expressing the speaker/audience relation, and the textual, expressing the mechanics of text formation like "in conclusion" (Halliday and Martin 1993, 29).

9. In *Against the Sophists,* when Isocrates is summarizing the skills of rhetoric (to choose elements that belong to a subject and to arrange them properly) he writes, "ἀλλὰ τοῖς

ἐνθυμήμασι πρεπόντως ὅλον τὸν λόγον καταποικῖλαι." This phrase is translated as "to adorn the whole speech with striking thoughts" (Conley 1984, 172). Clearly *enthymemasi* means something more than thoughts, something that belongs in that part of rhetoric concerned with final expression. Conley suggests that to Isocrates enthymemata means something like "smart sayings," "well-turned phrases," or "finely wrought periods" (172). In other words, figures.

10. Conley's case for an alternate meaning of enthymeme, one of several by twentieth-century rhetoricians (see Poster 1992), is well supported. It leads him to a convincing indictment of the exclusive focus on the Aristotelian enthymeme as an incomplete syllogism that invites audience participation. He believes that this view, which conflates rhetorical with syllogistic reasoning in a misleading way, derives from scholastic glosses on the ancient texts (Conley 1984, 175). It might, however, also be argued that the success and ubiquity of the mainstream understanding of the enthymeme argues for its usefulness too. There are certainly premise/conclusion pairs throughout most arguments, pairs that rely on inexplicit assumptions for their cogency. Whether these pairs should be expanded into canonical syllogistic form and held to a standard of formal validity is another matter to which most rhetoricians would answer "no." But overall, rhetorical theory can certainly handle both nuanced definitions of the enthymeme$_1$ as stylistic capper and the enthymeme$_2$ as truncated syllogism expressing a probabilistic argument.

11. A study that begins from attention to the sixteenth-century tradition of the *topoi* rather than to their figural epitomes and that concentrates on the interpretive purchase these provide for individual Shakespearean plays is Marion Trousdale's *Shakespeare and the Rhetoricians* (Chapel Hill: University of North Carolina Press, 1982). The opening chapters of this book provide an excellent introduction to Elizabethan language theory and the role of the topics.

12. Effectiveness does not necessarily mean persuasiveness. As the Belgians explain, "a figure may be seen as argumentative without its necessarily bringing about adherence to the conclusions of the discourse: all that is required is that the argument should be seen in its full value" (Perelman and Olbrechts-Tyteca 1969, 170).

13. In "The Figure and the Argument," Olivier Reboul has convincingly improved on *The New Rhetoric*'s case for the figure/argument connection. In answer to the question, "Can a figure of rhetoric be an argument?" Reboul illustrates figure/argument connections with examples from four categories of figures (words, tropes, schemes, and thought) and with a special section on metaphor. Reboul, however, would add to *The New Rhetoric*'s discussion a point that he believes Mme Olbrechts-Tyteca made in *Le comique du discours*: There is a pleasure or affect associated with the apt use of a figure so that "The essence of rhetoric is to not distinguish feeling from understanding. This is why a figure is stronger than the argument it condenses" (Reboul 1989, 178). Reboul also makes essentially the same point expressed in this chapter with its definition of figures as epitomes. "We may conclude that a figure is an argument as soon as it is impossible to translate, paraphrase or otherwise express it without weakening it" (181).

14. Some manuals have an alternate definition, reserving the term catachresis for a particularly far-fetched, strained, or outrageous metaphor. Appreciating this definition requires understanding that many rhetorical manuals specified the semantic fields from which typical metaphoric borrowings were taken. An excellent discussion of these competing meanings can be found in Patricia Parker's "Metaphor and Catachresis" (1990).

15. Newton's usage in "his light" may not represent a deliberate marked choice against the unmarked norm of "its light." In the sixteenth and seventeenth centuries, the possibility of using "its" for "his" only gained ground gradually. However, later in this article,

Newton does use "its" freely (e.g., Newton 1672, 3086) so it seems likely that he was using "his" in a marked way in his opening passage.

16. In England, Francis Bacon, Thomas Hobbes, and John Locke all produced memorable passages denouncing eloquence. One of the most famous of these diatribes occurs in Thomas Sprat's *History of the Royal Society*, a polemic written within a few years of the Royal Society's foundation.

> Who can behold, without indignation, how many mists and uncertainties, these specious *Tropes* and *Figures* have brought on our Knowledg? How many rewards, which are due to more profitable, and difficult *Arts*, have been still snatch'd away by the easie vanity of *fine speaking*? For now I am warm'd with this just Anger, I cannot with-hold my self, from betraying the shallowness of these seeming Mysteries; upon which, *we Writers*, and *Speakers*, look so big. And, in few words, I dare say; that of all the Studies of men, nothing may be sooner obtain'd, than this vicious abundance of *Phrase*, this trick of *Metaphors*, this volubility of *Tongue*, which makes so great a noise in the world. (Sprat 1667, 112)

Chapter 2

1. The following is the Greek text of this important definition, as printed in the Loeb Classics edition: "ἐναντίῳ ἐναντίον σύγκειται ἢ ταὐτὸ ἐπέζευκται τοῖς ἐναντίοις" (Freese 1926, 390).

2. The original versions of these two figures are as follows, according to the text reproduced by Freese: "συμβαίνει πολλάκις ἐν ταύταις καὶ τοὺς φρονίμους ἀτυχεῖν καὶ τοὺς ἄφρονας κατορθοῦν" (Freese 1926, 390), and "ἢ ζῶντας ἕξειν ἢ τελευτήσαντας καταλείψειν" (392).

3. The use of temporary, constructed opposites and the power of predicating opposites of opposites is seen in this simple opening sentence from a news magazine's back page editorial written in the first months of the Clinton administration: "Reaganism, at its core, proclaimed that government is the problem, not the solution. Clintonism, at its core, proclaims the opposite" (Starr 1993, 32). The careful parallelism in the construction of these two cola forces the reader to fill in the conclusion of the second as "proclaims that government is the solution, not the problem" (giving us also, incidentally, an antimetabole or inverted claim embedded in an antithesis as the second contrasted term.) But perhaps for economy and for creating a place for the audience to complete the arguer's thought cooperatively, the writer simply followed Aristotle's advice in an oddly literal way; he put "the opposite" in the appropriate place. In doing so, of course, he relied on his audience holding "Reaganism" and "Clintonism," terms in themselves figurative creations, as antithetical opposites. Months and years of such sentences from both parties created just such a presumption in the audience that the arguer at one specific point in time in one specific opening sentence could build on as an object of agreement. These are constructed, cultural antitheses temporarily part of the semantic antitheses available in a language.

4. Twentieth-century semanticists distinguish six types of antonymy or opposition: "1. Contradictory terms (perfect/imperfect); 2. Contrary terms (white/black); 3. Reverse terms (constructive/destructive); 4. Contrasted terms (rich/destitute); 5. Relative terms (brother/ sister); 6. Complementary terms (question/answer)" (Miller 1991, 197). The contrary, contrasted, and reverse terms in this list can all, from the perspective of dialectic, be treated as contraries. Furthermore, the kind of opposition that Aristotle terms possession and privation, like blindness and sight, seems indistinguishable from the kind of opposition we find between contraries, and indeed these pairs behave like contraries in premise formation.

5. In order for a pair of words to be taken as contraries, they must apply to the same domain and share all but one semantic feature. "Near" and "far," for example, describe distance in relation to an observer or fixed point of reference, but in one feature, relative proximity to that point of reference, they are opposed. Despite the considerable overlap in meaning, the members of a pair of contraries are not always "weighted" equally; one of the two will usually be the unmarked choice when questions are formed. Someone making small talk with a child will ask, "How tall are you?" not "How short are you?" And many commentaries on antonyms have pointed out that in their cultural contexts, one of a pair of opposed terms will usually be taken as more "positive" or highly valued than the other, light being preferred over darkness, right over left, and warmth over cold.

6. Admittedly one of these pairs is "more dependent" than the other; it is possible to be a student without a teacher but not a teacher without students, a doctor without patients, but not a patient without a doctor, a child without a parent, but not a parent without a child, etc.

7. For an ethical position based on paradoxically maintaining contrary single antitheses, see Matthew 5:43–44: "You have heard that it was said, 'You shall love your neighbor and hate your enemy.' But I say to you, Love your enemies and pray for those who persecute you."

8. In the final group of figures listed in Book IV of the *Ad Herennium*, including figures like "refining" that can pattern whole passages and even genres, the double classification of antithesis is acknowledged, and yet a third aspect of the figure is introduced when it appears for a third time in a reprise of devices of amplification.

> Through Antithesis [contentio] contraries will meet. As I have explained above, it belongs either among the figures of diction, as in the following example: "You show yourself conciliatory to your enemies, inexorable to your friends"; or among the figures of thought, as in the following example: "While you deplore the troubles besetting him, this knave rejoices in the ruin of the state. While you despair of your fortunes, this knave alone grows all the more confident in his own." Between these two kinds of Antithesis there is this difference: the first consists in a rapid opposition of words; in the other opposing thoughts ought to meet in a comparison. ([Cicero] 1954, 377)

Though this passage refers to the two kinds of antithesis already mentioned, it introduces the possibility that contrasted lexis can express "opposing thoughts" replicated over a longer passage in order to develop a comparison, in the example offered between "you" and the "knave." Each of the example's two sentences is a separate antithesis, but the sentences themselves are parallel, offering a pattern for repeated use of the figure in expanding a passage and an argument. In the earliest complete technical manual, then, rhetorical theory is perfectly comfortable with antithesis as a stylistic device, a source of premises and a means of amplification.

In the later style manuals of antiquity (treatises associated with the work of the grammaticus), antithesis is released from its borders, and the compressed verbal device becomes an arrangement strategy operating on a larger scale. Demetrius' *On Style*, for example, maintains the same double perspective on antithesis as a pattern of words and as a pattern of thought that may or may not be shaped into antithetical cola. In a text once thought to come from the century after Aristotle, but now placed in the late first century C.E., the author acknowledges two senses of the term antithesis.

> Periods can also be formed of contrasted members. The antithesis may lie in the thought, as "sailing across the mainland and marching across the sea." Or it may be twofold, of thought and of expression, as in this same period. (Demetrius 1982, 313)

The verbal antithesis, or antithesis of expression, in Demetrius' example comes from the presence of semantic opposites, *sailing* versus *marching* (not a particularly strong pair unless one thinks of the alternatives for moving an army) and *mainland* versus *sea*. The antithesis in the thought comes from reversing the expected pattern, "march across the mainland and sail across the sea," but neither half of the offered example expresses a premise for the other half.

9. Many of Quintilian's examples involve immediate juxtapositions of terms; in an inflected language, these can be complete predications, but a user of English, following Quintilian's advice precisely, could produce antithetical pairings of single terms like the oxymoron. Quintilian also recognizes that words of "similar termination but different meaning" can be placed at the end of corresponding clauses or that contrasted phrases can be separated by other phrases rather than placed in immediately adjacent phrases. Quoting Cicero, he includes "correspondence between subsequent particulars and others previously mentioned," by which he apparently means a scattering rather than a careful positioning of opposed terms. Quintilian even concedes that the contrast need not be expressed antithetically ("Nec semper, quod adversum est, contraponitur," in balanced, parallel cola [Quintilian 1921, III: 494–496]). And he includes antimetabole: "Antithesis may also be effected by employing that *figure*, known as *antimetabole* [Greek term], by which words are repeated in different cases, tenses, moods, etc., as for instance when we say, *non ut edam, vivo, sed ut vivam, edo* (I do not live to eat, but eat to live)" (497). Quintilian ends his exhaustive jottings with special praise for the elegance of using names antithetically.

10. Earlier, Quintilian claimed that all arguments come from either "things consequent or things opposite"; the latter could be called enthymemes (Quintilian II:193). See also III:287: "The term *enthymeme* may be applied to any concept of the mind, but in its strict sense means a *reflexion* drawn from contraries."

The enthymeme appears in Book I and again in Book II of Aristotle's *Rhetoric* as a device of premise-conclusion presentation characteristic of arguments in rhetorical situations. The antithesis is introduced in Book III as a stylistic device for achieving an urbane style. Though Aristotle points out that an antithesis is "like a syllogism, for refutation [*elenkos*] is a bringing together of contraries" (Kennedy 1991, 242), there is no suggestion in the *Rhetoric* that all enthymemes would be formed as antitheses.

11. Demetrius further illustrates his point by rewriting a lament on the fate of Athens from Aristotle's lost dialog *On Justice*—"What city had they taken from their enemies as great as their own city which they lost?"—into more balanced cola with rhyming terminations: "What so great city from their enemies had they taken as their own city which they had forsaken?" (Demetrius 1982, 317). The "ill-judged ingenuity" of this second version, he argues, would provoke mirth.

12. Since the overall purpose of Blair's treatise is to define tastefulness in usage, he comments on the possible faults in the use of all the figures. For antithesis, the fault is using it too much. And while Pope is praised for what looks like a string of antithetical juxtapositions, Dr. Young is criticized for a similar string in his *Estimate of Human Life*: "The peasant complains aloud; the courtier in secret repines. In want, what distress? in affluence, what satiety? The great are under as much difficulty to expend with pleasure, as the mean to labour with success . . . " (Blair 1965, I:354). The perfection of these antitheses in rapid succession is their undoing, but the device that Blair disavows here is precisely that congeries of antitheses recommended in the Renaissance manuals.

13. Campbell was actually not the first to suggest the heterodox possibility of a three-part antithesis. In one late seventeenth-century rhetoric, something new enters the discussion of antithesis in a text that otherwise looks like nothing more than a highly condensed summary of classical advice, Hobbes' *A Briefe of the Art of Rhetorique*. In his hasty reprise of rhetorical stylistics, heavily based on Aristotle, Hobbes gives the usual account of comma, cola, and periods (which he calls parts, members, and periods), and he acknowl-

edges that the parts of a period can be divided or contrasted. He labels a period with "opposition of parts" an antithesis. Nothing new. But then Hobbes introduces a surprising possibility:

A *Period* with opposition of *Parts*, called also *Antithesis*, and the parts *Antitheta*, is when *contrary Parts* are put together; or also joyned by a third. *Contrary parts* are put together, as here, *The one has obtained glory, the other Riches; both by my benefit.* (Hobbes 1986, 114)

Hobbes has apparently used the verb "put together" with great literalness, constructing a third colon that puts together the contrasted terms ("glory" and "riches" were perhaps a stronger contrast in Hobbes' time than in ours) with what they have in common, their source. Though Hobbes has nothing further to say than the two points quoted above, he nevertheless has defined stylistically the way to undo an antithesis argumentatively: by finding a third term, representing a ground or mediating substance, that absorbs the opposed pair into a common background. The anticipation of Hegelian dialectic is striking but hardly worked out in Hobbes' *Rhetorique.*

14. Bacon in effect described the procedures for using his tables as antithetical operations in the opening of Book II: "*Therefore it* [the subject investigated] *is always present when that nature is present,* and universally implies it, and is constantly inherent in it. Again, the form is such, that if it be taken away the nature infallibly vanishes. *Therefore it is always absent when the nature is absent, and implies its absence, and inheres in nothing else* (Bacon 1860, 121). (The antithesis is tighter in the Latin: *Itaque adest perpetuo, quando natura illa adest, atque eam universaliter affirmat, atque inest omni.* Eadem forma tali est ut, ea amota, natura data infallibiliter fugiat. *Itaque abest perpetua, quando natura illa abest, eamque perpetua abnegat, atque inest soli*" [Fowler 1889, 349].)

15. These days, what Darwin called signs of affection in the dog are interpreted as functional signs of submission to the pack leader. My thanks to Randy Alan Harris for pointing out to me that current explanations of canine behavior are organized by another antithetical pair, dominance/submission.

16. Though it is usually fatal to explain a joke, it is worth pointing out that without the possibility of construing this line as an antithesis and hence as humorous, it would literally refer to situations at two different times.

17. Thomas Wilson in *The Rule of Reason,* for example, distinguished between mediate contraries, where there are species between the extremes, and immediate contraries, where there are none (Joseph 1947, 322).

18. The opposition between normal and abnormal presented Ogden with a special problem because this pair, he believed, cannot be imagined on either side of a single cut nor on opposed ends of continuous, converging or diverging scales. Instead, normal, Ogden thought, seems to sit in the middle of a scale (Ogden could have used the image of the bell-shaped curve, the standard distribution), while "abnormal" signifies the extremes at either end (Ogden 1967, 89–90). Given the importance of appeals to the normal in argument, reconfiguring antitheses of the normal versus abnormal can be critical.

19. The human/brute antithesis is easily undone by pointing out that *animal* is a genus term and *human* a species term, and that therefore all humans are animals. But arguments about the human/brute distinction readily concede this fundamental identity while focusing on how humans are related to the rest of the animal kingdom.

20. Huxley also reinforces the closeness of apes and monkeys to humans by setting an absolute anatomical cut elsewhere on the scale at lemurs, an argumentative move that once again requires an antithesis.

Every lemur which has yet been examined has its *cerebellum partially uncovered,* its posterior lobe with the contained posterior cornu and hippocampus minor more or less *rudimentary. Every marmoset, American monkey, Old World monkey, baboon, or man-like ape,* on the contrary, has its *cerebellum entirely covered,* a large posterior cornu, and a *well-developed* hippocampus minor" (Huxley, qtd in Lyell 1863, 489; italics added).

21. The ability to distinguish [b] from [p] is essentially an ability to impose an either/or difference on a continuous phenomenon. In the articulation of a [b], voicing (vocal cord vibration) is immediate and with [p] it is delayed. Experimenters can precisely control the onset of voicing to the millisecond in synthesized syllables and present a range of such differences to subjects. As Wallman explains, "Subjects asked to identify each syllable as one or the other did so without difficulty. They made a sharp differentiation between those on either side of the 25 millisecond point, which happens to be the voice-onset time that divides a [b] from a [p] in English" (Wallman 1992, 121–122).

22. Aristotle records these ten pairs fundamental to the world view of the mathematical mystics of fifth-century B.C.E. Greece in his *Metaphysics*: limited/unlimited, odd/even, one/plurality, right/left, male/female, resting/moving, straight/curved, light/darkness, good/bad, square/oblong (Barnes 1984, I:986, II:1559). In the western tradition they function as a very enduring set of basic oppositions, usually taken as contraries without mediation or as contradictories, and they are often employed in scientific argument.

23. The distinction between "symbolic" versus "direct expression," also used in this newspaper caption, constitutes still another pair of opposites featured in arguments for sex differences in behavior and brain anatomy and activity. In the opening paragraph of the 1995 article by Gur's group, the expected summary of related work includes the antithesis, "In the domain of emotional regulation, men are more likely to express affect instrumentally, such as through physical aggression, whereas women use symbolic mediation, such as through vocal means" (Gur et al. 1995, 528). The instrumental/symbolic and physical/vocal pairs translate easily into the dichotomy spatial/verbal, noted above. The culturally popular correlations of women/verbal/symbolic mediation and male/spatial/instrumental or physical aggression represent something of an inversion of the older mapping of men/women onto the pair rational/emotional.

Chapter 3

1. Lincoln uses other unifying tactics such as common naming. His terms for the North in the opening lines are comprehensive terms: "fellow countrymen," "the nation," "the public." The country is the "Union," which has a "southern part"; thus "the Union" could serve as the ground, the frame, the encompassing term that could potentially contain the divided parts. That label, however, had been used exclusively for the North. In another move, Lincoln creates a special agent when he refers to the active enemy as "insurgents." These villains, who seek to destroy Washington and rend the nation, can be dissociated from the general population in the South.

2. When the words to be combined "cooperate," it is sometimes possible to create a blended or fused compound (like "spork" from spoon and fork). Evidently a facetious physicist once combined the irreconcilable analogies for electron behavior, particle and wave, into the compound coinage "wavicles" (Barnett 1957, 31).

3. Recently there has been a new and alarming nominee for the position of most primitive living form: the prion. Prions are proteins rather than nucleic acids, but they have the ability to replicate themselves in a host. They are hypothesized as the source of "mad cow" disease and of the related human malady, Creutzfeldt-Jakob disease.

4. The gradatio may possibly be alluded to in Book I of the *Rhetoric* when Aristotle, in explaining the topics of degree or magnitude, refers to the dramatist Epicharmus' man-

ner of "building up" [epoikodomein] phrases and clauses to make something seem greater. The reference here is thought to be to the same passage Aristotle half quotes in *On the Generation of Animals*, which is found whole elsewhere: "After the sacrifice a feast, after the feast, drinking; after the drinks, ... insult; after the insults, a lawsuit; after the suit a verdict; after the verdict, chains, stocks, and a fine" (Kennedy 1991, 73, n. 144).

5. There is a highly specialized variant of the gradatio in which the first and last terms of the series are the same, so the figure can be said to circle on itself. Montaigne used such a circular gradatio when anatomizing the foibles of human perception and reasoning in his "Apologie de Raimond Sebond": "Pour juger des apparences que nous recevons des subjects [*sic*], ils nous faudroit un instrument judicatoire; pour verifier cet instrument, ils nous y faut de la demonstration; pour verifier la demonstration, un instrument: nous voilà au rouet" [In order to judge the appearances we receive from subjects, it is necessary to have an instrument of judgment; in order to verify this instrument, we need to perform a demonstration, and in order to verify the demonstration, we need an instrument: thus we have a wheel.] (Montaigne 1962, 585). Peacham translates the first verse of the Gospel according to John as a circular gradatio: "In the beginning was the word, and the word was God, and God was the word" (Peacham 1954, 133). David Berlinski uses a circular gradatio to underscore the difficulty of defining the concept of "change": "Change is *growth*. But growth is *transformation*. And transformations are *changes*" (Berlinski 1995, 62).

Curiously, the *Ad Herennium* gives an example of a gradatio when it warns what not to do in the *narratio* of a forensic oration where brevity is a virtue and a story should be presented "in such a way that the facts that have preceded can also be known, although we have not spoken of them" ([Cicero] 1954, 27). To follow this advice, "we must guard against saying a thing more than once, and certainly against repeating immediately what we have said already, as in the following: 'Simo came from Athens to Megara in the evening; when he came to Megara, he laid a trap for the maiden: after laying the trap he ravished her then and there'" (27).

6. The first member of this series, the *eohippus*, was renamed to fit in with the others. It had been described and named *hyracotherium* (hyrax-like) in 1840 by Richard Owen as an isolated species (Simpson 1951, 86). When T. H. Huxley predicted that an "eohippus" had to come before the *orohippus*, it was discovered two months later, and only in the twentieth century recognized as identical with Owen's *hyracotherium* (Rudwick 1985, 252).

7. First, the steps in this series do not represent equal increments of time; one form may have persisted much longer than the other. Second, the change in size from one stage to another must ignore the fact that some individuals of the lower form were larger than some individuals of the next higher form. Third, the change across this series was not uniform. From *miohippus* to *parahippus*, for example, the dentition changed significantly, adapting the protohorse from browsing on foliage to grazing on grass (Simpson 1951, 133).

The typical museum illustration of ballooning horses could be called the most "accommodated" visual. Kovalevsky simply used a diagram that lines up the four names under each other and connects them with straight lines in a vertical arrangement of the linear incrementum (see the reproduction of this visual in Gould [1996, 66]). Marsh produced a visual that arranged specific changes in the fore and hind feet, forearm, leg, and upper and lower molars (visual reproduced in Rudwick [1985, 253]). Significantly, the more easily interpreted changes in the feet are lined up to the left where they can "bias" the interpretation of the less easily illustrated changes in the teeth.

8. My thanks to Stephen G. Brush, Department of History and Committee on the History and Philosophy of Science, the University of Maryland, for bringing this example, as well as Herschel's magnificent writing, to my attention.

9. Stephen Brush has pointed out that Herschel may seem to have an evolutionary analogy in mind in these arguments, particularly in the 1791 paper (Brush 1987, 250–252). "When I pursued these researches, I was in the situation of a natural philosopher who follows the various species of animals and insects from the height of their perfection down to the lowest ebb of life; when, arriving at the vegetable kingdom, he can scarcely point out to us the precise boundary where the animal ceases and the plant begins; and may even go so far as to suspect them not to be essentially different. But recollecting himself, he compares, for instance, one of the human species to a tree, and all doubt upon the subject vanishes before him" (Herschel 1791, 72). Herschel follows this passage with a series "through gentle steps" from a coarse cluster of stars to the nebula in Orion, where he compares the shock that occurs to the naturalist who looks from the perfect vegetable to the perfect animal to the realization that he is looking at a different order of phenomenon (73), namely, the nebula condensing to a star and clusters of stars.

10. St. Paul uses a causal sorites in the form of a gradatio when he wants to show the interlocking consequences that follow from a falsification of Christ's resurrection: "Now if Christ be preached that He rose from the dead, how say some among you that there is no resurrection from the dead? But if there be no resurrection from the dead, then is Christ not risen: and if Christ be not risen, then is our preaching vain, and [if our preaching is vain] your faith is also vain" (I Cor. 15:12–14).

We might unfold this sorites into the following syllogisms: 1. Christ was dead/ The dead never rise/ Therefore Christ did not rise; 2. That Christ did rise is not true/ We preach that Christ is risen/ Therefore we preach what is not true. 3. Preaching what is not true is preaching in vain/ We preach what is not true/ Therefore we preach in vain; 4. Our preaching is vain/ Your faith comes from our preaching/ Therefore your faith is vain. St. Paul, of course, made his premises hypothetical to show their disastrous consequences and then to contradict them firmly: "But in fact Christ has been raised from the dead" (I Cor. 15:20).

11. The causal argument, specifically described as a chain, is expressed as follows in the text of the piece: "In a hypothetical example given by Dr. Mech, a wolf kills a moose. The remains slowly disintegrate and add minerals and humus to the soil, making the area more fertile. Lush vegetation grows, which attracts snowshoe hares, which in turn draw foxes and other small predators, which coincidentally eliminate many of the mice that live nearby. A weasel that used to hunt the mice moves to another area and in so doing is killed by an owl. The chain could be extended indefinitely" (Stevens 1995, C4).

12. Leibniz produced an extravagant version of a definitional sorites in the following "proof" of the immortality of the human soul. Since his conclusion was probably already acceptable to his audience, it is likely that the following gradatio represents a *tour de force* use of this figure applied to a philosophical conception.

The human soul is a thing whose activity is thinking. A thing whose activity is thinking is one whose activity is immediately apprehended, and without any representation of parts therein. A thing whose activity is immediately apprehended without any representation of parts therein is a thing whose activity does not contain parts. A thing whose activity does not contain parts is one whose activity is not motion. A thing whose activity is not motion is not a body. What is not a body is not in space. What is not in space is insusceptible of motion. What is insusceptible of motion is indissoluble (for dissolution is a movement of parts). What is indissoluble is incorruptible. What is incorruptible is immortal. Therefore the human soul is immortal. (qtd in Copi 1972, 228–229)

This "container logic" was travestied by Molière in *La Jalousie de Barbouillé*:

Know, my friend, that if you were to give me a purse full of pistoles, if this purse were in a costly box, this box in a precious case, this case in a wondrous casket, this

casket in a curious cabinet, this cabinet in a magnificent room, this room in an agreeable apartment, this apartment in a stately castle, this castle in a matchless citadel, this
citadel in a famous town, this town in a fruitful island, this island in a wealthy province, this province in a flourishing kingdom, and this kingdom stretching throughout the world; [Molière then runs the whole thing in reverse]. (Cooper 1924, 37)

13. Unlike Locke a century earlier, Herder is not prepared to reason from the chain of
creatures leading up to humans that there must also be a series of beings leading from
humans to God: "Bei dem Menschen stand die Reihe still; wir kennen kein Geschöpf über
ihm, das vielartiger und künstlicher organisiert sei: er scheint das höchste, wozu eine
Erdorganisation gebildet werden konnte" [With humanity the series stops; we know of
no creature over him that is more variously and artificially organized: he appears the highest
to which an earthly organization can be shaped] (Herder 1989, VI:166).

14. The symmetry in this *gradatio* would be clearer without the definition Darwin
interpolated between the first and second members: "Certainly no line of demarcation has
as yet been drawn between species and sub-species . . . or, again, between sub-species and
well marked varieties, or between lesser varieties and individual differences. These [indi-
vidual] differences blend into each other by an insensible series, and a series impresses
the mind with the idea of an actual passage."

15. The wording of this passage was altered slightly by the sixth edition. "The representation of the groups, as here given in the diagram on a flat surface, is much too simple.
The branches ought to have diverged in all directions. If the names of the groups had been
simply written down in a linear series, the representation would have been still less natural; and it is notoriously not possible to represent in a series, on a flat surface, the affinities
which we discover in nature amongst the beings of the same group" (Darwin 1958, 392).
The branching tree diagrams used by Ernst Haeckel and others beginning in the 1860s
answer Darwin's objection.

Chapter 4

1. In Greek, the prefix ἀντι can mean over against, in opposition to, one against another, mutually, in return, instead, equal to or like, and corresponding. The noun μεταβολή,
meaning a change or changing, can be fruitfully combined with several of the potential
meanings of the prefix to yield a composite term meaning something like an opposed but
corresponding change. In *Figures of Speech: Sixty Ways to Turn a Phrase,* Arthur Quinn
prefers the term *epanados* for inverse repetition at the level of words and claims that
"antimetabole" is reserved for "an *epanados* which is also an antithesis" (Quinn 1982, 93).
However, the term *epanados* is not used in the *Ad Herennium*.

2. "All relatives are spoken of in relation to correlatives that reciprocate. For example,
the slave is called slave of a master and the master is called master of a slave; the double
double of a half, and the half half of a double; the larger larger than a smaller, and the smaller
smaller than a larger; and so for the rest too. Sometimes, however, there will be a verbal
difference, of ending" (Barnes 1984, I:11). Much of Aristotle's subsequent discussion is
devoted to explaining how relatives must be correctly expressed reciprocally. The genitive
case does not automatically produce a relative.

3. Breck strengthens his argument for a corrected reading of this passage by pointing
out that the Greek verb used in the last colon can only refer to attacking dogs (Breck 1994,
29).

4. Cicero, writing in *De Oratore* within decades of the *Ad Herennium*, includes perhaps
two references to the antimetabole in Crassus' off-hand catalog of devices that every orator must know. The editor, J. S. Watson, identifies the first, "conversion," as an "antithetic

position of words" with the live/eat example as an illustration, and claims that the second possible reference, called *declinatio* by Cicero, is the figure Quintilian identifies over a century later as the antimetabole (Cicero 1970, 254). Despite the editor's suggestions, it is difficult to know whether Cicero had a distinctive antimetabole in mind.

5. In one instance, Demetrius expresses the inversion typical of antimetabole by inflectional ending and not syntactic reordering: "ὁ Θουκυδίδης χρῆται, ὅμοια λαμβάνων τά τε ὀνόματα τῇ συνθέσει, τοῖς τε ὀνόμασι τὴν σύνθεσιν" (Demetrius 1982, 332). The most effective way to render this reversal in English is to use the figure: "Thucydides uses all expressions of this kind, assimilating the words to the composition and the composition to the words" (333). There is a controversy over the dating of Demetrius's *On Style*, some arguing that it is a Peripatetic manual belonging in the third century B.C.E. and others that it comes from the first century C.E. The fact that Demetrius ignores the antimetabole argues that he is closer to Quintilian's subordination of the figure than to the *Ad Herennium*'s emphasis on it.

6. In *The Art of Rhetoric* (1560), the lawyer Thomas Wilson defines a device called "regression" in a way that conflates this figure with other figures of repetition. It is only the examples that show that Wilson essentially has the antimetabole in mind.

That is called regression, when we repeat a word eftsoons that hath been spoken and rehearsed before, whether the same be in the beginning, in the midst, or in the latter end of a sentence.

In the beginning, thus: "Thou art ordained to rule others, and not others to rule thee."

In the midst, thus: "He that hath money hath not given it, and he that hath given money hath not his money still, but he that hath given thanks hath thanks still, and he that hath them still hath given them notwithstanding."

In the latter end, thus: "Man must not live to eat, but eat to live." "Man is not made for the Sabbath, but the Sabbath is made for man." "If man do any filthy thing and take pleasure therein, the pleasure goeth away but the shame tarrieth still." "If man do any good thing with pain, the pains go away but the honesty abideth still."
(Wilson 1994, 228–229)

Regression or ἐπάνοδος is a figure of repetition as defined by Quintilian (1921, III:464–465) but not of inversion. Quintilian offers as an example the following lines from the *Aenied*: "Iphitus too with me and Pelias came, /Iphitus bowed with age and Pelias/Slow-limping with the wound Ulysses gave" (465). The notion of defining the position of the repetition, beginning, middle, end, is certainly in the spirit of this section of Quintilian, but seems to make little sense applied to inverted phrases. Wilson's decision here is an example of how highlighting a different feature of a figure and thus its category can obscure its argumentative work. In the following century, Bernard Lamy also categorized antimetabole, though not by name, among the figures of repetition: "Sometimes in the same member the same words are used at the beginning, and then inverting the Order, placed in the end" (Harwood 1986, 276). Lamy's is entirely a theory of the aesthetic effects of the figures.

7. In one of Melancthon's examples, the antimetabole has been lost in translation. He writes "Si Evangelium approbat civiles mores, consequitur, ut hi, qui civiles mores improbant, Evangelii autoritatem graviter laedant," which is translated as "Inasmuch as the Gospel approves of the civil laws, then the authority of the Gospel is hurt by those who disapprove of the civil laws" (Melancthon 1969, 292). Melancthon's Latin antimetabole is the more appropriate form to convey the threat to the Gospel's authority expressed in this argument.

8. Richard Whately, the author of the last complete English rhetoric (the seventh and expanded edition appearing in 1846) cannot be accused, as Fontanier can, of ignoring the

argumentative dimensions of stylistic choices, because he also authored a highly successful logic text. But Whately, looking at corrective anitmetaboles, also folds a discussion of
reversals into his section on antitheses and thus focuses on the overall opposition of the
two halves: "Frequently the same words, placed in different relations with each other, will
stand in contrast to themselves," as in the example, "Persecution is not wrong because it
is cruel, but it is cruel because it is wrong" (Whately 1963, 324).

9. "εἰ φεύγοντες μὲν ἐμαχόμεθα ὅπως κατέλθωμεν, κατελθόντες δὲ φευξόμεθα ὅπως
μὴ μαχώμεθα" (Freese 1926, 314).

10. Aristotle did not find that converse sequence led to the formation of premises in
the case of correlatives, privation/possession pairs, and most contraries. But he did, however, claim that rare contraries require converse sequence. He gives only one example:
"health follows upon vigour, but disease does not follow upon debility [here is the typical
antithesis where opposite lies with opposite]; rather debility follows upon disease" (Barnes
1984, I:190). Aristotle makes a causal claim here: vigor causes health but disease causes
debility.

11. It is also possible for an antimetabole to support definitions by contrast. In the
Grammar of Motives, Kenneth Burke, a highly self-conscious user of figures, dissociated
religious from secular futurism by claiming, "Whereas both would merge present and
future, religious futurism does so by reducing the *future* to the *present* whereas secular
futurism reduces the *present* to the *future*" (Burke [1945] 1969, 334; italics added). Religious and secular futurism, then, differ because they symmetrically reverse a present/
future reduction. The kind of redefinition Burke engages in here is precisely defined in the
New Rhetoric as a dissociation that aims at purging a formerly unitary term, creating two
notions from one. A mark of the resulting dissociative definition is the creation of two terms
containing the same noun but modified by contrasting adjectives (e.g., religious futurism/
secular futurism). Burke used the antimetabole as further support for this dissociation.

12. The inversions of projective geometry are typical of other branches of mathematics and physics where inverse processes seem to abound. Thus, for example, however er-
roneously, people tend to pair mathematical operations as reversals—addition and subtraction, multiplication and division, raising to a power and finding a root, differentiation
and integration—the result of the second of each of these pairs of operations restoring the
original entity or function. Each of these pairs of reciprocal operations can be redefined
in terms of the first alone, subtraction being redefined as the addition of a negative number, division as multiplication by a fraction and taking a root as raising to a fractional ex-
ponent, and so forth.

13. Newton's Third Law is expressed in the original Latin version as follows: "Actioni
contrariam semper et aequalem esse reactionem: sive corporum duorum actiones in se
mutuo semper esse aequales et in partes contrarias dirigi" (Newton 1822, 16).

14. Since figures are such apt summaries of lines of argument, they are likely to occur
more frequently where there is a greater need for clarity, especially in texts addressed to
readers who need accommodation. Newton's choice of trenchant examples in the form of
antimetaboles to illustrate the Third Law seems to be the norm for popularizers or expli-
cators. Thus the eminent historian of science I. Bernard Cohen, in an article on "Newton's
Discovery of Gravity" for *Scientific American,* uses the same epitomizing antimetabole
repeatedly: "Not only does the sun attract each planet but also each planet attracts the sun"
(Cohen 1981, 20); "Newton had seen that if the sun pulls on the earth, the earth must also
pull on the sun" (21); "Newton first recognized that if the sun attracts the earth, the earth
must attract the sun with a force of equal magnitude" (25); and in a picture caption, "Not
only does the sun attract each planet but also each planet attracts the sun" (23). In his history of astronomy, John North also uses this verbal formula: "The planet attracts the Sun

as the Sun attracts the planet" (North 1995, 369). In their innovative textbook introducing physics from a historical perspective, Gerald Holton and Stephen Brush use the following particularly Newtonian antimetabole to explain the Third Law: "The earth is attracted upward to a falling apple as much as the falling apple is attracted downward toward the earth" (Holton and Brush 1985, 128).

15. "Cascade" is a term frequently used to describe biochemical processes where an initiating event triggers a chain of connected reactions. These reactions can be reciprocal: A causes or leads to B, B causes or leads to A which causes or leads to B, and so on. Each successive reiteration can be amplified; it can occur to a greater extent than the previous one. A current theory to explain the aging process depends on such a physiological cascade, described by an antimetabole in the following passage: "Proponents of the mitochondrial free-radical hypothesis of aging suggest that damage to mitochondria by free radicals eventually interferes with the efficiency of ATP production and increases the output of free radicals. The rise in free radicals, in turn, accelerates the oxidative injury of mitochondrial components, which inhibits ATP production even more" (Weindruch 1996, 51). The cascade that progresses through recurring pairs can be thought of as a combination of the figural logic of the antimetabole and the gradatio.

16. After reading the notice of Faraday's work in the popular Library of Useful Knowledge, Henry sought a better account. He could only find two paragraphs in the *Philosophical Magazine; and Annals of Philosophy* for April 1832. He quoted the part devoted to Faraday's discovery of magneto-electric induction in full in his own first announcement.

If a wire, connected at both extremities with a galvanometer, be coiled in the form of a helix around a magnet, no current of electricity takes place in it. This is an experiment which has been made by various persons hundreds of times, in the hope of evolving electricity from magnetism, and as in other cases in which the wishes of the experimenter and the facts are opposed to each other, has given rise to very conflicting conclusions. But if the magnet be withdrawn from or introduced into such a helix, a current of electricity is produced *whilst the magnet is in motion,* and is rendered evident by the deflection of the galvanometer. If a single wire be passed by a magnetic pole, a current of electricity is induced through it which can be rendered sensible (Henry 1886, I:74).

Henry could gain neither experimental design nor suitable language from this extract.

17. Henry is an extremely clear, precise writer, worthy of extensive study for his rhetorical abilities. Like Faraday, he began in poverty as an apprentice storekeeper but at 14 turned to acting. At 16, he had another change of heart and charmed his way into the Albany Academy as a student. Henry then received a crash course in the standard gentleman's education of the day, which would, of course, have included training in rhetoric and elocution (Wilson 1986, 63–64).

18. R. W. Burkhardt, Jr., points out that Lamarck is usually characterized incorrectly as attributing transformation to the inheritance of acquired characteristics when instead he imagined that two distinct forces were involved: "The state in which we now see all the animals is on the one hand the product of the increasing *composition of* organization, which tends to form a *regular gradation,* and on the other hand that of the influences of a multitude of very different circumstances that continually tend to destroy the regularity in the gradation of the increasing composition of organization" (Burkhardt 1984, xxv).

19. Another version is used to correct the mistaken belief of other naturalists who have noticed how the parts of animals are perfectly fitted for their uses and so have thought that

les formes et l'état des parties en avoient amené l'emploi: or, c'est là l'erreur; car il est facile de démontrer, par l'observation, que se sont, au contraire, les besoins et

les usages des parties qui ont développé ces mêmes parties, qui les ont même fait
naître lorsqu'elle n'existoient pas, et qui, conséquemment, ont donné lieu à l'état
où nous les observons dans chaque animal.

the forms and the state of their parts have led to their use: now, that is the error; for
it is easy to demonstrate, by observation, that it is, on the contrary, the needs and
the uses of the parts which have developed these same parts, which have even given
birth to them when they did not exist, and which, consequently, have given rise to
the state in which we observe them in each animal. (Lamarck 1960, I:236)

Lamarck also quotes his key insight in the form of an antimetabole from an earlier work.
It is not surprising that in quoting from himself, he picks his own most memorable lines
expressed figuratively.

Ce ne sont pas les organes, c'est-à-dire, la nature et la forme des parties du corps d'un
animal, qui ont donné lieu à ses habitudes et à ses facultés particulières; mais ce sont,
au contrarie, ses habitudes, sa manière de vivre, et les circonstances dans lesquelles se
sont rencontrés les individus dont il provient, qui ont, avec le temps, constitué la forme
de son corps, le nombre et l'état de ses organes, enfin, les facultés dont il jouit.

It is not the organs, that is to say, the nature and the form of the parts of an animal's
body, which have given rise to its habits and its particular faculties, but it is, on the
contrary, its habits, its manner of life and the circumstances in which the individuals
occur from which it arises, which have, with time, constituted the form of its body,
the number and state of its organs, and finally the faculties which it enjoys. (Lamarck
1960 I:237; cited by Lamarck as taken from *Recherches sur les corps vivans*, p. 50)

20. My thanks to David Kellogg of Duke University for bringing the antimetaboles in
Lewontin's essay to my attention. Once Lewontin introduces the antimetabole, he, like
Lamarck, uses the figure several times across a few pages. Other occurrences in the last
few pages of his article include "Because organisms create their own environments we cannot characterize the environment except in the presence of the organism that it surrounds"
(Lewontin 1995, 133) and the elegant statement of identity between what are usually taken
as antithetical terms, "Every act of consumption is an act of production and every act of
production is an act of consumption" (135).

Chapter 5

1. The classical rhetorical perspective on repetition has to be distinguished from repetition as characterized by twentieth-century text linguists who mention repetition as a
device present in cohesive texts. Among the cohesive devices in English identified by
Halliday and Hasan in *Cohesion in English* (1976), speakers and writers can maintain the
same subject from sentence to sentence by repeating key words as well as by using synonyms or by using pronouns that clearly refer to previously introduced nouns. Repetition also has its place in the descriptions of information flow achieved in Functional Sentence Perspective. Writers and speakers can use essentially the same topic in the openings
of consecutive sentences, the slot for "given" information, or they can pick up a new idea
introduced toward the end of one sentence in the beginning of the next. These kinds of
repetition can certainly have rhetorical importance, but the notions of cohesion or topic
maintenance used by text linguists are not found in classical rhetoric.

2. Also known as *apanaphora*.

3. It could be argued that the recurrence of "life" three times in this sentence inevitably divides it in three units so that by default "life" occurs at the end of each of these units.

4. Peacham also lists antanaclasis as "a figure which repeateth a word that hath two
significations, and the one of them contrary, or at least, unlike to the other. An example:

Care for those things which may discharge you of all care. Care in the first place signifieth to provide, in the last the solicitude and dread of the minde" (Peacham 1954, 56–57). Here is another interesting case where the same device can be described from the perspective of the double signification as a trope and from another, emphasizing the repetition, as a scheme.

5. For a similar lability according to the chosen figure of reading, see chapter 3 for the differences among the series figures.

6. The connection achieved by repeated adjectives can change from correlation to cause when the same word modifies what an arguer would like an audience to take as a cause-and-effect pair. In a letter to parents, a college president announced a donor's magnificent challenge grant in order to prepare for a funding campaign. He wanted the donor's generosity to spur the generosity of others and so he used repeated adjectives to make a causal connection: "I want you to know, however, that I have complete confidence in our ability to meet and even exceed the requirements of this challenge. Extraordinary events have a way of inspiring extraordinary response." The similarity in essence between a cause and its effect claimed by the repetition of "extraordinary" might be characterized as a fallacy, or a bit of shaman's word magic, but it is precisely the offered similarity that the president wants to establish in order to give the impression of inevitable future action.

7. A 1963 textbook, *The Microbial World,* second edition, credits Koch's teacher, Jacob Henle, with laying down the required causal criteria that Koch later instantiated. This text phrases "Koch's postulates" as follows: "(1) the microorganism must be present in every case of the disease; (2) the microorganism must be isolated from the diseased host and grown in pure culture; (3) the specific disease must be reproduced when a pure culture of the microorganism is inoculated into a healthy susceptible host; and (4) the microorganism must be recoverable once again from the experimentally infected host" (Stanier et al. 1963, 26).

In a 1977 textbook, James H. Otto and Albert Towle's *Modern Biology,* the postulates are given in the imperative as a set of directions, "(i) Isolate the organism suspected of causing the disease. (ii) Grow the organism in laboratory cultures. (iii) Inoculate a healthy animal with the cultured organism. See if the animal contracts the disease. (iv) If the animal contracts the disease, examine the animal and re-isolate the organisms that caused the disease" (Carter 1985, 353, n. 2).

In the third edition of a textbook intended for medical students, *Microbiology: Including Immunology and Molecular Genetics* by Davis, Dulbecco, Eisen, and Ginsberg, the postulates are phrased without the rigor of ploche, and in fact the "organism" in a sense disappears after the first step and only re-emerges in the fourth: "(1) the organism is regularly found in the lesions of the disease, (2) it can be isolated in pure culture on artificial media, (3) inoculation of this culture produces a similar disease in experimental animals, and (4) the organism can be recovered from the lesions in these animals" (Davis et al. 1980, 7). In most situations, language users readily resort to pronoun substitution (see steps one to two in the previous example) rather than to exactly repeated terms. Thus it is an index to a different kind of rhetorical situation when language users "decide" that they must repeat terms precisely. In the informal register of a popular work, the British microbiologist John Postgate is comfortable with a pronoun but uses it with the consistency of ploche: "One of the earliest bacteriologists, Dr. Robert Koch of Berlin, crystallized this dilemma [deciding if a particular microbe is really the cause of a disease] in a set of conditions known as Koch's postulates: a microbe may be accepted as the cause of a disease if (1) it is present in unusual numbers when and where the disease is active, (2) it can be isolated from the diseased patient, and (3) it causes disease when inoculated into a healthy subject" (Postgate 1992, 100).

8. Duesberg, like others, uses ploche in his presentation of the postulates: "First, the germ must be found abundantly growing in every patient and every diseased tissue. Second, the germ must be isolated and grown in the laboratory. Third, the purified germ must cause the disease again in another host" (Duesberg 1996, 35). A formulation later in the book uses the word "microbe" instead of "germ" (174–186).

9. "Zunächst war festzustellen, ob in den erkrankten Teilen Formelemente vorkommen, welche nicht zu den Bestandteilen des Körpers gehören oder aus solchen hervorgegangen sind. Wenn sich solche fremdartigen Gebilde nachweisen ließen, dann war weiter zu untersuchen, ob dieselben organisiert sind und ob sie irgendwelche Anzeichen von selbständigem Leben bieten, wohin besonders eigene Bewegung, mit welcher sehr oft noch die Molekularbewegung verwechselt wird, Wachstum, Vermehrung, Fruchtbildung zu rechnen sind. Ferner waren die Beziehungen zu ihrer Umgebung, das Verhalten der benachbarten Gewebsbestandteile, ihre Verteilung im Körper, ihr Auftreten in den verschiedenen Stadien der Krankheit und ähnliche Umstande zu eruieren, welche schon mit mehr oder weniger großer Wahrscheinlichkeit auf einen ursächlichen Zusammenhang zwischen diesen Gebilden und der Krankheit schließen lassen [sic]. Die auf diesem Wege gewonnenen Tatsachen können möglicherweise schon soviel Beweismaterial liefern, daß nur noch der äußerste Skeptizismus den Einwand erheben kann, daß die gefundenen Mikroorganismen nicht Ursache, sondern nur eine Begleiterscheinung der Krankheit seien. Oft wird dieser Einwand allerdings eine gewisse Berechtigung haben, und es gehört deswegen zur vollständigen Beweisführung, daß man sich night allein damit begnügt, das Zusammentreffen der Krankheit und der Parasiten zu konstatieren, sondern daß außerdem direkt diese Parasiten als die eigentliche Ursache der Krankheit nachgewiesen werden. Dies kann nur in der Weise geschehen, daß die Parasiten von dem erkrankten Organismus vollständig abgetrennt und von allen Produkten der Krankheit, welchen etwa ein krankmachender Einfluß zugeschrieben werden könnte, befreit werden, und daß durch Einführung der isolierten Parasiten in den gesunden Organismus die Krankheit mit allen ihren eigentümlichen Eigenschaften von neuem hervorgerufen wird" (Koch 1912, I:469–470).

10. According to K. Codell Carter, Koch formulated two different sets of general rules for establishing that a particular organism causes a disease. The first set appeared in his 1878 paper on wound infections, "Untersuchungen über die Aetiologie der Wundinfektionskrankheiten" and specified that an organism be found in every instance of the disease, that it correlate with and explain the disease, and that each disease be associated with a distinct micro-organism (357). The standard here is primarily one of association or correlation; it depends on the assumption that microorganisms are likely to cause disease. Koch's 1882–1884 work on tuberculosis adds the further criteria that the organism be isolated, cultured, and then inoculated into test animals, causing the disease. Both of these protocols combine in the passage from the 1884 paper cited in the text and together produce the current version of Koch's postulates.

11. Word play and specifically the creation of words that resemble each other was so well codified in Renaissance manuals that a set of figures was defined that marked the internal changes a word could be subjected to by certain additions, deletions, and transpositions of letters. *Prothesis* adds a letter or syllable to the beginning of a word and *aphaeresis* takes it away, *syncope* takes a letter or syllable away from the middle, and *epenthesis* puts one in; *apocope* removes an ending letter or syllable and *paragoge* adds one (Smith 1973, 170–171). Nothing in the word lore of rhetoric could seem further either from argumentative import or from the practices of scientists. Yet an *epenthesis* figures in the recent controversy over whether a meteorite from Mars shows signs of microbial life. The scientists making that claim used the notion first put forth by a geologist, Robert L. Folk, that there ex-

ists a hitherto unrecognized kind of extremely small microbial life, 0.05–.2 μm, which are extremely abundant and which "run most of the earth's surface chemistry" (Folk 1997). Folk calls these forms *nannobacteria,* the term, and the proposed type of life, picked up by the NASA scientists in their sensational announcement. The prefix that would indicate the range of size here is *nano* meaning one billionth, used in combined forms like nanometer and nanogram. But Folk deliberately used a spelling with an added *n,* conforming to the practice of geologists who have coined the term *nannoplankton* for minute ocean life (Wade 1997, C1). This spelling then is an act of addressing a disciplinary community more hospitable to his claims. It may also be a way of hedging on ultimate claims about size. (For a similar use of variant spelling, and specifically adding letters see Fahnestock [1993, 178, 327].)

12. Galton, who quotes Shakespeare frequently in his writings, may have drawn his pair from a passage in *The Tempest* where Prospero says of Caliban, "A devil, a born devil, on whose nature nurture can never stick" (4.1.187–189; see Gottesman 1997, 1523).

13. Peacham gives the derivational migration of a word the special name *paregmenon,* "a figure which of the word going before derivith the word following," as in his examples, "I will destroy the wisedome of the wise," "They have stumbled at the stumbling stone," and even "Never marvel at that which is so little a marvel, except it were more marvellous," an example that manages "three wordes of like affinity set in one sentence" (Peacham 1954, 55–56).

14. Another allied figure is *syllepsis.* In this figure, more appropriately classified as a trope, a word appears only once, but it governs two subsequent sentence elements in two different senses, so it works as two words in one: *She shot the rapids and her boyfriend.* Syllepsis produces a surprise, almost requiring a reader to go back and reparse the sentence to savor the double meaning of the word. In the case of a *syllepsis,* however, the second meaning does not usually change the word's function; in the example above, the two "shots" are both verbs, and it would be very difficult, if not impossible, to read a syllepsis that involved a grammatical change (e.g., *Paper rips and your walls,* where in the first sense, paper is a noun, and in the second, a verb). The *syllepsis* instead usually plays with competing meanings in the same part of speech. It is a bravura figure, meant to be noticed, but it is easy to imagine more subtle *syllepses* where one of the applications of a single word is not wholly different but merely conveniently stretched for the sake of the argument. In this case the *syllepsis* merges with *antanaclasis.*

15. Aristotle does briefly mention repetitions of the same root through "inflexion" in his passage on patterning in the double colas of periods (Kennedy 1991, 243). Such repetition is merely one among the several methods (including repetition of the same word or the same ending or the same number of syllables) that can impose resemblance on the two cola of a period. In his brief listing of these devices in Book III, he gives them no special argumentative force, and if this passing reference were the only mention, there would be no warrant for the importance of this device in the Aristotelian corpus.

16. Polyptotonic logic surfaced in the comments of a member of E Pluribus Unum, part of the patriot movement of the 1990s that suspects the federal government's power and frequently sees its hand in events. "Nothing," said the member, "occurs by accident. If it occurs, know that it was planned that way. To be planned, there must be planners. If you have planners, you must have a conspiracy" (Janofsky A18).

17. Arguments about speciation typically attempt to present forms in a graded sequence. See Fig. 5.3 for a series of hybrid forms that link two distinct species of sapsucker.

18. Electricity is spelled correctly in the table of contents for No. 308, Vol. 25 (1706–1707). Eighteenth-century spelling tended to be haphazard, but there was more variation in common terms than in special terms.

19. When Gray writes of these end point attractors, as he did in many of his letters, he also uses a variety of synonymous phrases to refer to them in their new state. For instance, in 1708, he found that his watch "was Electrical" just from being in his pocket (Chipman 1954, 36); in 1720, that bodies "acquire an Electricity" and become "strongly Electrical" (Gray 1720, 105, 106); and in 1731, that objects "had an Electricity communicated to them" (1731, 21), "became Electrical" (32), or "receive a greater Quantity of Electric Effluvia" (42); in 1732, "After it has been excited, not only the Dish, but the Water also, becomes Electrical" (1732, 228); and in 1735 to how "Metal had been made Electrical by the Tube" (1735, 17). By 1745, all of these constructions would have been looked on as unnecessary circumlocutions, perhaps only used for stylistic variety, since the past participle of the verb, "electrified," was available to make the same point succinctly.

Also favoring an inverted syntax, not necessarily the passive but the recipient as grammatical subject, is Gray's focus on the different substances that "become electrical." When, for example, in 1732, Gray succeeded in arousing cones, sparks, and streams of vapor by holding a rubbed tube over tiny ivory dishes brimming with water, he writes that "Water may have an Attractive Vertue communicated to it from an Electrick Body" (Gray 1732, 227) instead of "An Electrick Body communicates an Attractive Vertue to water" and "A body of Water receives an Attractive Vertue and also a Repelling one, by applying the excited Tube near it" (227).

20. Writing in the same year as Watson, Nollet in France also uses human agents: "Mr Bose . . . au lieu de tubes electricoit des globes de verre" and frequently uses the past participle as modifier: "homme electrisé" (Heilbron 1979, 280 n. 20). A description of French usage around 1745 would be interesting to see if it conforms to Watson's. I have not done such a study but would predict that it conforms. [On p. 276, Heilbron translates an article of Fontenelle on Dufay that appeared in the *Academies des Sciences Histoire* for 1737, with the phrase "attraction and repulsion of electrified bodies."]

21. The change of meaning obvious in Watson's use of the term "electricity" begins at least a decade earlier. Stephen Gray's uses of the noun and adjectives in 1729 show significant shifts from Hauksbee's usage. Gray prefers "Electrick Vertue" to "effluvia" as his term for the attractive property in electrics. The term "electrick vertue" emphasizes what is in a body, whereas "effluvia" suggests an accidental property, the result of excitation. The subtle shift to an inherent virtue is a natural corollary of the fact that, as Gray discovered, "the electrick vertue" can be moved from one place to another, endowing a new material with a property it did not have before. Thus, when the English Jesuit Turbervill Needham writes in 1746 of electrical experiments with larger transferred charges perfected in Paris, he clarifies his definition: "When I speak of the Power of Electricity in this Case, I would not be understood [sic] of the Power of attracting light Bodies . . . but I would only be understood of that communicated Virtue, which renders Nonelectrics *per se* electrical" (Needham 1746, 259).

References

[Ahumada, Teresa]. 1957. *The Life of Saint Teresa of Ávila*. Translated by J. M. Cohen. Edinburgh: Penguin.

Alberts, Bruce, Dennis Bray, Julian Lewis, Martin Raff, Keith Roberts, and James D. Watson. 1994. *Molecular Biology of the Cell*. 3d ed. New York: Garland.

Arbib, Michael A., and Mary B. Hesse. 1986. *The Construction of Reality*. Cambridge: Cambridge University Press.

Backman, Daniel G., and James C. Williams. 1992. Advanced materials for aircraft engine applications. *Science* 255 (28 February): 1086–1087.

Bacon, Francis. 1889. *Novum Organum* [Latin edition]. Edited by Thomas Fowler. Oxford: Clarendon Press.

Bacon, Francis. 1860. *Novum Organum*. Translated by James Spedding. In *The Works of Francis Bacon*. Vol. IV. London: Longman.

Bacon, Francis. 1952. *The Advancement of Learning*. Great Books, Vol. 30. Chicago: Encyclopedia Britannica.

Barnes, Jonathan, ed. 1984. *The Complete Works of Aristotle*. The Revised Oxford Translation. Princeton, NJ: Princeton University Press.

Barnett, Lincoln. 1957. *The Universe and Dr. Einstein*. 2d rev. ed. New York: Bantam.

Bazerman, Charles. 1988. *Shaping Written Knowledge: The Genre and Activity of the Experimental Article in Science*. Madison: University of Wisconsin Press.

Berlinski, David. 1995. *A Tour of the Calculus*. New York: Vintage Books.

Black, Max. 1962. *Models and Metaphors. Studies in Language and Philosophy*. Ithaca, NY: Cornell University Press.

Blair, Hugh. 1965. *Lectures on Rhetoric and Belles Lettres*. Edited by Harold F. Harding. Carbondale, IL: Southern Illinois University Press.

Boyd, Richard. 1993. Metaphor and theory change: What is "metaphor" a metaphor for? In *Metaphor and Thought*. Edited by Andrew Ortony. Cambridge: Cambridge University Press, pp. 481–532.

Breck, John. 1994. *The Shape of Biblical Language: Chiasmus in the Scriptures and Beyond*. Crestwood, NY: St. Vladimir's Seminary Press.

215

Briggs, John. 1989. *Francis Bacon and the Rhetoric of Nature.* Cambridge, MA: Harvard University Press.

Brogan, T. V. F., ed. 1994. *The New Princeton Handbook of Poetic Terms.* Princeton: Princeton University Press.

Bronowski, Joseph. 1986. The Creative Process. In *Scientific Genius and Creativity: Readings from Scientific American.* New York: Freeman, pp. 2–9.

Brush, Stephen. 1987. The nebular hypothesis and the evolutionary worldview. *History of Science.* 25:245–278.

Burke, Kenneth. [1945] 1969a. *A Grammar of Motives.* Berkeley, CA: University of California Press.

Burke, Kenneth. [1950] 1969b. *A Rhetoric of Motives.* Berkeley, CA: University of California Press.

Burkhardt, Richard W. Jr. 1984. The zoological philosophy of J. B. Lamarck. In *Zoological Philosophy*, by Jean Baptiste Lamarck. Translated by Hugh Elliot. Chicago: University of Chicago Press.

Campbell, George. 1963. *The Philosophy of Rhetoric.* Edited by Lloyd F. Bitzer. Carbondale, IL: Southern Illinois University Press.

Campbell, John Angus. 1986. Scientific revolution and the grammar of culture: The case of Darwin's *Origin. Quarterly Journal of Speech* 72:351–376.

Campbell, John Angus. 1990. On the way to the *Origin*: Darwin's evolutionary insight and its rhetorical transformation. The Van Zelst Lecture in Communication. Northwestern University School of Speech, May 24.

Cantor, Geoffrey N. 1985. Reading the book of nature: The relation between Faraday's religion and his science. In *Faraday Rediscovered: Essays on the Life and Work of Michael Faraday, 1791–1867.* Edited by David Gooding and Frank A. J. L. James. New York: Stockton.

Carter, K. Codell. 1985. Koch's postulates in relation to the work of Jacob Henle and Edwin Klebs. *Medical History* 29:353–374.

Chipman, R. A. 1954. An unpublished letter of Stephen Gray on electrical experiments, 1707–1708. *Isis* 45: 33–40.

Cicero, 1949. *De Inventione. De Optimo Genere. Oratorum Topica.* Translated by H. M. Hubbell. Cambridge, MA: Harvard University Press.

[Cicero]. 1954. *Rhetorica ad Herennium.* Translated by H. Caplan. Cambridge, MA: Harvard University Press.

Cicero. 1970. *On Oratory [De Oratore] and Orators.* Translated by J. S. Watts. Carbondale, IL: Southern Illinois University Press.

Cicero. 1988. *Brutus*, Translated by G. L. Hendrickson; *Orator*, Translated by H. M. Hubbell. Cambridge, MA: Harvard University Press.

Cohen, I. Bernard, ed. 1941. *Benjamin Franklin's Experiments: A New Edition of Franklin's Experiments and Observations on Electricity.* Cambridge, MA: Harvard University Press.

Cohen, I. Bernard. 1981. Newton's discovery of gravity. In *Scientific Genius and Creativity.* New York: W. H. Freeman, pp. 17–25.

Colepresse, Samuel. 1667/1668. An account of some observations made by Mr. Samuel Colepress at and nigh Plimouth, an. 1667. *Philosophical Transactions* 3:632–634.

Conley, Thomas M. 1984. The enthymeme in perspective. *Quarterly Journal of Speech* 70: 168–187.

Conley, Thomas M. 1990. *Rhetoric in the European Tradition.* New York: Longman.

Cooper, Lane. 1924. The climax. *Sewanee Review* 32: 32–43.

Copi, Irving M. 1972. *Introduction to Logic.* 4th ed. New York: Macmillan.

Corbett, Edward P. J. 1971. *Classical Rhetoric for the Modern Student.* 2d ed. New York: Oxford University Press.

Corbetta, Maurizio, Francis M. Miezin, Susan Dobmeyer, Gordon L. Shulman, Steven E. Petersen, 1990. Attentional modulation of neural processing of shape, color, and velocity in humans. *Science* 248: 1556–1559.

Crosland, Maurice P. 1962. *Historical Studies in the Language of Chemistry.* Cambridge, MA: Harvard University Press.

Dalton, John. 1808. *A New System of Chemical Philosophy.* Pt. I. Manchester: S. Russell.

Darwin, Charles. 1958. *The Origin of Species by Means of Natural Selection.* New York: Mentor. [Reprint of sixth edition, 1872]

Darwin, Charles. 1965. *The Expression of the Emotions in Man and Animals* [1872]. Chicago: University of Chicago Press.

Darwin, Charles. 1979. *The Origin of Species by Means of Natural Selection.* New York: Avenel. [Reprint of first edition, 1859]

Darwin, Charles. 1998. *The Expression of the Emotions in Man and Animals.* 3rd ed. Edited by Paul Ekman. New York: Oxford University Press.

Davis, Bernard D., Renato Dulbecco, Herman N. Eisen and Harold S. Ginsberg. 1980. *Microbiology: Including Immunology and Molecular Genetics.* 3rd ed. Philadelphia: Harper & Row.

Dawkins, Richard. 1976. *The Selfish Gene.* New York: Oxford University Press.

Day, Angel. 1967. *The English Secretorie.* Menston, U.K.: The Scolar Press Limited.

Dear, Peter. 1985. Totius in verba: Rhetoric and authority in the Early Royal Society. *Isis* 76: 145–161.

de Duve, Christian. 1995. *Vital Dust: The Origin and Evolution of Life on Earth.* New York: Basic.

Demetrius. 1982. *On Style.* Translated by W. Rhys Roberts. Cambridge, MA: Harvard University Press.

Devillers, Pierre. 1977. The Skuas of the North American Pacific Coast. *Auk* 94: 417–429.

Devlin, Keith. 1994. *Mathematics: The Science of Patterns. The Search for Order in Life, Mind and the Universe.* New York: W. H. Freeman.

Diels, Hermann. 1922. *Die Fragmente der Vorsokratiker.* 4th ed. Vol. II. Berlin: Weidmannsche Buchhandlung.

Douglass, Frederick. 1988. *Narrative of the Life of Frederick Douglass: An American Slave. Written by Himself.* Edited by Benjamin Quarles. Cambridge, MA: The Belknap Press of Harvard University Press.

Duesberg, Peter. 1996. *Inventing the AIDS Virus.* Washington, DC: Regnery.

Dufay, Charles. 1734. A letter from Mons. Du Fay, F. R. S. and of the Royal Academy of Sciences at Paris, to his Grace Charles Duke of Richmond and Lenox, concerning electricity. Translated from the French by T. S. MD. *Philosophical Transactions* 38: 258–266.

Du Marsais, [1953] 1977. *Traité des Tropes.* suivi de Jean Paulhan. Traité des Figures [1953]. Postface, Claude Mouchard. Paris: Le Nouveau Commerce.

Dupont Corporation. 1994. The world of DuPont. Promotional brochure.

Eigen, Manfred. 1993. Viral quasispecies. *Scientific American.* 269: 43–49.

Eiseley, Loren. 1957. *The Immense Journey.* New York: Vintage.

Erasmus. 1963. *On Copia of Words and Ideas.* Translated by Donald E. King and H. David Rix. Milwaukee, WI: Marquette University Press.

Euclid. 1952. *The Thirteen Books of Euclid's Elements.* Translated by Sir Thomas L. Heath. Great Books, Vol. 11. Chicago: Encyclopedia Britannica.

Fahnestock, Jeanne. 1993. Tactics of evaluation in Gould and Lewontin's "The Spandrels of San Marco." *Understanding Scientific Prose.* Edited by Jack Selzer. Madison, WI: University of Wisconsin Press, pp. 158–179.

Faraday, Michael. 1932. *Faraday's Diary; being the various philosophical notes of experimental investigation made by Michael Faraday during the years 1820–1862.* Edited by Thomas Martin. Vol. I. London: G. Bell and Sons.

Faraday, Michael. 1952. *Experimental Researches in Electricity.* Great Books, Vol. 45. Chicago: Encyclopedia Britannica.

Feduccia, Alan. 1993. Evidence from claw geometry indicating arboreal habits of *Archaeopteryx. Science* 259: 790–792.

Feynman, Richard. 1965. *The Character of Physical Law.* Cambridge, MA: The M.I.T. Press.

Fitzpatrick, John W., David E. Willard, and John W. Terborgh. 1979. A new species of hummingbird from Peru. *The Wilson Bulletin* 91: 177–186.

Folk, Robert L. 1997. Nannobacteria: Surely not figments but what under heaven are they? *naturalSCIENCE. A World Wide Web Journal.* Vol I, Article 3, 1997. [http://naturalscience.com/ns/articles/01–03/ns_folk.html]

Fontanier, Pierre. 1977. *Les Figures du Discours.* Introduction by Gérard Genette. Paris: Flammarion.

Fowler, Roger and Gunther Kress. 1979. *Language and Control.* London: Routledge.

Freese, J. H., trans. 1926. Aristotle's *Art of Rhetoric.* Cambridge, MA: Harvard University Press.

Galton, Francis. 1970. *English Men of Science: Their Nature and Nurture* [1874]. London: Cass.

Geison, Gerald L. 1995. *The Private Science of Louis Pasteur.* Princeton, NJ: Princeton University Press.

Genette, Gérard. 1982. *Figures of Literary Discourse.* Translated by Alan Sheridan. New York: Columbia University Press.

Gentner, Dedre and Michael Jeziorski. 1993. The shift from metaphor to analogy in Western science. In *Metaphor and Thought,* 2nd ed. Edited by Andrew Ortony. Cambridge: Cambridge University Press, pp. 447–480.

Gilbert, William. 1952. *On the Loadstone and Magnetic Bodies and on the Great Magnet the Earth [De Magnete].* Translated by P. Fleury Mottelay. Great Books, Vol. 28. Chicago: Encyclopedia Britannica.

Gladue, Brian A., Richard Green, and Ronald E. Hellman. 1983. Neuroendocrine response to estrogen and sexual orientation. *Science* 225: 1496–1499.

Gooding, David. 1985. In nature's school: Faraday as an experimentalist. In *Faraday Rediscovered: Essays on the Life and Work of Michael Faraday, 1791–1867.* Edited by David Gooding and Frank A. J. L. James. New York: Stockton.

Gottesman, Irving I. 1997. Twins en route to QTLs for cognition. *Science* 276: 1522–1523.

Gould, Stephen Jay. 1996. Mr. Sophia's pony. *Natural History* 105: 20–24, 66–69.

Gray, Stephen. 1720. An account of some new electrical experiments. *Philosophical Transactions.* 31: 104–107.

Gray, Stephen. 1731. A letter to Cromwell Mortimer, M.D. Secr. R.S. containing several experiments concerning electricity. *Philosophical Transactions* 37: 17–44.

Gray, Stephen. 1732. A letter concerning the electricity of water. *Philosophical Transactions.* 37: 227–230.

Gray, Stephen. 1735. Experiments and observations upon the light that is produced by communicating electrical attraction to animal or inanimate bodies, together with some of its most surprising effects. *Philosophical Transactions* 39: 16–24.

Gross, Alan. 1990. *The Rhetoric of Science.* Cambridge, MA: Harvard University Press.

Gross, Alan, and William M. Keith, eds. 1997. *Rhetorical Hermeneutics: Invention and Interpretation in the Age of Science.* Albany, NY: State University Press of New York.

Gur, Ruben C., Lyn Harper Mozley, P. David Mozley, Susan M. Resnick, Joel S. Karp, Abass Alavi, Steven E. Arnold, Raquel E. Gur. 1995. Sex differences in regional cerebral glucose metabolism during a resting state. *Science* 267: 528–531.

Halliday, M. A. K. and R. Hasan. 1976. *Cohesion in English*. London: Longmans.

Halliday, M. A. K. and J. R. Martin. 1993. *Writing Science: Literary and Discursive Power*. Pittsburgh: University of Pittsburgh Press.

Harris, Randy Allen. 1997. *Landmark Essays on Rhetoric of Science: Case Studies*. Mahwah, NJ: Hermagoras Press/ Lawrence Erlbaum.

Harwood, John T., ed. 1986. *The Rhetorics of Thomas Hobbes and Bernard Lamy*. Carbondale, IL: Southern Illinois University Press.

Hauksbee, Francis. 1706. An account of an experiment made before the Royal Society at Gresham-Colledge, touching the extraordinary elistricity of glass, produceable on a smart attrition of it; with a continuation of experiments on the same subject, & other phenomena. *Philosophical Transactions* 25: 2237–2335.

Hauksbee, Francis. 1707a. Several experiments shewing the strange effects of the effluvia of glass, produceable on the motion and attrition of it. *Philosophical Transactions* 25: 2372–2377.

Hauksbee, Francis, 1707b. An account of an experiment, confirming one lately made, touching the production of light, by the effluvia of one glass falling on another in motion. *Philosophical Transactions* 25:2313 [2413]–2415.

Hauksbee, Francis. 1708a. An account of the repetition of an experiment touching motion given bodies included in a glass, by the approach of a finger near its outside: With other experiments on the effluvia of glass and An account of some experiments, touching the electricity and light producible on the attrition of several bodies." *Philosophical Transactions* 26: 82–92.

Hauksbee, Francis. 1708b. An account of an experiment, touching the production of light within a globe glass, whose inward surface is lin'd with sealing-wax, upon an attrition of its outside. *Philosophical Transactions* 26: 219–221.

Hauksbee, Francis, 1709a. An account of an experiment, shewing that an object may become visible through such an opake body as pitch in the dark, while it is under the circumstances of attrition and a vacuum. *Philosophical Transactions* 26: 391–392.

Hauksbee, Francis, 1709b. An account of an experiment, touching an attempt to produce light on the inside of a globe-glass lin'd with melted flowers of sulphur, as in the experiments of sealing-wax and pitch. *Philosophical Transactions* 26:439–443.

Heathcote, Niels H. de V. 1967.The early meaning of electricity: Some pseudoxia epidemica— I. *Annals of Science* 23: 261–275.

Heilbron, J. L. 1979. *Electricity in the 17th and 18th Centuries: A Study of Early Modern Physics*. Berkeley: University of California Press.

Henry, Joseph. 1886. On the production of currents and sparks of electricity from magnetism. In *Scientific Writings of Joseph Henry*. Vol. I. Washington: Smithsonian Institution.

Herder, Johann Gottfried. 1989. *Ideen zur Philosophie der Geschichte der Menschheit*. Band 6. *Johann Gottfried Herder Werke*. Frankfurt am Main: Deutscher Klassiker Verlag.

Hermogenes. 1987. *On Types of Style*. Translated by Cecil W. Wooten. Chapel Hill: University of North Carolina Press.

Herschel, William. 1789. Catalogue of a second thousand of new nebulae and clusters of stars; with a few introductory remarks on the construction of the heavens. *Philosophical Transactions* 79: 212–255.

Herschel, William. 1791. On nebulous stars, properly so called. *Philosophical Transactions* 81: 71–88.

Herschel, William. 1811. Astronomical observations relating to the construction of the heavens, arranged for the purpose of a critical examination, the result of which appears to throw some new light upon the organization of the celestial bodies. *Philosophical Transactions* 101: 245–238.

Hesse, Mary B. 1966. *Models and Analogies in Science.* Notre Dame, IN: University of Notre Dame Press.

Holmes, Frederic L. 1987. Scientific writing and scientific discovery. *Isis* 78: 220–235.

Holton, Gerald and Stephen G. Brush. 1985. *Introduction to Concepts and Theories in Physical Science.* 2nd ed. Princeton: Princeton University Press.

Hoskins, John. 1935. *Directions for Speech and Style.* Edited by Hoyt H. Hudson. Princeton: Princeton University Press.

Huxley, Thomas H. 1871. *Evidence as to Man's Place in Nature.* New York: Appleton.

Huxley, Thomas Henry. 1897. On a piece of chalk. *Discourses Biological and Geological.* New York: Appleton.

Huxley, Thomas Henry. 1968. Paleontology and the doctrine of evolution. *Collected Essays.* Vol VIII, *Discourses Biological and Geological.* New York: Greenwood.

Isocrates. 1929. Against the Sophists. Translated by George Norlin. In *Isocrates*, Vol. II. Cambridge, MA: Harvard University Press.

Janofsky, Michael. 1995. Demons and conspiracies haunt a "Patriot" World. *New York Times*, 31 May, A18.

Jardine, Lisa. 1974. *Francis Bacon: Discovery and the Art of Discourse.* Cambridge: Cambridge University Press.

Johnson, Ned K. and Carla Bowman Johnson. 1985. Speciation in sapsuckers (Sphyrapicus): II. Sympatry, hybridization, and mate preference in *S. Ruber Daggetti* and *S. Nuchalis. Auk* 102: 1–15.

Joseph, Sister Miriam. 1947. *Shakespeare's Use of the Arts of Language.* New York: Columbia University Press. [Sister Joseph's overview of sixteenth-century compositional theory, Part I, and the definitions of rhetorical constructs and figures, Part III, were reprinted as *Rhetoric in Shakespeare's Time: Literary Theory of Renaissance Europe*, New York: Harcourt Brace, 1947.]

Kelly, Kevin. 1995. The gene in the machine. *New York Times*, 15 May, A17.

Kennedy, George A. 1980. *Classical Rhetoric and Its Christian and Secular Tradition from Ancient to Modern Times.* Chapel Hill: University of North Carolina Press.

Kennedy, George A., trans. 1991. *Aristotle On Rhetoric: A Theory of Civic Discourse.* New York: Oxford University Press.

Kerr, Richard A. 1995. Did Darwin get it all right? *Science* 267 (10 March): 1421–1422.

Kline, Morris. 1953. *Mathematics in Western Culture.* New York: Oxford University Press.

Kline, Morris. 1955. Projective geometry. *Science and the Arts.* New York: Scientific American.

Kline, Morris. 1972. *Mathematical Thought: From Ancient to Modern Times.* New York: Oxford University Press.

Knight, David. 1970. *Classical Scientific Papers. Chemistry: Second Series. Papers on the Nature and Arrangement of the Chemical Elements.* New York: American Elsevier.

Koch, Robert. 1987. *Essays of Robert Koch.* Translated by K. Codell Carter. New York: Greenwood.

Koch, Robert. 1912. *Gesammelte Werke.* Leipzig: George Thieme.

Kolata, Gina. 1995. Man's world, woman's world? Brain studies point to differences. *New York Times*, 28 February, C1, C7.

Kuhn, Thomas. 1970. *The Structure of Scientific Revolutions.* 2nd ed. Chicago: University of Chicago Press.

Kulkarni, S. R. 1997. Brown dwarfs: A Possible missing link between stars and planets. *Science* 276 (30 May): 1350–1354.

Lamarck, Jean Baptiste. 1960. *Philosophie Zoologique*. Reprint. New York: Hafner.

Lamarck, Jean Baptiste. 1984. *Zoological Philosophy*. Translated by Hugh Elliot. Chicago: University of Chicago Press.

Lasmézas, Corinne I., Jean Philippe Deslys, Olivier Rebain, Alexandre Jaegly, Vincent Beringue, Jean-Michel Peyrin, Jean-Guy Fournier, Jean-Jacques Hauw, Jean Rossier, Dominique Dormont. 1997. Transmission of the BSE agent to mice in the absence of detectable abnormal prion protein. *Science* 275 (17 January): 402–405.

Latour, Bruno. 1988. *The Pastuerization of France*. Cambridge, MA: Harvard University Press.

Lavoisier, Antoine. 1787. Mémoire sur la nécessité de réformer & de perfectionner la nomenclature de la Chimie. In *Méthode de Nomenclature Chimique*, Proposéé par MM. De Morveau, Lavoisier, Betholet (*sic*), & De Fourcroy. Paris: Cuchet, pp. 1–25.

Lavoisier, Antoine. 1952. *Elements of Chemistry*. Translated by Robert Kerr. Great Books Series Vol. 45. Chicago: Encyclopedia Britannica.

Lavoisier, Antoine. [1789] 1965. *Traité Élémentaire de Chimie*. Paris: Cuchet, Brussels.

Leech, Geoffrey and Michael Short. 1981. *Style in Fiction: A Linguistic Introduction to English Fictional Prose*. London: Longman.

Levine, Arnold. 1992. *Viruses*. New York: Scientific American Library.

Lewontin, Richard C. 1995. Genes, environment and organisms. In *Hidden Histories of Science*. Edited by Robert B. Silvers. New York: *New York Review*, pp. 115–139.

Lloyd, G. E. R. 1966. *Polarity and Analogy: Two Types of Argumentation in Early Greek Thought*. Cambridge: Cambridge University Press.

Locke, John. 1995. *An Essay Concerning Human Understanding* [1693]. New York: Prometheus Books.

Lyell, Charles. 1863. *The Geological Evidences of the Antiquity of Man*. Philadelphia: George W. Childs.

Magendie, François. 1822. Expériences sur les fonctions des racines des nerfs rachidiens. *Journal de physiologie expâerimentale et pathologique* 2: 276–279.

Marrou, H. I. 1956. *A History of Education in Antiquity*. Translated by George Lamb. New York: Sheed & Ward.

Marsh, O. C. 1877. Introduction and succession of vertebrate life in America. *Nature* 16 (20 Sept. 27 Sept. 4 Oct.): 448–450, 470–472, 489–491.

Mason, Stephen. 1962. *A History of the Sciences*. New York: Collier.

Mayer, Jane. 1996. Quitting the Mediaocracy. *New Yorker* 71 (12 February): 25–26.

McFadden, Robert D. 1994. Drifter's tale of serial death: Remorse prompts confession. *New York Times*, 11 March, A1, B4.

Melancthon, Philip. 1969. "Elementorum Rhetorices Libri Duo." Latin text with English translation and notes by Sister Mary Joan LaFontaine. Ph.D. diss., University of Michigan, Ann Arbor.

Miller, George. 1991. *The Science of Words*. New York: Scientific American Press.

Montaigne, Michel de. 1962. *Oeuvres Complètes*. Edited by Albert Thibaudet and Maurice Rat. Paris: Editions Gallimard.

Morell, Virginia, 1993. *Archaeopteryx*: Early bird catches a can of worms. *Science* 259: 764–765.

Moss, Jean Dietz. 1993. *Novelties in the Heavens: Rhetoric and Science in the Copernican Controversy*. Chicago: University of Chicago Press.

Murphy, James J. 1974. *Rhetoric in the Middle Ages: A History of Rhetorical Theory from St. Augustine to the Renaissance*. Berkeley: University of California Press.

Murphy, James J., ed. 1983. *Demosthenes' On the Crown: A Critical Case Study of a Masterpiece of Ancient Oratory*. Translation by John J. Kearney. Davis, CA: Hermagoras.

Murphy, James J. 1990. *Topos* and *Figura*: Historical cause and effect? In *De Ortu Grammaticae. Studies in Medieval Grammar and Linguistic Theory in Memory of Jan Pinborg*. Edited by G. L. Bursill-Hall, Sten Ebbesen, and Konrad Koerner. Amsterdam: Benjamins, pp. 239–253.

Needham, Turbervill. 1746. Extract of a letter from Mr. Turbervill Needham to Martin Folkes, esq; Pr. R.S. concerning some new electrical experiments lately made at Paris. *Philosophical Transactions* 44: 247– 263.

Newton, Isaac. 1672. New theory about light and colors [*sic*]." *Philosophical Transactions* 6: 3075–3087.

Newton, Isaac. 1822. *Philosophiae Naturalis Principia Mathematica*. Glasgow: Treuttel & Würtz.

Newton, Isaac. 1952. *Mathematical Principles of Natural Philosophy*. Translated by Andrew Motte and Rev. Florian Cajori. Great Books, Vol. 34. Chicago: Encyclopedia Britannica.

North, John. 1995. *The Norton History of Astronomy and Cosmology*. New York: W. W. Norton.

Nowak, Rachel. 1995. Staging ethical AIDS trials in Africa [Inset: A model collaboration built to last]. *Science* 269 (8 September): 1333.

Ogden, C. K. 1967. *Opposition: A Linguistic and Psychological Analysis*. Introduction by I. A. Richards. Bloomington: University of Indiana Press.

Ogden, C. K. and I. A. Richards. 1923. *The Meaning of Meaning*. New York: Harcourt Brace.

Ohanian, Hans C. 1989. *Physics*. 2d ed. New York: Norton.

Ortony, Andrew, ed. 1993. *Metaphor and Thought*. 2d ed. Cambridge: Cambridge University Press.

Paley, William. 1963. *Natural Theology*. Indianapolis, IN: Bobbs-Merrill.

Papin, Liliane. 1992. This is not a universe: Metaphor, language and representation. *PMLA* 107: 1253–1265.

Parker, Patricia. 1990. Metaphor and catachresis. In *The Ends of Rhetoric*. Edited by John Bender and David Wellbery. Stanford, CA: Stanford University Press.

Pascal, Blaise. 1952. *Pensées*. Translated by W. F. Trotter. Great Books, Vol. 33. Chicago: Encyclopedia Britannica.

Pascal, Blaise. 1966. *Pensées*. Translated by A. J. Krailsheimer. London: Penguin.

Pasteur, Louis. 1905. *Researches on the Molecular Asymmetry of Natural Organic Products* [1860]. Edinburgh: The Alembic Club.

Pasteur, Louis. 1922. *Oeuvres de Pasteur*. Edited by Pasteur Vallery-Radot. Vol I. *Dissymétrie Moléculaire*. Vol II. *Fermentations et Générations dites Spontanées*. Paris: Masson.

Peacham, Henry. 1954. *The Garden of Eloquence* [1593]. Gainesville, FL: Scholars' Facsimiles & Reprints.

Percival, W. Keith. 1983. Grammar and rhetoric in the Renaissance. *Renaissance Eloquence*. Edited by James J. Murphy. Berkeley: University of California Press, pp. 303–330.

Perelman, Chaim and Lucie Olbrechts-Tyteca. 1969. *The New Rhetoric: A Treatise on Argumentation*. Translated by J. Wilkinson and P. Weaver. Notre Dame, IN: University of Notre Dame Press.

Plett, Heinrich. 1983. The place and function of style in Renaissance poetics. *Renaissance Eloquence*. Edited by James J. Murphy. Berkeley: University of California Press, pp. 356–375.

Poster, Carol. 1992. A historicist recontextualization of the enthymeme. *Rhetoric Society Quarterly* 22: 1–24.

Poster, Carol, 1997. Being, time, and definition: Notes towards a semiotics of figural rhetoric. Paper delivered at the National Communication Association, Chicago, IL.

Postgate, John. 1992. *Microbes and Man.* 3d ed. Cambridge: Cambridge University Press.

Prelli, Lawrence. 1989. *A Rhetoric of Science: Inventing Scientific Discourse.* Columbia: University of South Carolina Press.

Priestley, Joseph. 1966. *The History and Present State of Electricity, with Original Experiments.* 3d ed. New York: Johnson Reprint Corp.

Puttenham, George. 1970. *The Arte of English Poesie* [1589]. Kent, OH: Kent State University Press.

Pylyshyn, Zenon W. 1993. Metaphorical imprecision and the "top-down" research strategy. In *Metaphor and Thought.* Edited by Andrew Ortony. 2d ed. Cambridge: Cambridge University Press, pp. 543–558.

Quinn, Arthur. 1982. *Figures of Speech: 60 Ways To Turn a Phrase.* Salt Lake City, UT: Gibbs.

Quintilian. 1921. *Institutio Oratoria.* Translated by H. E. Butler. Cambridge, MA: Harvard University Press.

Ragsdale, J. Donald. 1965. Invention in English "stylistic" rhetorics: 1600–1800. *Quarterly Journal of Speech* 51: 164–167.

Ray, John. 1977. *The Wisdom of God Manifested in the Works of the Creation* [1692]. New York: Arno.

Reboul, Olivier. 1989. The figure and the argument. In *From Metaphysics to Rhetoric.* Edited by Michel Meyer. Dodrecht, Netherlands: Kluwer, pp. 169–181.

Rehbock, Philip F. 1975. Huxley, Haeckel, and the oceanographers: The case of Bathybius haeckelii. *Isis* 66: 504–533.

Rennie, John. 1993. Who is normal? *Scientific American* 269: 14–17.

Retallack, G. J. 1995. Permian-Triassic life crisis on land. *Science* 267 (6 January): 77–80.

Rhetorica ad Alexandrum. 1984. In *The Complete Works of Aristotle.* Edited by Jonathan Barnes. Vol. 2. Princeton, NJ: Princeton University Press.

Rudwick, Martin J. S. 1985. *The Meaning of Fossils: Episodes in the History of Paleontology.* 2d ed. Chicago: University of the Chicago Press.

Rugg, Michael. 1995. La différence vive. *Nature* 373 (16 February): 561–562.

Shaywitz, Bennett A., Sally E. Shaywitz, Kenneth R. Pugh, R. Todd Constable, Pawel Skudlarski, Robert K. Fulbright, Richard A. Bronen, Jack M. Fletcher, Donald P. Shankweller, Leonard Katz, John C. Gore. 1995. Sex differences in the functional organization of the brain for language. *Nature* 373 (16 February): 607–609.

Shaywitz, Sally E., Michael D. Escobar, Bennett A. Shaywitz, Jack M. Fletcher, Robert Makuch, 1992. Evidence that dyslexia may represent the lower tail of a normal distribution of reading ability. *New England Journal of Medicine* 326: 145–150.

Simpson, George Gaylord. 1951. *Horses: The Story of the Horse Family in the Modern World and Through Sixty Million Years of History.* New York: Oxford University Press.

Smith, John. 1973. *The Mysterie of Rhetorique unvail'd* [1657]. New York: Hildesheim.

Smith, Robert F. 1981. Chiasm in Sumero-Akkadian. In *Chiasmus in Antiquity: Structures, Analyses, Exegesis.* Edited by John W. Welch. Hildesheim: Gerstenberg, pp. 17–35.

Smoluchowski, Roman. 1983. *The Solar System.* New York: W. H. Freeman.

Sonnino, Lee A. 1968. *A Handbook to Sixteenth-Century Rhetoric.* New York: Barnes & Noble.

Sprat, Thomas. 1667. *History of the Royal Society.* London: J. Martyn and J. Allestry.

Stanier, Roger K., Michael Doudoroff and Edward A. Adelberg. 1963. *The Microbial World.* 2d ed. Englewood Cliffs, NJ: Prentice Hall.

Starr, Richard. 1993. The Clinton counterrevolution. *Insight,* 28 February: 32.

St. Augustine. 1986. *On Christian Doctrine.* Translated by D. W. Robertson, Jr. New York: Macmillan.

Stevens, William K. 1995. Wolf's howl heralds change for old haunts. *New York Times,* 31 January, C1, C4.

Stock, A. 1984. Chiastic awareness and education in antiquity. *Biblical Theology Bulletin* 14: 23–27.

Sur L'Électricitiè. 1733. *Histoire de L'Academie Royale des Sciences avec les memoires de mathematique et de physique.* Tome 1: 5–17.

Thucydides. 1954. *History of the Peloponnesian War.* Translated by Rex Warner. London: Penguin.

Travis, J. 1996. Kids: Getting under mom's skin for decades. *Science News* 149(10 February): 85.

Trousdale, Marion. 1982. *Shakespeare and the Rhetoricians.* Chapel Hill: University of North Carolina Press.

Turner, Mark. 1991. *Reading Minds: The Study of English in the Age of Cognitive Science.* Princeton, NJ: Princeton University Press.

vanSpronsen, J. W. 1969. *The Periodic System of Chemical Elements: A History of the First Hundred Years.* Amsterdam: Elsevier.

Varga, A. Kibédi. 1983. Rhetoric, a story or a system? A challenge to historians of Renaissance rhetoric. *Renaissance Eloquence.* Edited by James J. Murphy. Berkeley: University of California Press, pp. 84–91.

Vickers, Brian. 1968. *Francis Bacon and Renaissance Prose.* Cambridge: Cambridge University Press.

Vickers, Brian. 1981. Rhetorical and anti-rhetorical tropes: On writing the history of *elocutio.* In *Comparative Criticism: A Yearbook.* Edited by E. S. Shaffer. Cambridge: Cambridge University Press, pp. 105–131.

Vickers, Brian. 1988. *In Defence of Rhetoric.* Oxford: Clarendon.

Vossius, Gerardus Joannes. 1655. *Rhetorices Contractae Sive Partitionum Oratoriarum. Libri V.* Oxford: Jos. Godwin.

Wade, Nicholas. 1997. Mars meteorite fuels debate on life on Earth. *New York Times,* 29 July, C1, C6.

Wallman, Joel. 1992. *Aping Language.* Cambridge: Cambridge University Press.

Wang, Andrew H.-J., Gary J. Quigley, Francis J. Kolpak, James L. Crawford, Jacques H. Van Boom, Gijs van der Marel, and Alexander Rich. 1979. Molecular structure of a left-handed double helical DNA fragment at atomic resolution. *Nature* 282 (13 December): 680–686.

Watson, William. 1745. Experiments and observations, tending to illustrate the nature and properties of electricity. *Philosophical Transactions* 43: 481–501.

Watson, William. 1746. Further experiments and observations tending to illustrate the nature and properties of electricity. *Philosophical Transactions* 44: 41–50.

Weaver, Richard M. 1948. *Ideas Have Consequences.* Chicago: University of Chicago Press.

Weaver, Richard. 1985. *The Ethics of Rhetoric* [1953]. Davis, CA: Hermagoras.

Weindruch, Richard. 1996. Caloric restriction and aging. *Scientific American* 274: (January): 46–52.

Weiner, Jonathan. 1995. Evolution made visible. *Science* 267 (6 January): 30–33.

Welch, John W. 1981a. Chiasmus in ancient Greek and Latin literatures. In *Chiasmus in Antiquity: Structures, Analyses, Exegesis.* Edited by John W. Welch. Hildesheim: Gerstenberg, pp. 250–268.

Welch, John W. 1981b. Chiasmus in Ugaritic. In *Chiasmus in Antiquity: Structures, Analyses, Exegesis.* Edited by John W. Welch. Hildesheim: Gerstenberg, pp. 36–49.

Westfall, Richard S. 1980. *Never at Rest: A Biography of Isaac Newton.* Cambridge: Cambridge University Press.

Weyl, Hermann. 1952. *Symmetry.* Princeton, NJ: Princeton University Press.

Whately, Richard. 1963. *Elements of Rhetoric* [1846]. Carbondale, IL: Southern Illinois University Press.

Wheler, Granvile. 1739. Some electrical experiments, chiefly regarding the repulsive force of electrical bodies; communicated in a letter from Granvile Wheler, Esq; F. R. S. *Philosophical Transactions* 41: 98–111.

Wilde, Oscar. 1985. *The Picture of Dorian Gray*. London: Penguin.

Wilford, John Noble. 1995. Big telescope is first to find brown dwarf, team reports. *New York Times*, 14 June, B7.

Williams, Joseph. 1989. *Style: Ten Lessons in Clarity and Grace*. 3d ed. New York: Harper Collins.

Wilson, Mitchell. 1954. Joseph Henry. In *Scientific Genius and Creativity*. New York: W. H. Freeman, pp. 62–66.

Wilson, Thomas. 1994. *The Art of Rhetoric* [1560]. Edited by Peter E. Medine. University Park, PA: Pennsylvania State University Press.

Index

agnominatio, 165–168
AIDS, 163
alchemy, ordering of metals, 105
allegory, 7
alliteration, 165
amplification, devices of, 9, 12, 13
anadiplosis, 94, 158
anaphora, 20, 36, 157
anastrophe, 7
antanaclasis, 159, 169, 194, 210 n. 4
antimetabole
  in ancient texts, 122–123
  as antithesis, 129
  argumentative uses of, 131–133
  in Aristotle's *Rhetoric* and *Topics*, 131–133
  and bilateral symmetry, 134–135
  in causal reversals, 141–143
  not chiasmus, 123–124, 126–128
  in Cicero, 206 n. 4
  as commutative principle, 133–135
  corrective, 151–153, 208 n. 10
  dispersed, 41
  in Faraday and Henry on
    electromagnetism, 144–150
  in geometry, 135–137
  history of the figure, 126–131
  illustrating figure/topic relationship,
    24–26
  use by Lamarck, 152–153

  use by Lewontin, 154–155, 210 n. 20
  mirror-imaging, 137–139
  in *New Rhetoric*, 36
  in Newton, 142–143
  in Pasteur, 139–141
  physical antimetaboles, 137–138
  predictive power, 124
  as reading frame, 127
  for refutations by reversal, 150–151
  semantics and syntax, 123–126
  visual form, 41, 137–138
Antiphon, 130
antithesis
  with antimetabole, 124, 129, 131, 201
  uses in argument, 58–59
  Aristotle's definition of, 46–47
  in Bacon's *Novum Organum*, 59–65
  in Blair, 57
  in Campbell, 57
  conflation with enthymeme, 55–56
  with contradictions, 48
  with contraries, 48
  with correlatives, 49
  cut versus scale oppositions, 72–75
  Darwin's "principle of antithesis," 65–69
  in Demetrius' *On Style*, 200 n. 8
  dissociation into stylistic and probative
    kinds, 55
  in early electrical lexicon, 177–178

antithesis (*continued*)
excluding emotion, 56
using existing semantic contrasts, 59
as figure of thought versus figure of
speech, 200 n. 8
in Fontanier, 57
history of the figure, 53–58
human versus brute antithesis, 75–80
in Lavoisier, 195 n. 1
male versus female antithesis, 80–85
in Melancthon, 12
Pascal's "false window," 69–72
in Peacham's *Garden of Eloquence*, 56–57
Quintilian's treatment of, 55–56, 201
semantics of, 47–49
syntax of, 49–51
three-part antithesis, 201–202 n. 13
two types, single and double, 47, 52
undoing antithesis, 87–90
antonomasia, 7, 159
apes, in human versus brute debates, 76–80
aphaeresis, 212 n. 11
Aping Language (Wallman), 78–80
apocope, 212 n. 11
aposiopesis, 6, 22
apostrophe, 19
archaeopteryx in bird versus dinosaur
controversy, 71–72
argument from design, 172
Aristotle. *See also Rhetoric; Topics*
on antimetabole in *Rhetoric* and
Topics, 131–133
on antithesis in dialectical and
rhetorical invention, 51–53
definition of antithesis, 46–47
form/function view of figures, 26–28
on gradatio, 203–204 n. 4
on polyptoton in *Rhetoric* and *Topics*,
170–171
on repetition, 213
articulus, 18, 91–92
assonance, 165
asyndeton, 26–27

Bacon, Francis, use of antithesis in
Novum Organum, 59–65, 202 n. 14
Bathybius haeckelii, 86–87
Bianca, Diana, 137
bilateral symmetry and antimetabole,
135–135

Biot, Jean Baptiste, 137
bird-reptile categories, 112–113
Black, Max, 5
Blair, Hugh, 38, 57, 201 n. 12
Bose, Georg, 178
Bovine Spongiform Encephalopathy
(BSE), 163
brain function localization, 162
Breck, John, 126–127
Bronowski, Jacob, 5
brown dwarfs, 104–105
Brown, William Jr., 119–120
Browne, Sir Thomas, 179
Brush, Stephen, 204 n. 8, 205 n. 9
Burke, Kenneth
use of antimetabole, 141, 208 n. 11
on gradatio, 94–95
on identification through formal
devices, 34

caloric, theories of heat, 3–4
Campbell, George, 57, 130
Candolle, Alphonse de, 167
Carter, K. Codell, 163
cascade, 209 n. 15
catachresis, 7, 37
Categories, by Aristotle, 125
category merging with series, 112–114
chain of being, 102–103
chiasmus
in Biblical exegesis, 126–127
definition of, 123–124
distinguished from antimetabole, 123–
124, 126–128
Cicero, 18, 28, 31
circular gradatio, 204 n. 5
climax, 93. *See also* gradatio
Colepresse, Samuel, 41–42
Collinson, Peter, 182, 190
Colonna, Fabio, 177
communicatio, 197 n. 5
commutative principles, 134
concessio, 11
congeries, 92
Conley, Thomas, 29–30, 198 n. 10
constitutive, theory of figuration, 21–22,
40
contentio, as a form of antithesis, 54, 55,
200 n. 8
continuum. *See* gradatio; incrementum

continuum of life forms, 90
contradictions, in antitheses, 48–49
contraries, in antitheses, 48, 200 n. 5
contrarium, form of antithesis, 54, 55
co-ordinate terms in argument, 170
correlatives, in antitheses, 49, 200 n. 6,
    206 n. 2
cut-based antitheses, 72–74

Dalton, John, 3–4, 195–196 n. 1
Darwin, Charles
    use of antimetabole, 125
    category blending, 113–114
    use of competing series, 118–120
    continuum between domestic and
        natural selection, 114–115
    limits of linear series, 121
    principle of antithesis in *Expression of*
        the Emotions, 65–69
    repetition of adjectives, 161
    series reasoning in *On the Origin of*
        Species, 113–121
    views reversed by Lewontin, 154
Day, Angel, 92
de Candolle, Alphonse, 167
de Duve, Christian, 89
degree, arguments from greater or lesser,
    95–96
De Kruif, Paul, 162
Demetrius of Halicarnassus, *On Style*,
    129, 200 n. 8, 201 n. 11, 207 n. 5
Demosthenes, 93, 129
Desargues, Gérard, 136
descriptio, 11
Devlin, Keith, 134
diaeresis, 91
dialectical reasoning, 51–53, 132, 170–171
diaphora, 159, 160
DNA (deoxyribonucleic acid), 90, 137
Döbereiner, Johann, 103
Donatus, *Ars Maior*, 32
double hierarchy arguments, 105–108
double homology in archaeology, 108
Douglass, Frederick, 45–46, 56
duality, principle of, 136
Duesberg, Peter, 163
Dufay, Charles, 177, 184–186
DuMarsais, 32
duplicatio, 159
dyslexia, 113

écart, theory of figuration, 15
ecphonesis, 14
effictio, 8
Eiseley, Loren, 133
electricity, studies of in eighteenth
    century
    adjustment of vocabulary to
        experimental parameters, 187–190
    antithesis in, 177–178
    Franklin's use of *electri*, 190–193
    metaphors in, 177
    nouns and modifiers from *electri*, 178–
        182
    ploche and polyptoton in, 177–194
    polyptotonic path of *electri*, 193–194
    verb forms from *electri*, 182–190
electromagnetism, 89
emotion
    as conveyed in figures, 19, 21–22
    opposite emotions in Darwin's
        Expression of the Emotions, 66–69
enantiomorphs, 135, 137
enthymeme, 29–30, 51, 102, 151,
    198 n. 10, 201 n. 10
enumeratio, 91
eohippus, 204 n. 6
epanados, 206 n. 1
epanalepsis, 17, 157
epenthesis, 212 n. 11
epistrophe, 20, 50, 157
epitome, definition of, 24
Erasmus, 11, 14, 92
Euclid's *Elements*, 135–136
eutrepismus, 91
The Expression of the Emotions in Man
    and Animals (Darwin), 65–69

Faraday, Michael, 144–149
Feduccia, Alan, 71–72
female/male opposition, 80–85
Feynman, Richard, 111, 133–135
figures of speech
    in early modern treatments, 11–14
    figure/topic separation of, 31–32
    formal versus functional descriptions
        of, 14–15
    as grammatical errors, 197
    historical view of form/function
        rationale, 26–31
    in Quintilian's *Institutio Oratoria*, 8–11

figures of speech (*continued*)
  for repetitions, 157–158
  in the *Rhetorica ad Herennium*, 7–8
  scholarly restorations of figure/topic
    connection, 32–36
  in scientific discourse, 43–44
  series-forming, 91–95
  verbal spread of, 40–41
  visual representations of, 41–42
figures of speech, theories of
  boundary problems with, 37–40
  as constitutive or iconic, 21–23
  écart, 15
  as epitomes, 24, 40
  as expressions of the emotions, 21–22
  fixed number impossible, 23
  as not normal versus not typical, 15–17
  as ornament versus armament, 18–19
  redefinition of the category "figure," 23, 40
  revised in *New Rhetoric*, 34–36
  substitution, 17
  as value added, 20–23
figures of thought, 8, 10–11, 12, 196–197
    n. 5
Folk, Robert, 212–213
Fontanier, Pierre, 16, 32, 57, 130–131
fossil horse sequence, 98–100, 204 n. 6
fossil plant sequence, 99
fossil shell in illustration, 177
fourfold exegesis, 17
Fowler, Roger, 160–161
Fox, Everett, 122
Franklin, Benjamin, 177, 178, 182, 190–193

Galton, Francis, 167–168
Gaudry, Albert, 98
Genette, Gérard, 6
geometrical progression, 171
Gilbert, William, 89, 178–179
Gladue, Brian, 101–102
Goffman, Erving, 197 n. 5
Godfrey, John, 182
Gooding, David, 144
Gorgianic figures, 50
Gorgias, 45
Gould, Stephen Jay, 98
gradatio
  use in argument, 95–98
  in argument from design, 172
  in Aristotle's *Rhetoric*, 203–204 n. 4

  circular, 204 n. 5
  definition of, 93–95
  as emboîtement strategy, 111
  in fossil plant sequence, 99
  in geographical distribution, 120
  in great chain of being, 102–103
  in ineffective narrative, 204 n. 5
  in Lamarck, 152, 209 n. 18
  in Leibniz, 205 n. 12
  in Molière, 205 n. 12
  as sorites, 108–112
  for wolves in ecosystem, 109–110
Gray, Stephen, 182–186, 214 n. 19
Gross, Alan, 174
Gur, Ruben C., 84–85

Haeckel, Ernst, 86, 90
Halliday, M. A. K., 197 n. 8
Harris, Randy Allen, 202 n. 15
Hauksbee, Francis, 179–182
heat, Francis Bacon's study of, 61–64
Heathcote, Niels, 180
Heliangelus regalis, 174–175
Henle, Jacob, 211 n. 7
Henry, Joseph, 149, n. 16
Heraclitus, 141
heratio, 159
Herder, Johann Gottfried, 111–112,
    206 n. 13
Hermogenes, *On Types of Style*, 28–29, 129
Herschel, William, 104–107, 205 n. 9
Hertzsprung-Russell chart, 104–105
HIV infection, 52, 163
Hobbes Thomas, three-part antithesis,
    201–202 n. 13
homoeoteleuton, 50
Hoskins, John, 89, 108, 165
human versus brute antithesis, 75–80
Huxley, Thomas Henry
  on ape-human scale, 76–78
  on *Bathybius haeckelii*, 86–87
  on bird-reptile blending, 113
  on *eohippus*, 204 n. 6
  Evidence as to Man's Place in Nature,
    77–78
  flanking an antithesis, 90
  on lemurs, 202–203 n. 20
  on series inference, 119
hyperbaton, 7
hyperbole, 7

hypophora, 196 n. 5
hysteron proteron, 124

iconic, figures as, 21–22, 40
incrementum
  use in argument, 91–93
  definition of, 91–93
  in fossil horse sequence, 98–100
  in Herschel's catalogs, 106–108
  in Hertzsprung-Russell chart, 104–105
  in Lamarck, 152
  in mathematical series, 101
  in Titius-Bode series, 104
  visual incrementum, 176
  with visual polyptoton, 176
inheritance of acquired characteristics,
  152–154
inter se pugnantia, 14
irony, 11
isocolon, 50
Isocrates, 29, 197–198 n. 9
isomers, discovery of by Pasteur, 137–139
IUPAC (International Union of Pure and
  Applied Chemistry), 173

Johnson, Mark, 4
Joseph, Sister Miriam, 33

Kellogg, David, 210 n. 20
Kepler, Johannes, 105, 142
Koch, Robert, 162–165
Koch's postulates, 162–165
  early versions, 212 n. 10
  text-book versions, 211 n. 7
Kolata, Gina, 82–83
Kovalevsky, Vladimir, 98, 204 n. 7
Kress, Gunther, 160–161
Kuhn, Thomas, 178, 181

Lakoff, George, 4
Lamarck, Jean Baptiste, 152–154, 209 n.
  18, 209–210 n. 19
Lamy, Bernard, 207 n. 6
language capacity, apes versus humans,
  77–80
Lavoisier, Antoine, 4, 172–173, 195 n. 1
Leibniz, definitional sorites, 205 n. 12
left/right dichotomy, 84
Lewontin, Richard, 154–155, 210 n. 20
licentia (freedom of speech), 197 n. 5

Liebig, Justus von, 139, 140
Lilienthal detectives, 104
Lincoln, Abraham, Second Inaugural
  Address, 87–88, 203 n. 1
lines of argument. *See* topics
Locke, John, 102–103
Longinus, *Sublimity*, 31
Lund, Nils, 126
Luther, Martin, 124
Lwoff, André, 159

Magendie, François, 70–71
male/female opposition, 80–85
Marcy, Geoffrey W., 105
Marsh, Othniel C., 98, 204 n. 7
Maxwell, James Clerk, 150
Mayr, Adolf, 164
Melancthon, Philip, 12, 30–31, 129, 207 n. 7
membrum, 18
mempsis, 14
Mendeleev, Dimitri, 103
merismus, 91
metalepsis, 6
metaphor
  compared to *catachresis*, 37
  dominance of, 4–5
  in double hierarchy arguments, 108
  in early study of electricity, 177
  in *Rhetorica ad Herennium*, 7
  in science studies, 5–6
  systems of metaphor, 114
metonymy, 7, 36, 194
Molière, satirical gradatio in *La Jalousie
  de Barbouillé*, 205–206 n. 12
Montaigne, Michel de, 204 n. 5
Murphy, James J., 32

nannobacteria, 212–213 n. 11
Nash, Walter, 19
natural theology, 25, 172
nature versus nurture, 154, 167
Needham, Turbervill, 214 n. 21
nerves, motor versus sensory, 70–71
neuroanatomical differences, male/
  female, 81
The New Rhetoric (Perelman and
  Olbrechts-Tyteca), 34–36, 159. *See
  also* Perelman, Chaim
A New System of Chemical Philosophy
  (Dalton), 3–4

Newlands, John, 103
Newton, Isaac
  paper on light in 1672, 38–40
  Principia and antimetabole, 143, 208 n. 13
  series use in approximations, 101
  third law of motion and antimetabole,
    142–143, 208–209 n. 14
nomenclature, in chemistry, 172
  in molecular biology, 174
  in organic chemistry, 173
nonce antonyms, 47, 69
notatio, 8
Novum Organum (Bacon), 59–65

Ogden, C. K., 72–74, 202 n. 18
Olbrechts-Tyteca, Lucie, 34–36, 198
    n. 13. *See also* Perelman, Chaim
onomatopoeia, 7
On the Origin of Species (Darwin), 86,
    113–121
opposition
  kinds of, 48, 133
  Pythagoreans' ten fundamental
    oppositions, 203 n. 22
  in twentieth-century semantics, 199 n. 4
ornamentation, as theory of figuration,
    18–19
Owen, Richard, 76, 202 n. 6
oxymoron, 89

Paley, William, 172
palilogia, 159
palindrome, 124
paragoge, 212 n. 11
paralepsis, 11
paregmenon, 213 n. 13
parison, 50
Parker, Patricia, 198 n. 14
paronomasia, 166
partitio, 91
Pasteur, Louis, 137–140
Peacham, Henry
  on *antanaclasis*, 210–211 n. 4
  on antimetabole, 130
  on antithesis, 56–57
  on ploche, 159
  on series-making figures, 91–93
  on *traductio*, 160
  treatment of figures in *The Garden of
    Eloquence*, 13–14, 36

Perelman, Chaim, 34–36, 112, 160
periodic table of elements, 103
periphrasis, 7
permissio, 8
personification, 38
pH scale, 75
Piazzi, Giuseppe, 104
ploche
  as aesthetic defect, 162
  argumentative effects, 160–162
  definition of, 20, 158–160
  in Koch's postulates, 162–165
  prevalence in uninflected languages,
    168
  in science of electricity, 177–194
  visual representation of, 166
polyptoton
  and antimetabole, 128, 131
  argumentative uses of, 170–172
  definition of, 20, 50, 168–170
  in derivational changes, 169
  in nomenclature and taxonomy, 172–
    177
  in science of electricity, 177–194
  visual representation of, 174–176
polysyndeton, 27
Pouchet, George, 139
predicables, four in Aristotle, 132
Priestley, Joseph, 180–182, 185–186
Principia Mathematica (Newton), 142–143
prions, 203 n. 3
projective geometry, 136
prose style, discussion of in Aristotle's
    Rhetoric, 46
prosopopoeia, 17, 196–197 n. 5
prothesis, 212 n. 11
Puttenham, George, *The Arte of English
    Poesie*, 169
Pythagoreans' ten fundamental
    oppositions, 203 n. 22
Pythagorean thoerem, 135–136

Quinn, Arthur, 206 n. 1
Quintilian
  analogies between body and language,
    8–9, 196 n. 4
  on *antanaclasis*, 159
  on antimetabole, 128–129
  on antithesis, 55–56, 201 n. 9
  on repetition, 157

separating tropes and schemes, 196 n. 3
on series-forming figures, 92
treatment of figures in *Institutio Oratoria*, 8–11

Ragsdale, J. Donald, 33
Ray, John, 25–26
reading frames for figures
 antimetabole, 127
 repetitions, 159, 170
 series, 92
Reboul, Olivier, 167, 198 n. 13
reciprocal causality, 141–150
reciprocal processes in mathematics, 208 n. 12
refutation by reversal, 150–151
regression, 207 n. 6
repetition, figures of, 157–158
 with altered sense, 159
 with antimetabole, 206 n. 6
 aural, 166
 consistency of reference intended, 159–160
 random, 158–159
 for text cohesion, 210 n. 1
rhetoric, 31–32. *See also* Aristotle; *Rhetoric*
Rhetoric (Aristotle), 26–27, 51–52, 53, 128, 132, 141, 170, 201 n. 10, 203 n. 4
Rhetorica ad Alexandrum, 53–54, 128
Rhetorica ad Herennium
 on antimetabole (as *commutatio*), 128
 on antithesis (as *contrarium* and *contentio*), 54
 on *licentia*, 197 n. 5
 on polyptoton, 168
 treatment of figures of speech, 7–8, 27
rhetorical question, 36, 196 n. 5
Rich, Alexander, 137
RNA (ribonucleic acid), 90
Rudwick, Martin, 175–176
Rukeyser, Louis, 135

Sandemanians, 146
scale-based antithesis, 73–75
Scaliger, 14, 159
Schade, 11
schemes, 9, 11, 13, 15
scientific argument and the figures of speech, 43–44

scriptio continua, 127
Second Inaugural Address (Lincoln), 87–88, 203 n. 1
series. *See also* gradatio; incrementum
 constructed by figures, 91–95
 creating places with series, 98–102
 in Darwin's *On the Origin of Species*, 113–121
 in double hierarchies, 105–108
 incomplete series, 102–105
 length of, 100–101
 mathematical series, 101–102
 merging categories, 112–114
 as sorites, 108–112
 and star formation, 105–107
sermocinatio, 8
sexually transmitted diseases, 52–53
sexual orientation experiments, 101–102
Shaywitz, Bennett A., 81–83
Shaywitz, Sally, 81–83, 113
Sidney, Sir Philip, *Arcadia*, 165
Simpson, George Gaylord, 98–99
sorites, 108–112, 205 n. 10 and n. 12
speciation, 113–114, 174–175
Sprat, Thomas, 199 n. 16
spontaneous generation, controversies over, 139–140
St. Augustine, 123
Steele, R. B., 124
St. Paul, 45, 93, 205 n. 10
St. Theresa of Ávila, 45
Sturmius, 12
style, three levels of, 19
subjunctio, 158
Susenbrotus, 11, 159
syllepsis, 213 n. 14
symploche, 20, 158
syncope, 212 n. 11
synecdoche, 7

Talon, Omer, 14
tautologia, 160
temperature scales, 74
third law of motion from Newton's *Principia*, 141–143
Thucydides, 70, 88
Timaeus by Plato, 93
Titius-Bode sequence, 104
Topica (Cicero), 24

topics
  with antitheses, 51–52
  arguments from greater and lesser
    degree, 95–96
  with co-ordinate terms, 170–171
  as lines of argument, 23–24
  from reversals, 131–133
Topics (Aristotle), 24, 51–52, 95–96, 132–
    133, 151, 170–171, 206 n. 2, 208, n. 10
traductio, 158, 160
transposition, 7
tropes, 7, 9, 11, 196 n. 3
Trousdale, 198 n. 11
Turner, Mark, 4, 5
two domain theory of language, 17, 40

Uranus, 104
urschleim, 86

value-added theories of figuration, 20–23
Varga, A. Kibédi, 32–33
Veronese, Guarino, 197 n. 7
Vickers, Brian, 6, 18, 19
virtues of style, 17
viruses, 159, 164–165
Vossius, Gerhard, 14, 101

Wallman, Joel, *Aping Language*, 78–80
Watson, William, 186–190
Weaver, Richard, 38, 94
Weyl, Hermann, 134–135
Whately, Richard, 125, 207–208 n. 8
Wheler, Granvil, 182, 186
White, Hayden, 4
Wilson, E. O., 119–120
Wilson, Thomas, 93–94, 202 n. 17,
    207 n. 6

Printed in the United States
134738LV00008B/34/A